From Suffering to Solidarity

From Suffering to Solidarity

The Historical Seeds of Mennonite Interreligious, Interethnic, and International Peacebuilding

Edited by
ANDREW P. KLAGER

Foreword by
MARC GOPIN

☙PICKWICK *Publications* • Eugene, Oregon

FROM SUFFERING TO SOLIDARITY
The Historical Seeds of Mennonite Interreligious, Interethnic, and International Peacebuilding

Copyright © 2015 Wipf and Stock Publishers. All rights reserved. Except for brief quotations in critical publications or reviews, no part of this book may be reproduced in any manner without prior written permission from the publisher. Write: Permissions, Wipf and Stock Publishers, 199 W. 8th Ave., Suite 3, Eugene, OR 97401.

Pickwick Publications
An Imprint of Wipf and Stock Publishers
199 W. 8th Ave., Suite 3
Eugene, OR 97401

www.wipfandstock.com

ISBN 13: 978-1-62564-800-6

Cataloguing-in-Publication data:

From suffering to solidarity : the historical seeds of Mennonite interreligious, interethnic, and international peacebuilding / edited by Andrew P. Klager ; foreword by Marc Gopin.

xviii + 410 p. ; 23 cm. Includes bibliographical references.

ISBN 13: 978-1-62564-800-6

1. Mennonites. 2. Peace-building. 3. Conflict management. I. Klager, Andrew P. II. Gopin, Marc.

BX8128 F35 2015

Manufactured in the U.S.A.   10/22/2015

This book is dedicated to my children:
Charlie
Ida
Elliot
Jane

"God put the sense in the head. Why? Do you know? So that we cannot see ourselves. Yes! So that we see only the Other and love only the Other. And so that we see ourselves only in the eyes of the Other."

—Mother Gavrilia (twentieth-century Greek Orthodox nun)

Contents

Foreword by Marc Gopin | xi
Acknowledgments | xiii
List of Contributors | xv
Abbreviations | xvii
Introduction | 1

Part One: Historical Conditions of Anabaptist-Mennonite Peacebuilding Approaches

1. The Roots of Anabaptist Empathetic Solidarity, Nonviolent Advocacy, and Peacemaking
   John Derksen | 13

2. The Testing of Mennonite Peacemaking in Twentieth-Century Soviet Russia
   Walter Sawatsky | 37

3. Privilege, Right, and Responsibility: Peace and the North American Mennonites
   Royden Loewen | 58

4. The Beginnings of Mennonite Central Committee and Its Ministry of Peace
   Esther Epp-Tiessen | 71

5. Historical Conditions of Mennonite Peacebuilding Approaches: Global Anabaptism and Neo-Anabaptism
   John D. Roth | 90

Part Two: Analysis of the Historically Conditioned Mennonite Peacebuilding Approaches

6 From Resolution to Transformation: Experience, Encounter, and Solidarity in the Peacebuilding Work of Mennonite Practitioner-Scholar, John Paul Lederach
   Janna Hunter-Bowman | 115

7 Formative Mennonite Mythmaking in Peacebuilding and Restorative Justice
   Carl Stauffer | 140

8 Mennonites and Contemporary Human Rights
   Lowell Ewert | 162

9 Mennonite Women: Making Positive Peace
   Marlene Epp | 178

10 Transforming the Peacebuilder: Building Trust and Local Capacity through Containment of Ego and Cultivation of the Inner Life
   Ron Kraybill | 193

11 Called to Be Snakebirds: Mennonite Historical Conditions as Inspiration for Peace Work
   Virgil Wiebe | 204

Part Three: Application of Mennonite Peacebuilding Approaches in Conflict Settings

12 Authentic Grassroots Conflict Transformation in Egypt: Interreligious Hospitality and the Gift of Pessimism in Mennonite Approaches to Peacebuilding
   Andrew P. Klager | 231

13 Communities of Hope: Colombian Anabaptist Churches Bridging the Abyss of Suffering with Faith
   Bonnie Klassen | 251

14 Religious Violence, Peacebuilding, and Mennonites: The Case of Indonesia
   Sumanto Al Qurtuby | 274

15 Remembering a Perforated Land: Strategies of Peacebuilding in Palestine-Israel
   Alain Epp Weaver | 298

16 The Mennonite Peacebuilding Response to Interethnic Division in the Democratic Republic of the Congo
   Fidele Ayu Lumeya | 309

17 Overcoming Trauma, Grievance, and Revenge in Bosnia-Herzegovina and Kosovo: Fostering Nonviolent Reconciliation Efforts
   David Steele | 330

Bibliography | 367
Index | 395

Foreword

Marc Gopin

This extraordinary volume on Mennonite peacebuilding is significant for a number of reasons. The focus on history is crucial. Religion and peacebuilding is best understood by looking at its deepest structural roots in history. In particular, what we always want to understand is how religion and peacebuilding emerges out of a religion's history intact. For example, many religious traditions begin with deep nonviolent roots, but they do not end up that way. It is hard to imagine Jesus and his immediate disciples being the spiritual foundations of the Crusades, with all their torture, mass murder, and forced conversions. But this is the reality of history. The same is true for the legacy of many other prophets and founders.

Menno Simons did not give rise to an entire religious sect of peacebuilders by any means, and there is no sanctification here of Mennonites as such. But there is a remarkable trajectory between Menno's pacifism and today's Mennonite peacebuilders. That needs study and understanding in its historical, anthropological, and theological roots. This volume provides that, and it matters greatly to the future of religion and peacebuilding, because if we want to analyze where religion at its root goes right and where it goes wrong, then we must look carefully at history and texts in their details.

Roughly speaking, as an outside observer, it certainly looks as if there is paradoxical serendipity at play here. The powerlessness and vulnerability of the Mennonite community, their subjection to persecution, scarred them physically and emotionally. At the same time, the powerlessness kept intact the most demanding psychological stringencies of nonviolent spirituality. It is not easy to keep a religion nonviolent once it has temporal power over people's lives and their resources. But the separation from mundane state and police power kept Mennonite nonviolent political ethics in an incubator. It was an incubator that would one day flourish not just as pacifism, but something much more crucial for the future of the planet—religious peacebuilding, especially as it is embodied in some of the great exemplars of the Mennonite contribution, Lederach, Zehr, Schirch, Kraybill and many others. We must understand this evolution as if we were looking at the microscopic roots of a cancer cure. So history is one of the great contributions of this volume.

The other great contribution is the analysis of fragmented diversity in Mennonite peacebuilding. I am struck as an outsider by the fact that the Mennonite community is not only a tiny fraction of the global community, but a fraction of the Christian global community. Furthermore, within the Mennonite community, peacebuilders are a minority. And yet this volume deliberately welcomes the analysis of a great diversity of styles and methods within this tiny community. This is striking to any veteran student of religion and conflict analysis and resolution. Many religious institutions and thinkers write extensively and voluminously about interfaith dialogue and peace, and yet sometimes one senses in every sentence a tone of imperialism, triumphalism, and even totalitarianism. "We have the answers, the answers are with us, and we are one." And then you know why that theological interpretation tended to get too many people killed. Yet here, among proven peacebuilders, one senses an indulgence in fragmented diversity. Therein may lie another secret of Mennonite nonviolence and why its contribution has been so outsized statistically given the small number of Mennonites globally.

An indulgence in fragmented diversity is a marker of humility, as I have pointed out in my own Mennonite writing, and humility—making space for the Other (a) in the world and (b) in one's consciousness seems to be a central gateway on the road not to Damascus but to "Do no harm." There is no decent peacebuilding without the bedrock of (a) humble "Do no harm," and (b) making space for the Other. Both of these Taoist-like traits, nonviolence and humility, which also emerge from some of the great Abrahamic roots in the Old and New Testaments, and rabbinic and Sufi traditions, make for a powerful foundation of advanced peacebuilding for our large and complicated planet that has become overrun by the human race.

These are just a few of the excellent characteristics of this highly erudite, well-fashioned volume that should be studied by any student of conflict analysis and resolution today who wants to move the field in the best direction possible.

Acknowledgments

I always enjoy expressing my gratitude toward the many people and voices—both encouraging and dissenting—that helped shape my work. I first want to thank the Orthodox Peace Fellowship and Mennonite Central Committee BC for funding and otherwise supporting my peace research trip to Egypt in 2012, which eventually became the primary inspiration for the volume that you hold in your hands. More specifically, I am indebted especially to Jim Forest and Alex Patico of the OPF, Jon Nofziger and Wayne Bremner of MCC BC, and Tom and Judi Snowden and Ayman Kerols of the MCC office in Egypt for your warm hospitality and the excellent itinerary that you put together for my trip.

I would also like to thank the Anabaptist-Mennonite Centre for Faith and Learning at Trinity Western University—especially the Director, Myron Penner, and the Executive Board—for investing in the publication of this volume through their generous financial support and for showing interest in extending the scope of the book's influence through promotional work and related symposiums. Korey Dyck & Wendy Barkman and the Mennonite Heritage Centre Archives, Winnipeg, Manitoba also contributed financially to this project, of which I am very appreciative. I am also grateful for the support of the Centre for Mennonite Studies at the University of the Fraser Valley where I teach, and especially the encouragement of the Director, Steven Schroeder. I would be remiss if I didn't also acknowledge the inspiration of the Mennonites and Human Rights conference (October 18–20, 2012) that was organized by Royden Loewen, Chair of Mennonite Studies at the University of Winnipeg. Not only did this conference inform some of the themes and ideas expressed in this book, but it gave me an opportunity to meet several of the authors who appear in this volume, including John Derksen, Royden Loewen, Lowell Ewert, Virgil Wiebe, Bonnie Klassen, and Alain Epp Weaver.

I was also fortunate enough to complete a short research fellowship (Spring 2014) at the Centre for Studies in Religion and Society at the University of Victoria (British Columbia) and would therefore like to thank the Director, Paul Bramadat, for offering the time and space necessary to more deliberately analyze the data that I collected in Egypt, some of which informs the contours of my chapter in this volume and the themes that underlie the book project as a whole. Several colleagues at Trinity Western University and the University of the Fraser Valley have shown interest in my work and this book, and countless individuals have also helped refine its scope and objectives as well as my own evolving peace thought; three such individuals are worth mentioning for the many conversations that have helped shape my commitment to peace and nonviolence as they underpin this volume: Ron Dart, Mark Northey, and Brad Jersak. I am also grateful for the questions, concerns, critiques, and fine-tuning in early correspondences as this book project was beginning to unfold, especially by Jeremy Bergen and James Urry. Further personal correspondence with and otherwise scholarly influence of Marc Gopin, John Paul Lederach, Howard Zehr, Stanley Hauerwas, and Noam Chomsky have profoundly shaped my peace research and conflict analysis as well. For your dedication to seeing this book through to its eventual publication, I would also like to thank my indexer, Stephen Ullstrom, as well as Wipf and Stock and my assistant managing editor, Matthew Wimer, and typesetter, Ian Creeger.

And last but furthest from the least, I am grateful for the love and encouragement of my wonderful and infinitely supportive wife, Laurie-Jane, and for the welcome intermittent distraction of my children—Charlie, Ida, Elliot, and Jane—for constantly reminding me of what's actually important in life. This book is dedicated to all four of you.

Contributors

Sumanto Al Qurtuby is Assistant Professor of Anthropology, King Fahd University of Petroleum and Minerals, Dhahran, Saudi Arabia.

Fidele Ayu Lumeya is the Executive Director, Congolese American Council for Peace and Justice and a graduate in Peace and Conflict Studies, Eastern Mennonite University, Harrisonburg, Virginia.

John Derksen is Associate Professor of Conflict Resolution Studies, Menno Simons College, Winnipeg, Manitoba.

Marlene Epp is Professor of History and Peace and Conflict Studies, Conrad Grebel University College, University of Waterloo, Waterloo, Ontario.

Esther Epp-Tiessen is the Ottawa Office Public Engagement Coordinator for Mennonite Central Committee Canada.

Alain Epp Weaver is the Director of Strategic Planning for Mennonite Central Committee and has served previously as co-representative for Palestine, Jordan, and Iraq for Mennonite Central Committee and was a project coordinator in the Gaza Strip.

Lowell Ewert is the Director of Peace and Conflict Studies, Conrad Grebel University College, University of Waterloo, Waterloo, Ontario.

Janna Hunter-Bowman is Assistant Professor of Peace Studies and Social Ethics, Anabaptist Mennonite Biblical Seminary, Elkhart, Indiana.

Contributors

Andrew P. Klager is on faculty at the Centre for Mennonite Studies, University of the Fraser Valley, Abbotsford, British Columbia and is a Research Associate at the Anabaptist-Mennonite Centre for Faith and Learning, Trinity Western University, Langley, British Columbia, where he is also Adjunct Professor.

Bonnie Klassen is the Mennonite Central Committee Area Director for South America and Mexico.

Ron Kraybill is Senior Advisor for Peace and Development for the United Nations in the Philippines, a position he previously held in Lesotho. From 1995–2005, Ron was also a professor in the Conflict Transformation program at Eastern Mennonite University, Harrisonburg, Virginia.

Royden Loewen is the Chair in Mennonite Studies and Professor of History, University of Winnipeg, Winnipeg, Manitoba.

John D. Roth is Professor of History at Goshen College and the Director of the Institute for the Study of Global Anabaptism, Goshen, Indiana.

Walter Sawatsky is Emeritus Professor of Church History and Mission, Anabaptist Mennonite Biblical Seminary, Elkhart, Indiana.

Carl Stauffer is Assistant Professor of Development and Justice Studies, Center for Justice and Peacebuilding, Eastern Mennonite University, Harrisonburg, Virginia.

David Steele is Adjunct Lecturer, Brandeis University, Boston, Massachusetts and is an independent consultant in international conflict transformation for a variety of organizations.

Virgil Wiebe is Professor of Law, University of St. Thomas, Minneapolis, Minnesota. Virgil is also the Co-Director of the Interprofessional Center for Counseling and Legal Services and the Robins Kaplan Director of Clinical Education.

Abbreviations

CGR *Conrad Grebel Review*
JMS *Journal of Mennonite Studies*
JPR *Journal of Peace Research*
MCC *Mennonite Central Committee*
MQR *Mennonite Quarterly Review*

Introduction

IN AN INTERVIEW WITH Miroslav Volf by the online self-described "visual liturgy library" called *The Work of the People*, Volf aptly observes, "I don't think it's an accident that the idea of the love of the enemy emerged from marginalized groups . . . I think that the position of marginality lets you have an insight into the true character of human relations."[1] Likewise, in Steven Pinker's somewhat controversial book, *The Better Angels of Our Nature: Why Violence Has Declined*, the author—a well-known public intellectual and psychology professor at Harvard University—makes the bold claim that one of the reasons why violence has actually declined in recent decades despite perceptions to the contrary is that we have become more sensitive to the plight of the victim and to acts of victimization.[2]

In a similar vein, this book and the chapters in it explore the historical conditions—usually in the form of various experiences of suffering—that cultivated empathetic solidarity with the Other and shaped the various innovative peacebuilding approaches for which Mennonites have become known throughout the world. This is an ambitious project for a number of reasons: to my knowledge, no study has taken on the task of determining the manner in which the Mennonite historical context has influenced their peace work in such a comprehensive manner; this project requires expertise in Anabaptist-Mennonite history, Mennonite-inspired peacebuilding approaches, and their applicability and actualization in different conflict settings around the globe; and the subject matter needs—if at least

---

1. Miroslav Volf, "Love Your Enemy," *The Work of the People*, http://www.theworkofthepeople.com/love-your-enemy.

2. Steven Pinker, *The Better Angels of Our Nature: Why Violence Has Declined* (New York: Penguin Books, 2012). Cf. Kevin Miller, "Victimhood: A Double-Edged Sword," *Patheos*, http://www.patheos.com/blogs/hellbound/2014/08/victimhood-a-double-edged-sword/. For examples of the impact of victimization on the peace thought and behavior of early sixteenth-century Anabaptists, see Klager, "From Victimization," 119–132.

a movement toward objectivity is desired—the voices of both scholars and practitioners, analysts and field workers, Mennonites and non-Mennonites, "insiders" and "outsiders," women and men. As such, I determined in the early stages of this project that no single author could adequately tackle such a formidable challenge with the requisite sophistication, precision, and nuance. Therefore, I have enlisted an eclectic mix of authors who together reflect the above diversity with the intent to ensure the highest quality of all sections and chapters of this book equally.

Mennonites have been able to assemble a rich and enduring historical infrastructure that has allowed them to preserve and disseminate their stories, memories, and myths to inspire love of enemies after they themselves were enemies, empathetic solidarity with those who suffer after they themselves had suffered, nonviolent forms of conflict transformation after they themselves experienced violence. The red thread that unites these historical conditions, the resulting preservational infrastructure, and the enduring means of inspiration and education is empathetic solidarity: We know how it feels to be the targets of violence and injustice, so we will help anyone who now faces these same threats, but through nonviolence and the pursuit of justice—that is, a 'just peace' that avoids making *anyone* a target of violence or viewing anyone as an enemy.

So, what is the main objective of this volume? Very simply, to show, through the lens of a particular ethno-religious group, how a historical infrastructure that preserves and disseminates narratives, stories, memories, and myths of suffering and nonviolence—either through withdrawal early on in their history or positive action and advocacy in recent decades—in the midst of persecution can inspire identity groups, whether ethnic, religious, or otherwise, to act in solidarity with those who suffer in similar ways today and work for peace and justice on their behalf in nonviolent and transformative ways. Far from an uncontested romanticism, the chapters in this book collectively exhibit both the effectiveness and challenges of this Mennonite heritage.

The title of this book is *From Suffering to Solidarity*, but this transition is a complex one. It is not a straight line or an unfiltered cause-and-effect dynamic. The fidelity of Mennonites to the sense of empathetic solidarity with those who suffer today in the same way that they suffered in the past varies. The psychological scars and difficulty translating complicated experiences into new political landscapes loom large. Sometimes a wide-angle lens of more assimilated Mennonites is needed. This is not to say that assimilated Mennonites have a superior outlook than Mennonites who emigrated from Russia in the 1870s and the early and mid 20th century. But the combination of a more panoramic perspective and later inspiration—rather than a direct experience of suffering in the turmoil of the moment—with a growing and sophisticated awareness of today's global challenges has created an effective cocktail for encouraging relief, development, and peacebuilding in many of the world's trouble spots. Even the awakening among new generations of Mennonites that some of their ancestors either knowingly or unwittingly persecuted others (e.g., Jews in Russia—while some Mennonites also assisted Jews during the pogroms—and First Nations peoples in North America) has heightened their sensitivity to this type of discrimination today.

In this sense, the shift from suffering to solidarity doesn't entail the abandonment of suffering and certainly did not for the Mennonites in the history that this volume explores. The two are by no means mutually exclusive. Solidarity with those who suffer implies sharing in their suffering and increasing our own. If anything, the shift is from suffering in the past to the addition of the suffering of others today—this is the essence of solidarity, in peacebuilding, social activism, relief and development, and reconciliation and trauma healing. It is inherently self-sacrificial and self-denying—in the spirit of the sixteenth-century Anabaptist principle of *Gelassenheit* or "yieldedness"—and, for these Mennonites, it demands that we take up our own crosses and traverse the same treacherous path that Jesus first trod: the narrow way. And this way is narrow because it's a path we all want to avoid; it's a difficult path that seems to demand too much of us. In this sense, the suffering of Mennonites compelled them—despite lingering hesitancies—to work for the elimination of this same sensation on behalf of others, even if it meant compounding the sensation personally. This is the transformation of suffering from a debilitating experience to an empowering and mobilizing stimulus. The hope, however, is that this shared sensation of suffering will be temporary—that by knowing "the things that make for peace," we can dry the tears of the Prince of Peace who weeps over Jerusalem by wiping away the tears of the least of these who suffer under systems of oppression today (Luke 19:42; Matt 25:31–46).

With this in mind, the present volume operates under the conviction that Mennonite peace thought and practice did not develop in a vacuum. There were tangible historical events—from the very large, including early Anabaptist persecution and political isolation; the pattern of persecution, migration, and re-settlement; the Bolshevik Revolution and the Russian Civil War; World War II; and the civil rights movement mainly in the U.S., to the amalgam of a near infinite number of more minor recurring phenomena—that triggered, shaped, and transformed the Mennonite community's peace witness and approaches to peacebuilding. Parallel to these historical events and conditions is a peace theology and commitment to the gospel of peace, nonviolence, and love of enemies—the internalization of a cruciform

Christology—that provided the religious resources for preserving this peace witness (where it still existed) and shaping their approaches to peacebuilding. Historical events and a "lived theology" within periods of intense persecution and hardship helped to inspired contemporaneous Mennonites and new generations of Mennonites to engage in relief, development, and peacebuilding globally. These experiences in turn shaped the unique combination of Mennonite approaches to peacebuilding and underlying attitudes, including a suspicion of governments, grassroots focus on building peace from the ground-up, an equal—even if vexingly nebulous—accent on peace and justice together, the need for access to genuine decision-making that Anabaptists were long denied, relationship- and trust-building, the advantage of building one's credibility in a foreign conflict setting, conflict transformation rather than mere resolution, and a restorative rather than retributive view of justice, among many others that this book explores.

As the authors in this volume will show, however, the connection between historical inspiration and inspired behaviour is complex and far from linear; streamlined myths give way to multi-faceted and heavily layered narratives. But these memories and stories—however redacted for the sake of convenience—have nevertheless made a profound impact on Mennonite peacebuilding sensibilities. This book is therefore primarily about the role of history; Mennonites' collective synthesis of historical data; the inspiration of history, narratives, stories, memories, and myths; history that galvanizes peacemaking responses by solicitous observers and that animates the behavior of actors within a violent conflict; and historically conditioned memories that inspire empathetic solidarity with those whose historically conditioned memories drive their quest for peace and justice amidst violent conflicts today. History, therefore, has a dual function: it inspires the peacebuilders and reminds the sufferers, it is the content of "remembering what it was like" for peacebuilders and the content of "remembering what we lost" for victims.

So, what do we hope to accomplish with this volume? Primarily, to inspire any other groups—ethnic, religious, etc.—that, like Mennonites, have faced persecution, violence, and injustice to harness this experience for encouraging empathetic solidarity with others who face similar threats. This is, at its core, about thrusting a stick in the spokes of the cycle of violence. As Mennonites generally did not retaliate when confronting violence and injustice (though exceptions certain did exist), this books seeks to answer why—from a historical perspective—this was the case and, at least more implicitly, what other groups can do to encourage the same response—i.e., the refusal to fuel, perpetuate, or laud the cycle of violence and its benefactors. All of this requires the preservation of narratives, stories, memories, and myths; the mechanisms for their dissemination including storytelling, role-playing, and myth-building; and the infrastructure to support these objects of preservation and forms of dissemination. This is also the recommendation of the present volume for other groups as much as it is an encouragement to the Mennonite community to continue and enhance their existing historical infrastructure. These are therefore the things I want my readers to think about as they read through this volume. Ultimately, the authors of this volume hope to inspire influential leaders among other groups who have faced violence and injustice to ask, How can we also preserve and disseminate our stories, memories, and myths in ways that will encourage non-participation in the ongoing cycle of violence and instead acting in peaceful ways to resolve conflicts and cultivate reconciliation? And, related, how can we harness—where applicable—religious resources as a way to catalyze and shape nonviolent forms of conflict transformation and restorative forms of justice? These are two areas that Mennonites have found some success—even if uneven in places—that can inspire other groups around the world to do the same.

As the reader may already notice, this book is for both Mennonites and non-Mennonites alike, though perhaps for different purposes. There is much that is instructive for Mennonites and the way in which they might implement their historically conditioned peacebuilding approaches. At the same time, the authors of this volume do not shy away from both successes *and* failures in the Mennonite community to live up to their own ideals, which can be instructive also for non-Mennonites. The diversity of authorship and anticipated audiences of this book is reflected in other ways too. The various chapters in this book purposefully present an uneven spectrum of scholarly rigor; some contain copious amounts of footnotes and academic paraphernalia, while others are equally as valuable firsthand accounts, analyses, and recommendations. Both approaches dispense invaluable wisdom equally.

For my part, I am an academic on the research and analysis end of peacebuilding and a non-Mennonite (ethnically and religiously); as an Eastern Orthodox Christian, I nevertheless benefit from a conspicuous Anabaptist-Mennonite residue happily left over from when I used to attend a Mennonite church and completed my undergraduate studies at a Mennonite college. I also earned a PhD in Ecclesiastical History from the University of Glasgow with a focus on sixteenth-century Anabaptist origins and have been influenced by neo-Anabaptist impulses since my early years in college. As well, I maintain strong ties to the wider and local Mennonite community as an observer and encourager, teaching Mennonite Studies at the University of the Fraser Valley and carrying out research in partnership with Mennonite Central Committee (MCC) in Egypt on interreligious peacebuilding between Coptic Christians and Muslims. My wife, however, was born and raised in a thoroughly ethnic and religious Mennonite family and sat at the feet of her maternal grandmother to listen to and internalize her traumatic experiences of immigrating from the Chortitza Colony in the Great Trek to Germany and finally (for her) to Canada. This has inspired my wife's own nonviolent stance, objection to war, advocacy for peaceful resolutions to conflict, simple living as non-participation in the systemic violence of wealth, and support of MCC. So, my perspective is as both an "insider" and "outsider." Aside from the macro-historical continuity, these meaningful personal encounters—especially when taken collectively—are the subject of this book as well. Given the various Anabaptist-Mennonite impulses that have influenced me, my peace studies in the Middle East, and my academic pursuits and family dynamics, I am—in a sense, for better or worse—a living sample and test case of what this book portrays. It is therefore not a stretch to contend that the present volume contains semi-autobiographical elements. I imagine this is the same of all authors in this book, though for different reasons and from unique combinations of personal backgrounds and resulting priorities.

At times, the paradox of Mennonite peace thought—passive-ism vs. pacifism, nonresistance vs. active nonviolence, peace vs. justice, public vs. private—pop up from time-to-time in the various chapters of this book. Mennonites and peace—as this book is unafraid to venture—is a messy marriage that challenges the many trite caricatures and facile romanticism. And although this book accomplishes much, it also asks new questions that are as yet unanswered. One recurring question in many of the chapters—even if only implicitly—is, To what degree was the pioneering work of Mennonites in peace and conflict studies simply an attraction to and commandeering of secular peace movements especially in the 1960s and 70s? Was there something unique about the Mennonite appropriation of these emerging peace impulses? Did Mennonites simply copy or otherwise take advantage of the underpinning intellectual theories and demonstrations of these anti-war movements or were these reinterpreted within a Mennonite historically conditioned framework to give them a unique shape and character? Rather than take a negative (perhaps even humble) view of Mennonite mimesis, did Mennonites and other peace churches instead actively contribute to the emerging peace movements to give it a prominence that it otherwise might not have attained? And what of the *positive* and *transformative* features of peacebuilding—even if we concede that the shift from passive nonresistance to active nonviolence was the product of its time, is their room to demonstrate—and even celebrate—the *pro-peace* theory, methods, initiatives, and strategic peacebuilding and conflict transformation that transcends the *anti-war*, and therefore predominantly negative, impulses of the 1960s and beyond? This book certainly answers some of these questions by drawing on the historical conditions and experiences that have molded Mennonite intellectual, practical, and psychological sensitivities in the midst of violent conflict from the early sixteenth-century to the present, but there are still many questions—or aspects of questions—that still need to be answered more fully, especially if they are to inform other ethno-religious groups that have experienced persecution, marginalization, and the sensation of being someone else's enemy.

One interesting unintended dynamic of this book is worth noting. Although not a hard-and-fast rule, on the whole, the Mennonite authors in this volume seem to be more self-critical when they consider the Mennonite contributions to peacebuilding than are the non-Mennonite authors. They are more willing to draw attention to the flaws of Mennonite peace and conflict sensitivities and actions; this, I believe, is important, as it is only in the recognition of deficiencies that we can make improvements. Perhaps this is simply a testament to the latent or unacknowledged humility of Mennonites or else the reality that Mennonites definitely do frequently fall short of their own ideals—or perhaps a mix of both. While I am of the latter group—a non-Mennonite who admires and respects the many peacebuilding contributions of Mennonites—I am also not under the delusion that theirs was a self-evident, painless, effortless foray into serious and deeper peacebuilding and conflict transformation practices; there is much to learn from Mennonites, and much that Mennonites still need to learn. However, I also believe that Mennonites could stand to take a few steps back and survey their positive contributions, especially in contrast to the relatively meager or underdeveloped—even antagonistic and undermining—perspectives of other groups. This book, while certainly pointing out room for improvement, celebrates the Mennonite contributions to peacebuilding, even—I must admit—at the reluctance of some authors in this volume. As a non-Mennonite, I admire Mennonite contributions and perspectives and have incorporated them into my own ethical life and vocation. My experience in Egypt with MCC and interviews with directors and participants of MCC's partner organizations in Egypt—all of whom enthusiastically heaped praise on MCC for its innovative peacebuilding perspective, tireless development assistance, and commitment to nonviolence—has also persuaded me that Mennonites have a lot of unique positives in the realm of peace and conflict studies on which to hang their collective hat. Mennonites need to know and own this more, I think. In this sense, I hope that the areas in need of improvement will not drown out any recognition—by Mennonites and non-Mennonites alike—of the many fine contributions that Mennonites have made over the previous decades and centuries and continue to make today.

Along these lines, within the many attempts to make connections between the Mennonite past and the present in service of the future, the authors in this volume have also provided innovative insights into new horizons in peace and conflict studies. While this book has a specific focus and purpose, it is also an outlet for these experts in their fields to introduce new peacebuilding theories, strategic considerations, practices, and initiatives within the parameters of the book's mandate. Part 1 of this book is a chronological exploration, from the sixteenth-century Anabaptist origins to the present, of the historical seeds of contemporary contributions to conflict transformation by Mennonite peacebuilding scholars and practitioners. Each chapter picks up on various common thematic threads that run throughout the nearly five hundred-year Mennonite history and give attention to unique components in each era and geographical location. Part 2 connects the past to the present within the exclusive sphere of Mennonite peacebuilding and conflict transformation. By analyzing the influence of the historical seeds of Mennonite peacebuilding emphases, theory, methods, and strategies from the previous section (Part 1), each chapter demonstrates how this Mennonite heritage and its historical development has informed and inspired Mennonite peacebuilding today through devices such as memory, inter-generational storytelling, myth-building and -preservation, and the location of oneself in the grander Mennonite narrative. This section is concerned most with the Mennonite third-party conciliator, but also acts as a resource for subsequent application by either Mennonites or non-Mennonites working with other ethnic and/or religious groups. And, finally, Part 3 gives the opportunity for conflict analysts and peacebuilders to *adapt* and *apply* the historical components, experiences, memories, stories, and myths that have preserved and informed Mennonite peacebuilding sensitivities, theories, and methods for use by either Mennonites or non-Mennonites for the benefit of *other* ethnic and/or religious communities. Contributors to this section use their own particular paradigms for drawing historical components, stories, memories, and myths from other religious or ethnic communities that are similar to—and may therefore be just as efficacious as—those of Mennonites, and perhaps determine how to adapt and apply them to a particular interethnic or interreligious conflict.

This three-part arrangement reflects the aforementioned paradigm that informed the title of this volume: from group suffering to internal reflection and refinement of responses to outward-looking empathetic solidarity and nonviolent conflict transformation. The transmission of various narratives from generation-to-generation and the invitation to new generations to also live in these narratives today, the deep historical consciousness and infrastructure that supports its preservation, and the internalization of the stories and myths of this persecution and marginalization is a combination that separates the Mennonite community from many other ethno-religious groups; determining how to adapt these lessons for other ethnic and religious groups in meaningful, profound, and permanent ways is the responsibility of peacebuilding scholars and practitioners. This book is an invitation to begin the conversation.

The iconic copper etching of Dirk Willems rescuing his pursuer by Jan Luyken from *The Martyrs' Mirror* appears on the front of this book. Admittedly, I wanted to find a different image—one that conveyed the same dynamic but perhaps within the last century, or from the Soviet experience, or the growing Mennonite church in developing, conflict-ridden countries around the world—as this etching has, in my opinion, been overused to the point of losing its jolting cognitive dissonance and becoming a trite commentary on the love of enemies. But when it finally came down to it, this remains perhaps the single best encapsulation of the dynamic between the sensation of being *someone else's* enemy while still loving *one's own* enemies, the shift—captured in a single instant—from suffering to solidarity. This image, therefore, best captures the Mennonite experience outlined in this book.

Andrew P. Klager, PhD

PART ONE

Historical Conditions of Anabaptist-Mennonite Peacebuilding Approaches

1

The Roots of Anabaptist Empathetic Solidarity, Nonviolent Advocacy, and Peacemaking

JOHN DERKSEN

Introduction

MUCH OF MENNONITE NONVIOLENT advocacy and peacebuilding today finds its roots in sixteenth-century Anabaptism. But sixteenth-century Anabaptists were diverse. In keeping with the polygenesis view of Anabaptist origins, this paper assumes diversity in the geography, origins, cultures, shaping influences, spiritual orientations, attitudes to violence, and other expressions of Anabaptists.[1] We define Anabaptists as those who accepted (re)baptism or believer's baptism and the implications of that choice. Various Anabaptists had sectarian, ascetic, spiritualist, social revolutionary, apocalyptic, rationalistic, or other orientations, and the distinctions between them were often blurred. Geographically, they emerged in Switzerland in 1525, in South Germany-Austria in 1526, and in the Netherlands in 1530. Many agree that the Anabaptists displayed

---

1. Stayer, Packull, and Deppermann, "Monogenesis," 83–121; Coggins, "Definition"; Stayer, *Sword*. Surveys of Anabaptist history that incorporate the polygenesis perspective include Snyder, *Anabaptist*, and Weaver, *Becoming Anabaptist*. Works that explore Anabaptist unity beyond polygenesis include Weaver, *Becoming Anabaptist*, and Roth and Stayer, *Companion*.

both Protestant and Catholic characteristics in different configurations. "Negatively, there was anger against social, economic, and religious abuses . . . but responses to this discontent varied widely. Positively, the 'Word of God' served as a rallying point for all, but differences . . . emerged over how it was understood and used."[2] While Swiss Anabaptists tended to favor sectarianism after the 1525 Peasants' War, South German and Austrian Anabaptists tended more toward spiritualism, and early Dutch Anabaptists tended toward apocalyptic thinking. As they spread across Europe, there was much religious, intellectual, and cultural cross-fertilization. In the wake of much persecution that decimated the spiritualist and apocalyptic Anabaptist communities, after 1540 an increasingly uniform sectarianism emerged. By 1600 the Anabaptists had crystallized into the Swiss Mennonite, Dutch Mennonite, and Hutterite varieties that continue into the twenty-first century.

Certainly the Anabaptists were not perfect. Some were rigid, narrow-minded, short-tempered, and intolerant. But their legacy continues in Mennonite nonviolent advocacy and peacebuilding today. Why have Mennonites emphasized this? Where did this come from and what are its roots? What sixteenth-century external historical conditions and influences (political, social, economic, religious, persecution, suffering, etc.) gave rise to Anabaptist peaceful responses? What teachings, practices, actions, and experiences emerged from these conditions that inspired later Mennonites to engage in peacebuilding and shaped their peacebuilding approaches? Without being comprehensive, this paper suggests seven multifaceted factors that gave rise to Anabaptist service, solidarity with the marginalized, nonviolent advocacy, and peacemaking: (1) Medieval Catholic spirituality, (2) Renaissance Humanism, (3) the experience of socio-economic, political, and religious oppression, (4) the Protestant Reformation, (5) disillusionment and persecution after 1525, (6) the experience of a healing alternative community, and (7) emphasis on the centrality of Jesus and the New Testament.

Medieval Roman Catholic Spirituality

In the centuries before the Protestant Reformation, the medieval Roman Catholic Church saw many reform movements that sowed seeds for Anabaptism and later Mennonite peacemaking. A number came in the wake of the fourteenth- and fifteenth-century Avignon schism and scandals that for

---

2. Derksen, *Radicals*, 15. See Goertz, *Die Täufer*, 40–48; Hillerbrand, "Radicalism," 31–32, 36; Snyder, *Anabaptism*, 48–49.

a time saw the papacy controlled by France and, among other things, two and three rival popes. Reformers urged four major directions:

1. Conservative reformers called on the Catholics, leaders and commoners alike, to repent of sins and live purer lives. They did not challenge institutional structures.

2. Liberal reformers called on the entire church to return to the simpler and purer pattern of Christ and the New Testament church. This implied a dismantling of institutional structures and traditions.

3. Monastic reformers sought a purer faith outside the structures of the institutional church.

4. Lay reformers such as the Waldensians, the Beguines, the Union of the Brethren, and the Lollards sought to live simple, Christlike lives of poverty and service without the interference of the official Church.[3]

Medieval Catholic spiritual traditions that influenced Anabaptists included monastic ascetic traditions, mystical and spiritualist traditions, apocalyptic traditions, a medieval theology of martyrdom, and ethical, *imitatio Christi* traditions.[4] Monastic asceticism set a sharp distinction between the church and the world. Those under the reign of Christ were to keep themselves pure and separate from the world with a holy life. This emphasis appears in the Swiss Anabaptists after the Schleitheim Confession (1527), the Dutch Anabaptists under Menno Simons (1496–1561), and the Hutterites in Moravia. This had an ethical import. To live in the reign of Christ in purity and separation from the world meant to live in love and give up violence, even toward the enemy. These emphases contributed to an Anabaptist ethic of nonresistance and peacemaking.

In the tradition of Meister Eckhart (c. 1260–1327), John Tauler (c. 1300 –1361), and an anonymous book entitled *The German Theology* (*Theologia Deutsch*), mysticism and spiritualism emphasized openness and yieldedness to God (*Gelassenheit*), loving oneness with God and Christ, growth in holiness, and cooperation with God's grace for salvation. Anabaptist leaders with mystical inclinations included Hans Denck (c. 1500–1527), Hans Hut (c. 1490–1528), Leonard Schiemer (d. 1528), and Hans Schlaffer (d. 1528) in South Germany and Austria and Melchior Hoffman (c. 1495–1543) in

---

3. Davis, *Asceticism*, 54; Ozment, *Reform*; Brock, *Varieties*, 9–12.

4. See Davis, *Asceticism*, 54–63, 109–17, 128, 131–96, 202–92, 297–98; Snyder, *Anabaptist History*, 11–19, 71–79, 159–72; Weaver, *Becoming Anabaptist*, 65–77, 111–60; Packull, *Mysticism*, 17–34, 48–61, 66–76; Williams, *Radical*, 73–108; Deppermann, *Melchior*, 160–219, 354–58, 363–65; Hillerbrand, "Anabaptism," 407–18; Gregory, *Salvation*, 198–249, 344–52; Krahn, *Dutch Anabaptism*, 8–79.

Strasbourg and the Netherlands. To be one with Christ in *Gelassenheit* implied submission to God, to the community, and to suffering without violent resistance, even toward enemies.[5] These emphases cultivated a peaceable Anabaptist worldview and ethic.

Medieval apocalypticism, widespread across Europe throughout the Middle Ages and the sixteenth century, also shaped Anabaptist orientations and behaviors. When crises and uncontrollable threats such as war, plagues, famine, and inflation loomed large, apocalypticism offered people meaning in life and helped them cope by asserting that God was in control and would soon save the righteous.[6] It inspired missionary zeal, apathy toward government, and a willingness to suffer and die.[7] Among Anabaptists, Hut, Schiemer, Schlaffer, Hoffman, and Ursula Jost (d. 1530) and Barbara Rebstock in Strasbourg, were widely influential apocalyptic preachers. Their messages expressed solidarity with the suffering and oppressed, an egalitarian thrust that all would come under God's judgment, and an anticlerical note that God would judge clerics and rulers who dominated and exploited the poor.[8]

Related to asceticism and mysticism was the medieval theology of martyrdom—the view that true followers of Christ must expect suffering. Anabaptists found this both in the Bible and in their experience. They found that their dangerous move of (re)baptism to join a separate church threatened the existing alliance of church and state, and often led to suffering and death. Soon after the Peasants' War of 1525, Anabaptists in Switzerland, Germany, Austria, and Moravia faced severe persecution, especially from Catholic authorities, as did Dutch Anabaptists after the disastrous 1534 Kingdom of Münster. Between 1525 and 1550 some 2500–3000 Anabaptists died for their faith, and they developed a martyrological mentality.[9] Upper Austrian Anabaptists interrogated in 1527 confessed, "No one may be saved, except through suffering, that is genuine baptism by blood, into which they themselves consent through baptism by water."[10] Hans Hut, who

---

5. Packull, *Mysticism*, 17–34, 48–76, 159–75; Snyder, *Anabaptist History*, 69, 76–79; Snyder, "Mysticism," 195–215; Weaver, *Becoming Anabaptist*, 65–78; Stauffer, "Martyrdom," 234–35.

6. Barrett, "Ursula Jost," 277–78, 282; Petroff, *Medieval*, 6.

7. Williams, *Radical*, 1303–7.

8. Packull, *Mysticism*, 77–87, 101, 106–17; Snyder, *Anabaptist History*, 70–72, 75–77, 143–45, 164–72; Weaver, *Becoming Anabaptist*, 65–74; Barrett, "Ursula Jost," 273–87; Deppermann, *Melchior*, 354–58, 363–65; Derksen, *Radicals*, 70–71.

9. Gregory, *Salvation*, 198–99, 207, 211, 249, 344–52; Gregory, "Martyrdom," 477–79.

10. Gregory, *Salvation*, 211.

died in prison in 1528, wrote, "No man can come to salvation, save through suffering and tribulation which God works in him, as also the whole Scripture and all the creatures show nothing but the suffering Christ in all his members."[11] Suffering had purpose because God, salvation, eternity, and Truth were at stake.[12] And so emerged an ethic of Anabaptist nonresistance in the face of violence and solidarity with others who suffer.

In the Netherlands, the ground for Anabaptism was prepared by movements of monastic and lay piety such as the *Devotio Moderna* of the Brethren of the Common Life, and the Sacramentists. Both called for church reform, sought Christlike simplicity, and offered service to the poor. The Brethren of the Common Life educated children and emphasized following Christ in humble service. Many, including Anabaptists, cherished the book *Imitatio Christi* by the well-known Brother, Thomas à Kempis (c. 1380–1471).[13] The Sacramentists, an anticlerical reform movement led largely by clerics and artisans, favored a symbolic interpretation of the Eucharist. Many of them became Anabaptists.[14] For example, Menno Simons, a former Catholic priest, was well aware of sacramentism and the piety of the *Devotio Moderna*.[15] Like the Sacramentists and the *Devotio Moderna*, the Anabaptists expressed solidarity with the laity and the poor, and emphasized following Jesus in purity, humility, and obedience.

Medieval Catholic spirituality sowed seeds for Anabaptist nonresistance, nonviolent advocacy, egalitarianism, service, and solidarity with the marginalized. Like the reforming ascetics, Anabaptists sought to be pure, holy, and close to God apart from the corrupt Church institution. Like the medieval mystics, Anabaptists sought a direct relationship with God without the mediation of priests and the church institution, and growth toward Christ-like love for all. Like apocalypticists of the Middle Ages, Anabaptists preached that with Christ's imminent return, all would come under God's judgment and that God would judge authorities who oppressed the poor. Like Christ and the martyrs who had gone before, Anabaptists displayed a readiness to accept suffering and death without violence, and a hope stronger than death. This stance, and solidarity with others who suffer, implied criticism of the church and lay rulers who administered the suffering and a radical egalitarianism in the conviction that, on judgment day, all stand as

11. Hans Hut, "Mystery," 50–51.

12. Gregory, *Salvation*, 344–52.

13. Davis, *Asceticism*, 55–57, 63, 243–66; Williams, *Radical*, 95–108; 528–34; Ozment, *Reform*, 17, 79, 96–98; Krahn, *Dutch Anabaptism*, 22–25.

14. Waite, "Netherlands," 254–56, 265; Krahn, *Dutch Anabaptism*, 39–40, 44, 58, 71–72, 118–19; Williams, *Radical*, 95–108, 528–34; Davis, *Asceticism*, 55–57, 63.

15. Dyck, "Spirit," 119; Krahn, *Dutch Anabaptism*, 69.

equals before God. Like the *Devotio Moderna*, Dutch Anabaptists sought simplicity, service, purity, and Christ-likeness that challenged the institutional church. Like the Sacramentists, they challenged Church doctrine and stood in solidarity with the oppressed. These seeds that Medieval Catholic spiritual traditions sowed blossomed not only into Anabaptist faith and life but also into later Mennonite peacemaking.

Renaissance Humanism

A number of scholars have identified Renaissance Humanism as formative for Anabaptists.[16] In Italy from the fourteenth century onward, and then in northern Europe, the intellectual and cultural movements that became known as the Renaissance encouraged the revival of classical learning and the concept of human dignity, known as Humanism. The emphasis on human dignity led to a greater emphasis on education, rationalism, and human free will in the moral life. The call to return "to the sources" (*ad fontes*), which included a call to return to the Bible rather than merely church tradition, implied criticism of the Church. Growing literacy, the 1450 invention of printing, and the proliferation of pamphlets spread reforming ideas. Christian Humanism influenced Anabaptists to criticize the corruption and hubris of church and secular leaders, to uphold both the Spirit and the Word of God, to center on Jesus and the New Testament, and to embrace ethical living.[17]

The greatest Renaissance humanist scholar was Desiderius Erasmus (1465–1536), who had studied with the Brethren of the Common Life and cherished "their regard for simple living and simple Biblical truth."[18] Society, he argued, was entangled in corruption because of having lost sight of the simple teachings of the Gospels. To rectify this he offered (1) clever satires to show people the error of their ways, (2) serious moral treatises to guide people toward proper Christian behavior, and (3) scholarly editions of Christian texts. In his satires (e.g., *Praise of Folly*, 1509) he lampooned society (the folly of war, individual and national pride), the church (hair-splitting theologians, ignorant monks, power-loving bishops), and the common folk for their superstitions (fasting, confessions, indulgences, pilgrimages).

---

16. See, for example, Friesen, *Erasmus*, 20–42, 44, 54, 96, 109; Burger, "Erasmus"; Davis, *Asceticism*, 266–92; Hall, "Possibilities," 149–70; Fast, "Dependence," 104–19; Kreider, "Humanism," 123–41.

17. Davis, *Asceticism*, 266–92; Burger, "Erasmus," vi; Weaver, *Becoming Anabaptist*, 28–29.

18. Littell, *Origins*, 50.

Of his serious moral treatises, in *Handbook of the Christian Knight* (1501) he urged a simple life, tolerance, and a Christ-like ethic. In *Complaint of Peace* (1517) he pleaded, especially to the papacy, for an end to Europe's incessant wars and for Christian pacifism. As for scholarly texts, in addition to reliable editions of the Church Fathers, Erasmus produced a new authoritative Greek New Testament (1516) together with explanatory notes and his own Latin translation. Like many humanists, he believed that once people understood Christ's message and the good, they would do it. Piety and charity would become the rule. So steep people in the Word of God.[19]

Many Anabaptists came to rely on Erasmus's translation and explanatory notes for their understanding of Christian baptism and ethical Christian living, and their views of grace, salvation, free will, moral reform, and the authority of Church councils versus that of the Bible.[20] They echoed Erasmus in their pleas for freedom of conscience and faith. In 1534 Leopold Scharnschlager wrote to the Strasbourg city council,

> I am convinced that each one of you who loves the truth desires a free, voluntary access to God, . . . uncoerced, without pressure. And if someone would force you to a faith, which . . . you could not accept in peace of conscience, you would desire to be free in that. Therefore I sincerely request that you remember and take to heart that this is the situation with me and my associates. . . . You urge us to depart from our faith and accept yours. That is the same as if the Emperor were to say to you that you are to give up your faith and accept his.[21]

The Regensburg Anabaptist, Hans Umlauft, pleaded similarly in 1539, "We are people and human as you and those of your kind created in the image of God, a creation of God, having God's law, will and word written in our hearts (Rom. 2:[15]). Therefore you should grant to us a gracious God as well as to yourselves."[22]

For some the plea for freedom of faith implied that others also ought to be free to follow their conscience. Kilian Aurbacher, a preacher in Moravia, wrote in 1534, "It is never right to compel one in matters of faith, whatever

---

19. Nolan, *Erasmus*, 8–23; Latourette, *Christianity*, 661–62; Krahn, *Dutch Anabaptism*, 25–28.

20. Friesen, *Erasmus*, 20–42, 44, 54, 96, 109; Nolan, *Erasmus*, 8–23; Burger, *Erasmus*, 43–128, 150–54; Davis, *Asceticism*, 266–92; Williams, *Radical*, 42–46.

21. Scharnschlager, "Strasbourg Council," 214–15.

22. Hans Umlauft, "Letter," 294–95.

he may believe, be he Jew or Turk."[23] Hans Denck in 1525 argued that such tolerance would be positive for society:

> Such a security will exist also in outward things, with practice of the true gospel that each will let the other move and dwell in peace—be he Turk or heathen, believing what he will—through and in his land, not submitting to a magistrate in matters of faith . . . I stand fast on what the prophet says here. Everyone among all peoples may move around in the name of his God. That is to say, no one shall deprive another—whether heathen or Jew or Christian—but rather allow everyone to move in all territories in the name of his God. So may we benefit in the peace which God gives.[24]

Influences of Erasmus and Christian Humanism on Anabaptists included (1) critiques of the religious establishment, (2) critiques of the political establishment, (3) an emphasis on the Bible as the fundamental Christian source, (4) a focus on Jesus and the Gospels, (5) alternate interpretations of New Testament texts, (6) a call for moral reform, and (7) a refusal to coerce people on questions of faith and conscience. This led Anabaptists to eschew the wars of their rulers, including those against the Muslim Turks who in the 1520s posed a great military threat. At the trial that led to his 1527 execution, Michael Sattler confessed, "If the Turk comes, he should not be resisted, for it stands written: thou shalt not kill. We should not defend ourselves against the Turks or our other persecutors, but with fervent prayer should implore God that he might be our defense and our resistance."[25] The call of Erasmus and other Humanists to return to the sources, including the Bible and the New Testament church, implied an egalitarianism that invited all to bypass the institution and tradition of the Catholic Church in the search for Truth. Their emphasis on human dignity challenged the church's doctrine of original sin and predestination, and implied free will and tolerance for those who are different.[26] Against the tradition, wealth, and violence of the church institution, Christian Humanism offered a return to the simplicity, service, and peace of Christ. Here lay seeds of Anabaptist egalitarianism, empathetic solidarity with the marginalized, tolerance of others, nonviolent advocacy, peacemaking, and service.

---

23. Aurbacher, "1534," 293.
24. Denck, "Commentary," 292.
25. Sattler, "Trial," 72.
26. Klager, "Mennonite Religious Values," 139–44.

Experience of Socio-economic, Political, and Religious Oppression

The experience of socio-economic, political, and religious oppression also influenced Anabaptist nonresistance, solidarity with the marginalized, and nonviolent advocacy. The feudal system in medieval society featured two main social classes—the lords and the serfs who worked for them. Despite a population increase and a rise in cities from the twelfth century onward that brought a rise in trade, a money economy, and a merchant class, in the sixteenth century peasants still constituted over 85% of the population.[27] Apart from some leaders before 1530, almost all the Anabaptists came from the artisan or peasant classes. Many were familiar with peasant poverty and they shared in the hardships that common folk shared.

The largest landowner was the church, and many peasants worked church lands. Everyone was aware of peasant unrest, which had much to do with agricultural production and economic conditions. After about 1450 inflation rose sharply as low yields forced prices higher, and church and secular taxes increased. Peasants suffered an ever greater economic pinch. Exacerbating these economic conditions were long-standing grievances against lay rulers, the clergy, and the church over compulsory tithes, rents, usury, and land seizures. Anger over recurrent poor harvests, rising costs, and political powerlessness, targeted at religious and secular landlords, erupted in peasant revolts every few years, as in the 1493–1517 *Bundschuh* movement.[28]

Religious and political abuses also bred anger and social unrest. The church imposed taxes on all parts of Europe to finance the church hierarchy, art collections, luxurious lifestyles, political diplomacy, buildings, and wars. As national consciousness rose, people grew less willing to pay taxes to distant Rome. As taxes did not generate enough revenue for the church, other money raising schemes included simony (buying and selling church offices), indulgences (forgiveness of sins in exchange for a financial donation), annates (the church takes a priest's first year's salary), and reservations (when a bishop dies the church collects his salary but does not replace him),

---

27. On late medieval and sixteenth-century social conditions, see Kamen, *Iron Century*; Blickle, *Revolution*; Stayer, *German Peasants' War*, 19–60; Scribner, *German Reformation*, 26–32, 37–41; Scribner, "Religion," 2–22; Cohn, "Anticlericalism," 3–31; Ozment, *Reform*, 190–204; 272–85; Williams, *Radical*, 137–74.

28. Brady, Jr., *Ruling Class*, 202; Cohn, "Anticlericalism," 6–28; Derksen, *Radicals*, 21, 38; Rott, "Strasbourg," 199; Ozment, *Reform*, 190–99.

relics of saints, and pilgrimages to holy sites. Further, clergy were often uneducated and/or immoral.[29]

Martin's Luther's 95 theses posted to a church door in 1517 were in response to these church abuses, and many Anabaptists sympathized with these sentiments. For many, economics and theology were inseparable. People who felt oppressed economically concluded that the church's teaching must be off, for their experience was of injustice, often imposed by the church. When preachers such as Luther preached that a true church with true teaching should offer social and economic justice and equality to all, this was music to the commoners' ears. Luther's words on freedom and "the Gospel" gave new vigor to the *Bundschuh*'s concepts of "ancient rights" and "divine right." Meanwhile, apocalyptic preachers, other reformers, and provocative pamphlets exacerbated unrest. So while preachers such as Luther touched a chord with scholars, artisans, and peasants, the mass response of commoners gave power to the reformers' preaching.[30]

In the years 1524–26, economic oppression, political marginalization, ecclesiastical corruption, and disillusionment over the lack of meaningful involvement in religion came to a head. In what is known as the Peasants' War, some 300,000 peasants and artisans rose to protest their grievances, and to pursue visions of a better society inspired by the "Word of God" with its proclamations of justice and freedom.[31] The clearest expression of the commoners' vision was a pamphlet of 1526 or 1527 by a Nuremberg printer named Hans Hergot. Entitled *On the New Transformation of the Christian Life*, the pamphlet describes a Christian society of equality and sharing. With an oft-repeated theme of "for the honor of God and the common good," Hergot offered the following images:

> In order to promote the honor of God and the common good, . . . God will humble all social estates, villages, castles, ecclesiastical foundations and cloisters . . . The villages will be come rich in property and people, and all their grievances will be redressed. The nobility of birth will pass away, and the common people will occupy their houses. Cloisters will lose the four mendicant orders and the right to beg, and the other rich cloisters will lose what they possess in payments and rents . . . All resources—such

29. Ozment, *Reform*, 204–22; Cohn, "Anticlericalism, 3–31; Snyder, *Anabaptist History*, 15–19; González, *Christianity*, 6–13.

30. Baylor, *Radical*, xi; Stayer, *German Peasants' War*, 19–60; Cohn, "Anticlericalism," 3–31; Derksen, *Radicals*, 25–26, 31, 35–42; Rott, "Strasbourg," 199.

31. See Blickle, *Revolution*, 25–67; Baylor, *Radical*, xi–xvii; Stayer, *German Peasants' War*, 5; Gerber, "Sebastian Lotzer," 80–83; Ozment, *Reform*, 272–80; Snyder, *Anabaptist History*, 32–33; Goertz, "Karlstadt," 3–4.

as woods, water, meadows, etc.—will be used in common . . . And all things will be used in common, so that no one is better off than another.[32]

This new society would also be spiritual: "The people will believe in God, and prove this with works, prayers, fasting, and by reflection on God's suffering, divine mercy, and other matters . . . Then the 'Our Father' will be fulfilled and the word which the lord often uses in the 'Our Father' will be meaningful: our, our, our."[33] More specific grievances and political plans appeared in Peasants' War programs such as *The Twelve Articles of the Upper Swabian Peasants*.[34]

Of course the establishment—the rulers, the upper classes, the Catholic Church hierarchy, and even reforming intellectuals such as Luther—did not like this. They feared that all of society would be overturned. So rulers, supported by the church hierarchy and Luther, brutally crushed the uprising—and the commoners' quest for a social revolution. Some 100,000 commoners were killed.[35] Survivors "were left with a choice either to abandon their dream by returning to Catholicism or the [Protestant] reform, or to pursue it down alternative paths," such as apocalypticism, spiritualism, or sectarianism.[36]

Most Anabaptists were familiar with these developments. Their own experiences of economic hardship and moral, ethical, and theological abuses led to resentment against the church hierarchy, compassion for the suffering, solidarity with other dissenters, a reminder that Christ too had been poor and persecuted, and a commitment to recover the simple, peaceable model of Christ and the New Testament church. Memory of these experiences came to influence Anabaptist peacemaking, egalitarianism, empathetic solidarity with the marginalized, and nonviolent advocacy.

The Protestant Reformation

In several ways the Protestant Reformation was the nest in which Anabaptism was born, and it influenced Anabaptist biblicism, egalitarianism,

---

32. Hans Hergot, "Christian Life," 210–12.

33. Ibid., 210–13.

34. Other peasant programs included "The Eleven Mühlhausen Articles," "The Memmingen Federal Constitution," "The Document of Articles of the Black Forest Peasants," "The Forty-six Frankfurt Articles," and "Michael Gaismair's Territorial Constitution for Tyrol," in Baylor, *Radical*, 227–60.

35. Snyder, *Anabaptist History*, 32; Ozment, *Reform*, 280–85.

36. Derksen, *Radicals*, 42.

and peacemaking orientations. (1) Reformers such as Martin Luther (1483–1546), Ulrich Zwingli (1481–1531), and Andreas von Karlstadt (c. 1480–1541) articulated the grievances against the Catholic Church and gave commoners a voice. At the same time, the embrace of the masses gave the reformers social power and made the Reformation possible.[37] Anabaptists emerged out of this movement and in some ways carried it further. (2) The Reformation placed new emphasis on the Bible, its availability, and the right of ordinary people to read and understand it. Anabaptists highlighted this. (3) The Reformation placed new emphasis on the grace of God and faith in Christ for salvation, apart from saints, clerics, and the institutional church. While Anabaptists interpreted grace and faith somewhat differently from the mainline reformers, they all embraced the need for God's grace and faith. (4) The Reformation imagined and articulated a new vision for the church, one different from the Catholic Church and closer to the New Testament church, in which all believers were priests.[38] Anabaptists embraced this vision, and when it fell short, they tried to carry it further.

In his 95 theses and in his preaching Martin Luther gave eloquent expression to the widespread criticism of Catholic Church tithes and abuses, and the popular agitation for social justice and meaningful worship. His emphasis on spiritual freedom by faith through the grace of God carried connotations of socio-economic freedom and offered hope to burdened peasants and artisans. His *sola scriptura* principle reinforced peasant demands for justice in line with the "Word of God." His use of the printing press hastened the spread of pamphlets with messages of reform. His translation of the Bible into German encouraged people to read it for themselves. His emphasis on Jesus Christ alone contributed to the criticism of the church's hierarchy, sacraments, confessions, and other forms of social control. Colleagues of Luther such as Karlstadt pushed his reforms further and encouraged image removal and attacks on monasteries. Were it not for Luther's break with the Catholic Church and the popular impetus he offered for reform, the Anabaptist movements might have been stillborn.[39]

The first Anabaptists emerged in the context of the Swiss Reformation, led by the Humanist priest and Bible preacher Ulrich Zwingli. Like Erasmus and Luther, Zwingli's emphasis on the authority of the Bible reinforced the criticisms of the Catholic Church and society. Zwingli's popular Bible-based

37. Stayer, *German Peasants' War*, 43, 60.

38. See Snyder, "Recovering," 12–16; Snyder, *Anabaptist History*, 43–49; Weaver, *Becoming Anabaptist*, 224–31; Roth, "Recent Currents," 530–35.

39. Derksen, *Radicals*, 34, 36–39; Weaver, *Becoming Anabaptist*, 27, 30–33, 44–49, 53; Pater, *Karlstadt*; Snyder, *Anabaptist History*, 19–22, 25–28; Goertz, "Karlstadt," 1–20.

preaching and his success in persuading the Zurich city council to accept reform (albeit gradually) enabled Humanist intellectuals in the city and priests and commoners in the countryside to hope that thoroughgoing reform, with social justice and meaningful worship might truly be on the way. Only when intellectuals in Zurich and priests in the countryside became impatient with the slowness of Zwingli's reform did they break from him in pursuit of a more radical reformation of the countryside, which became caught up in the Peasants' War.[40]

Although Anabaptists ended up diverging from the mainline reformers, in many ways the Reformation made the birth of Anabaptists possible. By energizing the protests against poverty and church abuses, by giving hope for change, by focusing people's attention on the authority of the Bible rather than church tradition, by energizing peasants and artisans to call for a transformed society in line with the "Word of God," by focusing worshipers' attention on Jesus and the New Testament, by stimulating pamphlets to spread ever more radical ideas of reform, and by spawning other reformers throughout Europe, the Protestant Reformation prepared the way for Anabaptism. Its early call to restore the New Testament church invigorated the Anabaptists. The Reformation's *sola scriptura*, *sola fide*, and *sola gratia* principles opened the way for Anabaptists to approach God and study the way of Christ without saints and priests to mediate Truth for them, and to stand in solidarity with others who sought to ground their lives and societies in "the Word of God." In the Reformation's emphasis on the priesthood of all believers, Anabaptists affirmed the dignity of all, including women, peasants, artisans, and the poor. Thus the Protestant Reformation gave the Anabaptist movements fertile soil in which to take root.

Experience of Disillusionment and Persecution after 1525

Despite the hope engendered by Christian Humanism and the Protestant Reformation, by 1526, many common folk and radicals, including future Anabaptists, were disappointed and disillusioned. The published programs of the Peasants' War movement such as the "Twelve Articles," had justified their demands with "the Word of God." And Martin Luther's movement had disseminated hopeful slogans such as "the pure Gospel," "Christian liberty," and "the priesthood of all believers."[41] Rejecting both secular and

---

40. Snyder, "Swiss Anabaptism," 48–79; Snyder, *Anabaptist History*, 51–65; Weaver, *Becoming Anabaptist*, 27–50; Stayer, *German Peasants' War*, 61–92; Goertz, "Karlstadt," 3–4.

41. Baylor, *Radical*, xi, 231–38; Ozment, *Reform*, 272–87.

ecclesiastical hierarchies, leaders of the rural communal Reformation had envisioned "an egalitarian Christian communalism." Each local community would "hear the gospel preached in pure form and regulate its life according to the gospel." Community members would have rights to manage certain local affairs, oversee the local church, choose their own minister, and allocate their own tithes.[42]

But hopes were dashed. Although Luther had expressed support for such reforms in 1522, by 1524 he opposed them.[43] The commoners' uprising of 1524–26 was crushed. Zwingli was not willing to move his reform faster than the Zurich city council was willing, for like all others, he envisioned not a new, separated church, but a *Volkskirche*, a church of the community that would include the city council. Idealists such as Conrad Grebel, Felix Manz, and other young Humanist intellectuals in Zurich, wishing to enact the "Word of God" immediately, grew impatient. Rural priests such as Wilhelm Reublin and Simon Stumpf and their parishioners were frustrated by Zurich's continued control over their pastors and the use of their tithes. A public debate on baptism in 1525 resulted in condemnation of the radicals' viewpoint, and in January 1527 Felix Manz became the first Anabaptist to be executed by drowning.[44] The radicals, including the Anabaptists, were disillusioned and marginalized.

Some disappointed radicals persisted in their quest for a social revolution. Other recast it in apocalyptic terms. Others chose a more individualistic spiritualism. Still others, the Anabaptists, "formed separatist communities in which to realize their radical ideals. Whatever the path, to some degree the radical movements from 1526 onward were a sublimated form of the commoners' revolt of 1525."[45]

But even these alternative directions involved disappointment. A broad social revolution never happened. Among the apocalypticists, the predictions of Hans Hut, Melchior Hoffman, and others of Christ's return in 1528, 1529, 1533, and other years were all proven wrong. Those who turned to spiritualism tended over time to die out because they lacked institutional structures for the long term. And Anabaptists had to rethink their view of the church. The first Anabaptists in Switzerland had envisioned a *Volkskirche*, a reformed church of the community. The disastrous Peasants'

42. Baylor, *Radical*, xvi, xxi; Goertz, "Karlstadt," 3–4; Gerber, "Sebastian Lotzer," 82–83.

43. Baylor, *Radical*, xvi; Ozment, *Reform*, 280–85; Cohn, "Anticlericalism," 5–6.

44. Weaver, *Becoming Anabaptist*, 27–64; Snyder, *Anabaptist History*, 12–15, 32–34, 51–65; Stayer, *German Peasants' War*, 61–65.

45. Derksen, *Radicals*, 42; Baylor, *Radical*, xx–xxvi; Stayer, *German Peasants' War*, 73.

War led them to question both the method of violence and the possibility of a Christlike *Volkskirche*. Led by men such as Michael Sattler in Switzerland, Jacob Hutter and Peter Riedemann in Moravia, Pilgram Marpeck in South Germany, and Menno Simons in the Netherlands, and as seen in 1527 Schleitheim Confession, many Anabaptists committed to a voluntary church separate from the existing alliance of church and state.[46] This invited the hostility of political and ecclesiastical authorities.

An economic disappointment was the ongoing practice of usury. Fridolin Meyger, a Strasbourg notary who drafted contracts for "rents and debts payable to the aristocracy," confessed that the failure of the Peasants' uprising and the ongoing practice of usury among the upper classes "drove him to the Anabaptists."[47] Hans Pfistermeyer, a Swiss Anabaptist leader, declared in 1531, "I have been offended by [the clergy's] remuneration since it has its source in usury. I know full well that he who serves with the gospel is entitled to a sufficient living from it. However, it may not come from interest or from usury. It is unrighteous gain."[48]

Another disappointment was hostility from the clergy and the lack of moral discipline in the Lutheran and Reformed churches. In the village of Wangen, at the funeral of the Anabaptist Hans Weibel, the pastor permanently alienated Weibel's wife and children by calling him "a godless and hellbound man." According to Hans Hagenawer, in the Reformed church "people lived unethical lives, and the pastor punished the pious, ignored blatant sinners, and slandered people rather than preach the word of God."[49] The Strasbourg Anabaptist, Leonhard Jost, refused to join the Reformed church for fifteen years because morals were not improved. When he finally joined in 1539, it was "because the ban had finally been established in the church and not every blatant, gross sinner [was] admitted to the eucharist."[50] Menno Simons complained in 1539,

> I wish to admonish you in faithful brotherly spirit one and all, Roman Catholics, Lutherans, and Zwinglians . . . What is your entire ambition and conduct if not world, carnality, belly, and life of luxury? . . . Some of you parade in ermine, in silk and velvet, others live in headlong revelry, others are avaricious and hoard; some disgrace virgins and young women, others defile

---

46. Weaver, *Becoming Anabaptist*, 51–64, 159; Snyder, *Anabaptist History*, 51–63.
47. Derksen, *Radicals*, 49, 96, 112.
48. "Conversation with Pfistermeyer, 1531," 124.
49. Derksen, *Radicals*, 218.
50. Ibid., 124.

the bed of their neighbor, the chastity of others is like the chastity of Sodom.[51]

Worse than hostility and slander was outright persecution from secular rulers such as Ferdinand II and the Catholic, Lutheran, and Reformed clergy. Between 1525 and 1550 thousands of Anabaptists were imprisoned, tortured, exiled, and executed.[52] As seen in *The Martyrs' Mirror*, this bred in the Anabaptists a deep empathy for others who suffer and are marginalized.

The radicals' sense of betrayal in Luther's reversal, the crushing of the peasants, Zwingli's cautious approach to reform, the end of the earliest Anabaptists' dream of a truly Christlike *Volkskirche*, the lack of moral improvement in Protestant churches, and outright persecution from secular and church authorities all shaped the early Anabaptists' worldview. These disappointments bred a commitment to an alternative community in line with the New Testament church. Here members would love each other, be radically equal, stand in solidarity with others who suffered, and accept persecution nonviolently. Thus disillusionment with developments after 1525 influenced early Anabaptist nonresistance, egalitarianism, solidarity with the suffering, and nonviolent advocacy.

Experience of a Healing Alternative Community

In the face of disillusionment and persecution, the support, encouragement, hope, and healing that Anabaptists found in their gatherings empowered them in their commitment and engendered later Mennonite peacebuilding and nonviolent advocacy.

One form of support was economic. Among the Hutterites this meant sharing all things in common. Among the Swiss Brethren, the Marpeck communities, and the Dutch Anabaptists, this generally meant generous sharing with those in need.[53] Swiss Brethren in Strasbourg testified in 1526 that they gathered in homes for worship. Emphasis fell on baptism following faith and mutual ethical obligations, including pacifism and sharing material possessions with the needy.[54] When Pilgram Marpeck, Jakob Kautz, Wilhelm Reublin, and Fridolin Meyger were arrested in 1528, they were collecting money for refugees, foreigners, and the poor in Strasbourg.[55]

---

51. Menno Simons, "Foundation," 207–8.
52. Gregory, "Martrydom," 478; Stayer, "Swiss-South," 108–9.
53. See Stayer, *German Peasants' War*, 95–106.
54. Derksen, *Radicals*, 46.
55. Ibid., 62.

Another form of support was social and moral. Meyger, distressed that neither the Peasants' War nor the Reformation had eliminated the use of usury against the poor, found "sincere love of God and neighbor" among the Anabaptists.[56] Some who were ostracized in the established churches found acceptance in Anabaptist circles. In Wangen, Simon Bentzen investigated the Anabaptists to see if they were as evil as the pastor had described them. He discovered that "they did good and avoided evil. Earlier he had been godless but now in their circle he sought to do good and be pious."[57] Moral support included a voice for all. All could interpret the Scriptures and contribute their insights. In meetings led by Leonard Schiemer in Rattenberg in 1527 and probably Pilgram Marpeck in later years,

> members met frequently to pray for each other. During meetings persons spoke in order while the others listened and evaluated the message, and they celebrated the Lord's Supper . . . Offerings were used to meet mutual needs. The dissolute were disciplined by the group. Each individual, then, was accountable for the group's life, worship, discipline and ministry.[58]

Participatory worship enabled mutual caring and accountability.

Women, who normally were voiceless in the sixteenth century, often found a voice and a ministry in Anabaptist congregations. Since worshipers usually gathered in homes, women, as hosts, held the congregations and the entire movement together in crucial ways. Ministry opportunities arose especially in communities where the work of the Holy Spirit received emphasis. Ursula Jost and Barbara Rebstock, for example, were known for their preaching and had a loyal following. In places, women taught, preached, evangelized, interpreted Scripture, wrote letters and songs, carried messages, nourished believers in hiding, hosted sewing circles and Bible readings, distributed alms, and housed traveling ministers and refugees.[59] As the examples of Margareta Sattler (1527), Elsbeth Hubmaier (1528), Margret Hottinger (1530), Katherina Hutter (1538), Anneken Jans (1539), and Elisabeth Dirks (1549), and Soetken van den Houte (1560), and others show,

---

56. Ibid., 49.

57. Ibid., 214.

58. Ibid., 62–63; Boyd, *Pilgram Marpeck*, 61–62.

59. See Roper, *Holy Household*, 253–54; Haude, "Gender Roles," 430–31, 439; Stjerna, *Women*, 15–17; Hecht, "Review," 406–15; Wyntjes, "Netherlands," 276–89; Wyntjes, "Reformation Era," 165–91; Sprunger, "Radical Reformation," 46; Umble, "Women," 135–45; Klassen, "Women," 548–71; Snyder, *Anabaptist History*, 251–74; and, generally, Snyder and Hecht, *Profiles*.

women displayed amazing courage in the face of imprisonment and death. Companions in faith, mission, and martyrdom, they were spiritual equals.[60]

To strengthen each other in the face of torture and death, the Swiss Brethren assembled a biblical concordance with passages pertaining to persecution. Clustered passages under headings such as "'Persecution,' 'Bearing Witness,' 'Be Not Afraid,' and 'Patience'" helped them to internalize the Bible verses with which they answered their interrogators and faced death.[61]

In their church communities, early Anabaptists discovered hope, love, acceptance, equality, inclusion, mutual sharing, and mutual support. Economic support, whether in sharing all things in common, or in generous sharing with those in need, expressed solidarity and equality with all. Social and emotional support communicated acceptance, equality, and solidarity. Radical equality emerged both in the relatively prominent place of women and in the participatory worship where all could interpret the Scriptures and contribute their insights. Here Anabaptists encouraged each other to follow Christ in holiness and service, and in suffering and death if necessary. Thus the experience of a healing alternative community nurtured early Anabaptist nonresistance, service, egalitarianism, and solidarity with the suffering.

Emphasis on the Centrality of Jesus and the New Testament

Finally, the Anabaptist emphasis on the centrality of Jesus and the New Testament shaped later Mennonite peacemaking. Early Anabaptists differed in their geographical and cultural backgrounds, in their patterns of worship, in the degree of their economic sharing, in their attitudes to the state, in their approach to the sword, on the relative importance of the Word and the Spirit, and in other ways. But they agreed on the centrality of Jesus and the New Testament. Whether Swiss, German, Austrian, Moravian, or Dutch; whether Biblicist or spiritualistic; whether peasant or artisan or scholar, they agreed that Jesus and the New Testament were central to their faith. The Swiss Balthasar Hubmaier wrote in 1525, "Now this person surrenders himself inwardly in the heart and intention unto a new life according to the rule and teaching of Christ, the physician who has made him whole, from

---

60. Van Braght, *Martyr's Mirror*, 481–83; Snyder and Hecht, *Profiles*; Weaver, *Becoming Anabaptist*, 57–58, 139–40, 219; Snyder, *Anabaptist History*, 117, 119, 254–58; Stjerna, *Women*, 17; Williams, *Radical*, 762; Sprunger, "Radical Reformation," 53–54.

61. Gregory, "Martyrdom," 471–72.

whom he received life . . . Christ lives in him, is life in him."[62] The Hutterite Peter Riedemann wrote in 1542, "In him and in none other is salvation . . . He is the Saviour who has robbed death of its power, torn its bond and snare asunder and set us, his people, free."[63] The Netherlander Dirk Philips wrote in 1558, "Man does not live by other words which proceed from the will of man, but alone by the words of God (Mt. 4:4), which have been made known to us by Jesus Christ and his apostles. Here is the bread of heaven; here is the water of life."[64]

Influences that nurtured this orientation included Erasmus and the Christian Humanists who called people to return to the sources such as the New Testament, the new availability of the Bible for laypeople in their own language, the long tradition of monasticism that sought the pure pursuit of God, the medieval theology of suffering and martyrdom in identification with Jesus, medieval mysticism that sought oneness with Jesus, the Medieval *Devotio Moderna* emphasis on imitating Christ, and the Anabaptists' rejection of abuses and violence in the Catholic and Reformation Churches.

Biblical inspiration came from the teaching, life, death, and resurrection of Jesus, and from the New Testament church described in Acts 2–4. The teaching of Jesus, especially the Sermon on the Mount on seeking first God's reign and returning good for evil (Mt. 5–7), undergirded the Anabaptists' determination to be separate from the sinful world. In the Schleitheim Confession, the Swiss Brethren confessed,

> We have been united concerning the separation that shall take place from the evil and the wickedness which the devil has planted in the world, simply in this: that we have no fellowship with them . . . The commandment of the Lord is also obvious, whereby he orders us to be and to become separated from the evil one, thus He will be our God and we shall be His sons and daughters.[65]

Peter Riedemann wrote similarly, "Thus is Christ king of all kings; . . . therefore he says, "My kingdom of not of this world . . . Thus he sets up quite a different kingdom and rule and desires that his servants submit themselves to it and become like him."[66]

One implication of separation from the world and returning good for evil for the Anabaptists was nonresistance in peace and war. In the words of

62. Hubmaier, "Summa," 85.
63. Peter Riedeman, "Account," 29.
64. Dirk Philips, "True Knowledge," 38–39.
65. Yoder, *Michael Sattler*, 37–38.
66. Peter Riedemann, "Account," 261.

the Schleitheim Confession, "Thereby shall also fall away from us the diabolical weapons of violence—such as the sword, armor, and the like, and all of their use to protect friends or against enemies—by virtue of the word of Christ: 'you shall not resist evil.'"[67] Dirk Philips wrote, "True Christians must here be persecuted for the sake of truth and righteousness, but they persecute no one on account of his faith."[68] Many Anabaptists went even further to demand conscientious objection to war. Conrad Grebel wrote to Thomas Müntzer in 1524, "True Christians use neither the worldly sword nor war, for among them killing has been totally abolished."[69] Peter Riedemann repudiated not only military service but also the manufacture of arms: "Now since Christians must not use and practice such vengeance, neither can they make weapons by which such vengeance and destruction may be practiced by others that they be not partakers of the other men's sins. Therefore we make neither swords, spears, muskets nor any such weapons."[70] Anabaptist nonresistance, readiness for martyrdom, conscientious objection, and refusal to make weapons of war all developed in response to the teaching of Jesus.

Aspects of Jesus' life that inspired Anabaptists included his healing, his identity with common folk, and his openness to Gentiles. Menno Simons wrote, "They show indeed that they believe, that they are born of God and are spiritually minded; that they lead a pious, unblamable life before all men . . . They walk in all love and mercy and serve their neighbors."[71] For Menno and others, this commitment was concrete: "True evangelical faith cannot lie sleeping . . . It clothes that naked, feeds the hungry, comforts the sorrowful, shelters the destitute, serves those who harm it, binds up that which is wounded; it has become all things to all people."[72] Further, wrote Menno, Christians extend this service also to enemies: "This is the nature of pure love, to pray for persecutors, to render good for evil, to love one's enemies."[73]

For some Anabaptists, Jesus' openness to Gentiles implied an openness to all including heretics, Jews, and Muslims. Balthasar Hubmaier wrote in 1524,

> The inquisitors are the greatest heretics of all, because counter to the teaching and example of Jesus they condemn heretics to fire

---

67. Yoder, *Michael Sattler*, 37–38.
68. Philips, "Church," 298.
69. Grebel, "Müntzer," 42–43.
70. Riedeman, "Account," 278–79. See Stauffer, "Martyrdom," 235.
71. Simons, "Confession," 505–6.
72. Simons, "Writing," 307.
73. Simons, "Foundation," 200.

> ... A Turk or a heretic cannot be overcome by our doing, neither by sword or by fire, but alone with patience and supplication ... To burn heretics appears to be confessing Christ (Titus 1:16), but indeed it is to deny him ... The law [which provides] for the burning of heretics is an invention of the devil.[74]

Melchior Hoffman wrote in 1533, "All are created for eternal salvation ... The holy Paul witnesses in Rom. 11 that God will have mercy on all. Of such witness the biblical Scriptures are full that Christ Jesus did not suffer for half a world but for the whole world, that is the whole seed of Adam."[75] Hans Umlauft wrote in 1539, "We must listen to Christ when he says that many, who are today called Turks and heathen, will come from east and west and eat with Abraham in the kingdom of God."[76] Thus Jesus' life of service, healing, and openness to outsiders inspired Anabaptists to serve the needy, stand with the suffering, and embrace the outcast.

Jesus' suffering and death inspired Anabaptists to accept persecution without resistance and to stand in solidarity with others who suffered. Menno Simons named "oppression and tribulation for the sake of the Lord's Word" as one of the true marks of the Church of Jesus Christ.[77] In a 1534/35 letter to Tyrolian prisoners in Austria, Jacob Hutter wrote, "Do not be ashamed of the bonds and suffering of Christ, but rejoice greatly in your hearts, for you know that nothing else has been promised you for your life on earth except suffering and death, tribulation, anxiety, distress and great persecution, pain, torture, insult and shame at the hands of godless men."[78] This kind of exhortation came not only from Anabaptist leaders. On the morning of her execution, a young mother, Anneken Jans of Rotterdam, wrote in 1539,

> My son, ... behold, I go today the way of the prophets, apostles, and martyrs, and drink of the cup they all have drunk. Matt. 20:23. I go, I say, the way which Christ Jesus ... himself went ... and who had to drink of this cup, even as he said, "I have a cup to drink of and a baptism to be baptized with ..." Having passed through, He calls His sheep, and His sheep hear His voice and follow Him whithersoever He goes.[79]

---

74. Hubmaier, "Heretics," 62, 64, 66.
75. Hoffman, "June/July 1533," 59–60.
76. Umlauft, "Letter," 294–95. See also Packull, *Mysticism*, 41–46.
77. Simons, "Reply," 742–43.
78. Hutter, "Letter," 91–92.
79. Van Braght, *Martyr's Mirror*, 453.

The concordance that clustered passages pertaining to persecution and faithfulness helped Anabaptists remain steadfast when interrogated and facing death.[80] Anabaptist songs also helped them internalize the biblical calls to discipleship and suffering. The first stanza of an early hymn that was later incorporated into the first Anabaptist hymnbook, the *Ausbund* (1564), reads as follows: "He who would follow Christ in life / Must scorn the world's insult and strife, / And bear his cross each day. / For this alone leads to the throne; / Christ is the only way."[81] The nonviolent suffering and death of Jesus was a model.

Faith in the resurrection of Jesus and eternal life gave Anabaptists hope and courage to persist in their difficult calling. Jacob Hutter, who was burned at the stake in 1536, wrote to encourage fellow believers, "Whoever battles like a true knight of Christ and is victorious will be crowned and will attain the prize. He will enter upon peace and joy, eternal rest and glory with all the chosen and with the heavenly host. He will be with the Father, his dear Son, and all the saints for ever and ever in the covenant of eternal life."[82] Menno Simons wrote similarly,

> The messenger is already at the door, who will say to us, Come ye blessed, enter into the glory of thy Lord. Then will our brief mourning be changed to laughter, our momentary pain into endless joy ... All our persecutors, executioners, and torturers will cease ... Neither ill nor pain nor pangs of death will touch us longer, but we will forever exalt, praise, and thank in expressively great joy and glory the Lamb who sits upon the throne.[83]

The Anabaptists centred on Jesus as teacher, model, and savior. His teaching inspired their separateness, peacemaking, and service for others. His life inspired compassion and service. His death inspired nonresistant service to others and solidarity with the suffering. Faith in his resurrection gave Anabaptists hope and courage to carry on in their path of nonresistance, service, solidarity, and sacrifice.

Also inspiring for Anabaptists was the model of the New Testament church seen in Acts 2–4. Although Hans Hergot was not an Anabaptist, his widely shared vision of a Christian society of equality and sharing echoed aspects of Acts 2–4 and is very close to what Anabaptists imagined in Switzerland and attempted in Moravia:

80. Gregory, "Martyrdom," 471–72.
81. Wagner, "Christo," 88. See also Gregory, "Martyrdom," 474–75.
82. Hutter, "Fourth Epistle," 325.
83. Simons, "Encouragement," 1047–48.

> In order to promote the honor of God and the common good, ... God will ... institute a new way of life in which no one will say, "That is mine." ... All resources—such as woods, water, meadows, etc.—will be used in common ... And the people will all work in common, each according to his talents and his capacities. And all things will be used in common, so that no one is better off than another ... The people will believe in God, and prove this with works, prayers, fasting, and by reflecting on God's suffering, divine mercy, and other matters ... All crafts will also be practiced as they should, and desires for selfish gain will be done away with. And a longing for the common good will prevail over the whole village. Then the "Our Father" will be fulfilled and the word which the lord often uses in the "Our Father" will be meaningful: our, our, our.[84]

To some degree Anabaptists brought this dream to reality. While the Swiss Brethren, Marpeck's followers, and Dutch Anabaptists practiced voluntary sharing with the needy, the Hutterites realized this dream of "our, our, our" "for the honor of God and the common good" more radically.[85] This vision and lived experience laid the groundwork for later Mennonites to nurture a society of equality and sharing, even as Jesus as teacher, model, and savior inspired nonresistance, compassionate service, and hope.

This paper argues that (1) medieval Catholic spirituality, (2) Renaissance Humanism, (3) the experience of socio-economic, political, and religious oppression, (4) the Protestant Reformation, (5) disillusionment and persecution after 1525, (6) the experience of a healing alternative community, and (7) emphasis on the centrality of Jesus and the New Testament gave rise to Anabaptist service, solidarity with the marginalized, nonviolent advocacy, and peacemaking. These, in turn, inspired later Mennonites to engage in peacebuilding and shaped their peacebuilding approaches.

These factors point to external influences, lived experiences, and inner commitments. Among external influences, medieval Catholic traditions of monastic asceticism, mysticism, apocalypticism, practical service, the imitation of Christ, and a martyrdom theology were prominent. Renaissance Humanism influenced Anabaptists to critique the religious and political establishment; to uphold the Word of God as the fundamental Christian source; to embrace ethical living and Christlike peace and service; and to affirm human freedom and dignity, especially in matters of faith and conscience. The Protestant Reformation helped birth Anabaptists by energizing protests against Church abuses, encouraging people to read the Bible,

---

84. Hergot, "Christian Life," 210–13.
85. See Stayer, *German Peasants' War*, 151–52, 162; Baylor, *Radical*, 210–13.

engendering hope for a transformed society in line with the "Word of God," and proclaiming a church in which God's grace and faith in Christ alone brought salvation, and all believers were priests. Lived experiences included the socio-economic, political, and religious hardships that peasants and most commoners suffered before the Peasants' War; disillusionment with the Reformation and persecution from church and secular authorities after 1525; and belonging, healing, and empowerment in the Anabaptist community. Inner commitments included commitments to follow Jesus in daily life and even in suffering, to relive the New Testament church, and to support others toward healing and hope in the Anabaptist community. Together these influences, experiences, and commitments moulded the character of Anabaptists and their biological and spiritual descendants. Later Mennonites drew on these memories, traditions, and character to engage in peacebuilding.

2

The Testing of Mennonite Peacemaking in Twentieth-Century Soviet Russia

Walter Sawatsky

Whose Narrative and Why?

THE RUSSIAN MENNONITE EXPERIENCE during the 20th century is seldom told and scarcely known outside its own more recent diaspora. Yet its traumas and ambiguities are worth knowing and pondering and may teach better the way of peace than does the extensive literature about American Mennonites and their peace theology. Here we can merely sketch out themes, cite vignettes, point out misperceptions, and offer more accurate main themes. A dominant way of telling the Russian Mennonite story for the past century was to focus on the agricultural success of 19th century Russian Mennonite colonists, similar to other German colonists in Russia who were Catholic, Lutheran, or Moravian, all of them contributing to the modernization of agriculture. One misperception was that it was the Ukrainian wheat fields that still constituted the bread basket of the Russian Empire, whereas an advancing frontier of settlement across eastern Russia, Siberia and Central Asia had already shaped the developmental dynamic of the second half of that century.

By 1890 more than half of the Russian Mennonite colonists were no longer in the south Russian imperial heartland. That eastward settlement process continued during the 20th century, so that since 1950 virtually all

Russian Mennonites were living in the Soviet Union's Asiatic regions. The standard story, however, was to stress the out-migration of Russian Mennonites, especially the immigration of 18,000 (1874–78) and 23,000 (1923–26) Mennonites to the plains of Canada and the United States. A vivid image in the movie *And When They Shall Ask* shows a train leaving the Soviet Union as the liberated Mennonites break into a song of thanksgiving. It seems God went with the Mennonites to North America, and those left behind disappeared from the storytelling.[1] The continued story, until quite recently, was to examine the immigrants' impact on the United States, Canada, and Paraguay. Indeed, between 1930 and 1956, contact and access was nearly impossible, and relatives were afraid to cause harm by speaking publicly about the fate of their loved ones. It was also a period of such excessive anti-communist rhetoric, so often framed in Christian language, that the north American Mennonites also learned to assume that Christians, including Mennonites, had disappeared in that atheist land.

The word 'colony' took on a specific meaning in 19th century Russia. It applied to free entrepreneurial immigrant groups from Germany, Greece, and other regions in contrast to the fourteen strata of Russians and their serfs. Serfdom officially ended in 1861, but the freed peasants were soon deeply indebted. Categories of citizenship also began emerging after 1861, steadily challenging the special arrangements for foreign colonists. The latter were self-administered colonies, with oversight from a special tsarist bureau of guardians.[2] Religious rights were also negotiated with the authorities who issued a formal *Privilegium* as the basis for colony life.[3] For Mennonites, this pattern of settlement had similarities with what they had practiced during the previous three centuries in Polish and east Prussian territories. There already, in a diversity of ways (depending on local condi-

---

1. When the dramatized movie appeared in 1983 it marked an effort to tell a fuller story, but the final out-migration in 1929 was the high drama moment. James Urry, anthropologist from Britain, began publishing well researched articles, and then a monograph on the first century (1789–1889): cf. Urry, *None but Saints*. A more recent social political analysis by Urry, *Mennonites, Politics, and Peoplehood*, while full of judicious insights and critiques, nevertheless retained the framework of moving the story and issues to Canada after 1929. As retired Reformation scholar, Abraham Friesen, drew heavily on the extensive papers of his relatives to write *In Defense of Privilege*. It too has long and fascinating quotes from his sources, but it not only retains the Urry pattern of moving to Canada, but also assigned the Russian Mennonites the Swiss version of the Anabaptist vision as normative for theological critique, something Urry no longer found useful.

2. Still a reliable guide for comparison is Bartlett, *Human Capital*.

3. The technical meaning of *Privilegium* was already noted in Friesen, "Mennonites in Poland"; currently, the best survey noting the many variants over three centuries is Klassen, *Poland and Prussia*.

tions) their religious rights, including freedom from military service, were maintained, because local Polish or German overlords had valued their industry and moral character enough to agree to the military exemption. Progressive restrictions as the Prussian Empire grew, specifically shrinking rights to avoiding military service and a need for more land, accounted for large Mennonite group migrations to the Russian Empire starting in 1789.

Until about 1850, Mennonite colonists in Russia tended to focus on basic survival and adaptation to new conditions, while relying on spiritual and other types of counsel from those who had remained in Polish & Prussian lands. Already more connected through literature, itineration of preachers, and personal contact with other Protestant communities through the Pietist renewal movements, by 1850 the Russian Mennonites had also developed ties with the variety of voluntary societies for spiritual and humanitarian needs that had emerged in Russia. For example, Mennonites cooperated with the Russian Bible Society when it opened branches in Mennonite regions in 1813. They also contributed to related societies for prison reform and to the British Baptist mission society, to which the Dutch and German Mennonites also contributed. Soon after the Dutch Mennonites formed their own mission society (1849) to send missionaries to the Dutch East Indies (now Indonesia), it was the Russian Mennonites, between 1860 and 1910, who were disproportionately active in sending missionaries to Indonesia and supporting them.[4] This included attempts at establishing mission colonies with agricultural projects, as the Moravian missionaries had done since their beginnings in 1731 and whose programs in Russia during the second half of the 19th century were known to the Russian Mennonites. That is a brief way of saying that the values of shared community life in the colony structure, a deep commitment to a way of peace, and a missional engagement with society around them, were firmly established.

The American world tended to forget about the larger body of Russian Mennonites who had remained, still over 100,000 strong, because the large group migrations of Russian Mennonites to the United States and Canada in the 1870s, and again in the 1920s, generated a major impact on the forms of American and Canadian Mennonite engagement in society. For example, they established service and mission societies after 1900 and became involved in more activist social engagement because of alternative service experiences during World War II. During Civil War clashes across Mennonite colonies in the Ukraine, some desperate Mennonites formed an armed self-defense league or *Selbstschutz*. It achieved little, and within 18 months, church leaders who had reluctantly agreed to the effort, publicly

---

4. Hoekema, *Dutch Mennonite*, 75–96.

reversed their support by admitting that they had sinned and again called for nonviolence as the biblical way.[5]

This episode of betrayal of principle has had two long-term impacts: on the one hand Soviet authorities treated it as evidence of Mennonites supporting the reactionary tsarists and disloyalty to Soviet power. Given the Mennonite pacifist influence on the Russian evangelicals who had emerged around them and establishing church unions after a toleration decree in 1906 with written constitutions that contained pacifist clauses, the persistent pacifist impulse within the free church movements of the 20th century was a key reason, as recent access to documents confirms, that Soviet authorities soon devoted disproportionate effort to break their pacifism.[6]

The other unfortunate long term impact was that Mennonite communities in the United States and Canada—who had Swiss and South German Anabaptist roots—gained knowledge of this Russian Mennonite betrayal of the way of nonviolence but were unaware of the subsequent pacifist martyrs during the 1920s, rendering these Russian Mennonites as no longer worthy of teaching them. What also seems forgotten is that in the first decades of the 20th century, the Russian Mennonite colonies were then the largest, well organized Mennonite communities anywhere, stretching from several large and smaller daughter colonies in the Dnepr region, the Volga region, Caucasus and already by 1909 to western Siberia, Kazakhstan, and Kyrgyzstan. Respected for their industry by the state, their school system, teacher training, hospitals, and other charitable projects would have continued to make them a model for other Mennonites, had not war and revolution, and then collectivization and the war on religion destroyed their way of life.

The Soviet Mennonite Experience as a Helpful Paradigm for Lived Peacemaking

The actual Russian Mennonite story of the struggle for the way of peace is probably a more helpful paradigm for free church communities around the world today facing serious testing as minorities in hostile settings.[7] First we should note that although around 18,000 Mennonites left Russia for the United States and Canada, the larger majority that stayed had man-

---

5. Still an accurate balanced analysis is Loewen & Urry, "Protecting Mammon," 34–53.

6. Savin, "'Divide and Rule,'" 1–18. Savin has produced large volumes of documents from state archives with critical commentary. This short essay offers insight into the attitudes of Tuchkov and other Bolshevik officials.

7. See Sawatsky, "Historical Roots," 149–180.

aged by 1880 to negotiate their own alternative service program. Financed and managed by self-assessed taxes of the colonies, this community service (forestry service initially) worked effectively, and even crossed the denominational boundaries that had emerged after about 1860.[8] Indeed, by the turn of the century, all Russian Mennonites were represented in an All-Russian Mennonite Conference, which negotiated with state authorities, as the latter—first Tsarist, then Soviet—increasingly attempted to encroach on their religious freedoms. During the conscription of World War I, Mennonites managed to find a compromise by serving in the medical corps. It turned out to be a learning experience for many young men about the extent of poverty and suffering of the peasants, whose sons were the cannon fodder during that hopeless war. As the Bolshevik government sought to strengthen its power and spread its influence after the Civil War, it attempted to manipulate the free church groups, including the Mennonites, toward their purposes. That testing of faith turned out to be very costly.

Several close associates of Lenin had long links to the Evangelical sectarian groups, hoping to build socialist models on the higher moral character of Evangelical sectarian communities (when compared to the typical Orthodox peasant), but persuading them to abandon religious superstitions. They were also challenged by the impressive practical democracy these sectarian groups demonstrated by organizing themselves across the vast reaches of the Soviet Union.[9] So initially one of the first decrees of the new Soviet state (spring of 1919) was to grant the right to alternative military service to persons able to demonstrate their objections to killing for reason of conscience and who could claim affiliation with an organized religious body supporting their views. A Council of United Religious Communities was organized soon after the military exemption decree, presided over by Vladimir Chertkov, who was a Tolstoyan and whose pedigree included aristocratic Evangelical Christians. Mennonite leaders C. F. Klassen and Peter Froese served on the council alongside Baptists, Evangelical Christians, and Molokan leaders to review the applications from their communities. The project was deeply troubled from the start because of poor communication, occluded command channels during early Bolshevism, and the challenges of a major famine. Many military service resisters were shot or sent to prison before at least some of them were given a hearing. After 1923, very few applicants succeeded in receiving alternative service assignments, and much later the decree was annulled.[10]

8. Klippenstein, "Mennonite Pacifism."
9. A point well-argued in the opening chapters of Coleman, *Russian Baptists*.
10. For more detail based on the Chertkov archive, see Sawatsky, "Pacifist

At the same time that the effort to crush the Russian Orthodox central administration was proceeding, the authorities pursued a manipulative dance of granting some freedoms to the free churches to secure their loyalty, while other elements within the Soviet leadership were organizing themselves for re-educating the sectarians to undercut their reliance on religious superstitions. So Baptist, Evangelical Christian, Pentecostal, and Mennonite national church unions were permitted to meet in congress in 1923 even though they were carefully watched and the agenda was manipulated. In 1926, when many of these church unions met in national congress again, security police played a prominent role, publicly arresting leading Evangelical Christians and insisting that the congress elect more acceptable leaders. They also insisted that these church bodies drop their pacifism clause from their faith statements (constitution) and declare their loyalty to Soviet power. In all cases, a narrow majority (often when enough delegates had left to make it possible) did as was demanded of them. Nevertheless, this still precipitated splits, with one wing of the denomination going underground.[11]

In the Mennonite case, its last all-Russian congress was held in 1925. It approved a statement of specified demands for religious freedom that included pacifism, even though its preamble stated Mennonite loyalty to Soviet power.[12] Subsequently, that 1925 Mennonite Congress was remembered as the Martyrs' Congress because the vast majority of delegates were soon after arrested to either suffer for many years in prison, face possible death, or try to survive in Gulag camps. Another portion of their number decided there was no future for them in the USSR and managed to emigrate to Canada in 1926. In global Mennonite terms, there had been proposals from the Russian Mennonites for a world Mennonite congress or conference well before 1925 (also true of Baptists and Evangelical Christians) hoping that their fellow believers would appeal to the Soviet authorities on their behalf by supporting their pacifism. What happened instead was that only one Rus-

---

Protestants." English original from author.

11. Since I have reviewed the story in my *Soviet Evangelicals* volume and later articles, and Coleman treats the pacifism as less widespread, I refer the reader for further sources to the fifth chapter of Kahle, *Evangelische Christen*, the typed Russian translation in the EAAA cd series, vol. 3, and to Nikol'skaia *Russkii Protestantizm*, 47–48, 61–62, 86–90.

12. Toews, *Mennonites in Russia*, 428–439. Documents and excerpts appear in German, drawn from the participant's personal archives, with introductions in English. This is the stenographic report of the January, 1925 All-Russian conference; the 8-point statement appears on pp. 430–31, as discussed and approved. The loyalty statement referred to above appeared in the Russian version that was sent to the Interior Ministry's Liquidation Committee, responsible at the time for religious affairs, which I examined during my research in Moscow in 1994.

sian Mennonite delegate, Elder Jakob Rempel, then chair of the All-Russian Mennonite Committee for Church Affairs, was able to attend. Rempel had been a doctoral student at St. Chrischona (Pietist school in south Germany near Basel), but had returned to take on pastoral duties before completing the dissertation. Rempel as a Soviet citizen, was not permitted entry into Basel, Switzerland where the first Mennonite world conference was held but received daily briefings at the train station before returning home to work for his people. He remained when others had emigrated, failed to get permission for a Bible school project, and with the extension of the war on religion to all religious bodies in 1929, was arrested and began a near two decade long career in prison and exile before being shot. His letters of encouragement to family and church have also begun to enrich the spirituality of others finally able to read about him in English.

A major testing for all Russian Mennonites took place from 1929 to at least 1933, and then especially during the great purge of 1937.[13] In 1929, the Soviet Union launched a five-year collectivization campaign that included dissolving the colony structure of the Mennonites; Marxist administrators had already been forced upon them in many places,[14] their schools were nationalized, and the Society of Agriculturalists of Dutch Origin was closed in 1928 (as was its international partner, the American Mennonite Relief organization, then engaged in agricultural development projects, and its Moscow files were confiscated). Also in 1929, a new law on religious societies was announced, which remained in effect (with a few revisions) until 1990. It served largely to provide legal justification (often *post facto*) for the closing of local religious societies (the Soviet term for parish or congregation). The Bolsheviks usually shut down religious life by arresting clergy and school teachers (especially in the Mennonite case) or other prominent community leaders. Some were able to return after shorter prison sentences, either for violating some clause of the "law on cults" of 1929 or breaking other tax laws that had been introduced against parasites such as the clergy, or they were accused of subservience to Mennonite structures abroad and therefore labeled treasonous. Until 1937, some forms of Mennonite church life (often in secret) had been possible. In the Asiatic parts of the Soviet Union, these restrictive policies took effect in somewhat delayed fashion, but as the incarceration of leaders increased in 1937, most forms of organized church life stopped. For the Mennonites, who some years later were

---

13. For a serious attempt at a statistical survey of the numbers arrested, killed, dekulakized, deported, or forcibly repatriated, see Letkemann, "Volga-Ural Region," 181–200, in which he included data from other regions as well.

14. I am using shorthand for space reasons. There were Mennonites who joined the Bolsheviks; extensive detail is in Neufeldt, "Separating," 221–91.

also caught within the *Spetskomandatura*, church life did not resume until after the initial lifting of *Spetskomandatura* restrictions in 1955.[15]

Instead, the faith practice of persistent believers became a secret faith, meeting in small groups irregularly enough not to attract attention. Large quantities of religious literature had been confiscated so that the post-war story of the rebirth of faith practice included long periods of spiritual drought, years of separation from family and kin, and then gradual recovery. Someone with a Bible became a copyist, others recalled and transcribed songs, or visiting evangelists found isolated groups of believers and offered whatever spiritual substance they could. For many other Mennonites, as was true of other fellow believers, faith in God lapsed or they compromised themself morally in order to survive. That is, there was a period of the death of organized Christian practice, a death of organized ministry and service, a death of theological and spiritual discourse. To process this theologically required a renewed appropriation of the dimensions of divine grace. During the first post-war decade, this recovery of the grace of forgiveness, restoration, and spiritual growth was largely individual, but eventually small group revival events emerged—especially after religious persecution eased upon Stalin's death in 1953—and gradually more organized church life began to develop (necessarily inter-evangelical initially). Then came (1958–75) the Khrushchev anti-religious campaign that closed down as many as one third of the congregations once again.

The Mennonites first succeeded in securing a purely local registration for a congregation in 1967 in Karaganda, Kazakhstan.[16] In the following two decades, more such local registrations were possible, more often so in the final decade of the USSR. But restrictions and interference continued, and any centrally organized All-Union Mennonite Conference was specifically forbidden. When Peter Froese had attempted in 1967 to bring a group of Mennonite leaders together to discuss forms of inter-congregational fellowship, he was immediately arrested and sentenced to another prison term.

---

15. References to the *Spetskomandatura* appear in much memoir material, as well as in the quarterly issue of *Aquila* magazine, with a more systematic description of the policies and phases of change in my chapter, "Soviet Mennonites" 299–337. See also the detail and extensive archival sources cited in Neufeldt, "*Spetspereselentsy*," 269–315. Neufeldt's term *Spetspereselentsy* (special settlers) and *Spetskomandatura* (special command) apply to the forced resettlement and to the conditions of several decades of 'settlement' respectively.

16. Aileen Friesen's broad discussion of 'sect' or 'confession' in her "Siberian Sect," 139–48 is instructive more for the varieties of classification tossed about since 1806, but "registration" in the 1960–80s, as noted above, were of a religious society without the distinctions between 'traditional' faiths and sects or foreign imports that have been debated since 1997.

Only in the final few years of the USSR (during Perestroika) did such leaders from Central Asia and Siberia manage a day of fellowship once every three months for sharing information.

From Gulag to Rebirth

The Gulag era was profoundly transformative, negatively so, but also promising for a people of peace. First some background in broad strokes. With the German invasion of the USSR in the fall of 1941, Mennonites were affected in two ways. The initial progress of the German Wehrmacht was so rapid that the Mennonite colonists on the west side of the Dnepr river became part of the German occupation, and their leaders were drawn into the administration of the occupied region. There was also a brief flowering of church life. When the Germans withdrew in 1943, the majority of the Russian Germans still in the Ukraine, including Mennonites, became part of a tortuous trek back into German lands. After Germany collapsed, some Mennonites were able to live in refugee camps (maintained by Mennonite relief agencies) until they were either resettled in Germany or able to emigrate to Canada or Paraguay. Others who had survived the trek were gathered up by Soviet agents and repatriated to the USSR, some for sudden death, others for extended stays in the Gulag.

Those Mennonites living in European Russia east of the Dnepr River in the fall of 1941 were ordered (along with all other Russian Germans) to present themselves at train stations on short notice for deportation eastward. Usually those who survived the boxcar journeys were deposited somewhere in central Asia or Siberia to fend for themselves, although some also joined existing Mennonite communities from Orenburg eastward. Nevertheless, all of them were declared a potential German fifth column and forced to report to the authorities. In addition, an army of laborers (*Trud Armiia*)[17] was formed and placed in forced labor camps stretching from the Caucasus to the Far East and Central Asia in order to establish industrial resources lost by the rapid invasion of the Russian territories. The workers' army included all able-bodied men and all women whose children could be left with a grandparent. Communication between work camps and their families' homes was impossible. Following the war, these conditions continued for the Germans, including Mennonites who were placed under a special command of the security police (*Spetskomandatura*), reporting weekly, and

---

17. Neufeldt, "*Spetspereselentsy*" includes reference to recent publications on the Trud Armiia as a whole. I would add to that Bacon, *Gulag at War*, especially its appendices on structure and statistics.

later monthly, their location and performing forced labor. They disappeared from the national census, until with the visit of German Chancellor Adenauer in 1955, some restrictions were eased, and eligible males were now conscripted into the Soviet Army. This special control helps account for the fact that a generation of Soviet Mennonites entered adulthood without the benefit of an education, with many illiterate. As a result, the high culture of the Russian Mennonites had been effectively destroyed.

Between approximately 1963 and 1989, a form of "normalized" Mennonite life re-emerged. These were post-Gulag believers, deeply linked with all other Soviet evangelicals.[18] There were rural communities of Mennonites, especially among those who had settled in Siberia and Central Asia before the internal deportations and whose colonies had been taken over by collective or state farms. Most of those among the displaced ended up living in new factory towns or cities, where the enterprising types among them managed to obtain semi-skilled labor. As an unofficially tolerated church practice developed, it was often the urban congregations that now took the lead, sometimes incorporating nearby rural communities as affiliates of their congregation. There were, however, some inter-Mennonite conflicts that shaped the story, so that the gradual normalization of relationships by 1989 also requires the use of "normal" in quotation marks. It may also be worth reminding the reader at this point how much the word "normal" presupposes a common pre-history, or at least an awareness of how much the normal or routine ways of living are highly situational. In his short summary of his 860-page history of the Omsk Mennonite Brotherhood, Peter Epp chose to list arrests and imprisonments from his group right through to 1988; that was their understanding of "normal."[19]

In contrast to the widespread penchant to anchor a Christian tradition in statements from its early beginnings, which for Mennonites often means the recovery of the "Anabaptist Vision," this chapter pursues a different approach. Applied particularly to the Reformation era of 16th-century Western Europe, historians have long recognized that the splits away from Roman Catholicism were situationally specific. Yet once separate Reformation church traditions had formed, it was common to emphasize distinct features of Lutheranism, Calvinism, Anglicanism, and Anabaptism; similarly, again when efforts to renew these Protestant churches' doctrinaire ossification in later centuries resulted in Methodism, Pietism within Lutheran, Catholic, Mennonite and Calvinist traditions, plus Quakers, Baptists, and Dissenters. The historical theological threads of Christianity as a whole,

---

18. For more on the changes, see Sawatsky, "Changing Mentalities," 315–363.
19. Epp, "Omsk Brotherhood," 113–32.

by the 20th century already a complex tale over nineteen centuries, were shaped by appeals to early church emphases and understandings (as in the New Testament) and by efforts to translate them into ever-changing situations.[20] Hence, to acknowledge the polygenetic beginnings (i.e., geographically diverse) while asserting commonalities of distinctives has tended to blur the similarities and differences within which Reformation traditions in their lived theologies found their way to new places and changing times.

My emphasis on Russian Mennonite testing—within the context of the pervasive Orthodox ethos of the Russian Empire that influenced all 'foreign' confessions, and within the context of indigenous renewal movements that produced a variety of forms of "Soviet Evangelicals"—treats 16th-century pronouncements as distant, often less known than the Bible, a scarce book throughout much of the 20th century. So it probes implicitly why it was the Dutch Doopsgezinde tradition that from the sixteenth century forward was the statistically larger branch of Mennonites (or Anabaptists), as those who did not know the rigidly sectarian stance of the Schleitheim Confession of 1527 but persisted in updating the Dordrecht Confession of 1632. It highlights the growth of institutional structures for teaching, service, and mission, and the highly organized alternative service program of the Russian Mennonites. The greater readiness to engage society and culture, often used to dismiss Dutch Mennonites as liberal and unfaithful to the Anabaptist Vision, helps account for their engagement in cross-cultural mission, and it is no surprise that the Russian Mennonites supported Dutch missions in the Indonesian islands by 1860. But when tested by the upheavals of history, that story necessarily becomes one of both failures and betrayals and witness unto death within the community of Russian Mennonites. What is so interesting for 21st-century peacemaking is observing the recovery of faith practices and to what were central commitments that were most reluctantly surrendered and which re-emerged with the resumption of church life.

Tracing out those recurrent central points of a Dutch-Russian Mennonite theology and practice in the 20th-century Russian Mennonite story reveals five key commitments: the Lordship of Christ, discipleship, mission, mutual discipline, and pursuit of the way of peace.[21] They were not so much theological teachings, but commitments to faithful Christian practice, never quite lost and never completely achieved. But they marked the terrain for discourse within and beyond their communities. To notice those key

---

20. Rare and instructive as social history are the extended sections comparing the varieties of Calvinist Reformed churches over the first 250 years, in Benedict, *Christ's Churches*.

21. Sawatsky, "Historical Roots," 149–80.

commitments (also in more or less qualities) in other confessional traditions provides the bridge for common Christian discourse.

During an earlier phase of renewal movements among the Russian Mennonites in the mid-19th century—some seeking greater ethical rigor, others a personal conversion experience, still others following an eschatological vision, or seeking to find a place in the central Asian desert free of government to preserve their pacifism—there developed a clear division between Mennonite Brethren stressing personal conversion and immersion baptism and the larger Mennonite body that received the label 'churchly' (tserkovniki in Russian). The split resulted in two religious denominations with separate spiritual leadership structures, but both groups were permitted to participate in colony land and daily life. By 1910, the religious differences had moderated, less so in the new colonies in Siberia, but they never quite disappeared. When church life started to return in the 1950s from its death phase, at first all that mattered was whether one was a believer.[22] By the mid 1960s, with more leaders from an earlier era returning from the camps, old denominational differences re-emerged. Soviet authorities had agreed during the war to permit a Protestant free church to be registered, provided that all Protestants joined one centralized body, initially known as Evangelical Christian Baptists, soon after including Pentecostals, and in 1963 also Mennonites. But this included only the Mennonite Brethren (except for several dissenting communities) and not the *tserkovniki Mennonity* (Church Mennonites) because the latter's practice of adult baptism by pouring or sprinkling was not recognized.[23] Even so, the announcement of Mennonite Brethren joining this larger free church union was an artifice to counter the image of a major split within the Evangelical Christian Baptists, a split effected by hostile Soviet authorities to a large extent.

---

22. For a recent analysis, see Dyck, "Dry Ground," 97–112. See also Weiss, "Causes and Results," 133–38, which concentrates on the Reform Baptists, very heavily Mennonite in the Slavgorod region.

23. A recent issue of *Aquila* magazine contains an article by retired Canadian Mennonite University Old Testament professor, Waldemar Janzen, about his father Vladimir Janzen, who was released from the Gulag after 8 years in 1947 and had attempted in the early 1950s to participate in a Baptist congregation in Karaganda, Kazakhstan that refused him communion as a former minister because he had not been immersed when baptized. This keenly felt inability to join in the fellowship of the Lord's Supper changed in his case when a Mennonite Brethren congregation made an exception for him. *Aquila* 2, no. 13 (April-June 2013), 24.

The Role of Mennonites in Contrasting Ways of Seeking Faithfulness

Much has been written about the division within Soviet Baptists (to use a common shorthand), including by this writer, and revisiting those events following the opening of some official archives and private collections by new scholars continues to throw more light on what was long a murky story. The point to be made here is to notice the interesting role played by Mennonites on both sides. During the second major anti-religious campaign under Khrushchev (1958–64, then gradually easing by 1975), the authorities required the heads of Orthodoxy and of the Evangelical Christian Baptists to participate in their own inner undoing by forcing them to issue by fiat new church regulations (Polozhenie in Russian) for enforcement by superintendents in their regions. Among the more egregious demands were requirements to keep children and youth away from worship, forbid evangelism, and to concentrate solely on meeting the religious needs of believers. It coincided with the return to churches of leaders who had never learned to manage church life in underground and semi-legal ways, as had the official leaders since 1945. At first the resistance was expressed in religious terms, with calls to the central leadership, then to all the churches for fasting and spiritual sanctification. When it became apparent that state authorities were constantly interfering, charging arrestees with violation of the Law on Cults (secretly revised with more restrictions), the dissenters organized themselves and pursued a human and religious rights campaign. Their key tool, hard to counter by the authorities, was the dissemination of self-published literature underground, and sent abroad for publication and marshaling public support.

A few key leaders among the Reformers bore Mennonite surnames. Soon it became noticeable that this was also true of the lists of persons imprisoned for their faith. These lists were distributed with amazing regularity as Samizdat (self-published) Bulletins by the Council for Prisoners Relatives, whose first leader was Lydia Vins (Wiens as Mennonites spelled it). She was the widow of Peter Wiens, an early leader of the evangelicals in the Far East and around Omsk region who became a martyr soon after his son Georgi was born. Georgi became known by the mid 1960s as the general secretary of the Council of Churches of Evangelical Christian Baptists CCECB), seeking legal registration to replace the other compromised council. Drawing on early Baptist and Anabaptist traditions, they challenged any interference by the state in church affairs, insisting on full separation of church and state.

One device to counter the influence of the Reform Baptists was to present to leaders the option of imprisonment or emigration. Since many regional leaders in the Baltic and Central Asian republics were of German Mennonite or Baptist origin, they were able to emigrate to West Germany in the family reunification program that began to develop in 1973. Within a few years, Georgi Vins, who had been in prison for a second five-year term, was traded with other human rights activists for some Soviet spies held in the United States. Vins, who did know of relatives among Mennonites in Ontario and California, quickly formed a missionary branch of the CCECB to organize publicity and provide support for his fellow believers. Almost simultaneously, younger regional leaders emigrating to West Germany formed the Friedensstimme mission for a similar purpose; its key leaders were named Penner, Loewen, and Janzen. In this way, the capacity for wider distribution of Samizdat increased.

On the other hand, the All-Union Council of Evangelical Christian Baptists (AUCECB) began cultivating the Mennonites, assigning a full-time staff person to represent them in Moscow, to tour the Mennonite regions to assist in church formation, and by 1966 another Mennonite as leading minister of a Russian/German congregation in Novosibirsk, Siberia was elected to the AUCECB presidium. A decade later, a Mennonite named Traugott Quiring was appointed superintendent of the Central Asian republics, and a deputy superintendent represented German Baptists and Mennonites in Kazakhstan (where the majority of Mennonites then lived). It was an inter-evangelical experience for these leaders and their churches. When something was written about the Mennonites in the official church paper (carefully censored), leaders like Jakob Fast emphasized that they shared a basic common theology, although there were struggles in places over whether to maintain the old practice of foot-washing. The issue of pacifism has been laid to rest, he claimed, so Mennonites too were serving the motherland with weapon in hand when called upon. Mennonite visitors from the West began speaking of the Russian Mennonites having lost their doctrine of nonresistance, even though they emphasized high faithfulness to biblical authority. Through this writer's visits and interviews, subsequently confirmed by the new scholarship from regional and central state archives, it became clear that a commitment to the way of peace, and to witness or mission were not really forgotten. Their forms of expression had shifted.

In both Evangelical Christian Baptist traditions (and Mennonites in both), when their young men were drafted into the army, there was a problem and a blessing. In places like Karaganda, so atheist propaganda literature complained in the 1970s, church leaders had managed to inculcate pacifism into their youth. As that appeared in personal testimonials during interviews, the believing Baptists and Mennonites sought to avoid shooting to kill humans, at worst shooting into the air. Many of them stuck out upon induction for refusing to swear the military oath with its atheist claims, so some were imprisoned, others got assigned to clean the latrines. Yet given the alcohol and drug problem of so many recruits, good officers on occasion chose a sectarian believer (including Mennonite) for staff work thanks to their honesty and reliability. The believers were not so much activist evangelists, but sought free moments for prayer and fellowship with other believers (as others were doing in prison) and this attracted new converts.

Post-Communist Witness for Service and Reconciliation

In a larger sense, what became evident after the dissolution of the USSR in 1990 was that there was an accumulated 'social capital' of profound respect for believers, in particular for the Protestant sectarians. What was less well known was that before the Soviet war on religion expanded to all religious groups in 1929, not just Orthodoxy since 1918, there had been much experimentation in social ministries. That is, a feature of post-Communist Christian activity has been to recover a social ministry.

Here I can merely cite a few illustrations of a broader phenomenon of searching for a social and moral recovery. When visiting the Karaganda evangelicals in 1991 who had formed an interchurch mission and charity committee (Evangelical Christian Baptists, Mennonite Brethren, Church Mennonites), I listened to them describe numerous ways that calls for speakers were coming in—to address school children about ethics and faith, to do a question and answer session with teachers in a large school (who this time listened with respect and gave thoughtful follow up questions), to hold services by the warden's request at a nearby prison, and to speak to large gatherings in the public square. As was true nearly everywhere in eastern Europe and the regions of the post-Soviet Union, there were no initiatives to get revenge on their former communist persecutors. Initially there was a wave of searching the archives to compile lists of persons sentenced to the Gulag or executed for trumped-up political reasons and publishing the names in newspapers. The Memorial Society that emerged searched out mass graves, and sought to identify the dead in unmarked graves by, for example, sending data and remains to the relatives of fallen enemy (e.g., German) soldiers from Volgograd.[24] The Evangelicals rarely joined this society but did participate in many other charity (*milocerdie*) societies that sprang up, whose programs invariably included distribution of relief, running soup kitchens, and visiting the sick in institutions, all justified by the widely felt need to recover the quality of graciousness (*milocerdie*).

24. Smith, *Remembering Stalin's Victims*.

Even though there was a massive out-migration of Russian Germans, including nearly all Mennonites (at least 100,000), the inter-church charity and mission society continued to function to the present, maintaining, for example, a seniors' retirement center in Karaganda. The Aquila relief organization has managed to provide reliable shipment of relief supplies through its own staff and volunteers (as the Kazakh, other central Asian countries, and western Siberia remained economically depressed with extreme unemployment challenges), doing reviews of their work and reporting on it extensively. The majority of the support—financial and through volunteers—came from that recent Russian German immigrant community. Also, very revealing is the reality that although the religious/theological conflicts and church splits that have accompanied their twenty-year acclimatization process in Germany have persisted, all of them have cooperated as possible and necessary through Aquila and a half dozen similar organizations. Generally they have managed to keep a greater distance from the initial efforts of Western (especially American) Evangelical missions with limited missiological sensibilities seeking to transform the Russian/Slavic evangelical community into their image. That too, is an indicator of a profound commitment to spiritual fraternity with fellow believers in the former Soviet territories, even though so many of the Mennonites decided it was unwise to trust the early promises of religious freedoms. Given developments in all those areas over the past decade, they may well be right. Nevertheless, those immigrant mission agencies continue to draw attention to patterns of religious restriction and call for prayer in various publications.[25]

Within their own circle, the post-communist era has provided the opportunity to tell the story more fully, accurately, and irenically. Further, they quickly availed themselves of study and research opportunities to rebuild their spiritual culture with care. Earlier immigrants led the way by writing memoirs, including pastors like Hartfeld, Reimer and Heidebrecht who wrote historical fiction accounts in German for fellow church members and other Germans. The Aquila mission launched its own publishing arm called Samenkorn. New immigrant leaders with master's degrees from MBBS in Fresno, CA soon parted company with a long-established American mission to foster their own theological education by extension (TEE) programs as early as 1986. This allowed them to gain access to locations in the Soviet Union because they had the connections and still had USSR passports. This mission, called LOGOS, also launched its own press for Russian and German language literature, and initiated its own theological seminars in Germany. During the 1990s, more than a dozen persons completed PhD studies,

---

25. See Tissen, "News from Kazakhstan," 25–6.

some in German universities, others in the United States, and still others became part of the theology and missiology programs fostered by UNISA (University of South Africa). Several students of the late missiologist, David Bosch—specifically Johannes Reimer and Peter F. Penner—wrote their dissertations in Russian, which were then published and used in the newly emergent theological colleges and seminaries. Penner opted to return, with his wife Katherine and children, first to assist in the foundational work in the early years of what is known as St. Petersburg Christian University. He served as Dean at a time when the University was starting to cooperate with Orthodox teachers (and their missiology organization that began to foster missiological and ecumenical themes) and with German Lutherans working to plant Lutheran churches and establish a seminary. Penner was consistently a leader with other heads of evangelical theological schools to foster common standards. This resulted in the formation of the Euro-Asiatic Accrediting Association (EAAA) that not only developed an extensive accreditation program, but through annual conferences also fostered a theological journal, an oral history project, and the extensive gathering of archival materials that were digitized and circulated through the theological schools network. Numerous times, it was the ties to Mennonites elsewhere, particularly through staff from MCC, that the low costs for the digital or archives projects were funded.

The irenic part emerged in at least two ways, neither of them headline-grabbing. With the mass out-immigration of Mennonites from the Soviet territories (1987–1993), there was soon a dramatic increase in the number of young men of conscription age in Germany who volunteered for alternative service assignments through Christliche Dienste (CD), which was run by the south German Mennonites. These assignments included social services in Germany and abroad, often arranged through the international Mennonite network. Peace teaching and peace practice were carried out in the congregations and also in the Bible schools that emerged in Germany.

The research program became another way to demonstrate (unintentionally) openness to the Other, to former enemies from the periods of persecution. Samenkorn Press assisted with history seminars and editing manuscripts to publish over a dozen thick histories of the evangelical movement, including at least four volumes on regions of Kazakhstan alone as well as elsewhere in Siberia. When scholars met for a conference at the Moscow Baptist Theological Seminary on that history in 2011, for example, it was co-sponsored by the Baptist Union, the History & Theology Research Center at Bonn BibelSeminar, and by the Russian Humanitarian University. Presenters represented still other secular universities, where professors and new doctoral students reported on findings from the archives on the evangelical movement during the Soviet era. Striking of course was the appreciative, insightful, and knowledgeable ways the scholars tried to understand religious and Marxist perspectives, tracking patterns of change and the reasons for them. One senior sociologist, whose work I had read in his scientific atheism days, kept on repeating that he was not a believer but respected believers. He could say so more openly now, but had learned to respect them as good human beings long ago and undeserving of the persecution meted out to them.

More to the point for this chapter was what the Baptist and Mennonite scholars were doing, as well as the leading clergy of the denomination. Over coffee, they engaged the secular guests naturally, did not argue self-righteously, but often lamented together the times when dialoguing together had not been possible. The organizer, an archivist for the Baptist Union, announced plans for another conference at a university in the Far East (a half dozen scholars had come from there) and freely shared his findings and archival resources, as they did with him. So, the digital archival resource base (at least researchers' file summaries, but often complete texts obtained with scanners) would be a shared resource. That event illustrates others, that I have either attended or learned of, that have been proceeding in this fashion. More Western Mennonite involvement in the future requires some sense of the history, preferably of the necessary research languages, but above all a readiness to engage in an extended dialogue process that has thus far been too episodic.

Unfortunately, the more recent story of the Russian Mennonite relationships with the Mennonite World Conference "global church" has not gone so well. After that first problematic 'meeting' with Jakob Rempel in the German side of the Basel train station in 1925, there was no further representation from the Russian Mennonites at subsequent MWC assemblies until a delegation was permitted to attend the Wichita assembly (1978). At that event, plus several later ones, historians of the Russian Mennonites from the west—Frank Epp and I—wrote the background stories for the handbooks. Then in 1990, a self-financed 14-person delegation arrived in Winnipeg for a very large Mennonite World Conference. Led by Viktor Fast, this mixed group of Church Mennonite, Mennonite Brethren and Evangelical Christian Baptist Mennonites, were welcomed with prolonged applause. They gave an afternoon workshop presentation, which drew several thousand sitting on bleachers in a gymnasium. The presentations (in Russian, Low German dialect, German (with translation), and some English) kept that audience attentive for two hours with their songs, poetry, personal testimonies, and sermons. There were commitments later from partner groups in Canada (MCC, mission boards, foundations) that resulted in some startup funds for purchasing printing equipment, and Mennonite Economic Development Associates (MEDA) launched some programs with the Russian Mennonites. Some of those projects continued and the Mennonite agencies became involved in small projects, including pamphlet and book publishing in Russian and a library and seminar center in Moscow, but the western financial and personnel support had dwindled in little more than a decade.

When there were renewed efforts in 2009 to organize a series of workshops involving the Russian Mennonite immigrants, now in Germany, for the Mennonite World Conference in Asuncion, only one immigrant conference, already a member of MWC, sent representatives. When both Viktor Fast of the independent Mennonite Brethren (and Aquila) and Hermann Heidebrecht (elder, writer and immigration staff person for years) of the Church Mennonites were asked to present papers, they found themselves needing to decline. They were of course deeply interested in the scholarly exchange of information and ideas, but their fellow leaders had in the intervening years developed such a depth of distrust of the orientation of Mennonite World Conference since 1990 that they felt the presence of Fast and Heidebrecht at the conference would signal an endorsement they were no longer ready for. Yet both groups, as well as other organized church bodies among those immigrants from Russia, were already doing mission in Bolivia (seeking to encourage spiritual renewal among conservative Russian Mennonite colonists) and were visiting the Chaco on speaking tours.

This illustrates another side of peacebuilding that was problematic for western Mennonites—reaching out to the more distant Other in dialogue, while no longer able to maintain engaged dialogue with a large wing (100,000) of one's own community that lacks the perspective of the peacebuilders. So peacebuilding also becomes an integrity issue. It seems that the question "what makes for peace" needs constant revisiting.

Reflection on the Beatitudes in Light of Modern Russian Mennonite History

Starting with the first immigration movement to Russia in 1789, to its near conclusion two centuries later, the theme of saying no to war, to killing, to the way of violence was always a red thread in the story. There had been many ambiguous issues along the way—by the time of the last migration group of 1860 to the Volga region, the generosity of the *Privilegium* was much reduced, and fellow Mennonites in Prussia were gradually abandoning their pacifism. It had seemed prudent to emigrate to Canada and the United States in the 1870s, but the North American Mennonite ability to resist conscription during World War I was less inspiring than was the program of self-managed alternative service of the previous three decades in Russia. Then came the deeper tests of facing exemption committees between 1919 and 1933, where local and even central officials ignored many applications for conscientious objection by refusing to approve alternative service. Eventually, all war-resisters were sentenced for treason or shot. During the *Spetkomandatura* (at least from 1941–1966), the Mennonite men did not exist as conscripts; every one of the Germans were in *de facto* prison camps doing forced labor or dying. The recovery phases from that death period required new creativity for resisting the urge to kill other human beings. Plus, there were also many Mennonites who no longer had any religious bonds, even if living next door to believers. When the widespread emergence of nonviolent resistance to injustice resulted in a series of moral or "velvet" revolutions in Europe, whose rhetoric even when not explicitly Christian was nevertheless rooted in Judeo-Christian understandings of the good civil society, most Soviet Mennonites (of whatever label) were not among the activists (as was true in the West too). But they did note the opportunities for a more explicit Christian witness, and were often among the leaders for organizing ministry initiatives no longer explicitly condemned. Their way of peace now linked them with many other people across those vast regions, those whom Vaclav Havel called the "powerless" in his "Power of the Powerless" article.

That the meek (the powerless) will inherit the earth seemed a profound recognition in 1989. The emerging "politics of decency" gained a broad support. One scholar wrote about the "ignorant perfection of ordinary people" when seeking to make sense of what qualities in the leadership of Gandhi, Martin Luther King, and Solzhenitsyn the simple, meek people resonated with.[26] Vincent Harding, watching the people tear down the Berlin Wall while singing *We Shall Overcome*, also realized there is a transnational bond, a trans-religious bond on basic values, on the way to a necessary peaceful coexistence.[27] Yet soon an alternative historiography about the ending of the Cold War claimed that America won with its massive weapons of destruction, so that the Russians blinked. The "New World Order" that the American authorities proclaimed assumed the right to global dominance with unfettered capitalist exploitation of the losers. From this writer's setting, indicators persist that many north American Mennonites, including

---

26. Inchausti, *Ordinary People*; Jonathan Schell already spoke of the Politics of Decency in 1986, but it was articulated for a broader readership by Ash *Uses of Adversity*.

27. Harding, *Hope and History*.

their intellectual leaders, accepted this interpretation and agreed to the myth of redemptive violence. Why was that?

Mennonite peacemaking was tested more deeply during the 20th century Soviet experience than anywhere else. Many Mennonites failed the test for a time, others passed it by paying the ultimate price with their lives, but its essential role in a Russian Mennonite lived theology never disappeared. The testing resulted in broader expressions of living a way of love, meekness, and counted blessings than their more prosperous and untested American Mennonites knew—their peacemaking was less programmed, more serendipitous. Lived-through testing is a deepening of faith; to fail a testing was not the end of the story, but a recovery of the mercy and love of a gracious God who restored them.

3

Privilege, Right, and Responsibility
Peace and the North American Mennonites[1]

Royden Loewen

Introduction

At the core of Mennonite identity in North America is the religiously derived idea of peace. It may come in many names: either as nonresistance or pacifism; as an "absolute pacifism"[2] or a "goal directed"[3] nonviolence; as the "intrinsic dimension of the gospel of Jesus Christ"[4] or an "absolutistic . . . love ethic."[5] But in each case it constitutes a teaching of peace within Mennonite history. Over their 300-year history in North America, Mennonites have made a name for themselves as an historic peace church, opposed to military service, the swearing of oaths of allegiance, and the use of courts to pursue personal rights.

No matter the treasured nature of this inheritance, the idea of peace has not been a static gift. Indeed it has come by various names and suggests

---

1. A portion of this essay first appeared as "Privilege, Right, and Responsibility: Peace and Mennonites in the U.S. and Canada" in Mennonite Central Committee's quarterly publication *Intersections*, Volume 3, No. 1 (Winter 2015).

2. Chatfield, "Thinking about Peace," 44.

3. Ackerman and Duvall, *Force*, 497.

4. Weaver, *Anabaptist Theology*, 27.

5. Kaufman, "Jesus," 123–25.

an evolution over time, reflecting the demands of war, the effects of migration, and the social status of Mennonites. The very idea has also changed as nations changed. With the rise of nationalism, that emotional tie to the "imagined community" of the nation state, the notion of peace bumped against notions of patriotic, universal military service.[6] And within the inexorable flow of modernization came the very idea of individual rights, including the right to resist universal military service. Eventually, Mennonites in both Canada and the United States experienced military exemption as a personal right, at first in a rather roughshod fashion, but by World War II with judicial sleekness and highly organized civilian service opportunities. A rights-based, personal approach to military exemption stood the test of time within the Mennonite community, even beyond the end of the draft in the 1940s in Canada and the 1970s in the United States. But in the postwar era, a significant diversion occurred. Both the idea of "privilege" and the idea of "rights" were premised on an old, Anabaptist "two-kingdom" theology, but now new articulate voices insisted on the Mennonites' responsibility to share their historic teaching. Indeed, some insisted that the peaceful Christ become "lord" over all of society. In broad strokes, then, the idea of peace has shifted from a group privilege, to a matter of personal right, to an imperative of social responsibility.

History, however, is never just about change, but also continuity. The fact of the matter is that the old two-kingdom theology is still deeply rooted in the North American cultural landscape. Moreover, peacebuilding initiatives are not unique to the late decades of the twentieth century. Local cultures of peace existed in rural societies; they were taught to children in the home and practiced in the village, addressing numerous potential points of conflict. This culture was reproduced in urban places, with more complex institutions that addressed issues of physical health, mental health, old age, and education, including institutions that served populations beyond the historic peace church community. Although this short chapter considers change over time, an essay of equal length could easily have been produced on signs of continuity overtime.

The Privilege of Military Exemption

In any case, this narrative on peace begins in 1683 when Mennonites first began settling English-speaking North America: they came as victims of religious persecution, seeking privilege in Quaker-run Pennsylvania where they hoped to be exempted from all military service and, idealistically, from

---

6. See Anderson, *Imagined Communities*.

strife of any kind. But it was not all about idealism. They would participate in politics and accept modern ideas of state-guaranteed private property, in part because Pennsylvania itself was committed to pacifism.[7] And, as Aaron Fogelman argues in his *Hopeful Journeys*, settlers in early Pennsylvania seemed mostly concerned with securing more land for "generational succession" for the increasing number of children and the chance to build communities marked by "ethnic cohesiveness."[8] Still, as Richard McMaster argues, the Mennonites were known as pacifists, hardworking simple folk, refugees from hostile Switzerland; as a Church of England missionary from Lancaster County put it at the time, perhaps the Mennonites were people who had "acquired riches and plenty," but they "chuse [sic] rather to leave their Properties and Liberty exposed to the first Invader, than bear arms in their Defence."[9] Early stories recounted the cost of this idea; perhaps they were the privileged—encroaching on the lands of the underprivileged Native American—but as the 1764 murder of the entire John Roads family shows, they came to be known in time as a people who would not defend themselves under any circumstances.[10]

This world, marked by humility and nonresistance, however, would not remain for long. Indeed, it confronted the new Enlightenment-derived impulse of individual rights and patriotic military service during the War of Independence. When hostilities broke out in 1775, following the Boston Tea Party, the Mennonites were in a quandary, for their traditional stance, based on Romans 12 and 13, taught humility and submission to state authority, even to King George III. Moreover, they had no appetite for the absolute right of the individual that stood at the heart of the Declaration of Independence. And yet, isolation would not be an option with the patriotic fervor that followed. Mennonites would need to articulate their stance. Hence, a November 1775 petition noted that they were simply "not at Liberty in Conscience to take up arms to conquer our Enemies." Significantly, the petition did not claim a right but a religiously rooted willingness to suffer: its authors stated that the Mennonites would "crave the patience of all the inhabitants of this country—what they think to see . . . in the Doctrine of the blessed Jesus Christ, . . . finding ourselves very poor [in spirit]."[11] Their appeal may have earned them an exemption in the various Militia Acts of the time, allowing for equivalency "in lieu of military service," but they also had to deal

---

7. Loewen and Nolt, *Seeking Places*, 30.
8. Fogelman, *Hopeful Journeys*, 71.
9. McMaster, *Land, Piety, Peoplehood*, 229.
10. Dyck, *Mennonite History*, 200.
11. McMaster, *Land, Piety, Peoplehood*, 256.

with new ideas on citizenship. In Pennsylvania, for example, Mennonites faced the need to provide a personal "Assurance of Allegiance" or face double taxation, the loss of property, and even jail. Their worlds rooted in group privilege had been severely challenged.

In the generation following the War of Independence, Mennonites endured the tension of life in a new republic. At least some Mennonites still considered a monarchy the most godly form of government. When, in 1791, the British North American province of Upper Canada was formed, followed by a Militia Act a few years later that offered commutation fees in lieu of military service, a number of land-hungry Mennonites made the historic trip inland, following the paths northward of the Loyalists. The British crown might not prosper the sectarian Mennonites, but it recognized them as a group. As Steven Nolt observes, "two different North American political environments" emerged, "a Canadian one marked more by stability and the language of privilege, and a United States one shaped by liberal claims of progress and citizens' majority rule," and one might add, individual rights.[12]

In the first half of the 1800s, Mennonites in both the United States and Canada were left alone on the matter of nonresistance. In the War of 1812, pitting Britain (including Canada) against the U.S., and then in the United States war against Mexico in the 1840s, it was volunteers who fought in the U.S., and the terms of the Militia Act of 1793 in Canada allowed Mennonites an exemption based on commutation fees.[13] Indeed, pressure to serve militarily was so tenuous, that publisher John F. Funk later asserted that "the doctrine of non-resistance had almost been forgotten," neither taught nor "impressed on the minds of the young men."[14]

But reinforcing the idea of peace was the task of the second major wave of Mennonite immigrants (now including Amish) to the "new world," that is, both the United States and Canada. Steven Nolt writes that this migration, beginning after the Napoleonic Wars and continuing till the Civil War, occurred in the context of modernization in Europe. He points out that "the sorts of privileges that local pockets of lease-holding Mennonites had negotiated with individual landlords collapsed in the face of new notions of universal citizenship that assumed all residents had a stake in the success of an emerging nationalism and modernizing society."[15] Ironically, the Mennonites and Amish headed for the "new world" to seek tracts of farm

12. Loewen and Nolt, *Seeking Places*, 33.
13. See, Steiner, *Promised Lands* and Schlabach, *Peace, Faith, Nation*.
14. Schlabach, *Peace, Faith, Nation*, 175.
15. Loewen and Nolt, *Seeking Places*, 13. For context, see Moch, *Moving Europeans*, 11, 105–7.

land in rural isolation to preserve an "old order" that would sustain a "two kingdom" theology and the idea of group military exemption.

Still, this understanding would be tested in 1861 when the United States divided in civil war over the issue of slavery and a year later when the North introduced the first federal American draft. Mennonites moved quickly to seek a reaffirmation of old privileges as humble subjects of government authority. One idea was to compose a letter addressed to "our most noble President," asserting a willingness to suffer ("if the Lord intends to chasten us we can not escape his hand"), and seeking exemption from being "forced or compelled to take up arms." But in the end, it was not the president but federal legislators who enacted a military exemption upon the payment of a $300 commutation fee, or the hiring of a substitute. Some Mennonites, especially in the north, were drawn into the war, revealing an ambivalence about military service, national glory, and civic responsibility.[16] But voices of peace were common and unequivocal. Representative was the lament of Barbara Ziegler Herr, a mother who had lost two sons as small children, but during the Civil War grieved even more intensely, weeping "day and night," to see the three boys who reached adulthood join the army.[17]

A reassertion of such a commitment occurred with the third major wave of migration of Mennonites from Europe beginning in 1874. Eventually, 17,000 Dutch-North German Mennonites from New Russia (present day Ukraine) settled on the North American grassland, 7,000 in the Canadian province of Manitoba and 10,000 in the western Midwest. The context of this migration resembles the arrival of the Swiss-South German migrants of the first half of the 1800s. A post-war commitment to modernization in the "old world" was pushing the Mennonites to the North American interior in search of an old order. Following its loss in the Crimean War of the 1850s, Russia pursued a program of relentless modernization, thus sweeping away the basis of its "old order," built on "layers of social status," in which no "common body of rights shared by everyone by virtue of their membership in society" existed, according to historian Jerome Blum.[18] Most notably, Russia ended serfdom in 1861, but within a decade it also ended special privileges, including self-governance and military exemption, for foreign colonists. Mennonite leaders employed an old tactic: they appealed directly to the head of state, Czar Alexander II, as humble subjects. They appealed to him "as your children," trusting "in your paternal heart," and they humbly sought the privilege "to live out our beliefs undisturbed," exempted "from all

---

16. See, Lehman and Nolt, *Civil War*.
17. Schlabach, *Peace, Faith, Nation*, 188.
18. Blum, *Lord and Peasant*, 4.

civil and military service" even if it meant "restrictions, special conditions and increased tribute money."[19]

When the Russian government refused their request and insisted on a national alternative service, a third of the Mennonites elected to migrate to North America instead. The group choosing the United States vied for a replication of the privileges they were losing in Russia. Some leaders secured an audience with President Ulysses Grant, and Congress debated a "Mennonite Bill" that sought special privileges, including a land reserve and sweeping military exemptions. Both Grant and Congress would not yield on the individualistic principles of a republic, and in the end it was state laws alone that recognized the Mennonites' religious scruples. The group of Mennonites that chose Canada found a more accommodating federal government, willing to promise special group privileges, including military exemption, block settlement, and control over their education. Legally secured in a special Order-in-Council, Mennonites quickly came to refer to the legal document, securing that promise, as their "Privilegium." When just a few years after settlement, the Manitoba Mennonites were visited by none other than the Queen's representative, Governor General Lord Dufferin, reasserting the promise of military exemption under "the aegis of the British constitution," they responded "with thankfulness [as] we acknowledge your fatherly protection."[20]

The Right to Alternative Service

The great test of these promises came a long generation later during the so-called "Great War," later redubbed World War I. As a British dominion, Canada entered the war from the get-go in 1914, while a more isolationist United States waited until 1917 to join the fracas. Mennonites in both countries were smug in the first years of the war; Daniel Kaufman, editor of the *Gospel Herald*, no doubt spoke for most Mennonites when he penned that "in the midst of suffering . . . we [must] manifest a meek, submissive spirit." Only in 1917 when both countries introduced universal military service bills was there much concern. Even then the Military Service Act in Canada cited the 1873 *Privilegium* as a tool of exemption, while Ontario Mennonites were simply given an informal way out by sympathetic officials.

In the United States, the 1917 Selective Service Act provided for conscientious objection, yet on unprecedented grounding. Each drafted young man would have the "right" to seek personal exemption, but the requirement

19. Quoted in Loewen, *Family, Church*, 63.
20. Reimer, *75 Gedenkfeier*, 48. Quoted in Loewen, *Family, Church and Market*, 84.

to make this appeal at the military training to which he had been assigned, made this opportunity somewhat tenuous. Secretary of War, Newton Baker, for example, might legally recognize the rights of the conscientious objector, but he was famously quoted as insisting that "war was the purest mission that a nation ever espoused."[21] Baker's strategy was simple, writes James Juhnke: "get the Mennonite men out of their narrow sectarian communities and into military cantonments. There the . . . enthusiastic [military] spirit might catch them up."[22] Draftees indeed found the military bases hostile places, complete with psychological torture and hazings, and imprisonment and physical cruelty, so harsh in one instance that two young Hutterite men died in camp.[23]

But an even greater problem ensued outside the camps, in the general society, leading ultimately to two significant intra-North American migrations. In the United States, writes Juhnke, a "patriotic frenzy . . . took hold at the grass roots" as "draft board officials, liberty bond collectors, military camp officers and a host of vigilant volunteer citizens sallied forth to make the world safe for democracy."[24] In Michigan and Oklahoma, churches were burned, in Kansas mobs threatened Mennonites who taught children not to salute the flag, and from Kansas, Ohio, Montana, Iowa and other states came stories of severe pressure to purchase war bonds, amidst near lynchings and public humiliation.[25] The spirit of the time was similar in Canada. The *Winnipeg Free Press* denounced Mennonites as an "undesirable" "people of 'peculiar' religions . . . clinging to an alien tongue," who did not deserve to live in Canada. In Berlin (Ontario), British Canadians forced the city to adopt the new name of Kitchener, a British naval hero. And in Saskatchewan as in Manitoba, zealous Anglo-conformist provincial governments closed German language private schools.

In both countries, distressed Anabaptists prepared to leave. From the United States, about 700 Mennonite boys and 11 of 17 Hutterite colonies relocated north to Canada for quieter waters, the Hutterites employing their own *Privilegium* negotiated but never realized during the Spanish-American War in the 1890s.[26] The hostile spirit of patriotism in Canada also lay behind the emigration of 8,000 Mennonites to Mexico and Paraguay in the 1920s. Leaders may have cited public English-language education as

21. Juhnke, *Vision, Doctrine, War*, 230.
22. Ibid., 232.
23. See, Mock, *Writing Peace*.
24. Juhnke, *Vision, Doctrine, War*, 217.
25. Loewen, "American Nationalism," 118–36.
26. Stoltzfus, *Pacifists in Chains*, 211.

the cause behind the exodus, but it was the cultural underpinnings of this pedagogy that worried them. Mennonites saw within the new school laws nothing less than "an inextinguishable enthusiasm for the art of war" and a plan that "militarism be instilled in every child" with the rallying cry "one king, one country, one fleet, one flag, one all-British empire: love and sacrifice for the Fatherland."[27] Mexico and Paraguay would guarantee the use of the nonviolent German language and allow the Mennonites to circumvent Canada's English-language militancy.

What World War I hinted at was confirmed during World War II. Military exemption could no longer be viewed as a group privilege. Mennonites would never again be exempted as a people, and within a rapidly urbanizing world throughout North America, they felt pressured to turn their teachings on pacifism into instruments of wider social good. Especially in Canada, doors opened in support of yet another large migration, the coming of 20,000 so-called Russlaender Mennonites from the war-torn Soviet Union, bringing with them stories of rape, plunder, murder, and botched attempts at self-defence. In the United States, a similar spirit pervaded with the founding of Mennonite Central Committee and its outreach to Mennonites caught in the Soviet crises. But as Paul Toews argues, during the inter-war period, American Mennonites were also attracted to liberal peace movements that foreshadowed a deep questioning of the old two-kingdom approach to peace.[28]

World War II would establish a new reality, although pressure was once again surprisingly subdued as the idea of "rights" for pacifists took firm hold in both countries. As in World War I, the Canadian government was extremely hesitant about introducing conscription, and the American government, again, hesitated entering a war on another continent. Coincidentally, just as in World War I, both governments introduced universal military conscription in the same year: 1940. Canada did so only after the German *Blitzkrieg* pulverized Holland and France, forcing the retreat at Dunkirk in June 1940, but even then Canadian Prime Minister, William Lyon Mackenzie King, did so hesitatingly. To placate an anti-war Quebec, he had the National Resources Mobilization Act (NRMA) only induct young men for home guard, and, reflecting his close ties to Mennonites, the bill's very text exempted members of historic peace churches. Indeed it made special reference to the 1793 Militia Act, the 1873 Order-in-Council, and to the immigrants of the 1920s. The United States passed the Burke-Wadsworth

---

27. Dyck, "Emigration." This book was published most recently as Dyck, *Die Auswanderung*, 13. See also, Dyck, *Anfangs Jahre*; Dyck, *Hinterlassene*.

28. Toews, *Mennonites in American Society*.

bill a full year before the December 1941 bombing of Pearl Harbor, and when it passed, it too provided a clause for conscientious objection. Despite early talks in Canada of a full group-based exemption, the American and Canadian provisions were very similar. In the U.S., Mennonite leaders presented a plan for a Civilian Public Service, not dissimilar from the Canadian Alternative Service Work plan.

In both countries young men appeared before officials to claim their right not to fight on the basis of religious commitment, and then they served as conscientious objectors in areas of national service. In both countries men worked at meaningful roles in mental hospitals, held adventurous roles as forest fire fighters or northern teachers, and engaged in less thrilling work in soil conservation, road construction, and forestry.[29] The CO boys in both countries eagerly embraced a broader world in the camps. Robert Kreider writes that even as a University of Chicago graduate, he made new friends outside his familiar Mennonite circle, including Holdeman and Mennonite Brethren, Plymouth Brethren, and Jehovah's Witnesses. But he also writes of a restlessness among the COs and his longing to do work of "real . . . national importance."[30]

The Responsibility to Building Peace

This restlessness was expressed in a number of ways. In both countries large groups of Mennonite boys—about 35% (4,500 in total) in Canada, and anywhere from 30% to 50% in the United States, depending on how conscientious objection is defined—answered the call to arms.[31] The young men included pilot Hans Pankratz of Canada who spoke of his service as the "highlight of my life," gladly given as "Canada gave our [immigrant] parents a new life."[32] They included young men in the United States, like Roland Juhnke who enlisted because he felt a "sense of duty" to his close friends and "to his country," and David Warkentine who went because he lived "in a non-Mennonite community [and] . . . felt little pressure [not to serve] from that quarter."[33]

---

29. See, Klassen, editor, *Alternative Service*; Matthews, *Smoke Jumping*.

30. Kreider, *My Early Years*, 19.

31. Even though the 50% figure has been accepted as the percentage of U.S. Mennonite draftees who went to war, this figure is disputed by Steven Nolt and others who suggest that not nearly all pacifist Mennonite boys were drafted. Personal email correspondence with Steven Nolt, 28 September 2014.

32. See, Regehr, "Lost Sons," 461–480.

33. Bush, *Two Kingdoms*, 101, 103.

The restlessness of the conscientious objector was also internalized. In sharp contrast to the bravado of the enlisted men, the COs were often tainted with the designation of cowards or "yellow bellies," and this stigma followed the Mennonites after the war. Marlene Epp writes that in Canada, "nonresistant teaching may have offered a nonconformist stance with respect to militarism, but it did not counter the male image of 'fighter,' 'warrior,' 'protector.'"[34] John Howard Yoder concluded later that in the United States, "those who want to show themselves liberated from the ethnic culture tend to think that the peace witness is a part of something the Mennonite have outgrown."[35]

Especially after the war, the more educated Mennonites in particular—spurned by Reinhold Niebuhr's charge that Mennonites were irresponsible "parasites on the sins of others"—began looking for new ways of expressing their pacifism. Indeed, a new resolve to become more socially useful after the war took root. In their book, *Mennonite Peacemaking*, Leo Driedger and Donald Kraybill describe how the "plausibility of biblical nonresistance was crumbling as younger scholars . . . sought to fashion a new theology of peacemaking for Mennonites in the modern world." In particular, they shifted "their focus from their ethnic community to civic responsibilities in the larger society as they became more urban, educated and mobile."[36] In November 1950 at a MCC-supported conference at Winona Lake, Indiana, Mennonite thinkers pondered how at "this critical time in a generation marked by widespread and disastrous wars and shadowed by the threat of still more ruinous warfare," one might live as a person of nonviolence. A new vocabulary was evident in the final communiqué as the word "nonresistance" became eclipsed by the words of love, service, and discipleship. It spoke unequivocally about "responsibility . . . to the total social order of which we are a part."[37] Harold S. Bender, who had identified peace and love as fundamental aspects of sixteenth-century Anabaptism in his watershed article, "The Anabaptist Vision," just a few years earlier, addressed the meeting, lamenting that Mennonites had "largely left unfulfilled our obligation to witness . . . for the way of love and nonresistance."[38]

During the 1960s as the Cold War threatened and the Vietnam War inducted young Americans, a new generation of Mennonite thinkers, linked to the Concern Movement, demanded more than to simply "witness for the

---

34. Epp, "Heroes," 110.
35. Bush, *Two Kingdoms*, 271.
36. Driedger and Kraybill, *Mennonite Peacemaking*, 84.
37. Ibid., 85.
38. Ibid., 86.

way of love." In his book, *Anabaptism: Neither Catholic nor Protestant*, Walter Klaassen reflected the new ethos: "Anabaptists were radical," he wrote, "not simply because they were more biblicistic, but also because . . . [t]hey were dangerous people; their views of church and state challenged positions held and supported by authorities . . . They were revolutionary . . . in non-violent ways . . . bring[ing] about change . . . [that would] more nearly [be] representative of God's will."[39]

Historian T.D. Regehr illustrates this fundamental shift in thinking by recalling two meetings with two different Canadian prime ministers. In a February 1960 meeting with Prime Minister John Diefenbaker, Mennonite leaders—self identifying as members of the "Historic Peace Churches," and seemingly priding "themselves on being 'the quiet of the land'"—spoke of their "deep-rooted conviction against active participation in war" and their desire for privileges of military exemption "which we have enjoyed since our church fathers came to this country in 1790." In sharp contrast was another meeting between a Prime Minister and Mennonites in 1970; this time the leaders hailed from the newly minted MCC Canada, and the national leader was the young intellectual, Pierre Elliot Trudeau. This meeting was televised and the exchange combative, as the Mennonites came asking not for privileges for themselves but with demands for others. Among their requests were the acceptance of American draft dodgers, a recognition of Communist China, and the creation of "peace chairs" for Canadian universities. The word "privilege" had been eclipsed, writes Regehr, by "political process, and politics."[40]

This culture was in keeping with new "peace" initiatives in both countries. In both Washington in 1968 and in Ottawa in 1975, MCC opened advocacy offices to seek to influence national policies. Their aim now was to advocate for the rights of others: African Americans and Aboriginal Canadians, for women and immigrants, and for nuclear disarmament, and indeed, peace around the world. As the Washington office director, Delton Franz, put it, here was a chance to "sensitize the powerful to the impact of their actions on the world's powerless."[41] Quite suddenly MCC offices in Akron and Winnipeg spoke of a new authority. As Keith Graber Miller noted at the time, "the stories, whether told by service workers or MCC staff persons [in other countries], have implications for American policy."[42]

---

39. Klaassen, *Anabaptism*, 9–10.
40. Regehr, *Mennonites in Canada*, 383–84.
41. Loewen and Nolt, *Seeking Places*, 316.
42. Miller, *Wise as Serpents*, 8.

This culture of peace took hold of the North American communities in numerous ways. High profile utterances linked to the Mennonite World Conference captured the imagination of Canadian and American Mennonites toward the end of the twentieth century. Two organizations in particular, Mennonite Conciliation Service, established in 1977, and the Christian Peacemakers Teams (CPT), founded in 1989, spoke of the responsibility to seek international justice and "to address systemic conditions that created injustice and violence."[43] The latter organization was founded after Ronald Sider challenged the delegates at the 1984 Mennonite World Conference in Strasbourg "to form groups of Christians who were to physically place themselves as peacemakers between hostile people." One of its volunteers, Patricia Shelly of Kansas, would write in a 1997 publication, *North American Mennonites and Peace,* that the idea of peace needed rethinking, moving it away from the binary of "personal" versus "political." Indeed, it must be seen in its broader context, wrote Shelly, as an attitude toward all of life, including consumer greed and the attending "need to protect what we have" amidst "an ethos that glorifies violence."[44] In an address in Winnipeg in 1990, Elizabeth Soto, a visitor from Puerto Rico, offered a similarly frank admonition, calling upon North Americans to learn to adopt "a new evangelical style" that would reject an historic "passive position against injustice," that is, "comfortable, inactive pacifism."[45]

Conclusion

On the 300-year anniversary of their sojourn in North America, many Mennonites still seemed quite comfortable in a continued "quiet in the land" approach to peace, and indeed most of those who voted, did so for governments noted for non-intrusive policies. And when seeking to spread the message of peace, progressive leaders continued to frame the question of peace in highly personal terms. In 1983, John Howard Yoder, author of the highly influential, *The Politics of Jesus,* appealed to a wider readership with an anthology entitled *What Would You Do?* "if a violent person threatened to harm a loved one." Meanwhile in 2002, writing in the shadow of the U.S. "war on terror," John Roth published his *Choosing Against War: A Christian View.*[46] Oftentimes effective peacebuilding came not from confrontational words, but in action that encouraged cross-cultural understanding and

---

43. Miller, "History," 16.
44. Heisey and Schipani, editors, *Theological Education,* 39.
45. *Proceedings,* 32.
46. Yoder, *What Would You Do?*; Roth, *Choosing Against War.*

solidarity with the poor, such as the work of SELFHELP Crafts, Mennonite Economic Development Associates (MEDA), or the workers of MCC who spoke of "standing with" those who suffered injustice.[47]

And yet the tone of these messages should not belie the fundamental shift that characterized the history of peace among the Mennonites of North America. It had turned the question of "privilege" inside out. Peacebuilding in the wider society had become a Mennonite responsibility.

---

47. See, Loewen and Nolt, *Seeking Place*, 228–30; 316; 318–19.

4

The Beginnings of Mennonite Central Committee and Its Ministry of Peace

ESTHER EPP-TIESSEN

Introduction

WHEN THE SOVIET UNION collapsed in 1991, many North American Mennonites pressed for Mennonite Central Committee (MCC) to initiate a massive aid program to the economically devastated region. An agency of Mennonite and Brethren in Christ churches in the U.S. and Canada, MCC was established in 1920 as a response to the suffering of Mennonites and others in the USSR in the wake of war, revolution, and economic upheaval. Between 1922 and 1926, the fledgling organization had saved many people from destitution and death through its provision of relief and rehabilitation assistance. But after 1926, the doors for direct MCC involvement in the Soviet Union remained firmly closed. When those doors opened quite suddenly and dramatically in 1991, many MCC constituents clamored for MCC to "do something" before the opportunity was lost once more.[1]

North American constituents, especially Canadians with more recent ties to the USSR, had many reasons for pressing MCC to get more involved in the former Soviet Union. Some of them were naturally concerned about relatives there who had struggled for years under difficult circumstances.

1. Raber, "Soviet Union," III–2.

Some were eager to support evangelistic efforts in the formerly atheist regime. Others felt it important for MCC to return to the place of its beginnings and resume the ministry that it had begun in the 1920s. Still others were motivated to somehow "redeem" the tragedy and suffering of their own Soviet experience, and they believed that MCC could help facilitate this.

A particular project undertaken in 1992 gave expression to this search for redemption. The project involved the shipment and distribution of 9,000 boxes of groceries to hospitals, orphanages, and the elderly in the Moscow area. North American constituents eagerly supported this shipment of material aid, which, for many, represented much more than feeding hungry people. Their donations signified a desire to reach out in friendship and forgiveness to a people and a place, which, for them or their families, represented terror and trauma. George Thielman of Winnipeg was one individual who donated money specifically for the food shipment. He said his donation was a way of offering forgiveness to the country that had abducted, tortured, and murdered his father in 1938 when he was only a small boy. Former executive director, J.M. Klassen, whose family managed to escape Soviet Russia under very difficult circumstances in late 1929, put it this way: "[The Soviets] were our persecutors—they took everything we had. And now we have a chance to show Christian love and forgiveness, to demonstrate that we bear them no malice."[2] Another person put it this way, "We . . . choose to be wounded healers, serving with wisdom and compassion where our relatives were once executed and exiled."[3] For many of the people who contributed to the food shipment and who desired MCC to "do more," theirs was a search for a healing of their Soviet experience and for a way of making peace with former enemies.

This essay explores the development of MCC's ministry of peace since its beginnings in the context of the desperate suffering of Mennonites in Soviet Russia. It analyzes the ways in which a commitment to peace—both as theological understanding and practical embodiment—pervaded MCC's work from those very beginnings and how that commitment has informed subsequent activity. It explores the question of how the Soviet experience has left its mark on Mennonite peacemaking through MCC.[4]

---

2. News release, February 28, 1992, Volume 4000, File 278 R 1992 Y, Mennonite Central Committee Canada Collection, Mennonite Heritage Centre, Winnipeg, MB.

3. Letter, Art DeFehr to Ray Brubacher, January 15, 1992, Volume 5039, File 922R 1993Y, Mennonite Central Committe Canada Collection, Mennonite Heritage Centre, Winnipeg, MB.

4. It should be noted that traditionally MCC has understood "peace" activity very broadly, from nurturing nonresistance, to providing alternative service options, to advocating for justice, to transforming conflict, to building relationships, etc. This

The Early Years of MCC's Existence

MCC was formed in 1920 in response to the intense suffering of Mennonites in "South Russia" in the wake of war, revolution, terror, and famine. A study commission of four representatives, sent by the Mennonite colonies, brought firsthand accounts of that suffering and pleas for assistance to co-religionists in the United States and Canada. U.S. Mennonites had already mobilized their denominational committees to help based on letters from relatives and reports in Mennonite periodicals. But it was the call of the study commission for a single centralized relief effort, combining the efforts of all the denominational committees, that led to the founding of Mennonite Central Committee in Elkhart, Indiana on July 27–28, 1920. Five separate U.S.-based relief committees joined to form MCC. Canadians supported the work of MCC through their own denominational channels and through a short-lived Canadian Central Committee, which was established in 1920 and was subsumed in the Canadian Mennonite Board of Colonization in 1922.

In those early years, MCC described its work as "relief." Its calling was to provide emergency aid to people confronted with starvation. Years later, the organization would recognize that it was also "doing development." By providing not only food, but also seeds, animals, and tractors, it was enabling people to regain the capacity to feed themselves. More recently, MCC personnel have pointed out that the early ministry in the Soviet Union also incorporated a peacemaking approach. A 2010 essay suggests that an integrated approach of "relief, development and peace" has been a "hallmark" of MCC's activities since its founding in 1920.[5] Indeed, for its nearly one hundred year existence, MCC has played a key role in the shaping of the peace understandings and commitments of North American Mennonites and Brethren in Christ.

Between 1920 and 1926, North American Mennonites donated $1.3 million to feed 75,000 people, preventing the starvation of an estimated 9,000 people in the Soviet Union. Their gifts also included clothing, as well as seed, draft animals, and tractors to help restore agricultural productivity. Between 1923 and 1929, Canadians, through the Canadian Mennonite

---

broad sweep has led many people to say that "everything that MCC does is peace." Only recently has MCC begun to bring greater specificity to its definition of peace and the myriad activities that have been identified as part of a peace agenda. See Alain Epp Weaver and Krista Johnson, "Peace, Peace: Making Distinctions," *Intersections* 1:1 (Winter 2013), 3–7. Because this essay provides a general overview of past experience, it relies on the broader definitions of peace and peacemaking.

5. Reimer and Guenther, "Relationships," 356.

Board of Colonization, also welcomed and helped to re-settle some 20,000 Mennonite refugees from the Soviet Union. This two-pronged initiative was later described as the Mennonites' "greatest outpouring of corporate benevolence in their history."[6]

Although MCC did not use the word "peace" to describe its work in these early years, the fledgling organization nevertheless was rooted in an Anabaptist peace church tradition, and it demonstrated a commitment to relieve suffering in a way so as to reduce conflict between peoples, to build understanding, and to demonstrate a life-giving—rather than life-destroying—ethic. A commitment to peace undergirded its efforts.

A primary example of MCC's early commitment to peace was the connection that its leaders made between the relief of suffering and nonresistant faith. When MCC was organized, Mennonites in North America were still reeling from the impact of World War I. In both Canada and the U.S., Mennonite convictions about nonparticipation in war had been put to the test. In the U.S., despite assurances that conscientious objectors (COs) would not be ill-treated, some 200 were imprisoned, and many were subjected to physical and psychological abuse. Canadians COs fared somewhat better, but in both countries Mennonites were soundly criticized for their resistance to military service, especially in light of the wartime profits they made from growing grain. Key church leaders insisted it was critical for Mennonites to demonstrate the integrity of their nonresistant convictions by actively and sacrificially helping to relieve the suffering of war. In Canada, Ontario Mennonites organized a Non-Resistant Relief Organization (NRRO) in 1918 to gather money for war relief as a way of expressing these commitments and as a gesture of goodwill to the Canadian government and public. In the U.S., the Mennonite Relief Commission for War Sufferers also solicited money for war relief, in addition to appointing young men and women as relief workers with the American Friends Service Committee and Near East Relief to assist with post-war relief and reconstruction in Europe. Pressured by public opinion, many Mennonites began to see donating money for relief and doing relief service as integral to a faith-based refusal to perform military service.

This spirit and understanding found expression within the beginnings of MCC. Longtime MCC chairperson P.C. Hiebert wrote that the faithful witness of young men in relief service in the years immediately following the war awakened U.S. Mennonites to "a realization of their peculiar mission as a people who believe in saving life rather than in destroying it."[7]

---

6. Kreider and Goossen, *Hungry*, 41.
7. Hiebert, *Feeding*, 28.

Clayton Kratz, one of three initial MCC workers to South Russia and the one who lost his life there, wrote on his application form that he wished to help people in need, "because this great world catastrophe has not caused me any inconvenience."[8] In 1929, writing a comprehensive report about MCC's work in Russia, Hiebert wrote that the relief of suffering was

> ... of special importance to a people who are by creed and practice opposed to war and the destruction of life as well as to all other crime and deeds of violence. To be a true pacifist in the spirit of Christ implies more than to desist from injuring others, or in refusing to heed a government's call to arms. It doubtless includes the putting forth of every legitimate effort in preserving life.[9]

In other words, the active relief of suffering was the positive expression of a refusal to take up arms and to kill.

A second example of how MCC reflected an expression of peace in its very early years was the fact that it was a collective inter-Mennonite effort. Prior to the formation of MCC, the various Mennonite groups in the U.S. and in Canada did their mission and relief work independently. A great divide separated the Dutch/North German/Russian Mennonites from Swiss/South German Mennonites; even within these two traditions, there were distinct sub-groups that occasionally harbored suspicion and distrust of each other. In the words of James Juhnke, so great were the differences of dress, culture, language and theological nuance, that the two main traditions found it impossible "to share communion (the Lord's Supper) with each other, to accept each other's ordination, or to come together in a common denominational organization."[10] The founding of MCC as a "central committee," bringing together diverse groups to collectively address an urgent crisis, represented a significant breakthrough in inter-Mennonite relationships. The insistence of the study commission in 1920 that North American Mennonites unite in a single relief effort proved not only to be practical at many levels, it also built relationships, strengthened understanding, and facilitated peacebuilding amidst a fractured Mennonite family.

A third example of MCC's commitment to peace in the early years was the deliberate commitment to feed the hungry, regardless of their race, religion, or social status. To be sure, it was the suffering of fellow Mennonites that compelled North Americans to give generously, but the Soviets insisted that MCC relief be impartially given to all people, no matter what their race

---

8. Quoted in Kreider and Goossen, *Hungry*, 25.
9. Hiebert, *Feeding*, 416.
10. Juhnke, "Turning Points," 67.

or religion. And MCC workers were convinced of this mode of operation, especially when they observed that Mennonites, while suffering, were not starving in nearly the numbers as their non-Mennonite neighbors. Alvin J. Miller, director of MCC[11] operations in Russia, insisted that aid given only to Mennonites would heighten animosity between them and their Orthodox, Catholic, and Lutheran neighbors. He wrote, "To bring relief to Mennonites and refuse others would not seem christlike. It would also engender and increase the ill feeling against the [Mennonite] colonists..."[12] Another MCC worker, Arthur Slagel noted the need to generate a spirit of goodwill with the Soviet government and the Russian people in general.[13] Thus MCC fed the very neediest first, regardless of whether they were Mennonites or not. It also established feeding kitchens in several volosts (counties) where no Mennonites lived. Of the 75,000 people which it fed between 1922 and 1923, at least 15,000 were not Mennonites.[14] MCC relief operations were carried out in such a way as to ease hostilities and build understanding. And, in the sense that MCC had to negotiate with communist authorities, many of whom regarded Mennonites as enemies of their revolution, MCC was in a sense reaching out in friendship to an unfriendly regime. It was seeking to provide relief in a spirit of generosity, peace, and goodwill.

Yet another way in which MCC's early experience in the Soviet Union informed its later peacemaking ministry is with respect to advocacy to government. From the very early beginnings, MCC personnel addressed government on behalf of suffering people. MCC director Alvin J. Miller spent eighteen months negotiating with Soviet officials in Moscow, Kharkov, and elsewhere for permission to begin a relief program. The lengthy and difficult process nearly drove him to despair, as he realized that people were dying while food waited just beyond their borders. But his dogged persistence eventually bore results, and the aid began to flow in the spring of 1922. Advocacy was also carried out across the Atlantic, where Mennonite leaders sought permission for Mennonites from the Soviet Union to resettle. In 1919, the government of Canada had, through an Order in Council, barred Mennonites, Hutterites, and Doukhobors from immigrating into Canada. Officials of what became the Canadian Mennonite Board of Colonization

---

11. It should be noted that MCC's work in the Soviet Union was known as American Mennonite Relief (AMR). MCC was the name known in North America. For the sake of simplicity, I have chosen to use only the term MCC.

12. Letter, Alvin J. Miller to A. A. Friesen, April 4, 1921, Volume 1175, File 84: Mennonite Central Committee, 1921–1930, Canadian Mennonite Board of Colonization Collection, Mennonite Heritage Centre, Winnipeg, MB.

13. Quoted in Hiebert, *Feeding*, 208.

14. Kreider and Goossen, *Hungry*, 41.

(an MCC partner) now sought the rescinding of this Order in Council. Thanks to a federal election that brought victory to a sympathetic Opposition leader, the effort was successful. In 1921, the new government rescinded the offensive Order. Between 1923 and 1930, more than 20,000 Mennonites from the Soviet Union made a new home in Canada.

A fifth way in which the early beginnings of MCC illustrated a ministry of peace was in the welcome of these refugees and newcomers. In response to appeals from the Canadian Mennonite Board of Colonization and the churches that supported it, Canadian families opened their homes and hearts to provide hospitality. Many of them hosted large families, providing food, shelter, and sometimes work for extended periods. My own grandparents lived for many months with a Clemmer family near Waterloo, Ontario, paying nothing for room, board, and home, helping out by working on the farm. The Canadian hosts who welcomed the newcomers into their homes, often for months at a time, did not necessarily regard the hospitality they provided as a peace response. They simply saw it as a Christian response to human need. But down the road, the sponsorship of refugees and newcomers, driven from their homes by war and armed conflict, would indeed come to be seen as a peacemaking response.

We will return to these five expressions of a peacemaking ethos in MCC's work. But before that, it is important to explore how MCC's peace ministry unfolded subsequent to those early years.

MCC's Service and Peace Work during World War II

MCC entered a brief period of dormancy between 1926 and 1930, when a new movement of Mennonite refugees from the Soviet Union required resettlement. Canada was no longer accepting refugees after 1930, so MCC stepped in to transport and resettle in Paraguay approximately 1,000 refugees who needed a home. Another several years of limited activity ended with the outbreak of the Spanish Civil War in 1936, and in 1937 MCC took steps to formalize its existence through incorporation. When Germany invaded Poland in September 1939, igniting World War II, MCC increased its relief efforts. At the encouragement of Canadians, who found their country at war sooner than Americans, MCC sent money, clothing, and personnel to England. After the war ended in 1945, MCC moved onto the European continent and began a massive relief and reconstruction program. It also soon found itself working to locate, process, and resettle Mennonite refugees who had escaped the Soviet Union with retreating German troops in 1943 and were now scattered throughout the various zones of Germany.

Prior to engaging this massive relief effort, however, MCC became increasingly involved in addressing peace-related concerns at home. In the U.S., MCC administered a program of alternative service for conscientious objectors. At the outset of the war, a specially created inter-Mennonite peace committee had represented Mennonites in their negotiations for exemption from military service and alternative service. The task of directing this program, called Civilian Public Service (CPS), soon fell to MCC. So, in addition to soliciting money and material aid for war relief in Europe, MCC placed conscientious objectors in hospitals and institutions for the mentally ill, where they could perform an important service for their country without rendering military service. Eventually, this work led to the formation of the MCC Peace Section. Canada's alternative service program—consisting of firefighting, forestry, road construction, and service in hospitals and institutions—was run by the government, but several inter-Mennonite committees, led by the Conference of Historic Peace Churches (CHPC) based in Ontario, advocated for Mennonite exemption in Ottawa, and oversaw spiritual care of workers in camps. In 1944, the CHPC, along with several other Canadian organizations, became members of MCC through the appointment of representatives to the MCC board.

One of the realities that confronted Mennonites and Brethren in Christ as the war dragged on was that significant numbers of their young men were enlisting in active military service rather than claiming conscientious objector status. In both Canada and the U.S., estimates held that nearly 40 percent of Mennonite young men chose military service.[15] The reasons for those choices were varied. But Mennonite and MCC leadership clearly believed that young people—and perhaps the churches themselves—did not adequately grasp the biblical and historical foundations for Mennonite nonparticipation in war. A significant mandate of the Peace Section therefore was to interpret the meaning of nonresistance to the MCC constituency. The Peace Section published peace-related materials, held conferences, itinerated speakers, and fostered dialogue on nonresistance and peacemaking. In taking on this task, MCC became not only a ministry of but a ministry to the churches and denominational groups which supported it.

The tremendous suffering caused by the war, as well as the need to demonstrate to a skeptical public the authenticity of a refusal to participate in war, led MCC officials to articulate a strong connection between nonresistance and relief.[16] Mennonites were strongly encouraged to give sacrificially to the relief effort, as a way of giving a positive peace testimony.

---

15. Lapp, "Peace Mission," 285; Regehr, *Mennonites in Canada*, 35.
16. Lapp, "Peace Mission," 281.

For women, who traditionally gave through material aid, the preparation of clothing and food was their own expression of peacemaking.[17] A booklet on relief published by MCC in 1945 put it this way:

> The refusal to hate, harm or kill persons is in compliance with the command of God. God commands obedience to his own given ethical code which is consonant with his own nature. That nature is revealed as love. Love expresses itself positively in action to help all classes of people. It expresses itself negatively in refusal to harm in any way. Relief and peace are not separate entities. They are two aspects or phases of the doctrine that the Christian must express, the nature of God which is love, and obey his revelation.[18]

An MCC handbook also released in 1945 identified the organization's mission in the interconnected fields of relief and peace.[19]

Even before the war was over, various voices began to call for not only contributions of money and material aid, but *people* willing to locate themselves in contexts of great suffering to distribute food and clothing, to care for refugees and displaced persons, and to offer Christian love and compassion—in other words, people to serve. MCC had already placed some personnel in Europe (as was possible) early in the war, but it began to plan for a much larger contingent of workers for readiness at war's end. By 1950, MCC had personnel engaged in relief service in Europe, as well as in Asia, the Middle East, and Latin America. And in the post-war period, virtually every North American Mennonite extended family had at least one member who had completed a term of service with MCC.[20]

Relief service captured the imagination of many young Mennonites in North America as a way of expressing very concretely their desire to save life rather than destroy it. John Fretz, a young Ontarian who completed several years of forestry as an alternative service worker, signed up for two years of MCC relief service in France as soon as he could. Although not unhappy with his stint in forestry service, he desired to serve in a way that more directly and explicitly offered a message of peace and reconciliation. "[S]ervice such as in MCC is a more positive kind of witness."[21] Significantly, women volunteered for service as readily as men, demonstrating a commitment to peace, nonresistance, and conscientious objection that ran

17. Epp, *Mennonite Women*, 215.
18. Lehman, *Relief Work*, 34.
19. *Handbook*, 11.
20. Miller, "History," 6.
21. Quoted in Klassen, editor, *Alternative Service*, 79.

as deeply and steadfastly as their male counterparts who were usually the ones expected to offer a nonresistant peace testimony.[22]

The Post-War Years: Service as Peace Witness

In the 15-20 years after the war, service—offered through Christian individuals who were screened carefully for their faith testimony, their involvement in a church, and their commitment to nonresistance—was the primary way in which MCC expressed a peace witness to the world. When the U.S. imposed the draft during the Korean War, MCC created a special international PAX (peace) program for young male draftees to fulfill their draft obligations through reconstruction work, agricultural extension, and other forms of service. "During the war young Mennonite men had been *required* to do something in lieu of military service."[23] The belief was growing that young people—women and men—should readily serve a hurting world even when their country did not require this of them.

In addition to international relief service, MCC developed a variety of programs to facilitate service on the part of Mennonite and Brethren in Christ young people within the North American context. At the encouragement of a group of young women, MCC established a summer service program at two hospitals in the U.S. This initial experiment was so successful that it quickly spread through the country, as well as into Canada. Soon, MCC also developed year-round Voluntary Service options. Most of the young people who signed up for Summer Service or "VS" found themselves working among people struggling with poverty, disability, mental illness, or lack of social supports. In Newfoundland, which joined Canada in 1949, MCC began to provide nurses and teachers for a province that seriously lacked both. In the context of the Cold War and a booming North American economy, voluntary service, said one inter-Mennonite newspaper, was the "answer to the materialism and militarism of our age."[24]

Mennonite Disaster Service, a grassroots initiative that quickly came under the MCC umbrella, was yet another way in which service expressed a witness against war. Today, MDS is known almost exclusively for the way it rallies volunteers for clean-up and reconstruction in the wake of natural disasters such as floods, tornadoes and hurricanes. But it emerged in the early Cold War context and the fear of a Soviet attack against North America. In both the U.S. and Canada, Mennonites wanted to be helpful should such an

22. See Marlene Epp, *Mennonite Women*, 203–15.
23. See Redekop, *Pax Story*.
24. [Epp] "One Hundred," 2.

attack happen, but they were reluctant to participate in government-organized and sponsored civil defense programs because these programs were closely linked with the military. They wished to be able to mobilize trained volunteers for a swift response, but on their own terms. MDS was the result, first in the U.S. and then in Canada, in the 1950s.

MCC also provided leadership to Mennonite understanding and practice of peacemaking in other ways during this Cold War period. One of them was fostering cross-cultural exchange as a way of breaking down barriers and building understanding. As young American service workers worked alongside German youth, only a few years after their two countries had been at war, some of the hatreds and animosities of the war began to melt away. Learning from this experience, MCC established a farm trainee program, bringing to U.S. farms young international guests for the purpose of cross-cultural learning, as well as "international understanding and goodwill."[25] Over the next sixty years, this initial experiment evolved significantly, inspiring a whole range of other cross-cultural, educational and goodwill exchanges, intended to build bridges across significant divides.

The 1960s and 1970s: Addressing the Root Causes of Conflict

The 1960s and 1970s were years of change in the U.S. and Canada. In the U.S., the civil rights movement and the Vietnam War were paramount in shaping MCC. In Canada, the resurgent strength of indigenous people, the FLQ crisis, and a developing social safety net shaped a newly created MCC Canada.

An in-depth examination of the impact of the Vietnam War on MCC is beyond the scope of this essay, but it is essential to mention two important aspects. First, the war pushed MCC once again to be impartial in the delivery of emergency assistance. In the same way that MCC sought to feed Mennonites and non-Mennonites in the Soviet Union in the 1920s, MCC now attempted to provide aid to both South Vietnam (supported by the U.S.) and North Vietnam (supported by Communist China and the USSR). As Doug Hostetter, MCC worker in South Vietnam, put it, "[I]f MCC was to clearly demonstrate that the God it served was the God of all people—and not just the God of America—it must extend love and compassion to the people of North Vietnam."[26]

---

25. *Touch Any Corner*, 4.
26. Quoted in Epp-Tiessen, *Mennonite Central Committee*, 113.

Because MCC as a U.S.-based entity could not deliver aid to North Vietnam, it requested the newly formed MCC Canada to act on its behalf. The Canadians had only limited success, but their efforts, as well as the witness of several U.S. MCC workers who chose to remain in the country through the withdrawal of U.S. forces and the collapse of the South, spoke positively to the new regime. Not long afterwards, MCC was invited to establish an assistance program in the unified Vietnam, the first western non-government relief and development agency to be asked to do so. Once again MCC brought a peace perspective and a concern for impartiality to its work of emergency relief.

A second important learning for MCC's ministry was the need to address the root causes of suffering, not only their symptoms. By 1968, MCC had some 42 workers in South Vietnam, providing health care, literacy, agriculture, and refugee assistance. These workers witnessed the horrors of the war and the terrible suffering it inflicted. They became convinced that they could not continue to minister to the suffering without condemning the war itself. The words spoken by a North Vietnam ambassador to MCC worker Peter Dyck, who met with him in Algeria, also spoke loudly. According to Dyck, the ambassador "was very emphatic in pointing out that the biggest help we can give would be to bring about a change of heart in the Pentagon." In other words, MCC should be focused not on binding up the wounds of war, but in stopping America from inflicting more wounds.[27] The call to address root causes led MCC to speak out against the war to its constituency in North America and to the U.S. government.

Of course, MCC workers heard similar challenges in other parts of the world. In the Middle East, where MCC became involved in 1949, Palestinian refugees challenged MCC workers about their relief and development work, when the U.S. government supported Israel's occupation of the Palestinian territories. One individual in a Jordanian refugee camp, upon receiving an MCC Christmas bundle in the wake of the 1967 Six Day War, threw it back to the MCC worker with the cryptic comment, "We get Christmas bundles and the Israelis get Phantom jets. You keep your Christmas bundles and you have your country keep its Phantom jets."[28] Throughout Asia, the Middle East, Latin America, and even North America, the recipients of MCC assistance dared to challenge the organization to get to the root of the problem and develop more radical responses to human need. They demanded justice rather than simply charity or even development.

---

27. Dyck, "Theology," 262–80.
28. Quoted in Miller, *Wise as Serpents*, 38.

One of the outcomes of this challenge was the establishment of advocacy offices in both Washington, DC (1968) and Ottawa, Canada (in 1975). MCC in the U.S. and related organizations in Canada had for years appealed to government for policies or privileges that would be beneficial to Mennonites themselves, but for many people, the presence of MCC offices so close to government seemed much too "political." MCC therefore carefully described the offices to constituents as "listening posts"—small offices that would keep MCC and the churches abreast of relevant developments in government. But in reality they quickly became offices through which MCC could convey the concerns of MCC workers and partners with respect to government policy. They became vehicles through which MCC could advocate on behalf of poor and marginalized people around the world. Advocacy for justice and for policy change became an important part of MCC's peace witness.

Throughout this period, MCC was also becoming more attentive to conflict and injustice close to home. Indeed, its overseas service workers often heard the encouragement from partners to "go home and address the injustice in your own country." At its founding in 1963, MCC Canada received a mandate to address "peace and social concerns" within the country, and within its first fifteen years, it developed a variety of programs and initiatives to do just that. Voluntary service workers serving in aboriginal communities, among offenders and prison inmates, and among people with disabilities quickly recognized that the major problem for these marginalized groups were certain structures of oppression, as well as attitudes of mainstream society, including Mennonite churches. For indigenous people, the loss of land, culture, and identity—through colonial domination—lay at the heart of their suffering. For offenders and inmates, a punitive justice system stood in the way of healing and reconciliation with victims and communities. For disabled persons, physical barriers and attitudes of condescension prevented full participation in society. As MCC Canada sought to "walk with" the marginalized in Canada, it attempted to address the social, political, and attitudinal barriers that seemed to lie at the heart of so much suffering. And again, this meant seeking to speak to Mennonite and Brethren in Christ constituents about the ways in which they participated in the injustice. This was not always well-received. Similarly, in the U.S., MCC's Peace Section found itself grappling with racism, labor strife, and gender equality.

The 1980s and 1990s: Conflict Transformation and Peacebuilding

By the 1980s, MCC's understanding and practice of peacemaking had evolved tremendously. From a concern for military exemption for conscientious objectors, to administering alternative service in the U.S., promoting voluntary service as peace witness, addressing the root causes of social problems, and advocating for justice, the scope of its vision and activity had grown astonishingly. From a stance of quiet refusal to do military service, Mennonites and Brethren in Christ had become "steadily convinced" that "speaking out publicly against war, violence, and injustice was central to their Christian faith."[29] This evolution continued in the 1980s and 1990s.

A significant new development in the 1980s and 1990s was the emergence of the field of "peacebuilding." Arising in part out of practical experiments in victim-offender reconciliation and restorative justice, and in part out of the emerging academic field of peace and conflict studies, MCC helped to guide, support, and train people in mediation, conciliation, and conflict transformation. It sought to equip people with proven practical tools for resolving or transforming conflicts, thus opening the door to healing and reconciliation between individuals and groups. The establishment of Mennonite Conciliation Service (MCS) in 1979 by MCC with Ron Kraybill at the helm was a significant development in this new direction. Another one was the formation a decade later of International Conciliation Service under John Paul Lederach to provide training, consultation, and intervention in conflicts outside of the U.S.. One of Lederach's early invitations for intervention came in 1990 from Mohawk communities in Quebec when a dispute over a golf course on indigenous land led to an armed stand-off between the Mohawk and Quebec police, supported by the Canadian military.

Another important new direction for MCC was the work of Women's Concerns programs in both the U.S. and Canada on family violence and sexual abuse. As women in the wider society had begun to talk about physical, emotional, and sexual abuse, so did women in the Mennonite and Brethren in Christ churches. They began to come forward, saying they had experienced abuse at the hands of husbands, boyfriends, relatives, and even church leaders. MCC tried to provide a context for the churches to hear, respect, and support the victims, hold offenders to account, and equip pastors, caregivers, and others to provide a healing presence. It also did much to educate a constituency often in denial about the reality of abuse.

---

29. Miller, *Wise as Serpents*, 10.

This was extremely difficult and sensitive work, for it focused attention on a lack of peace *within* Mennonite families, congregations, and communities. It was always safer for MCC to address problems "out there" than so close to home. But the work struck a chord. MCC-sponsored conferences and workshops on family violence and abuse were widely attended, and its educational packets proved to be among the organization's most popular resources.[30] Some twenty years after some of these materials were produced, a comprehensive overview of Canadian church responses to abuse called MCC's packets "groundbreaking" for their radical but restorative justice approach.[31]

The 1980s and 1990s also spurred reflection and action within MCC about the place of apology, repentance, and forgiveness in the work of peacemaking. Some of this happened within the context of Women's Concerns and its work on abuse, but it also surfaced elsewhere. In 1985, for example, MCC Canada issued an apology to Japanese-Canadians for the ways in which some Mennonites in British Columbia had benefited when the Canadian government had interned and confiscated the property of Japanese-Canadians during World War II. In 1992, on the occasion of the 500th anniversary of Christopher Columbus' arrival on the shores of the Americas, the wider MCC system offered an apology to indigenous peoples for the various ways Mennonites had not fully recognized their humanity and dignity. Both of these apologies led to the establishment of educational and healing funds. Somewhat later, Wilma Derksen of MCC Canada explored the meaning of forgiveness in the context of violent crime. Her work had special poignancy because it emerged from her struggle to come to terms with the murder of her daughter.

In the years since the new millennium, MCC's approaches to peacebuilding have continued to evolve. Some of the most recent manifestations include trauma healing, interfaith bridge-building, human rights promotion, contextual conflict analysis, and greater efforts to integrate a "do no harm" approach into all the work, whether emergency response, community development, capacity building, or justice advocacy. MCC has also deliberately sought to be more specific in its use of the language of "peace" and "peacebuilding." I will not describe these more recent approaches and developments because many of them—and indeed many of the approaches already outlined in this essay—are explored in considerable depth in the remainder of this volume.

---

30. Graybill, "Writing Women," 248.
31. Trothen, *Shattering the Illusion*, 101.

Linking Past and Present

Clearly, the importance of Mennonite Central Committee in the development of an ethos and practice of peace among North American Mennonites is undeniable. As James Juhnke noted at MCC's 75th anniversary in 1995, "Since its founding in the wake of the First World War, the Mennonite Central Committee has played a significant role in the shaping of [the Mennonite peace] agenda."[32]

From its first intervention in the Soviet Union in the 1920s, MCC, a ministry of Anabaptist peace churches, embodied a commitment to nonresistant faith. In the context of World War I and the need for Mennonites to demonstrate a practical expression of their refusal to bear arms, the provision of relief to those in need became a tangible witness of peace, compassion, and goodwill. From the beginning, MCC insisted that its workers embrace an Anabaptist commitment to nonresistance because it wanted their actions to serve as a message of peace to all those it encountered. An explicit and inseparable connection between a commitment to nonresistance and loving service to the suffering became especially clear in World War II. In subsequent years, MCC has continued to articulate and witness to peace and nonviolence, nurture Anabaptist peace theology, and require all its workers to embrace a bedrock commitment to the nonviolent resolution of conflict.

Secondly, from the beginning, MCC brought together very different Mennonite groups in a united effort to relieve the suffering of co-religionists. That collective inter-Mennonite spirit, though tested at times, has continued to be another expression of peacemaking. A divided Mennonite family does not make a very strong witness for peace. Indeed, during World War II, while MCC jointly represented U.S. Mennonite concerns for military exemption to the U.S. government, Canadian Mennonites were divided, sending various groups of representatives to Ottawa to argue for different levels of military exemption. Some of the leaders were painfully aware of the irony of a supposedly peace-loving people not being able to get along.

Present-day Mennonites who take inter-Mennonite cooperation as a given may have difficulty understanding just how profound this MCC "experiment" has been. From the beginning, MCC has been a vehicle for the breaking down of barriers, the building of bridges, and the forging of relationships that might not have occurred otherwise. MCC, in effect, has been a means of peacemaking within the broader Mennonite fold. In subsequent years, MCC has pursued ecumenical dialogue and cooperation and

---

32. Juhnke, "War," 11.

also interfaith bridge-building. No doubt the experience of inter-Mennonite cooperation paved the way for bolder relationship-building.

Thirdly, from the beginning, MCC provided impartial relief assistance to those in need. This commitment has continued to the present, as has a deliberate commitment to provide relief, not only to feed the hungry, but also to reach out in friendship to nations and peoples deemed enemies. The offer of aid to North Vietnam in the 1960s, mentioned earlier, is one such example. Another example is the provision of food aid to North Korea in the late 1990s when severe famine overwhelmed the politically isolated country. As noted by MCC Canada representative Bill Janzen in *The Globe and Mail*, the offer of food aid was intended to sow the seeds of improved relations between North Korea and the west.[33] MCC's humanitarian assistance—food, medicine, school and health kits—to Iraq under Saddam Hussein is yet another example. From the earliest beginnings in Soviet Russia, MCC has sought to offer an emergency response to save lives and relieve suffering, but also to extend friendship and goodwill to people regardless of the political persuasions of their governments.

Fourthly, from the outset MCC engaged in advocacy to governments on behalf of suffering people. At the beginning, that advocacy was for fellow Mennonites. But as MCC workers scattered across the globe befriending people in all kinds of circumstances, MCC's advocacy extended to include others, particularly people who were suffering as a result of U.S. and Canadian government policies. Some North American constituents frequently criticized MCC when, for example, it urged an end to U.S. military interventions in Latin America or called for greater consideration of the plight of Palestinians. They called such activity "political" and inappropriate for a church agency that espoused a separation of church and state. Sometimes MCC needed to remind its constituents that advocacy on behalf of fellow Mennonites—as well as *not* speaking out on issues of injustice—was also political.[34] The establishment of the Washington and Ottawa Offices in the 1970s and a UN Liaison Office in the 1990s was the visible expression of an increased commitment to advocacy that continues to the present. Today, there is a recognition that not all MCC advocacy relates directly to violence prevention and reduction, but it does connect with a broader vision of peace and well-being for all.[35]

---

33. William Janzen, "Politics and Hunger in North Korea," *Globe and Mail*, 7 August 1997, A-17.

34. Epp-Tiessen, *Mennonite Central Committee*, 117.

35. Heidebrecht and Wiebe, "Advocacy," 9–12.

Fifthly, the impulse to welcome and help re-settle refugees, an urge present in the beginnings of MCC, has also continued to be a significant way that MCC offered a peace-filled response to the wars of the 20th and 21st centuries. This is especially true for Canadian Mennonites, many of whom had a recent refugee story of their own. Gradually, Canadian Mennonites extended their welcome to other people, not just Mennonites. In the late 1970s, TV images of "boat people" fleeing Vietnam touched the hearts of Mennonites across the country. As one man told an MCC staff person, the images brought back memories of himself as a young boy, clutching the hands of his parents and trudging along a road in their escape from the Soviet Union in 1943.[36] In 1979, MCC Canada worked out a master sponsorship agreement with the federal government, and within half a dozen years, Canadian Mennonite and Brethren in Christ churches had sponsored nearly 5,000 southeast Asian refugees. Refugee sponsorship through MCC, in the words of historians Royden Loewen and Steven Nolt, had become "a signature expression of service and Cold War peace witness on the part of Canadian Mennonites."[37] In the U.S. context, MCC has worked at immigration reform as a way of providing welcome to strangers.

Clearly, not all of the impulses that shape MCC peacemaking and peacebuilding today were present in the initial years. But certainly many of them were.

Conclusion

This essay has demonstrated that from MCC's beginnings in 1920 in response to Mennonites suffering in the Soviet Union, a commitment to peace informed its work, even if this was not explicitly articulated at the time. Many of the practices that would today be considered part of a larger peacemaking agenda were present in the 1920s.

But how much is the actual experience of Mennonite trauma in the Soviet Union itself responsible for MCC and Mennonite peace work as a whole? An answer to that particular question requires much more in-depth research. Certainly the story about the 1992 food shipment, at the outset of this essay, demonstrates that the need to redeem a traumatic past led some survivors of the Soviet experience to offer forgiveness and friendship and seek to make peace with former enemies. As such, the story provides a small entrée into such an exploration.

---

36. Epp-Tiessen, *Mennonite Central Committee*, 150.
37. Loewen and Nolt, *Seeking Places*, 187.

I suggest that it was not the suffering itself that spurred MCC and Mennonites to embrace a peace witness and practice that has become increasingly explicit over the years. Rather, I believe it was a deep faith commitment to a nonviolent Christ and his gospel of peace that provided the foundation for MCC's work and witness for peace. It is this faith commitment which constitutes the bedrock for MCC's story of peacemaking and peacebuilding. Moreover, it is this faith commitment which enabled at least some survivors of the Soviet experience to extend the hand of friendship to those who represented their persecutors rather than to retaliate or seek revenge.

If the Soviet story has impacted MCC's ministry of peace in an ongoing way, it is more related to "how" that ministry has unfolded. As demonstrated here, some of the lessons learned as a result of MCC's assistance to Mennonites in the Soviet Union in the 1920s—lessons about inter-Mennonite cooperation and relationship-building, impartiality in the giving of aid, service to others, hospitality to refugees and strangers, advocacy on behalf of the suffering—continue to inform MCC's peace ministry today.

5

Historical Conditions of Mennonite Peacebuilding Approaches
Global Anabaptism and Neo-Anabaptism*

JOHN D. ROTH

Introduction

IN *GOSPEL VERSUS GOSPEL*, a landmark history of the Mennonite Church mission movement, Theron F. Schlabach argued that Mennonite missionaries in the twentieth century were frequently conflicted about the nature of the gospel they were proclaiming.[1] Whereas the Anabaptist-Mennonite tradition[2] understood the gospel to be a holistic message of

---

* Liz Wittrig, a Goshen College Maple Scholar in the summer of 2014, provided significant help with research.

1. Schlabach, *Gospel*. Although Schlabach's focus was primarily on the (Old) Mennonite Church, the mission histories of the General Conference Mennonite Church and the Mennonite Brethren suggested a similar trajectory.

2. I use the term "Anabaptist-Mennonite" in this essay to describe a theological tradition, anchored in the Anabaptist movement of the sixteenth century, that can be generally characterized by the practice of believer's baptism, a strong emphasis on Christian discipleship, a commitment to biblical pacifism, and a view of the church as a gathered community whose witness to the way of Jesus is evident in mutual aid, shared discernment of Scripture, and a commitment to walking alongside the poor, marginalized, and dispossessed of society. That tradition has found expression in a variety of

reconciliation—inseparable from a life of Christian discipleship, a commitment to love in all human relationships, and the collective witness of a disciplined church—Mennonites missionaries, borrowing heavily from the language of contemporary American fundamentalism and evangelicalism, frequently promoted a different gospel. On the mission field, Schlabach argued, Mennonites tended to reduce the gospel to simple formulas of forensic salvation, marked by a conversion experience and characterized primarily by intellectual assent to a set of prescribed doctrines.

As a result, Schlabach said, the churches that Mennonite missionaries helped to establish in countries around the world did not look very different from those of their Protestant counterparts, particularly in terms of their peace witness. "Mennonite Church missionaries might have gone forth with the integrated, holistic 'gospel of peace' idea at the center of their message," he concluded. "Generally, however, they did not."[3] Since the mission movement was the primary means by which the Anabaptist-Mennonite tradition took on a global expression in the course of the twentieth century, the indigenous churches that emerged from those efforts seemingly had little grounding in the theology or practices of pacifism.

On the surface, Schlabach's argument—carefully argued and bolstered by a host of primary sources—seems compelling. Yet, from the longer perspective of history, his conclusions do not tell the full story. During the past three decades, the Anabaptist-Mennonite tradition has undergone a profound transformation. Between 1980, when *Gospel versus Gospel* appeared, and 2014, membership in the global Anabaptist-Mennonite church nearly tripled—growing from 600,000 to 1,700,000—with the largest portion of that growth occurring in Africa, Asia, and Latin America.[4] Parallel to this growth, and often the primary reason behind it, has been a general indigenization of ecclesial identity, in which church leaders have translated the gospel into the language, cultural forms, and ritual traditions of their particular contexts. In many of these settings, Anabaptist-Mennonite groups around the world are rediscovering and reclaiming their identity as "peace churches."

---

groups, including Mennonites, Hutterites, Amish, and, to a certain extent, Brethren in Christ and Church of the Brethren. Because "Mennonite" is often narrowly associated with an ethnic group of German origin, the more expansive term "Anabaptist-Mennonite" is intended to include all those groups who aspire to Anabaptist ideals and are members of Mennonite World Conference, but may not have any direct association with Mennonites of German heritage.

3. Schlabach, *Gospel*, 182.

4. Bender, Steiner, and Thiessen, "World Mennonite"; online World Directory compiled by Mennonite World Conference 2012 http://www.mwc-cmm.org/.

One expression of the global character of the Anabaptist-Mennonite peace witness is the emergence of several so-called "neo-Anabaptist" peace networks. Usually composed of individuals and congregations who retain their own denominational identities, these networks have brought together Christians from many different theological backgrounds into a common conversation around Anabaptist understandings of discipleship and the church, with themes of peacemaking and reconciliation at the heart of these encounters.

Even more significantly, a commitment to Christian nonviolence and peacemaking has emerged as a defining characteristic in many Anabaptist-Mennonite churches around the world today. That commitment is evident in a sustained hunger for theological education on biblical themes of peace and a growing eagerness for training in the practical skills of conflict resolution. It is also made visible in lived experience—in contexts of violent crime, civil unrest, ethnic tensions, interreligious conflict, and postwar trauma, many Mennonite churches around the world today are creatively and courageously bearing witness to the gospel of peace.

To be sure, interest in the theology and practices of Christian peacemaking within the global Anabaptist-Mennonite fellowship has been complicated and uneven, expressed in a wide variety of ways. Moreover, like the Historic Peace Churches in North America, a chasm sometimes exists between the official teaching position—as expressed in a confession of faith or other theological statements—and the realities of local practice. And Anabaptist-Mennonite groups around the world continue to struggle with the painful fact of conflict and division within their own circles. Nonetheless, in communities throughout the global Anabaptist-Mennonite fellowship, interest in connecting the good news of the gospel with a theology of nonviolence and reconciliation is flourishing. Although Schlabach's argument regarding the muted character of the gospel of peace in the early Mennonite mission movement is largely correct, a longer view of history suggests that the legacy of the Anabaptist-Mennonite peace witness ran deeper than he had surmised.

This essay begins with a review of the historical conditions during the second half of the twentieth century that provided the impetus for contemporary expressions of peace theology and practice in the global Anabaptist-Mennonite church. Then follows an overview of various expressions of peace witness in the global Anabaptist-Mennonite fellowship today, noting especially the influence of Mennonite mission agencies, Mennonite Central Committee, and Mennonite World Conference in these developments. In particular, the essay describes the rise of several "neo-Anabaptist" networks that have formed around a common commitment to peacemaking and then traces the ways in which themes of peace and reconciliation have been embraced and transformed by numerous Anabaptist-Mennonite groups in various parts of the world. The essay concludes with a reflection on the hopes and challenges that all peace churches today face.

Historical Context of the Globalization of the Mennonite Peace Witness

World War II . . . and New Motifs in the Mennonite Peace Witness

It was, ironically, a war—World War II, the first truly global war—that planted the seeds of the globalization of the Anabaptist-Mennonite peace witness during the second half of the twentieth century. In the years leading up to the war, a small group of North American denominations—collectively known as the Historic Peace Churches—collaborated to promote theological conversation and new forms of witness regarding their commitment to peacemaking. Already in the mid-1930s, for example, Quaker, Mennonite, and Church of the Brethren leaders developed a "Plan of United Action in Case the United States is Involved in War," which envisioned a joint appeal to U.S. lawmakers for the legal recognition of conscientious objectors if a draft should be reinstated, along with the creation of a program of alternative service for draft-eligible young men.[5] As a result of their efforts, the Selective Training and Service Act of 1940 included both: a range of options for conscientious objectors and a legal framework for the creation of the Civilian Public Service program in 1941 that enabled conscientious objectors to perform "work of national importance" as an alternative to military conscription.[6]

The war and its aftermath marked a symbolic turning point in the North American Mennonite peace witness—a shift from a posture of nonresistant, quietist separatism to more activist forms of social and political engagement that connected Mennonites to the broader world. In the years immediately following the war, hundreds of young North American Mennonites participated in relief work in Europe. There, amid the still-smoldering ruins of European cities—symbolic centers of Western culture—they confronted firsthand the sobering consequences of modern warfare. The sheer devastation of the war, symbolized by the firebombing of Dresden and the use of the atomic weapons in Hiroshima and Nagasaki, raised deep questions about the logic of "Just War" arguments and generated a new sense

---

5. This story is told in Toews, *Religious Community*, 107–53.
6. For a fuller account of this program, see Keim, *CPS Story*.

among many Christians that pacifism was no longer an eccentric conviction of a few religious minorities.

In 1948, when the World Council of Churches (WCC) convened for the first time in Amsterdam, representatives publicly acknowledged that "war as a means of settling disputes is incompatible with the teaching and example of our Lord Jesus Christ."[7] Although North American Mennonites were not formal members of WCC, the newly-established organization clearly recognized that theological arguments regarding pacifism merited a broader hearing in the global community. In 1951, when the WCC invited representatives of the Historic Peace Churches and the International Fellowship of Reconciliation to submit a written statement of their peace position, they responded with a booklet titled *Peace is the Will of God*.[8]

The discussions that followed marked the emergence of John Howard Yoder, a Mennonite Central Committee (MCC) relief worker and student of Karl Barth at the University of Basel, as the leading Mennonite spokesperson for the cause of Christian pacifism.[9] Between 1955 and 1962 Yoder played a central role at the Puidoux Conferences, a series of theological conversations in Europe between representatives of the Historic Peace Churches and mainline Protestant theologians that focused on the subject of biblical pacifism and the nature of the Christian witness to the state.[10] Yoder's influence on the global Mennonite peace witness would continue to echo for decades to come.

This growing engagement in ecumenical conversations, joined with the practical experience in international relief work in the years following World War II,[11] had several significant consequences for the globalization of the broader Mennonite peace witness. Most immediately, it helped to renew a commitment to Christian pacifism among European Mennonites, many of whom had been combatants on opposite sides of both WWI and WWII.[12] In France, for example, Pierre Widmer, a Mennonite pastor from

---

7. Hostetler, "Nonresistance," 49. In 1953 Yoder presented an address on "Reinhold Niebuhr and Christian Pacifism"—a careful rebuttal to the Realist position advocated by Niebuhr.

8. International Fellowship of Reconciliation. *Peace is the Will of God*.

9. Nation, *John Howard Yoder*.

10. Cf. King, "From Sectarianism." The theme of the conferences was "The Lordship of Christ over the State."

11. In addition to MCC-sponsored relief work, North American Mennonites also developed several other initiatives, including PAX and the Teachers Abroad Program, which gave hundreds of young people international exposure.

12. The 1948, MWC assembly in Goshen/North Newton was the first international gathering of Mennonites following the war. Not surprisingly, it included several tense encounters among the German, Dutch, and French Mennonite church delegates. But

Montbéliard, emerged as an energetic voice for recovering a biblical understanding of peace. As editor of the French Mennonite periodical *Christ Seul*, Widmer featured numerous essays on the gospel of peace. He also promoted the translation and publication of peace-related literature and offered strong support for the European Mennonite Bible School (better known as Bienenberg), a collaborative French/German seminary established at Liestal, Switzerland. In the years following the war, Dutch, German, and Swiss Mennonites all established active peace committees that joined to form a European Mennonite Peace Committee.[13] European Mennonites also played a significant role in creating "Church and Peace," an ecumenical network of peace-related organizations, and they worked hard to promote alternative service for conscientious objectors in Germany and Switzerland. Thus, in a European context where a Mennonite peace witness had nearly disappeared, the shock of World War II led to a significant recovery of a peace church identity.

Second, conversations among Mennonites in North America about peace following the war gradually shifted from a focus on "nonresistance" to a new, more active, language emphasizing "justice," "responsibility," "peacemaking," and "witness to the state." As sociologists Donald Kraybill and Leo Driedger have argued in *Mennonite Peacemaking: From Quietism to Activism*, a younger generation of Mennonite leaders, deeply shaped by their experiences of international service, increasingly insisted that merely seeking exemption from military obligations was not a sufficient peace witness.[14] Instead, they argued, Christian pacifists needed to explore more carefully how the social, political, and economic structures that created conditions of injustice or violence might be transformed. Not all Mennonites agreed with the theology or style of peace activism, but the new approach helped to re-energize the message of reconciliation, peacebuilding, and conflict transformation that made the Mennonite peace witness seem more relevant to global realities.[15]

Finally, postwar developments brought Mennonite conversations regarding peace into the Christian ecumenical mainstream. To be sure,

---

the conference proceedings also included a public declaration of apology by the German delegate, Dirk Cattepoel, "Mennonites of Germany," 14–22.

13. The groups that formed included: the Doopsgezinde Vredesgroep (Netherlands); the Deutsches Mennonitisches Friedenskomitee (Germany); and the Schweizerisches Mennonitisches Friedenskomitee/Comité Mennonite suisse pour la paix (Switzerland).

14. Driedger and Kraybill, *Mennonite Peacemaking*. See also Stutzman, From Nonresistance.

15. Cf. Miller, *Wise as Serpents* and Stutzman, *From Nonresistance*.

advocates of Christian pacifism did not convince everyone; but during the second half of the twentieth century, Mennonite peace theologians and ethicists gained increasing credibility in WCC and other ecumenical settings. Here, the contribution of John Howard Yoder was of special note. Building on his very active role in the Puidoux Conferences, Yoder became a regular conversation partner in interchurch dialogues, representing Mennonite peace theology in dozens of international gatherings. His landmark book, *Politics of Jesus* (1972), has been translated into twelve languages and has become a standard text on the biblical, theological, and ethical foundations of Christian peacemaking.[16] Mennonites also played an active role on the WCC Faith and Life Commission, especially on topics related to peace. And during the last decades of the twentieth century, Mennonites entered into formal dialogue with the World Alliance of Reformed Church, the Roman Catholic Church, the Lutheran World Federation, and the Seventh-Day Adventists. One powerful symbol of the ecumenical character of the Anabaptist-Mennonite peace witness crystallized in 1998 when delegates of the Eighth Assembly of the World Council of Churches in Harare, Zimbabwe—prompted by the urging of a German Mennonite pastor and theologian, Fernando Enns—declared 2000–2010 as a "Decade to Overcome Violence" and appointed Swiss Mennonite, Hans Ulrich Gerber, to lead the initiative.[17] The WCC-sponsored campaign resulted in several significant regional conferences devoted to themes of peacemaking and at least three significant publications featuring the contributions of numerous Anabaptist-Mennonite church leaders.[18]

Another symbol of ecumenical reconciliation occurred in July of 2010 when representatives of the Lutheran World Federation and Mennonite World Conference concluded a five-year international dialogue with a service of repentance and forgiveness at the Lutheran global assembly in Stuttgart, Germany. The event marked a significant step in the healing of a church division nearly five centuries old.[19]

---

16. Yoder, *Politics*; for the fuller context of The Politics of Jesus and an assessment of its impact, see Nation, *John Howard Yoder*.

17. "Decade to Overcome Violence, 2001–2010: Churches Seeking Reconciliation and Peace." www.overcomingviolence.org.

18. Enns, Holland, and Riggs, *Seeking Cultures*; Miller, *Seeking Peace*; and Miller, Guiton, and Widjaja, *Overcoming Violence*.

19. For the final report of the Lutheran-Mennonite International Study Commission titled "Healing Memories: Reconciling in Christ," see www.mwc-cmm.org/article/interchurch-dialogue.

New Models of Anabaptist-Mennonite Mission, Service, and Global Identity

New realities in the second half of the twentieth century also transformed the character of North American missions and the identity of the global Anabaptist-Mennonite church. In the decades following WWII, rapid economic growth in the West—marked by the emergence of global capitalism, a growing gap between the rich and poor, and the political tensions of the Cold War—led to revolutionary unrest in many countries. Anti-colonial movements throughout Africa, Southeast Asia, and Latin America found expression in the emergence of new ideologies of liberation and the assertion of indigenous identity. The independence movements that followed had ecclesial, as well as political, consequences.

Mennonite Missions

Like many other Protestant groups, North American Mennonite mission agencies responded to these new dynamics by transferring control of the schools, hospitals, and church structures they had helped to establish into the hands of local church leaders. This process of indigenization was complex—each setting had its own unique story. But the general pattern was clear. Increasingly, the ecclesial identity of Anabaptist-Mennonite groups around the world was being determined by local leaders.

Within the Mennonite Board of Missions of the (Old) Mennonite Church, a new model of missions gradually emerged that was focused less on proselytizing and more on "accompaniment," "mutuality," and "patient presence."[20] The new approach began with a high regard for indigenous culture and was deeply attentive to physical and social, as well as spiritual, needs. Moreover, it tended to define the gospel in the language of *Shalom*—reconciliation with God, with others, and with Creation—and cultivated a posture of humility and respect. Thus, in 1949, Ralph and Genevieve Buckwalter began a thirty-year ministry in Japan with peacemaking at the heart of their work.[21] Albert and Lois Buckwalter spent a lifetime walking alongside indigenous groups in Argentina.[22] In 1959 Mennonite Board of Missions, responding to a call from several African Independent Churches

---

20. Cf. Shenk, *Anabaptism*. See also, Yoder, *As You Go*. In 2000, the Mennonite Board of Missions joined with the Commission on Overseas Mission of the General Conference Mennonite Church to form the Mennonite Mission Network.

21. Hershberger, "Neo-Anabaptist Approach," 385–414.

22. Horst, *Mision sin Conquista*.

(AICs), began a long fraternal relationship with Francophone Christians focused on Bible study and leadership training.[23] In all of these examples, the foremost goal was not to create Mennonite congregations, but to be "salt and light," following the Anabaptist practice of simply reading Scripture together and asking what the teachings of Jesus meant in particular settings.

A similar approach to missions also found expression in Europe. There, under the visionary leadership of Wilbert Shenk, the Mennonite Board of Missions patiently supported the long-term ministries of Alan and Eleanor Krieder in England, Joe and Linda Liechty in Ireland, Neil and Janie Blough in France, and Dennis and Connie Byler in Spain.[24] In each of these settings, mission workers often established small congregations or house fellowships. But since their primary emphasis was reaching out to other Christians and local churches, inviting conversations on Christian discipleship, and being a catalyst for holistic ministries of peacemaking and reconciliation, the churches often took root in surprising and unexpected ways.

In the decades following WWII, Anabaptist-Mennonite peace theology found special resonance in Central and South America. Here many countries were struggling with deep social, economic, and political unrest that pitted land-poor peasants and urban youth against oppressive, sometimes brutal, military regimes. During the 1970s and 1980s Mennonites living in countries like Argentina, Colombia, El Salvador, Guatemala, Nicaragua, and Paraguay were inevitably affected by the violent conflict of those years. Traditionally, Mennonites were generally deferential toward political authority, even that of oppressive regimes. But some Latino Mennonites, influenced in part by the emergence of "liberation theology," began to take note of the remarkable similarities they shared with the Anabaptists of the sixteenth-century and they rediscovered the radical roots of their faith. Suddenly, Anabaptist theology—with its emphasis on the priesthood of all believers, mutual aid, the dignity of human life—and Anabaptist stories of costly discipleship to the point of martyrdom, took on a new relevance.

---

23. These efforts began with the pioneering work of Edwin and Irene Weaver, primarily in West African settings (Nigeria, Ghana, Liberia, and Benin). David and Wilma Shank, working along with James and Janette Krabill in the Ivory Coast, were among a succeeding generation who carried this model forward.—Cf. Krabill, "Evangelical and Ecumenical," 240–47.

24. See, for example, Yoder, *As You Go*; and Shenk, *Anabaptism*. Both Yoder and Shenk served as administrators of the Mennonite Board of Missions, and both published extensively on themes related to peace and reconciliation. Since then, those themes have been extended in profound ways by a host of mission workers, including Kreider, Kreider, and Widjaja, *Culture of Peace*; Liechty, *Moving Beyond*; and Byler, *Los Genocidios*.

Here again, the influence of John Howard Yoder was unmistakable. In 1970 Yoder spent a year in South America, lecturing at the Mennonite Seminary in Montevideo, Uruguay, and at the Union Seminary in Buenos Aires, Argentina. The themes of his presentations, drawn largely from his recently-published *The Original Revolution*, sparked enormous interest among a young generation of evangelical theologians like René Padilla and Samuel Escobar.[25] The Latin American Theological Fraternity that they helped to establish provided a congenial forum for ongoing theological engagement with the Anabaptist-Mennonite tradition in Latin America. Over time, Mennonite seminaries in Colombia, Guatemala, Paraguay, and Uruguay developed curricula oriented to Anabaptist-Mennonite theology, which often included courses specifically on peace and reconciliation.[26] And publishing concerns such as Semilla-Clara or Kairos helped to bring Spanish-language resources on peace and social justice into broader circulation.[27]

No one did more to popularize Anabaptist-Mennonite peace theology in the Spanish-speaking world, translating it into the practical realities of daily living, than John Driver. In 1967, Driver began working as academic dean and professor of Church History and New Testament at the Inter-Mennonite Seminary in Montevideo, Uruguay. For the next 40 years, he served as an itinerant ambassador for the gospel of peace and as an advocate for the poor and dispossessed in his various roles as a teacher, educator, pastor, and biblical scholar. Driver's numerous books, which circulated well beyond Mennonite circles, integrated the Anabaptist peace witness into the wider tradition of the Christian church and fused the new spirituality of the Pentecostal movement with a strong Anabaptist communitarian ecclesiology.[28] His teachings often inspired Christians to reorient their ministries toward a more holistic understanding of the gospel. In the early 1980s, for example, members of the Radical Christian Communities network in Spain invited Driver to offer a workshop based on his book, *Community and Commitment*. Out of those relationships, a worshipping community emerged in Burgos with a ministry focused on drug addicts and on hospice care for those suffering from AIDS.[29] A similar community emerged outside of Bar-

---

25. For example, René Padilla and Samuel Escobar. For more on Escobar's encounter with Anabaptist theology, cf. "Latin America," 75–88.

26. In some of these settings, especially Colombia, Uruguay, and Paraguay, members of the General Conference Mennonite Church and Mennonite Brethren Church also took an active role. Laverne Rutschmann and Jacob Loewen were especially noteworthy in their theological orientation toward nonviolence.

27. Cf. William, *La reforma radical*; and Yoder, Machain, and Vilela, *Textos escogidos*.

28. Cf. Driver, Community and Driver, *Radical Faith*.

29. Driver, "The Church," 122–25.

celona. Driver's ministry, which combined theological expertise with deep humility and the integrity of authentic relationships, became a model for another generation of peacemakers and teachers like John Paul Lederach, Jack Suderman, and Howard Zehr.

Mennonite Central Committee

Parallel to these new approaches to mission, Mennonite Central Committee—the relief and service organization of numerous North American Anabaptist groups—emerged during the second half of the twentieth century as another powerful voice in disseminating the Anabaptist-Mennonite peace witness in the global church and a catalyst for encouraging indigenous forms of peace witness that had already taken root in local settings. The story of MCC's extensive work is described in more detail elsewhere in this volume. Here, it may suffice to simply affirm that MCC workers and resources have been catalysts for peacemaking and reconciliation, both in North America and throughout the world. Beginning in 1942, the MCC Peace Section—and, several years later, the MCC Canada Peace and Social Concerns Committee—worked to strengthen the peace witness of the church in North America. Elsewhere in the world, MCC has promoted a broad and holistic vision of peacemaking: extending material aid to people in need, regardless of their political, ethnic, cultural, or religious affiliation; providing financial support to dozens of local peace-minded organizations; and seeking to address the structural roots of violence, poverty, racism, and injustice as advocates in solidarity with the poor and the marginalized.

MCC's broad vision of peacemaking has also helped to inspire several educational centers that have had a significant impact on the diffusion of an Anabaptist-Mennonite peace witness. In particular, the Center for Peacemaking and Conflict Studies at Fresno Pacific University (Fresno, CA) and the Center for Justice and Peacebuilding at Eastern Mennonite University (Harrisonburg, VA) have played a crucial role in training church leaders from around the world in principles of conflict transformation and peacebuilding.[30] Since its beginning in the fall of 1994, for example, the Center for Justice and Peacebuilding has hosted 1,500 students from 83 countries in its summer peacebuilding program. Alumni of the program have since established similar institutes in the Philippines, Ghana, and Zambia, with groundwork under way for additional programs in Fiji, Jamaica, and

---

30. More recently, similar programs have emerged at Canadian Mennonite University (Winnipeg, MB) and Conrad Grebel University College (Kitchener, ON).

Nepal.³¹ Although an explicit connection to Mennonite peace theology varies considerably in these programs, the commitment to peacebuilding skill development and theory are clearly an outgrowth of the Anabaptist-Mennonite tradition.

Mennonite World Conference and a New Global Identity

Yet another significant factor in the globalization of the Anabaptist-Mennonite peace witness has been the creative influence of Mennonite World Conference (MWC). Established in 1925 as an effort by European and North American Mennonites to support their co-religionists in Russia who were suffering from the aftershocks of the revolution, MWC initially was little more than an international assembly of church leaders who gathered for worship and conversation every five or six years. At the 1936 gathering in Amsterdam, however, twenty-five participants formed an international Peace Interests Committee with the goal of providing support for conscientious objectors and strengthening the Mennonite peace witness in the face of growing militarism. Although the painful realities of World War II soon disrupted that initiative, the vision of a unified peace witness was not forgotten. Themes of peace and reconciliation emerged repeatedly in successive assemblies in Goshen/North Newton (1948), Karlsruhe (1952), Basel (1956), Kitchener (1962), and Amsterdam (1967).³² At the MWC assembly in Curitiba, Brazil, in 1972, a provisional peace committee assigned biblical studies on peace to each region represented in MWC with the goal of presenting them at the 1978 gathering in Wichita, Kansas. The 1978 assembly marked the birth of the International Mennonite Peace Commission (IMPC), with one representative for each of MWC's five regions.

Initially, the IMPC, which met every two years, focused primarily on translating peace-related resources, organizing regional seminars, and

---

31. Zimmerman and Lofton, "From Dream," 3–7.

32. The stated purpose of the IMPC was *(1)* to maintain contact between the Mennonite peace groups in the various countries; *(2)* to furnish a channel for cooperative action by these groups as may be desirable; *(3)* to publish a news bulletin to serve the international Mennonite peace cause; *(4)* to provide international Mennonite peace conferences at regular intervals; *(5)* to support those Mennonites in various countries who suffer for conscience's sake because of their nonresistant convictions; (6) to aid in clarifying, deepening, and applying fundamental convictions in regard to biblical nonresistance; *(7)* to aid in a more effective nonresistant witness. Before IMPC, the assemblies had a "Peace section" or "Peace work group" that would listen to speeches on peace related topics and include a discussion or a panel . . . the other sections of MWC were often women, men, and youth.—Mennonite World Conference Records, 1923–2012. Box X-009. Mennonite Church USA Archives—Goshen. Goshen, Indiana.

reporting on situations of conflict that affected MWC member churches. At meetings in Nicaragua and Colombia in 1979, for example, the IMPC addressed "Church-State Relations" in sessions that included a paper by Michnio Ohno on "Tax Objection in Japan," reports from India on several peace conferences sponsored by the Mennonite Church, and a lengthy discussion of the situation in Colombia where Mennonites were facing the challenges of social injustice, violence, and revolution. A gathering in 1981 associated with the MWC General Council included workshops with case studies on the challenges of peacemaking in Ethiopia, Taiwan, and Zimbabwe. And the IMPC gathering in India in December of 1985 led to the creation of an annual International Mennonite Peace Sunday.

Although the IMPC always struggled to find sufficient resources for its work, the group continued to meet biennially, focusing on issues related to conscientious objection, the challenge of revolutionary violence, and the urgent necessity of integrating peace teachings into the theological training of pastors in all Mennonite groups. Between 1978 and 1990 the IMPC hosted peace consultations in Belize City (1978), Kenya (1979), Colombia (1985), Kinshasa (1986), and Zambia (1988) and provided workshops focused on peacemaking at the MWC assemblies in Wichita (1978), Strasbourg (1984),[33] and Winnipeg (1990). The committee also provided the impetus for the publication of several peace-related books,[34] worked with the WCC to develop educational materials on the theme of "Justice, Peace and the Integrity of Creation," and supported the efforts of Mennonites in Brazil, Guatemala, Honduras, Nicaragua, and Paraguay on behalf of conscientious objectors and alternative service programs.[35]

In 1993 the IMPC was restructured as the MWC Peace Council, which developed a Global Anabaptist Peace and Justice Network to promote the exchange of information, prayer requests, and resources within the global church. It also created a directory of print resources, groups, and people that could be helpful in training church members in peacemaking skills. When MWC revised its organizational structure in 2009, the Peace Council

---

33. At the 1984 MWC Assembly in Strasbourg, the plenary address by Ronald Sider included a powerful call to the global church to establish a peacemaking witness that was prepared to "stand in the way" of violent confrontations, even if it meant assuming the same risks of bodily harm that military combatants experience. The speech was widely credited with being the impetus behind the creation of the Christian Peacemaker Teams. Sider, "God's People Reconciling," 224–32.

34. Mennonite Central Committee, Peace Section, *The Kingdom of God*; Harder, *Biblical Way*; and Peachey, *Church in Society*.

35. Peace Council Records Mennonite World Conference Records, 1923–2012. X-009. Mennonite Church USA Archives—Goshen. Goshen, Indiana.

evolved into the Peace Commission with a broadened mandate that included a framework for addressing conflicts within MWC member churches.

Although the ecclesial authority of MWC is limited, based on the voluntary participation of its 101 member groups, its patient, persistent advocacy—attentive to context and local realities—has been a crucial catalyst in the emergence of a global Anabaptist-Mennonite peace witness. By the end of the century, the organization increasingly reflected the profound demographic shift from North to South that was taking place in the larger Anabaptist-Mennonite fellowship. That transition was symbolized by locating recent assemblies in Calcutta (1997), Bulawayo (2003), and Asunción (2009) and, even more dramatically, by the appointment of César García, a Mennonite Brethren pastor from Colombia, as MWC general secretary in 2011 and the transition of MWC headquarters from Strasbourg, France, to Bogotá, Colombia.

Many of the global peace efforts described thus far emerged out of initiatives in North America. As the center of gravity in the global Anabaptist-Mennonite church shifts from Europe and North America to Africa, Asia, and Latin America, the question remains whether the gospel of peace will become fully integrated into the identity of the global church. Although that story is still being written, two clear trends are worthy of note: 1) the emergence of several neo-Anabaptist networks formed around a shared commitment to peace and reconciliation; and 2) a cluster of creative indigenous initiatives in Anabaptist-Mennonite settings around the world that are actively translating a theology of peace into terms relevant to their own setting. What follows below is little more than a rough sketch of these significant developments.

Neo-Anabaptist Network

One unforeseen consequence of the new Mennonite approach to missions, with its emphasis on "accompaniment" and relationships, was the emergence of several networks of individuals and groups who were attracted to Anabaptist themes of discipleship, community, and peacemaking. In most instances, participants in these networks were Christians, drawn from a wide range of denominations, who were frustrated with the formalism of the institutional church and their church's alignment with symbols of wealth and power. The "neo-Anabaptist" networks they formed were not understood to be new churches—those involved usually did not leave their own denominations to become "Mennonite." But members in these networks were drawn to the Anabaptist-Mennonite tradition of peacemaking, finding in that tradition a source of encouragement, education, and renewal in their own efforts to bear witness to the gospel of peace.

The prototype for these "neo-Anabaptist" networks emerged in England in the early 1990s, largely as a result of the ministry of Alan and Eleanor Kreider. The Mennonite Board of Missions had supported the London Mennonite Centre ever since the end of World War II, when the Centre served first as base for postwar relief efforts and then as a guesthouse for immigrant students. Under the leadership of the Kreiders, however, the Centre took on a new ecumenical identity as a focal point for theological and ethical conversations on topics related to peace.[36] In the late 1980s, a study group emerged, united by a commitment to bring a biblical perspective to their protests against the nuclear arms race and the escalating tensions of the Cold War. In the early 1990s, Stuart Murray, an energetic Baptist pastor, began to promote the concept of an Anabaptist peace network. In 1991 he sent a letter testing the idea to 80 individuals. By the following year, the "Anabaptist Network" numbered 200 members and the fledgling organization launched a journal, *Anabaptism Today*.[37] In time, the network developed a set of Core Convictions[38] and a succinct description of its mission:

> The Network offers resources and perspectives from the Anabaptist tradition for reflection on Christian discipleship in a post-Christendom culture, where churches are on the margins rather than at the center. It encourages friendship and sharing of ideas between people wrestling with the challenges of this context and who are interested in this marginalized tradition. Above all, it wishes to stimulate and encourage faithful and creative forms of mission, church life and discipleship.[39]

Today, the Anabaptist Network has some 1,500 members or affiliates.[40] In addition to hosting frequent conferences, seminars, and workshops on topics related to peace and social justice, the Anabaptist Network has been

---

36. Kreider, "London Mennonite," 2–11; and Murray, "Anabaptist Network."

37. Anabaptism Today began publication in November 1992 and continued until 2005 when it was replaced by a quarterly newsletter called *Network News*. The journal's goal was to support theological research related to peacemaking and social concerns and to stimulate "reflection and action . . . earthed in local church life, mission and practical social concerns."

38. For a summary of the Anabaptist Network statement of convictions published in January 2006, see: www.anabaptistnetwork.com/coreconvictions.

39. Murray, "Anabaptist Network."

40. People joining the Network frequently express a sense of "coming home" to a tradition that embodies their convictions and provides an integrating framework.—Cf. Kreider and Murray, editors, *Coming Home*.

the catalyst for numerous publications, including the "After Christendom" series published in partnership with Paternoster Press.[41] The Network also maintains links with other Anabaptist-oriented organizations and groups in other countries and has been an advocate for Christian peacemaking in many ecumenical settings.

The Anabaptist Network has also provided a model for similar networks to emerge in other contexts. Thus, already in 1995, Mark and Mary Hurst, Mennonite Board of Missions workers living in Australia, collaborated with local church leaders to create the Anabaptist Association of Australia and New Zealand (AAANZ).[42] Like the Anabaptist Network, the AAANZ did not seek to start a new denomination. Rather, drawing on the inspiration of "Jesus, the early church and the convictions of the first Anabaptist communities," it hoped that its members would become "peacemakers and work for a more compassionate world." The organization hosts a biennial conference and sponsors an active website. Its quarterly journal, *On the Road*, features themes of general interest—topics such as women in leadership; the arts; interfaith dialogue; voting; and sexuality—rooted in biblical perspectives while drawing explicitly on the Anabaptist tradition. The network has also formed local "Groundbreaker Groups" that meet in nine major cities for study and encouragement. "Membership within our network," writes Doug Sewell, former president of AAANZ, "is not like membership of a church, which often comes with obligations or at least expectations . . . Membership in AAANZ is more about a journey together on a road of discipleship and peacemaking. We are connected by a shared experience, interest, and vision."[43]

Three other networks have emerged more recently that share many of these same goals. In 2008, Mennonite Partners in China—a longstanding educational exchange organization between Mennonite and Chinese colleges—created "China Vision" in response to requests from various Chinese pastors who were interested in Anabaptist perspectives. This largely-informal network of pastors has since grown to include several hundred churches. Although few pastors identify themselves as Anabaptists or Mennonites, they are attracted to the ideals of servant leadership, community, and Christian discipleship, and inspired by deepened friendships with like-minded believers.

---

41. Murray, *Church after Christendom*.

42. Huber, "Upside-down Kingdom," 2–3; Hynd, "Anabaptism Down Under," 21–24.

43. Huber, "Upside-down Kingdom," 1.

In South Korea, an indigenous renewal movement in 1996 resulted in the creation of Jesus Village Church, the first Anabaptist congregation in the country. Several years later, working in collaboration with Mennonite mission agencies in the U.S. and Canada, leaders of Jesus Village established the Korea Anabaptist Center in Seoul as a resource of information about Anabaptist theology and practice. The Center has an active educational program throughout Northeast Asia that provides workshops on conflict resolution and victim-offender reconciliation, and has also translated and published numerous books on Anabaptist peace theology and practice.[44]

In a similar way, the Anabaptist Network in South Africa (ANiSA), established in 2009 and based in Pietermaritzburg, "draws on the collective wisdom found within the Anabaptist movement" to support churches and organizations who are "exploring, embracing, and embodying a radical lifestyle centered on God's reconciling vision for the world" and seeking to "support and grow communities of peace, justice, and reconciliation within South Africa."[45] The network manages a peace library and resource center, holds workshops on peace and justice issues, and organizes quarterly dialogues for ANiSA members to gather and discuss practical responses to the regional injustices that they face.

The Peace Witness in the Global Anabaptist-Mennonite Church

Whereas these neo-Anabaptist networks have emerged largely in English-speaking contexts, embracing a commitment to nonviolence from a position of relative privilege, groups in the broader Anabaptist-Mennonite fellowship have more often developed their peace-church identity in settings of regional conflict—sometimes including persecution and suffering. The nature of these conflicts, the theological and practical responses they have evoked, and the depth of commitment to a Christian witness of peace vary enormously across regions and even within specific countries. As in North America, it is often difficult to gauge how deeply an "official" commitment to peace is embraced at the congregational level. And sometimes, individuals or institutions carrying the identity of an Anabaptist-Mennonite peace witness are actually at the margins of the church, more tolerated than embraced by its leadership. What follows, therefore, is not an exhaustive summary of

---

44. Kim, "Anabaptism in Korea," 311–14.

45. Quotes are drawn directly from the main page of their website at: www.ani-sa.org.za. See also Suderman, "Friendship."

every form of peace witness in the global Anabaptist-Mennonite church, but merely a window into the range of contemporary peacemaking efforts.

Activist Engagement

In some global settings, Anabaptist-Mennonite peace theology and practice has found expression in political action that directly confronts established authorities or publicly defends the interests of marginalized or oppressed groups. Thus, for example, in the 1980s the German Mennonite Peace Committee mobilized protests against the U.S. decision to station nuclear weapons in Western Europe and has participated in demonstrations advocating on behalf of Palestinians or of refugees from the wars in the Balkans. In Japan, a small group of Mennonites have participated in protests and sponsored seminars against the use of nuclear power, anchoring their position in a theology of peace that extends to Creation itself.[46] In 1990, a prolonged civil war in Colombia that killed or displaced thousands of peasants in that country prompted Mennonites to create Justapaz, an organization dedicated to peaceful forms of resistance to militarization and violence in their country. Justapaz has worked diligently to train local church leaders in the skills of conflict resolution and has called on U.S. Mennonites to resist legislation that helps to fund the Colombian military. In recent years, the organization has helped to train regional teams to record human rights violations against Protestant church members by interviewing victims, families, and church members and compiling reports into a database.[47] Not all Mennonites have affirmed these activist forms of peace witness; but defenders of such approaches can point to the sermon disruptions, oath refusal, and tax protests of the sixteenth-century Anabaptists as precedents for their action.

Work toward Conscientious Objector Status

Another form of peace witness within the global Anabaptist-Mennonite church has been an effort to introduce the principle of conscientious objection in countries that still require compulsory military service. Anabaptist-Mennonite groups are present in many countries that do not recognize

---

46. Shelley, "Asia Conference," 1–2. Peace themes were also a significant part of the agenda at the three meetings of the Asia Mennonite Conference (Dhamtari, India, 1972; Osaka, Japan, 1980; Taipei, Taiwan, 1986), especially at the third conference in Taiwan which sent a message of concern about nuclear issues to more than thirty governments around the world.

47. Lozano, "Violent Land," 291–309.

conscientious objection.⁴⁸ Some governments in Latin America—Mexico, for example—have occasionally granted Mennonite youth noncombatant options even though there is no official recognition for conscientious objection. In other countries such as Argentina, Brazil, Paraguay, Nicaragua, and Uruguay, Mennonites and other advocates have successfully developed programs for alternative service. But elsewhere, Mennonites are faced with difficult choices—and the youth in some groups routinely join the military. Currently, the Korean Anabaptist Fellowship is engaging this issue in a direct way. Although young men in South Korean Mennonite churches have traditionally complied with their country's compulsory military service, in the spring of 2014 two young men associated with the Grace and Peace Mennonite Church in Seoul were sentenced to eighteen months in prison for refusing to join the military. As a consequence of their actions, the men not only face a jail sentence, but will also likely suffer other forms of social discrimination and diminished employment prospects for the rest of their lives.⁴⁹

More recently, the Constitutional Court of Colombia formally recognized the right of conscientious objection in that country following more than twenty years of lobbying by the Mennonites and other peace-minded Christians. The energetic engagement of Justapaz was particularly crucial to the success of those efforts.⁵⁰

Interfaith Initiatives

In many parts of the world, Anabaptist-Mennonite groups confront the daily challenge of living in settings of interreligious tension. In Ethiopia, relations between the Meserete Kristos Church and the state-supported Ethiopian Orthodox Church have improved significantly; but there are still regions where MKC members must worship in secret and there are occasional reports of personal violence.⁵¹ In other parts of the world, tensions between

---

48. Currently, these countries include Angola, Bolivia, Chile, Colombia, Cuba, D.R. of Congo, Dominican Republic, Ecuador, El Salvador, Eritrea, Guatemala, Kazakhstan, Kyrgyzstan, Mexico, Mozambique, Singapore, South Korea, Thailand, Togo, Ukraine, Venezuela, and Vietnam. Cf. Center on Conscience and War (http://www.centeronconscience.org/co/12-international/38-military-service-alternative-social-serviceand-conscientious-objection-in-the-americas-a-brief-survey-of-selected-countries.html).

49. Roth, "Plight of COs," 9.

50. For a fuller description of these efforts, and the Constitutional Court's decision in Feb. 2015, see the reports posted at www.justapaz.org.

51. Assefa, "Creating Identity," 539–70.

Christians and Muslims are a pressing concern. The most serious situation currently is in Nigeria, where the Boko Haram militant group has destroyed several Church of the Brethren meeting houses, assassinated pastors, and kidnapped schoolchildren. In other countries—especially in Kenya, Indonesia, and the Philippians—Mennonite churches sometimes struggle to find an appropriate response to the aggressive actions of neighboring Muslim groups: arbitrary restrictions on building permits; the strategic use of loudspeakers; the destruction of church buildings; and outright acts of personal violence.

And yet evidence also abounds of creative nonviolent responses by Mennonites and Muslims. In some countries, Anabaptist-Mennonite groups have adopted approaches to mission that nurture personal relationships with Muslim neighbors and affirm the possibility of following Jesus while remaining in the mosque. Indonesian Mennonites have been at the forefront of creating a sense of trust with many of their Muslim neighbors by forging friendships and offering material aid across ethnic and religious barriers. In the African context, David Shenk, who grew up in Tanzania, has been a pioneer in Christian-Muslim dialogue, helping east African Mennonites (and many other Christians) come to a deeper understanding of Muslim faith and culture, and nurturing respectful relationships as an extension of the gospel of peace.[52]

Reconciliation / Trauma Healing

In many countries around the world, Mennonites have developed reputations as a people of integrity who can be trusted to act as mediators or honest brokers in situations of tension or conflict. The Mennonite Brethren seminary in Shamshabad, India, for example, recently established a center for peace and reconciliation that is highly regarded in Protestant circles. Paraguayan Mennonites have helped to introduce the Victim-Offender Reconciliation Program—a model of restorative justice developed by Mennonites in North America—as a legal option. SEMILLA, the Mennonite seminary in Guatemala, has helped to raise awareness of the reality of domestic abuse and has sponsored workshops addressing the issues around male chauvinism. And several Mennonite groups have organized centers for conflict transformation or developed programs to help victims recover from the trauma of abuse or genocide. All of these initiatives are part of a larger

---

52. Krabill, Shenk, and Stutzman, *Anabaptists Meeting Muslims*; and Haile and Shenk, *Teatime in Mogadishu*; and Kateregga and Shenk, *Islam and Christianity*.

effort to think of peacemaking as practices woven into the fabric of daily life, transforming every aspect of human relationships.

The Witness of an Ordered Life

Finally, in a quite different way, Mennonite groups around the world—but perhaps especially conservative groups with a German ethnic identity—have borne witness to the gospel of peace by modeling the practices of a well-ordered community. To be sure, the Mennonite colonies scattered across Belize, Bolivia, Brazil, Paraguay, and northern Mexico are far from perfect. But the recent highly-publicized scandals associated with some of these communities should not overshadow the very significant and positive role that many of these groups play in their host countries. Mennonite colonies tend to be highly productive—in Belize, Bolivia, and Paraguay they produce a significant percentage of their country's supply of dairy, meat, and grain. Their factories are an important source of employment for local workers. And in settings where corruption is often endemic, Mennonites are generally—though not always—known to practice high ethical standards. The recent experiment of Mennonites entering into national political life in Paraguay as legislators, cabinet members, and advisors to the president is inconclusive in its results. But the biblical mandate to "seek the welfare of the city" (Jer. 29:7)—as exemplified in the life of these Mennonite communities—can be understood as an extension of an Anabaptist-Mennonite peace witness if it includes a genuine concern for the dispossessed and the marginalized.

Conclusion

On December 26, 2004, a 9.2 magnitude earthquake—with its epicenter at the floor of the Indian Ocean just off the west coast of Sumatra, Indonesia—unleashed a deadly tsunami. Within hours, the devastating force of the tsunami struck the coastal town of Aceh, killing 170,000 inhabitants and leaving more than 500,000 people without food or housing. Among the many relief workers who quickly arrived in the aftermath of the crisis was an unlikely team of Mennonites and Muslims from the Indonesian town of Solo.

For decades, Solo had been known as a center of various conservative militant Muslim groups, including several who explicitly advocated the use of violence to achieve their aims. Solo also happens to be the home of a small group of Indonesian Mennonites, members of the Muria Christian Church of Indonesia. For many years, relations between Christians and Muslims in Solo were filled with tension, sometimes breaking out into bloody conflict. In 2004, Paulus Hartono, a Javanese Mennonite pastor in Solo and director of Mennonite Diaconal Services, initiated contact with the leader of the Hizbullah militia group offering to help mediate a dispute over the group's radio station. Initially, the Hizbullah commander brusquely turned him away. Yet Hartono refused to give up. As a cofounder of the Forum for Peace Across Religions and Groups, Hartono was determined to put his convictions into action. So he continued to stop by the Hizbullah offices for tea and conversation. Eventually, the commander allowed Hartono to mediate the conflict, and the two men slowly became friends.

When the tsunami struck Aceh several months later, Hartono made a bold proposal. He invited the commander and members of the Hizbullah group to join in a relief effort, led by the Mennonites of Solo and funded in part by Mennonite Central Committee. For several months in the spring of 2005, Mennonites and conservative Muslims worked alongside each other helping to restore destroyed homes and to repair damaged churches and mosques.

In the years since then, the Hizbullah commander has asked Hartono's peace organization to lead conflict transformation workshops for his group, including several seminars at Center for the Study and Promotion of Peace in Duta Wacana Christian University. His hope, the commander explained, was that participants would come to think of themselves as "agents of peace." One Muslim volunteer reported to Hartono, "Thank you for this disaster response program. We know now that the Christian church and people are not as we thought before."[53]

The story of Paulus Hartono offers a small glimpse into the remarkable globalization of the Anabaptist-Mennonite peace witness. In dozens of settings around the world, Anabaptist-Mennonite Christians, enlivened by local readings of Scripture, strengthened by the insights of many members, enriched by conversations with other Christians, and drawing heavily on the cultural wisdom of their contexts are giving new life to the gospel of peace in creative and courageous ways.

At the same time, however, it is clear that many challenges still remain. In 2012, the MWC Peace Commission conducted a "peace audit" of the organization's member churches. Virtually all of the respondents expressed a clear desire to have an identity as a "peace church," and many listed a range of significant ways in which they were working to strengthen that identity. Yet equally clear in the summary statement were notes of significant

53. Jantzi and Shenk, "Indonesian Mennonites," 4–6.

concern. Respondents consistently indicated that a gap existed between the official statements of their church and the everyday practice of congregations and individuals. They all recognized the need for more resources and training in their commitment to being a peace church. Most important, perhaps, respondents identified a series of significant challenges: the influence of conservative evangelicalism and sophisticated mass media marketing; pastors recruited into church leadership who do not share a foundational commitment to a theology of peace; the absence of contemporary stories of peacemaking and nonviolence; the challenges of internal divisions—often based on caste, ethnicity, and tribal identity—that compromise a public witness to peacemaking; issues of *machismo*, domestic abuse, and gender discrimination; the pressures of military conscription; and the stress of religious persecution.

The conclusion of the MWC Peace Commission audit summarizes well the contemporary reality of the global Anabaptist-Mennonite peace witness:

> The good news is that a consciousness of being a Peace Church is deeply embedded in the identity of the MWC member-churches that responded. The bad news is the pervasive complexity in moving from what is desired and written on paper, to becoming a bedrock part of the Christian life and community. It is evident that the challenges to being a Peace Church are enormous.[54]

---

54. Suderman, "Mennonite World."

PART TWO

Analysis of the Historically Conditioned Mennonite Peacebuilding Approaches

6

From Resolution to Transformation
Experience, Encounter, and Solidarity in the Peacebuilding Work of Mennonite Practitioner-Scholar, John Paul Lederach

JANNA HUNTER-BOWMAN[1]

Introduction

THE METHODS AND LANGUAGE of conflict transformation—a multidimensional relationship-oriented approach to conflict—have deeply influenced Mennonite international peacebuilding and peace studies in the past two decades. They orient Mennonite work in Colombia, Somalia, Afghanistan, Syria and elsewhere. The methods and pedagogical approaches also infuse North American Mennonite peace studies programs.[2] One aim of this chapter is to recap the critical theoretical shifts and innovations that led from reliance on what has been the predominant conflict resolution model to a transformative approach and its concomitant goal of a 'just peace' in the field of peacebuilding generally. Understanding key terms and definitions is critical to the chapter's broader purpose.

---

1. The author thanks Gerald Schlabach, Larissa Fast, and Jennifer Rodriguez for their comments and suggestions.

2. Koontz, "Peace Theology," 77.

In the pages that follow I suggest that a lived stance of empathic solidarity with communities around the globe influenced the theory-making of Mennonite conflict transformation pioneer John Paul Lederach. The engagement of other Mennonites in international conflict settings is also shaped and disciplined by this stance. My thesis addresses the relationship between historical experiences of Mennonites and the development of transformative approaches to dealing with conflict and, secondly, how elicitive models serve the goal of fostering a 'just peace.' To this end, I suggest that a posture of empathetic solidarity, or Mennonites' "love of neighbor," explains why Lederach was susceptible to the questions of suspicion posed by local colleagues and allowed the communities he served to interrupt his professional knowledge base. I aim to show that such experience and his Anabaptist imagination were parts of a circular hermeneutic process, which by definition exposes preconceptions as suspect—and not necessary shared—to allow for new understanding.[3] The virtuous circle of practice (experience) and Anabaptist theological vision enabled him to perceive, experience, and articulate something radically different from his professional colleagues in the field of conflict resolution without abandoning theoretical coherence and programmatic action.

Theoretical Innovation Through Reflection on "Experience"

John Paul Lederach is one of the principal proponents of the transformative approach and is recognized for offering the greatest theoretical clarity and specificity to this outlook.[4] Over the past three decades, this conflict transformation pioneer has attributed key innovations to "reflection on experience" emergent from his work with Mennonite Central Committee (MCC). His publications chronicle the ways that his extensive fieldwork in war zones in Central America and the Horn of Africa alongside fellow Mennonite practitioners influenced his language and informed his critical contributions to the field of peacebuilding.

Through "experience," Lederach became convinced that he was seeking not resolution to conflict but constructive change. He began actively inviting—eliciting—resources and tools from the local communities to

---

3. Lederach self-consciously adopts Paolo Freire's philosophy of education for transformation through participatory action-reflection, which was deeply influential in the Latin American and African contexts in which he worked early on: Lederach, *Preparing for* Peace, 19, 25–26, 32; Freire and Macedo, *Pedagogy of the Oppressed*. For one articulation of the epistemological work of the participant action-reflection process I refer to, see Fairfield, "Dialogical Education?" 555.

4. Botes, "Conflict Transformation," 1–27.

pursue transformation, giving rise to what he later began calling the "elicitive" method. Through his years of reflective practice, the predominant idea of a sustainable, static peace that avoided conflict gave way to the goal of a dynamic state of 'just peace,' in which specific problems and their root causes are engaged simultaneously through ongoing processes. The contextually-contingent conditions that foster a 'just peace' in a given setting became the critical referents for change processes.

Yet telling a simple story about "experience," as I've done in the above paragraph, does not explain why or how it was that "experience" impacted Lederach's work as it did. If he was the trained specialist, why should what happens in the course of working with local communities around the world call his theoretical knowledge base and professional expertise into question? An important part of the answer to this question is found in his writing directed towards a Mennonite audience and about Mennonite peacebuilding. There Lederach explains that some of the ideas that inform his work and reflection emerge from the Mennonite-Anabaptist Christian tradition. He emphasizes movements of discipleship-oriented politics, peace embedded in justice, reconciliation as right relationships, and nonviolence as a way of life from within this Christian framework and living community. Mennonites, he writes, "are people who give me a legacy and provide a compass for my journey."[5]

By emphasizing his experience as a practitioner and the Mennonite-Anabaptist tradition concurrently, I suggest that Lederach sheds light on a dynamic relationship rooted in experience that alters existing language and a sociolinguistic community that shapes perception. If the first aim of this chapter is to trace the movement from resolution to transformational approaches, the second aim is to explore the dynamic dialogical relationship between Lederach's international experience and his Mennonite-Anabaptist community. Both help respond to our guiding questions. Methodologically, I proceed through probing the site of "encounter" as the space of convergence between the comprehensive visions of a narrative community and contingent experiences. I propose a three-fold typology for thinking about "encounters" grounded in the German theologian Karl Barth's theological reflections on secularism. Barth's social ethic of solidarity constitutes one form of encounter with the Other. In the other two types, the Subject assimilates the Other she encounters and the Other assimilates the Subject. I suggest that some contemporary Mennonite peacemakers, Lederach included, practice empathetic solidarity and are intellectually disciplined by the Christ-centered ethic in their engagement with communities around the

---

5. Lederach, *Journey toward Reconciliation*, 15.

globe. Reflection on the mode of engagement in context aids understanding of the kind of experience and convictions that have deeply influenced professional peacebuilding and academic peace studies through Lederach's work.

Conflict Resolution and Conflict Transformation: Operational Differences

To make sense of the "shift"[6] from a conflict resolution (CR) paradigm to transformational approaches, it will help to have some clarity about the operational differences between the two. For Lederach and others who see conflict transformation (CT) as a theoretical departure from resolution, transformation includes some of the mechanisms of CR but goes beyond the approaches and understandings proposed by resolution-based language. In contrast with resolution perspectives that aim to eliminate or control conflict from the outside, transformation perspectives view conflict as a normal, ongoing dynamic within all relationships.[7] Lederach has analyzed the changes conflict generates in four categories: personally, relationally, structurally, and culturally.[8] CT views attending to each level adversely affected by conflict as necessary to deal effectively with broad-based social conflict.[9]

The more comprehensive and holistic transformative approaches view multilevel and multidimensional engagement as critical. To describe how

---

6. Lederach, "Comprehensive Network," 201.

7. Lederach, *Preparing Peace*, 8–9. Drawing on phenomenology and symbolic interactionism in social science, Lederach articulates a social constructivist view of social conflict as something that "emerges and develops on the basis of the meaning and interpretation people involved attach to action and events" (8). Based on this constructivist approach and the insight of conflict sociologist, Lewis Coser, that conflict serves social functions, Lederach posited conflict as a constructive, "natural, common experience" (9). The normalization of conflict is central to altering the frames from CR to CT and the professional peacebuilding landscape; See, Coser, *Functions of Social Conflict*, 19. Cf., Augsburger, *Conflict Mediation*.

8. Lederach, *Little Book*, 23, 27. Wolfgang Dietrich observes that in doing so he expands on Galtung's triangle of physical, structural, and cultural violence: Dietrich, *Elicitive Conflict*. There are also points of resonance with Vayrynen, who offers levels or stages of conflict transformation that address some similar dynamics: Raimo Vayrynen, *New Directions*.

9. Other CT scholars have articulated the change generated by conflict differently, for example in terms of the micro and macro changes in parties and the nature of the conflict. Yet the emphasis on change caused by conflict remains. Vayrynen, *New Directions*.

change happens, Lederach draws on Rupesinghe[10] to specify three social strata that he believes peace practitioners need to engage: elites, middle level, and grassroots. In contrast, CR tends to focus on the top-down approaches of "official actors" and elites[11] leading to what Lederach calls "trickle-down peacemaking" of diplomacy and resolution.[12] Instead, he advocates for "bottom up" and "middle out" mechanisms for dealing with conflict and theorizing social change. The change agents that he articulates intersect with but are not contained by the state and institutional structures. That is, the government is not the only area of concern of the peacemakers. Ever since his pioneering work *Building Peace*, peacemaking "from the ground up" has come into wide recognition as a relevant approach for dealing with the dynamics of contemporary armed conflict:[13] changing the subject of social change from state and institutions to grassroots actors and relationships at various levels was a game changer in the field of international conflict and peace. Transformational orientations also expand beyond the assumptions of positivism and secularism of international relations by attending to questions of memory, trauma, and what Appleby calls "first order religious discourse," like theologies and Scripture.[14] The movement towards holism and more comprehensive approaches reinforces the need for robust interdisciplinary engagement, which broadens international conflict processes and peace studies beyond their traditional disciplinary home in political science.

One key dimension broadening the foci beyond statist diplomacy and peace as science is CT's expansive time horizon. The interlacing timeframes of CT are essential. Lederach's accounts of time integrate immediate observation and short-term response with long-term transformation. They provide an alternative to the linear thinking that he describes as issuing causal formulas based on categories of past, present, and future, suggestive of a

---

10 Kumar Rupesinghe also argues that a multisectoral approach is needed to transform conflict: Rupesinghe, "Conflict Transformation," 65–92.

11. Lederach, *Building Peace*, 39. Cf., Mitchell, "Beyond Resolution."

12. Lederach identifies various presuppositions in this view that he finds problematic. First, he finds the assumption of centralized power problematic. Leaders do not represent the whole or have the authority that the processes assumes. Moreover, the top-level approach assumes an issue-oriented, short-term peace process carried out by top-level leaders. But the evolution of the process does not unfold neatly in this time frame or step-by-step, as people at lower levels inevitable engage in various ways. John Paul Lederach, *Building Peace*, 6–7.

13. Lederach, *Building Peace*. As suggested by Johannes Botes, "Conflict Transformation," 1–27; Fast, "Frayed Edges."

14. Appleby, *Ambivalence*.

"chemical reaction."[15] For Lederach, the problem is that conflict envisioned as a single line looks at change processes through short-term thinking and solutions and emphasizes the more visible and overtly destructive manifestations of the conflict.[16] As I have explored elsewhere,[17] Lederach draws on theological notions of time from Mennonite theologians to articulate an alternative to the suppositions of necessary sequence and causality associated with CR.

For Lederach, integrated time frames are necessary because transformation needs to continue through the de-escalation of a particular problem, or what Lederach calls an "episode" of conflict that could be resolved in a short timeframe, to seek the "epicenter" generating the crises.[18] Lederach therefore believes that the presenting episodes, such as spikes in direct and open violence, are evidence of social and political problems on a structural level, especially injustice. Like the proverbial canary in the coal mine, they signal that something is deeply wrong and needs to be addressed. In contrast, CR focuses on the presenting situation ("episode") itself rather than on political, economic, and social systems.[19]

These contrasting units of analysis signal another key difference: CT is about change leading to a 'just peace,' whereas CR focuses on de-escalation. Not only does the paradigm of transformation normalize conflict, transformation considers conflict an important catalyst for constructive change of social systems. Viewed in the light of the change necessary to reach a different state, conflict is an opportunity or a gift,[20] or at least a potential gift. For Lederach, constructive change depends on a willingness to maximize conflict's potential as a catalyst for growth through engaged response.

It is important to note that relationships are at the core of CT. In contrast with a tendency to focus on the substance of particular outbreaks of violence or problems generated by conflict singularly, Lederach maintains that in order to understand conflict and create appropriate change processes it is crucial to identify the various and subtle dimensions of the relationships involved. Issues are important and require careful attention. Yet

15. Lederach, *Journey Toward Reconciliation*, 78.
16. Lederach, *Moral Imagination*, 46ff.
17. DuBois and Hunter-Bowman, "Intersection."
18. Lederach, *Little Book*; Lederach, *Moral Imagination*, 46–47.
19. See, Burton and Dukes, *Conflict*. The "human needs" theory articulated by Burton broadens and deepens the view of conflict but does not substantively address the ways in which parties must be involved in the change, the nature of the change, or the timeframes of the change. That is, the focus remains resolution-driven without engaging the complexities of how change occurs.
20. Lederach, *Little Book*, 18–19.

relationships constitute the background of the conflict in which a given situation may become increasingly fragile or addressed swiftly. Lederach uses imagery of a spider web to convey the relational connections and underlying human ecology from which specific issues emerge and are animated.[21] The web image also clarifies the reach of the relational circles; we are invited to "imagine ourselves in a web of relationships that includes our enemies."[22] n the language of social change theory, we can say that if we want transformation, we will develop social processes to address the depth and breadth of relationships. Conceptualizing change as an organic process helps us to envision social transformation as a dynamic, ongoing, and multifaceted undertaking.

CT's open-ended, continuous process has as its goal a 'just peace,' defined by Lederach and Appleby as a "dynamic state of affairs in which the reduction and management of violence and the achievement of social and economic justice are undertaken as mutual, reinforcing dimensions of constructive change."[23] Through the key innovations described above, it moves away from managerial language and logic of sequence and causality associated with CR. For Lederach, the more holistic and comprehensive approach requires the capacity for "moral imagination," as cited above. The moral imagination animates this process by enabling people enmeshed in conflict to envision possibilities beyond and outside of it.

To summarize the differences between CR and CT, unlike CR's emphasis on eliminating conflict, the intervention of CT approaches and initiatives transform the dynamic of the conflict, relationships between parties, and the very originators of the conflict. CT also underscores the role conflict plays in transforming relationships and social organizations while it endures. The short timeframe in which CR aims to work contrasts with CT's long-term processes. Accordingly, in contrast with CR's dealings with episodes of conflict, CT emphasizes systemic change. Whereas CR purports to resolve the conflict episodes, CT envisions a continuous process. Social change towards a dynamic end state of a 'just peace' is the ultimate purpose of transformative processes.

21. Lederach, *Moral Imagination*, 82.
22. Ibid., 5.
23. Lederach and Appleby, "Strategic Peacebuilding," 23. Earlier iterations of the definition are slightly different due to an emphasis on the approaches that lead to a 'just peace' rather than the dynamic state of the 'just peace.' For example, in 2005, Lederach defined 'just peace' as "An orientation toward conflict transformation characterized by approaches that reduce violence and destructive cycles of social interaction and at the same time increase justice in any human relationship." Lederach, *Moral Imagination*, 182.

Transformational approaches normalize conflict in human relationships and view conflict as a necessary motor of change.[24] Transformation both attends to multifaceted grievances and cultivates healthy relationships and communities, locally and globally. Lederach's renowned conflict pyramid comprised of elite, middle, and grassroots levels clarifies the ways that actors relate across social strata and conceptualizes ways in which the local dynamics relate to geopolitics without being consumed by it. Cultivating and reconstructing healthy relationships is at the core of the model for constructive holistic change and the horizon towards which CT journeys. The goal—or horizon—is not a static end state (like harmonious peace) but rather a dynamic state of 'just peace' (as ongoing reconciliation). The concept of 'just peace' recognizes that each context is ever journeying towards wholeness.[25]

The Role of "Experience" in Shifting from Resolution to Transformation

In his field-shaping book, *Building Peace*, Lederach says from the outset that he uses an inductive process to bring "ideas emerging from a practice-oriented learning process . . . to the broader discussion of peacebuilding in the international arena . . . Thinking and approach," continues Lederach, "emerge from the standpoint of a practitioner rather than a theorist."[26] He also frames his contributions in *Preparing for Peace* as reflections on experience as a mediator in dispute resolution.[27] According to Lederach, the theoretical shifts occurred in moments of reflection following intense experiences as a practitioner. Lederach recounts that when he arrived in Central America in the 1980s, his pedagogical vocabulary was replete with terms and concepts of conflict resolution and management. Soon he discovered

---

24. Lederach, *Little Book*, 4–5.

25. For a discussion of CT's relational orientation that dislocates the notion of a static 'end-state', see Lederach, *Little Book*, 20. In 2003, Lederach proposed the following definition: "[C]onflict transformation is to envision and respond to the ebb and flow of social conflict as life-giving opportunities for creating constructive change processes that reduce violence, increase justice in direct interaction and social structures, and respond to real-life problems in human relationships": Lederach, *Little Book*, 14. In 2010, Lederach and Appleby wrote that conflict transformation approaches "include violence prevention and early warning, conflict management, mediation and resolution, social reconstruction and healing in the aftermath of armed conflict, and the long, complex work of reconciliation throughout the process": Lederach and Appleby, "Strategic Peacebuilding," 23.

26. Lederach, *Building Peace*, xvi.

27. Lederach, *Preparing for Peace*, 3–5.

that that his Central American colleagues had questions, reservations, and suspicions about the meaning and implications of this language.

"Conflict happens for a reason," Central American colleagues responded to resolution's implicit offer of neat, quick fixes to deep-seated social problems involving inherent and untenable tensions. "Is this resolution idea just another way to cover up the changes that are really needed?"[28] Lederach further reflected that conflict resolution, with its focus on resolving the visible or "presenting" conflict, did not attend to the deeper structural, cultural, long-term relational aspects of conflict.[29] During workshops in Guatemala, he discovered that presuppositions about conflict and how to handle it that were pertinent in one cultural setting but not necessarily applicable in others were entrenched in mediation processes. This meant that the "unintended residue of imperialism" was also embedded.[30] In Panama and Nicaragua as well, he found that conflict resolution paradigms and training methods were "too narrow, often out of context and presumptuous."[31]

Elicitive Model of Conflict Transformation

The question became: how do we foster a pedagogical project that respects and empowers people to participate in creating and strengthening appropriate models for working at conflict in their own contexts?[32] In response, he works to understand conflict from local perspectives and elicit—or draw out—context appropriate tools grounded in the cultural knowledge of a people.[33] Drawing on insights about cultural relevance from the popular education of Paulo Freire,[34] appropriate technology, and ethnography, Lederach emphasizes peacemaking approaches based on local cultures

28. Lederach, "Little Book.," 3.

29. Important CR advocates would agree with this assessment. Mitchell maintains that major structural changes do not necessarily have to occur prior to the achievement of a resolution. See Mitchell, "Beyond Resolution."

30. Lederach, *Preparing for Peace*, 38.

31. Lederach, "Journey from Resolution," 46.

32. Lederach, *Preparing for Peace*, 21–27.

33. Lederach, *Preparing for Peace*, 5–10.

34. The notion of discovery and transformative action by the poor and marginalized finds particular resonance in Lederach's work. Lederach, *Preparing for Peace*; Freire and Macedo, *Pedagogy of the Oppressed*. Drawing on Freire, Shaull stated, "There is no such thing as a neutral education process. Education either functions as an instrument which is used to facilitate the integration of generations into the logic of the present system and bring about conformity to it, or it becomes the 'practice of freedom,' the means by which men and women deal critically with reality and discover how to participate in the transformation of their world." Mayo, *Gramsci*, 5.

and traditions rather than imported models. "Cultural modalities and resources for handling conflict in a given setting are not only important to identify but should be seen as foundational for building a comprehensive transformative framework,"[35] he declares. This *elicitive approach* is premised on the conviction that each community possesses the power and resources to move towards wholeness. In the elicitive method of conflict transformation, the local community is recognized as a key resource and "indigenous knowledge" is seen as a way to discovery and appropriate action. However external actors work to identify resources, foster self-sufficiency and empower local leaders to participate in political processes.[36] Lederach offers the elicitive approach as an alternative to the prescriptive approaches of CR. It constitutes a key contribution to transformation theory and pedagogy emergent from experience.

Understanding the Shifts

A researcher concerned only with the conceptual and strategic differences between resolution and transformation may be satisfied with this explanation of language shifts and innovative techniques developed "through experience." From a conflict resolution perspective, it could be argued that the self-correcting mechanism built into the simultaneously theoretical and applied discipline worked: perhaps, as CR would have it, resolution theory and resolution practice interacted to provide new theories and practices. Or with an "experiential approach" from theological methods, we could interpret the interaction this way: the perspectives of Lederach's professional conflict resolution narrative community (also called a sociolinguistic community) interacted with experiences that eluded and thus altered the existing language and concepts. The emphasis in the experiential approach rests with contingency and the possibility of experience that cannot be captured by the extant paradigms and so reworks them.[37] In some ways Lederach's

---

35. Lederach, "Comprehensive Framework," 213. The discovery-based, elicitive method is articulated in his dissertation (1988) even though the oft-cited source, *Preparing for Peace*, was not published until 1995. These early works lean into phenomonological theory to contribute to a social constructionist view of conflict and its transformation; see, Lederach, "Nets, Nails"; Lederach, *Preparing for Peace*, 8–9.

36. Lederach, *Building Peace*.

37. There are narrative or hermeneutical approaches and experiential or epistemological approaches. Sometimes these are parsed as two starting points: linguistic expression and pre-linguistic experience. The first emphasizes the role that sociolinguistic community plays in shaping human capacity to perceive and experience (or not). The second emphasizes contingency and the possibility of experience that alters or eludes

findings do reinforce the integration of conflict resolution theory, practice (what Lederach and I have called experience), and research in what Larissa Fast identifies as a "triangle" that combines the three dimensions (theory, research and practice).[38] This framework alone, however, does not provide a fine-tuned explanation of how these fundamental shifts occurred. After all, plenty of benevolent and competent resolution practitioners applied the techniques and practiced the trade in situations of conflict without arriving at the same critiques of CR's presuppositions, methods, and practices. As such, we are now in a position to answer the following questions: Why did Lederach allow questions posed by Central American colleagues to challenge his professional expertise? Why should their questions so deeply disturb his knowledge base? Why should their observations provide a genuine challenge for his view, requiring a new answer? How did he come to perceive, experience, and articulate something radically different from his professional North American colleagues without abandoning theoretical coherence and programmatic action?

Looking more closely at this puzzle encourages us to examine what we mean by "experience." Saying "international experience" played a major role in his theory-making may be a little fuzzy: perhaps the phrase suggests that we all know what we are talking about and that we are talking about the same thing. That assumption is probably false. After all, there are any number of ways people experience international contexts. To complement the "experiential approach" of theological method, let's look at what has been called the "narrative approach."

The Anabaptist-Mennonite Background to Lederach's Peacebuilding Theory and Practice

The narrative approach in theological methodology emphasizes the role that sociolinguistic or narrative communities play in shaping perception or experience. I prefer "sociolinguistic" because the term makes the relationship between language and sociality explicit; together they inform our interpretation of the world and the way we experience it. This approach is also attentive to the inverse—the lack of human capacity to perceive or experience

---

existing languages and paradigms. Here I use this delineation only as a useful analytical construct; in reality, both facets of knowing and expressing are always already operating in dialogical tension with one another. For one scholar's exposition of these categories, among other methods, see Fiorenza, "Systematic Theology," 1–89. I thank my friend and colleague, Heather Dubois, for discussions of these approaches.

38. Fast, "Frayed Edges," 528–45.

certain things. Lederach participates in various communities. Through this lens we might consider the ways that the resolution community's practical language and frameworks were formative to Lederach's theory-making and peace work: since he developed paradigms that retrieved select elements and proved himself a critical interlocutor, he is indebted to them. Yet since "transformation" is increasingly accepted as a new paradigm—which the experiential method in dialogue with Lederach's resolution community does not fully or adequately explain—I now turn to the focus on ways that the Anabaptist-Mennonite linguistic community helps shape Lederach's perception and experience.

Lederach has made his work ripe for reflection from a narrative approach by self-consciously exploring the links between his work and his Christian heritage and commitments. He often refers to the centrality of the Anabaptist-Mennonite tradition to his vocation. In addition to claiming to receive a legacy and compass from Mennonites,[39] he declares that an "Anabaptist/Mennonite religious-ethical framework" shapes his imagination and informs his theories.[40] He emphasizes peace embedded in justice, reconciliation as right relationships, and Christlike nonviolence as a way of life as mainstays of his Mennonite framework.[41] The emphasis on boundary-crossing and willingness to take risks are traced to the "enemy love" of a practical, concrete, and embodied theology of discipleship.[42] He traces the distinctive time horizon of transformational frameworks to Mennonite theological notions of time, wherein the present and future—or Eschaton—overlap in the "already, not yet" kingdom of God.[43] His analysis of the inadequacies of the predominant models of diplomacy and resolution to address contemporary armed violence dovetails with the alternative theory of change he discovers in a practical Anabaptist theological vision of incarnational politics and ecclesiology orientated by eschatology.[44] "It is," he observes, "as various Anabaptist authors have coined in the titles of their books, the 'politics of Jesus' carried through a 'mustard seed conspiracy'

---

39. Lederach, *Journey Toward Reconciliation*, 15.

40. Lederach, *Little Book*, 4. Cf., Ledearch, "Journey from Resolution," 45.

41. Lederach, *Little Book*, 4. Cf., Lederach, "Pacifism."

42. Lederach, "Missionaries," 11–19.

43. John Paul Lederach, "Recollections and the Construction of a Legacy: The Influence of John Howard Yoder on My Life and Work," presented at the A Believers Church Conference (South Bend, IN: University of Notre Dame, March 7, 2002).

44. The social change orientation of active nonviolence, which Lederach has recognized as a third "tributary" of his early thinking, is here evident: Lederach, "Journey from Resolution," 45.

in the 'upside down kingdom.'"[45] The narrative approach helps us appreciate the ways that a stream of Mennonite convictions, values, and conduct shaped his perception and experience in his extensive work in Central America and later the Horn of Africa and Nepal.

After all, early key innovations and theoretical shifts followed on the heels of experiences not with professional colleagues from the resolution community alone but with Mennonite Central Committee (1975–1996). This included a service assignment in Central America (1985–1988), directorship of Mennonite Conciliation Services (1988–1990), and director of International Conciliation Service (1989–1996). The shifts are accurately understood in terms of the dialogical relationship between contextual experience and the language communities in which Lederach participated: the circular hermeneutic at the nexus is crucial. One of the merits of participating in multiple communities is that one can see problems with the language of one community from the perspective of another. Or, at least see that not all languages are the same. The narrative approach helps us appreciate the ways that a stream of Mennonite convictions, values, and conduct collectively shaped Lederach's perception and experience in his extensive international cross-cultural work. This approach complements the ways his theologically formed imagination has played a substantive role in creating transformative theories and strategic peacebuilding paradigms.[46] Here the theological dimension cannot be reduced to a text-based resource chest to be mined for peaceable motifs.[47]

The dynamic, historical, and contextual living community in which Lederach was enmeshed was definitional. Lederach's contributions unfolded on the heels of transitions in Anabaptist-Mennonite peace theology and engaged ethics. He was influenced by the theological shifts from two-kingdom theology to forms of more engaged peace theology and sociological movements captured by the book title "From Quietism to Activism."[48] He came of age in the wake of a new approach to theological ethics articulated by Harold S. Bender, Guy Hershberger, John Howard Yoder, and Paul Peachy. His earliest work explicitly engages these transitions. A 1993 Spanish publica-

---

45. Lederach, "Pacifism." Yoder, *Politics of Jesus*; Sine, *Mustard Seed*; Kraybill, *Upside-Down Kingdom*.

46. See DuBois and Hunter-Bowman, "Intersection," 2014.

47. The way groundbreaking works on religion and peacebuilding have been deployed has resulted in an emphasis on the selective retrieval of peace and justice related themes for peacemaking purposes. See, Philpott, *Just and Unjust Peace*; Czada, Held, and Weingardt, editors, *Religions and World Peace*; Appleby, *Ambivalence*; Gopin, *Between Eden*.

48. Driedger and Kraybill, *Mennonite Peacemaking*.

tion with the translated title of *Following Jesus* highlights Yoder's theological formulations of the shifts.[49] In *Journey Towards Reconciliation*, Lederach rebuffs two-kingdom theology and its "dishonest" withdrawal from the messy realities of life. Like Yoder, Lederach urges active, engaged costly discipleship and a focus on reconciliation among divided peoples.[50] Sociologically, his interventions are located squarely in what Joseph Miller has called the "third phase" of Mennonite peacemaking.[51] In Miller's view, the first phase was quietism and the second phase included speaking publically and protesting against war and injustice. For Lederach and other Mennonite practitioners writing at that time, the third phase complements the second phase's stance of refusal to participate in taking human life with active, constructive engagement.[52] Mennonite Conciliation Service (MCS) was the church's movement to become "instruments of conciliation, mediation and transformation" accordingly.[53] Ron Kraybill and Lederach, the early practitioners called by the church to work with MCS as directors, conceptualize their role as an "expression of a 400 year tradition."[54] This "expression" was shaped by exposure and sensitivity that people in more "elite" positions do not have. This is because Mennonites of previous generations did not have access to statist strata, and in recent and current generations Mennonites have been averse to association with the state that could be construed as complicity in the violence of the state. In both cases, grassroots and mid-level work were the only available arenas for decades of Mennonite witness and peacemaking practice. Our attentiveness to Anabaptist historical and sociolinguistic lineage helps explain Lederach's sensitivities. The acknowledgements in his books, numerous co-authored pieces as well as practitioner manuals, articles, books, and current pedagogical approaches of other Mennonites involved in this community of practice in the late 1980s and 1990s attest to the community of action and reflection engaged in this rich work.[55]

Similar convictions, values, and conduct led people affiliated with Mennonite Central Committee to share some of the same predilections about modes of engagement in international peacemaking.[56] By the 1970s, MCC's

49. Lederach, *Seguir a Jesús*, 38.
50. Lederach, *Journey Toward Reconciliation*, 48–177.
51. Miller, "History," 10.
52. Lederach and Kraybill, "Paradox," 358.
53. Miller, "History," 10.
54. Lederach and Kraybill, "Paradox," 356.
55. See, for example, Lederach, Kraybill, and Price, *Conflict Transformation*; Lederach and Chupp, *Conflicto y la Violencia*; Lederach and Kraybill, "Paradox," 356.
56. As the citations in this chapter indicate, this is widely attested in the volume edited by Sampson and Lederach, *From the Ground Up*.

framework of values emphasized service, justice, and reconciliation.[57] In a self-reflective manner, MCC sought to avoid models that contained and therefore re-inscribed paternalistic patterns that posited the Western agency as the source or donor and local people as recipients of knowledge. Also, in the transformative sense of Paulo Freire, it demonstrated sensitivity towards local ways of seeing problems and addressing them through local practices. Of special relevance here, in the same way in the 1970s Mennonite Central Committee became suspicious of "development models which emphasized technology transfer over local organizing and problem-identification, so it usually avoided models of peace education which defined Mennonites as the knowledge outsiders."[58] This criticism would apply to third-party interveners who adopted resolution approaches.

In 1978, participants in a peace theology colloquium sponsored by MCC's Peace Section under the leadership of William Keeney voiced criticisms of conflict resolution. At this very early phase of encounter with resolution, they identified and named a latent fear of conflict in the CR structure. Concerned that the model encouraged "premature resolution," they worried that the structure of CR interventions could short-circuit the constructive function that conflict plays, especially in asymmetrical conflicts. Some also expressed strong suspicion of the institutional orientation of CR. The tenor of their report foreshadows both Mennonite engagement through third-party intervention and the theoretical shifts from resolution to transformation approaches that Lederach formulates.[59] This meeting demonstrates what Lederach himself says: "[S]ensitivity within MCC to these issues [with the CR paradigm] was readily apparent long before I" articulated the critiques and developed alternative, discovery-based methodologies of learning and practice.[60]

Common sensibilities and relational dispositions between Lederach and other Mennonites are evident in Mennonite involvement in Somalia

57. Weaver and Weaver, *Salt and Sign*, 81–84.

58. Ibid., 88.

59. The clear and insightful critique of CR's conceptualization of conflict merits full quotation: "Intervention, especially if motivated by fear, may lead to premature resolution. A premature resolution may hinder a necessary healthy process of heightened tensions, leading to heightened awareness, heightened dignity, heightened responsibility, growing identity and empowerment of the complaint, a stronger challenge to the system, and a better final result. The premature solution itself may not serve the long ranger or the global cause of justice. It might well be important, in most of the causes we can think of, to be an advocate for the underdog than to be conciliating interveners." The colloquium was a part of a series of conversations that led to the development of the Mennonite Conciliation Services.

60. Lederach, "Journey from Resolution," 46 and Miller, "History," 3–29.

in the second half of the 21st Century. In the years between 1953 and the 1980s, deep interfaith relationships developed between Mennonite workers and their Muslim neighbors in a number of Islamic countries. Concurrently, the attitude toward and description of Islam shifted. Peter Sensenig, who was immersed in the Mennonite peacebuilding experience in Somalia as a child, described and reflected on various developments in his dissertation. According to Sensenig, attitudes of humility and openness, long-term commitments, and an understanding of Mennonite assignment as service and relationship-building led to deep bonds even before the theological and sociological transitions to engagement and activism occurred.[61] Workers from Eastern Mennonite Missions and MCC were constituted the Mennonite presence. One missionary declared that "listening and learning are intrinsic to the missionary task."[62] Over the years, "mingled lives"[63] and key relationships challenged preconceptions about Islam and created an environment propitious for collaborative approaches to contextual problems.[64] For Sensenig, this posture towards others, shaped by convictions on Christlikeness, violence, forgiveness, and costly discipleship, profoundly informed their approach to engagement in Somalia.[65] The resulting experience accentuated different aspects of Mennonite theology and ethics and precipitated fresh, self-critical contextual reflection and particular forms of engagement. At the same time, crucial referents informing the experience were already present in the posture they adopted. In that way, the Mennonites moved more deeply into relationship with their Muslim neighbors and more deeply into engaging in the complex situation by delving more deeply into their own traditions, theology, and assumptions. As Gopin observes, "[T]he hermeneutic circle of receptivity and two way transformation here is clear."[66]

Sensenig's description suggests the way that Mennonites engaged Somali Muslims informed their discoveries on the ground and what they found to be true of their hosts. Perspectival and relational developments set the stage for a more "elicitive" approach to reconciliation efforts and peacemaking when political crises and inter-clan violence resulted in a state of anarchy in the early 1990s. Lederach worked closely with Mennonites during that period to develop a response. Revisiting key notions of

---

61. Sensenig, "Peace Clan," 53–100.
62. Ibid., 98.
63. Ibid.
64. See, Lederach, "Mennonite Central Committee," 141–148; Sensenig, "Peace Clan," 53–57.
65. Sensenig, "Peace Clan," 28–34.
66. Gopin, "Religious Component," 238.

the elicitive method in context helps us make the situation and model concrete.⁶⁷ First, the Mennonite workers recognized their Islamic neighbors as a key resource, rather than recipients of their external expertise. Although initially ambivalent about clan structure, local customs, and Islam, the Mennonites developed a positive understanding of Somali peacemaking. Thus, and secondly, they could conceive of the "indigenous knowledge" as a pathway to discovery of appropriate action. They recognized that the notion of "kinship" provides a mechanism for dealing constructively with conflict through traditional channels of authority—the elders. The foundation of the traditional kinship system, the social contract (Xeer), is a key social and political tool that can usher conflict from destructive "cycles of retaliation toward restitution and even reconciliation."⁶⁸ By building peace from available local resources, the Mennonite workers, thirdly, fostered self-sufficiency and sustainability. Fourth, by identifying and naming the local, contextual responses of their hosts and applying them to contextual needs and presenting problems, they empowered traditional leaders and encouraged their participation in political processes. This move to build an "infrastructure for peace" with "middle range actors" encouraged Somalis to be more involved in transforming Somali problems.⁶⁹ In the Somali context, the elicitive model means respecting and building transformative processes from traditional Somali social organization. The elicitive approach made sense in light of the way the Mennonite workers understood their call, related to others and engaged socially and politically.

Mennonite "Ethos" and Boundary-Crossing Encounters

In his own work, Lederach refers to the convergences of convictions, values and conduct in terms of a Mennonite "ethos" that shaped his mode of engaging complex, historical realities.⁷⁰ By "ethos," he is referring to ways of being

---

67. Lederach, *Building Peace*; Lederach, "Mennonite Central Committee," 141–49; Lederach, "Building Peace in Somalia."

68. Sensenig, "Peace Clan," 196.

69. Lederach, "Mennonite Central Committee," 141–49; Lederach, "Building Peace in Somalia."

70. Ledearch, "Compassionate Presence: Faith Based Peacebuilding in the Face of Violence," Distinguished Lecture Series booklet from Kroc Institute of International Peace Studies (San Diego, CA: Kroc Institute, 17 Feb 2012), 34. This discussion rose in the course of a phone interview with Laura Taylor, conducted on Feb 17, 2012, the transcript of which is included in the published booklet. Personal conversations on ethos and ethics first brought the issue to the fore for this author in January through April of 2013.

present in concrete, particular situations that are often pre-reflective in the moment of action, yet he believes, buoyed by the tradition and practices of the Mennonite-Anabaptist community that engages in them. His notion of Anabaptist-Mennonite "transactive ethics," which contrast with prospective guidelines or retrospective ethics, describes much the same thing: actions and responses to everyday crises grounded in the community's way of being, on which one might later reflect theologically.[71] He has also used the term "posture" to discuss how "we" as Mennonite actors should "place ourselves" in relation to others in international contexts and the "stance" we take when we engage.[72] He simultaneously explicitly identifies, shapes and animates a particular mode of engagement, in situations of protracted conflict, that he believes to be normative for the church in light of her commitments. This highly reflexive stance is part of what is unusual about Lederach.

I want to draw attention to a simple point implicit in the observation that common sensitivities and perspectives existed within MCC and Lederach's presence, intervention, and peacemaking: there are many ways that people "experience" within international contexts and there is a particular one that some Mennonites share. I am not suggesting that all Mennonites share this perspective. Nor am I suggesting that this perspective is limited to Mennonites. One way to talk about some sort of distinct (though not unique, essential, unified, or homogenous, in light of internal plurality) "experience" that is common to at least some "third-wave Mennonites" more precisely is in terms of boundary-crossing *encounters*.[73] Already with what Lederach has discussed regarding ethos and posture and the observations of Mennonite Central Committee workers, we learn that one's normative stance influences one's presence and engagement. The 20th-century theologian Karl Barth's ideas about the encounter with the secular help us see that the way we encounter the Other shapes what we *discover*. What we understand about "ourselves" in relationship with our external environment and those in it *shape what we learn*. It follows that the way we encounter the other definitively shapes this critical phenomena we are calling "international experience." In other words, if there is a kind of encounter that typifies this engagement in overseas settings then we might have a better idea of what we are talking about with respect to Lederach's international experience with Mennonites and as a Mennonite. Looking at the mode of

---

71. Ibid.

72. Lederach, "Missionaries," 11–19.

73. The notion of essential characteristics or core distinctives of religious traditions has come under scrutiny, and rightly so.

encounter helps us reflect on how the "Mennonite" of "experience" has substantive bearing on Lederach's theory-making.

Encounter as the Site of Dialogical Convergence of Comprehensive Vision (Narrative Community) and Contingent Experiences

To bring further insight, I offer an analytical framework for reflecting on what "international experience" with and as a Mennonite could mean theologically and imply in practice. This framework is a typology of encounters between the subject and the Other. In this schema, the "Subject" is the third-party intervener (Lederach or the international Mennonite practitioner or service worker) and the "Other" is the receiving body or local community. This accompaniment framework, or framework for thinking about service to others, emerges from Barth's formulation of Christian ethics as attestation to the gift of God's grace. Barth insists that we ought to envision and live our ethical lives as recipients of the Word of God. I draw from Barth's description of the encounter with modernity described in *Church Dogmatics 4.2*, the essay "Man in the 18th Century" from *Protestant Theology in the Nineteenth Century*, and the interpretation of Barth scholar, Gerald McKenny,[74] whom I have to thank for the conversation that inspired these three types: (1) the Subject assimilates the Other she encounters; (2) the Other assimilates the subject; (3) the Subject is in solidarity with the Other.

In the first mode—*the Subject assimilates the Other*—the subject is autonomous, self-enclosed, and self-sufficient. He operates as a "solitary sovereign" who knows no limits: there is no one who calls the self-contained modern subject into question. In effect, he absorbs everything external and subverts it to his will. For Barth, in this stance, the subject "wishes to remain by itself, and does not wish to hear of something radically different from its own working and its possible change."[75] At the end of the day, this subject will not acknowledge anything beyond its own possibilities and constraints, and the good that it aims to accomplish will be proportionate to its capabilities and achievements.[76] Placed in the context of international peacebuilding, the "self-enclosed subject" presupposes superiority, expertise, prescribed solutions, and unidirectional gift-giving in multifold forms (e.g., training, intervention, humanitarian aid, or money for a church

---

74. See, Barth and Torrance, *Doctrine of Reconciliation*; Barth, *Protestant Theology*; Cf. McKenny, *Analogy of Grace*.

75. Quoted in McKenny, *Analogy of Grace*, 25.

76. McKinney, *Analogy of Grace*, 3.

plant).[77] To the extent that power dynamics can be recognized at all, power imbalances seem "natural" in relationships between external-subjects and insider-Others. Lederach critiqued these tendencies within resolution perspectives (and the liberal peacebuilding model more generally). Now, to be fair and honest, casually dismissing this type as necessarily a "Peacemaking Rambo" would be too easy. The constructive role for this type surfaces in issues of cross-cultural learning and sharing (vs. hoarding). Yet, as an ideal type, the movement is unidirectional: the transfer is one-way with the Subject refusing to receive from the Other.

The second modality—*the Other assimilates the subject*—stands in an inverse relationship to the first, though it is unidirectional as well. In this mode, the subject has failed to recognize the necessary limits of self-giving. She has modeled her life in correspondence with Christ's self-sacrifice without adequately appreciating that Christ's sacrifice is sufficient. If the subject re-presents Christ, then the subject's self-giving to the Other is limitless. The problem with this arises from the affirmation that God's work is complete in Christ. This truth determines the role of human subjects. It places limits on self-sacrifice. Barth teaches us that humans are to witness to what Christ fully accomplished, not re-present Christ; humans trigger what is already accomplished in Christ, they do not re-present him. Granted, in contrast with the *eros* of the first type, self-giving *agape* love indeed appears to be the persistent undertow. For Barth, the tug towards self-giving arises in light of humanity's correspondence with Jesus Christ. Yet re-reading Barth helps us discover that the self-giving that "depletes" the subject for the benefit of the Other is not actually *agape* love after all. This is because a self-depleted subject is neither recognizing her own humanity as one God is for, nor free to be for God's cause of humanity.[78] The "Messiah complex" is an example in the realm of accompaniment. In this overcorrection of the self-absorbed sovereign, the subject has an inflated sense of personal ability and confuses divine and human agency. This focus obscures subjectivity in relation to others and may well be inimical to others.[79] Because she is human and not God, the subject gets lost in the other in this modality. The Other draws the subject into itself. Persons who have an inflated sense of worth or little sense of social value, an inflexible notion of correspondence with Christ's cross, or a porous sense of identity may be vulnerable to this loss.

---

77. Carolyn Shrock-Shenk and other Mennonite practitioners explored and incorporated this insight into their training pedogogy; see, Schrock-Shenk and Stutzman, *Mediation*; Schrock-Shenk and Ressier, editors, *Making Peace*.

78. Barth and Torrance, *Doctrine of Reconciliation*.

79. Feminist theological critiques of sacrifice extend and enrich these themes, including in ways that deeply problematize Barth's concepts.

A third way of encounter is solidarity, or *moral accountability to the Other*.[80] This overcomes the problems of one-way assimilation moving in both directions. It is characterized by the acceptance of limitations, a posture that supports the Other, and a willingness to be questioned and contested by the Other. For Barth, this is a right response to God's call and aligns with God's cause of reconciliation. On a basic level, it is a matter of answering with one's *life conduct* the claim grace has on one's life. It is incarnational in that humans find in the incarnation the way in which human beings are to be oriented—for the Other.

The stance is shaped by recognition that the Word of God is always free to speak in places where it is not explicitly acknowledged. As Weaver and Dula remind us, Barth insists that God's word is present "beyond the walls of the church," or outside of Christian scripture and proclamation, through "secular parables of the kingdom."[81] For Barth, Christ's Lordship over all the universe not only allows Christians to discover new things of God that seem strange and foreign but prompts us to expect them: all people and all creation originate from the cross of Christ, from the reconciliation accomplished by Christ, and are "ordained to be the bearers" of Christ's word.[82] Consequently, the posture is open to discovering new things of God that seem strange and foreign. The subject operating by this logic develops the capacity to hear God in strange and unfamiliar voices and see God working in unfamiliar ways. This openness to discovery presupposes—because it is conditioned upon—questioning and challenge from the Other. This is Barth's social ethic of solidarity.

Expanding further on this typology is beyond the scope of this chapter. My aim is simply to provide some definition that is rooted in the theological ethics of what Lederach might mean by a Mennonite "ethos" in international settings—what we are calling "international experience"—and a couple of points of contrast. As is surely clear, I suggest that some "third wave" Mennonite peacemakers—Lederach included—express and are disciplined by the third mode: engagement in solidarity. I initially drew on Barth with the aim of providing a framework that is both at home amidst Mennonites, due to its focus on Jesus Christ, and that could be deployed by a broader audience to analyze diverse actors. Along the way I discovered that Barth's insistence on God's presence outside church walls influenced the Mennonite theology that Lederach read, since we know Lederach was deeply influenced by Yoder, and offers a theological rationale for the elicitive

80. McKenny, *Analogy of Grace*.
81. Weaver, "Parables," 411–40; Dula, "Theology of Interfaith," 160–70.
82. Weaver, "Parables," 427.

approach he commends. Barth provides theological justification for Lederach's conviction that each community possesses the resources to move towards wholeness, since all are under the Lordship of Christ. And Barth insists that as a Christian body we are not only free but called to attest to God's grace through receiving the "words" shared by those we accompany. We can understand the elicitive "model" to emerge from practicing love of neighbor in the hard places of a fractured world and the knowledge born of that sacred, grace-filled space.[83]

This Christological description sheds light on the kind of encounter that ideally gives recent Mennonite international experience its distinctive shape.[84] I say "ideally" because what I have described is an ideal type: of course we fail knowingly and unknowingly, sometimes in very damaging and painful ways. Lederach does not shield his own fumblings and disappointments. Yet with all our faults, mistakes, and failures, this stance helps us understand what is going on when we talk about the significance of experience with Mennonites and as a Mennonite in Lederach's theory-making. It also provides a theological lens through which to interpret the value and contributions of a particular sociolinguistic frame in peacemaking.

It is my hope that elevating the site of encounter will help us to better understand the dialogical relationship between sociolinguistic community and experience. On a formal methodological level, it demonstrates the complementary relationship between the narrative approach and the experiential approach.[85] In terms of theologies, it reflects and deepens a shift from "two kingdom theology" to in-breaking eschatologies that support mutual dialogical, boundary crossing relationships.[86] Talk of separation

---

83. The eschatology underpinning the elicitive approach and Barth's solidarity ethic are at odds with some contemporary peace theologies, such as Ted Koontz' reappropriation of two-kingdom theology and other less realized eschatologies and related categories. Ted Koontz, "Thinking Theologically about War against Iraq," The Mennonite Quarterly Review 77, no. 1 (January 2003): 93–108. His concern is not with the elicitive method, per se, but with the need to acknowledge a limited role for the church in situations of political crisis. Yet two-kingdom sensibilities might raise the question, What keeps Lederach from sliding into a realized eschatology propping up humanism that doesn't need (or cannot "tolerate") Christ? I maintain that this move would jettison the posture of solidarity in favor of type two: the Other assimilates the subject.

84. The experiential approach helps us understand how a variety of experiences can be held in the Anabaptist-Mennonite tradition.

85. Suggesting the complementarity of two approaches runs counter to some theologians' accounts. In *The Nature of Doctrine* (Philadelphia: Fortress Press, 1984), theologian George Lindbeck gives one account of these two modes, naming them "cultural linguistic" and "experiential expressivist." Whereas Lindbeck argued for the former against the latter, here I see them as complementary.

86. See n. 37 above. As noted, for Lederach the elicitive model reflects the conviction

further gives way to discussions on the in-breaking kingdom of God and the kingdom of God in our midst. Applied, it represents the dynamic nexus of "third-wave" Anabaptist-Mennonite commitments as both conduct and experience.

Such experiences of engagement help explain how Lederach was able to (1) receive the questions posed by his Central American colleagues; (2) question CR's paradigms; and (3) propose new ones on the heels of intense experience. He gives us a glimpse of what this confrontation and questioning by the Other looked like in his early years in Central America. I quote at length from the first pages of his 1988 dissertation:

> Cross-cultural experience has the unique quality of "shocking" us into unexplored worlds. This is most obvious when we first enter their world: we experience and struggle with different ways of doing things that do not always make sense to us but seem to make perfect sense to them. The cross-cultural experience can also launch us into a less obvious unexplored world: our own taken-for-granted ways of thinking, being and doing.[87]

An openness to confrontation and questioning from the Other nurtures interdependent relationships. This is only possible through relationships that are developed through deep presence. Serving while anchored within grassroots communities is an embodiment of this posture in that it remains present with the Other. The accompanier (the "Subject") comes to recognize the need for the Other in various ways, including for their own comprehension of a situation and even physical safety. MCC protocol on presence and partnerships and Lederach's decades-long commitments to the communities he accompanies around the world express this posture. As a relational orientation underscores, it is the living tissue of the matter in the everyday, year after year, activities that count in our encounters.

Experience shaped by encounter in solidarity with the Other helps explain the positions that emerge. Epistemologically, supporting the Other with vulnerability, openness, and accountability rebuffs assumptions of superiority and power inequality. The notion of knowledge and resources moving in a single direction is rejected and the relationship of "expert" to "know-nothing" is undermined.[88] It presses against the attitudes, models,

---

that each community possesses the resources to move towards wholeness. In a Barthian theological key, God's work is already complete and humans' job is to trigger that which already is already present in the everyday. Our job is to develop the capacity to hear God speaking in unfamiliar voices and see God working in unfamiliar ways.

87. Lederach, "Of Nets, Nails," 4–5.

88. Lederach draws on Curle, who also makes the transition from the paradigm

and strategies of trickle-down imperialism as a form of neocolonialism. The normative stance of empathic solidarity does not undercut cross-cultural and international exchange, on the one hand, or imply false humility, on the other. Rather, what it means to exercise the role of third party intervener and engage others in light of acquired knowledge and experience is reoriented.

The exposure and sensitivities of MCC and Lederach's posture of solidarity help explain his attentiveness to the liabilities and problems endemic to the professional field of conflict resolution. The ways Lederach problematizes conflict resolution (as well as statist diplomacy and the liberal peace) have conceptual links with theories contributing to what Galtung called structural violence—unintended or indirect violence exercised through economic models, political or social structures, or cultural norms.[89] These include the less visible forms of "cultural violence"[90] and "symbolic violence."[91] MCC's suspicion and Lederach's critique of resolution are sensitive to condescending behavior by local and foreign elites[92] and the systematic denial of local knowledge and culture,[93] which are included within theories of violence. These concepts enrich the critique of expertise training models and the attendant assumptions that are made in cross-cultural settings by third-party interveners. Being present on behalf of the Other as a matter of accountability encourages the search for alternative ways of seeking transformation that are context relevant and contribute to the movement towards the contextually contingent process of a 'just peace.'

Conclusion

The "experience" in the field presented an opportunity that Lederach could have denied or ignored to keep his resolution paradigm intact and dominant. Rather, he honored his interpretation of a Mennonite ethos with its incarnational sense of vulnerable, relational presence to interact with the

---

of "experts" and empty vessels to discovery-based tools of transformation. This vulnerability and openness to exchange at the point of encounter is reflected in Mennonite theologies. Consider, for example, this passage in Huebner, *Precarious Peace*, 19–20: "The peace of the church, however, is a vulnerable exchange of gifts. It is not safe, but dangerous . . . It moves as if from below, from the underground. Its vision consisting of glimpses and brief snatches, never putting itself above the realities it encounters." Curle, *Tools for Transformation*.

89. Galtung, "Cultural Violence," 293ff.
90. MacGregor and Rubio, "Rejoinder."
91. Bourdieu, *et al.*, *Logic of Practice*.
92. Colin and Losch, "'Touche," 83–99.
93. Rupesinghe and Correa, editors, *Culture of Violence*.

productive disjunctures and allow new processes and outcomes as a result. Unlike the relatively tidy goal of negative peace to "stop the fighting," he opted for an emphasis on the process rather than closure. Key to this is that one draws parties into relationship because each holds some stake in their preferred future. By operating in what Barth calls a solidarity mode, Lederach rejected the role of a dispenser of expertise in conflict resolution to instead become a learner and elicitor within the place-based, local communities he was encountering. Lederach journeys with the processes of transformation by avowing to learn as much as sharing the skills that he had developed elsewhere. It is not only Lederach who has been shaped in this way, however. Presence in solidarity, which is love of neighbor taken to its logical conclusions, is a way of getting at the dialogical, dynamic relationship between experience and comprehensive vision of some recent Mennonites engaged in peacebuilding. As this chapter demonstrates, this form of presence is not only linked to the Anabaptist-Mennonite tradition, it actively shapes it.

7

Formative Mennonite Mythmaking in Peacebuilding and Restorative Justice

CARL STAUFFER

Introduction: Comprehending Mythmaking

MYTHMAKING IS A NATURAL phenomenon. Myths are foundational to the social scripts (narratives) that order our human configurations of existence. We as humankind are predisposed to constructing founding stories, rituals, symbols, and belief systems that shape our understanding of the world and how we view the meaning of life, value in relationships, and the comprehension of the Divine. Mary Midgley argues in her book *The Myths We Live By* (2003) that "We are accustomed to think of myths as the opposite of science. But in fact they are a central part of it: the part that decides its significance in our lives . . . Myths are not lies. Nor are they detached stories. They are imaginative patterns, networks of powerful symbols that suggest particular ways of interpreting the world."[1]

In its broadest sense, the conceptions and applications of mythology have been an integral part of our human experience since before recorded history. Age-old oral traditions of storytelling, wisdom-sayings, proverbs, parable, poetry, ritual, and drama have functioned to affirm and validate social configurations of human relationship for centuries. The pivotal role of oral tradition in the transmission and preservation of history, worldview,

1. Midgley, *Myths*, 1.

cultural and socio-religious values and practices among ancient pre-literate civilizations is well researched and documented.

According to Jean-Francois Lyotard, myth was the knowledge base of pre-modern societies. Lyotard conjectured that myth was considered knowledge in these ancient clan or tribal formations, not because it represented 'facts' but because it established and propagated social norms and structures, the rules of life that functioned as the glue to hold groups of people together in social cohesion.[2] As to the function of myth, Claude Levi-Strauss argued that myth may not give us a material power over the environment but it does give us the illusion that we can and do understand the universe.[3]

As Mennonites, a historically marginal people, we have formed multiple myths to explain who we are and why we do what we do. One of the Mennonite meta-myths is that of being and acting as peace-loving and justice-serving communities. All myths are encoded with particular historical realities while at the same time being embedded with both constructive and destructive legacies and aftermaths in current application. This chapter explores three typical, formative peace and justice myths from past Mennonite narratives: Dirk Willems of Asperen (1569), Russian Mennonite Persecution (1917–20), and the first Restorative Justice case in Elmira, Canada (1974). For each of these founding myths there are counter-narratives that both positively and negatively influence the expressions of Mennonite peacebuilding and restorative justice practice today.

Analytical Frameworks

Central to the process of mythmaking is the dynamic of collective memory. John Paul Lederach,[4] a Mennonite professor and one of the founding voices in the contemporary peacebuilding field, describes at least four layers of 'nested' memory that constitute what it means to link the past, present, and future into a meaningful whole. Firstly, all accounts of history carry with them deep pulses of *narrative discourse*, which he defines as the unspoken, even subconscious, value-laden meaning (worldview) that is ascribed to the socio-cultural text (either written or spoken) by different members of a particular group. Secondly, the next thread woven into collective memory is called *remembered history*—that part of the ancient story that is generationally transmitted through oral tradition and reinforced in behavior

---

2. Lyotard, *Postmodern*.
3. Levi-Strauss, *Myth and Meaning*, 17.
4. Lederach, *Moral Imagination*, 141.

mimesis (imitation). Thirdly, from the repository of remembered history, people overlay their rational and emotional memories with the conforming or nonconforming reality of *lived experience*. Finally, all of these nuanced memories function as the bedrock for the meaning that we attribute to *current events*.

A critical analysis of mythmaking draws from three major streams of knowledge: literary criticism, new historicism, and social constructivism. *Literary criticism* refers to the processes of discourse analysis and/or textual critique of written literature. Literary criticism, while concerned with content, is even more importantly concerned with the interpretive interaction between the 'voices' of the author(s) and the reader(s) and the meaning generated from that interface. *New Historicism* is concerned with the interplay between what has been termed the "dominant and subjugated narratives"[5] of society. New Historicism questions the 'objectivity' claim of past historians. While deeply sceptical of the dominant historical narrative (and its Euro-centric, militaristic, male agenda), the New Historicist eagerly undertakes the project of historical revisionism by surfacing the subjugated voices of marginalized peoples who have never had a chance to give 'voice' to, much less write history, but who represent the lived experience of history. *Social Constructivism* is concerned with the 'production of reality' through social narratives by which the members of any given society live and configure their institutional structures. For example, one form of social constructivism is called dramaturgical studies. Dramaturgical study applies theatrical performance frames and language (plot, script, actors, audience, stage, and props) to better understand the *ordering* meaning of seemingly chaotic social phenomena.

Mythology is primarily concerned with what has been termed the 'interpretative turn,'[6] and flowing from this production of meaning comes "the social construction of preferred realities."[7] With the rise of globalization and the accompanying technologies of social media, it is becoming increasingly apparent that our world is constructed as much from symbolic exchanges as from material transactions.[8] Mythmaking then, as it is used in this chapter, is comprised of three elemental parts: *content* (meaning), *structure* (form) and *performance* (interaction)[9]. Unpacking these three

---

5. Foucault, *Power/Knowledge*.
6. Geertz, *Interpretation of Cultures*.
7. Freedman and Combs. This term 'social construction' was first coined by: Berger and Luckmann.
8. Richards, *Fighting*, xxiii.
9. Elliot, *Using Narrative*.

factors as they have played out in the history of three particular founding myths of Mennonite peace and justice work is the central focus of this chapter.

Functions of Mythmaking

Mythmaking serves a number of functions both positive and negative. In their bold work on *"Transforming Historical Harms,"* Anderson-Hooker and Potter-Czajkowski discuss two salient outcomes of historical harms—*legacies and aftermaths*. They define these concepts as follows: *Legacy and Aftermath:* in relationship to the multigenerational transmission of trauma, *legacy* is the collection of beliefs, ideas, myths, prejudices, biases and behaviors that are disseminated and then inherited by and/or about differing groups. *Aftermath* refers to the institutions, laws, political and economic structures and the official narrative conveyed and enforced by a society's supporting systems (education, religion, social services, criminal justice, etc.) that were formed to enforce or reinforce particular aspects of a legacy.[10]

While not all myths refer to or are linked to 'historical harms' in the case of the Mennonite peacebuilding myths I am discussing in this chapter, each one has its origins in what could be termed historical violence. In that way, I will argue that these myths have been accompanied by certain legacies and aftermaths, both constructive and destructive, in the Mennonite peacebuilding experience. It is precisely because of these legacies and aftermaths that these myths, based on events that may have occurred decades or many hundreds of years ago, seem to be larger than life. These enduring legacies and aftermaths that have built up over generations and continue to morph with each subsequent generational transmission seem to have taken on a life of their own. This is what the central inquiry of this essay is about.

The Mennonite peacebuilding myths that I refer to throughout this chapter are not myths in the purest sense of the word. Indeed, they are not simply guiding, symbolic metaphors, they are also grounded in historical happenings and it might therefore be more appropriate to identify them as "mythico-histories," a concept coined by Stanford University Anthropologist, Dr. Liisa Malkki coming out of her work among Hutu refugees living in Tanzania. According to Malkki, the concept of "mythico-history" "went far beyond merely recording events. It represented, not only a description of the past, nor even merely an evaluation of the past, but a subversive recasting

---

10. Hooker and Czajkowski. *Transforming Historical Harms*: http://comingtothetable.org/wp-content/uploads/2013/10/01-Transforming_Historical_Harms.pdf (emphasis mine).

and reinterpretation of it in fundamentally moral terms. In this sense, it cannot be accurately described as either history or myth. It was what can be called a mythico-history."[11]

The three Mennonite peacebuilding "mythico-historical" narratives that I have chosen to explore in this chapter share at least two common characteristics. Firstly, they are all *founding* myths, meaning that they have been located in a particular place and time that has allowed them to take on a specific role and function in the identity formation of the global Mennonite community. Secondly, each of the three stories has developed into *purity* narratives, meaning that as they have grown in popularity, they have been simplified and used for moral categorization and contrast. In essence, these scripts have been purified of complexities and contradictions in order to be presented as morally prescriptive and as a form of sacred instruction in order to build up and edify the community. In short, the Mennonite peacebuilding myths highlighted here are both rooted in the reality of Mennonite history and are emblematic of the symbolic power of social discourse to give a sense of inspiration, guidance and solidarity to a worldwide community of Mennonites.

Mennonite Peace Myth #1: Dirk Willems & the Ethic of Enemy-Love

Compassion For The Enemy—Dirk Willems, Asperen, 1569
No story of an Anabaptist martyr has captured the imagination more than the tale of Dirk Willems. Dirk was caught, tried and convicted as an Anabaptist in those later years of harsh Spanish rule under the Duke of Alva in The Netherlands. He escaped from a residential palace turned into a prison by letting himself out of a window with a rope made of knotted rags, dropping onto the ice that covered the castle moat.
Seeing him escape, a palace guard pursued him as he fled. Dirk crossed the thin ice of a pond, the "Hondegat," safely. His own weight had been reduced by short prison rations, but the heavier pursuer broke through.
Hearing the guard's cries for help, Dirk turned back and rescued him. The less-than-grateful guard then seized Dirk and led him back to captivity. This time the authorities threw him into a more secure prison, a small, heavily barred room at the top of a very tall church tower, above the bell, where he was probably

---

11. Malkki, *Purity and Exile*, 54–55.

> locked into the wooden leg stocks that remain in place today. Soon he was led out to be burned to death.
>
> Some inhabitants of present-day Asperen, none of them Mennonite, regard Dirk as a folk hero. A Christian, so compassionate that he risked recapture in order to save the life of his drowning pursuer, stimulates respect and memory. Recently Asperen named a street in Dirk's honor.[12]

This brief account of historical Anabaptist 'enemy-love' is probably the quintessential myth of Mennonite pacifism-in-action of all time. In the first place, it has been immortalized in the annals of the Mennonite martyrdom publication, *The Martyrs Mirror*,[13] a detailed litany of the gruesome deaths and the supernatural faith and hope of the early Anabaptists of the Reformation period in the 1500–1600s. This showpiece anthology of martyrs was probably the most well read and revered book second to the Bible in most Mennonite homes up until two generations ago. My wife and I have our own modern day version tucked away with family photographs, educational certificates, important documents and other valuable memorabilia that we are keeping for posterity. *The Martyrs Mirror* remains a source of historical and literary study and research even until today.[14]

In the second place, this story has become the touchstone text for all that it means to be Anabaptist to the rest of the world outside the purview of Mennonite circles as evidenced by the honor Willems has received from the non-Mennonites who live in his village today. Because of its succinct descriptive power and its profound brevity, this account has often been used in church tracts, Mennonite institutional brochures, publications, websites, and other publicity and marketing materials as an 'identity descriptor' for who the Mennonites are and what we believe. Multiple testimonies of those outside of the Anabaptist tradition cite this story as a drawing point to their entry into the Mennonite Church. Not that it has only inspired, it has also intrigued and even confused non-Mennonite groups for years. My former professor, colleague, and friend, Rabbi Dr. Marc Gopin, fondly tells the story of his excitement when he first encountered Mennonites through the Eastern Mennonite University's Center for Justice and Peacebuilding where he has taught off and on for a number of decades. In his zeal for wanting to tell the 'amazing' peacebuilding story of this obscure religious group called

---

12. Oyer and Kreider, *Mirror*, 36–37.

13. Originally referred to as the "The Bloody Theater," the first edition was published in 1660 in the Dutch language by the Dutch Mennonite elder and author Thieleman J. van Braght (1625–1664).

14. See Beachy, *Thumb Screws*.

the Mennonites, he presented the Dirk Willems story to a group of Jewish religious leaders/scholars. But instead of being met with a response of heroic affirmation as he expected, his Jewish friends and colleagues responded in bewilderment asking, "Was this Willems guy stupid or what?"[15] Whatever the response to this 'sacred' narrative, it has become a signature piece for Mennonite peace identity.

A positive legacy of this founding myth has been a powerful inspiration for practical application of pacifism based on Jesus' teachings in the Sermon on the Mount (Mt. 5–7), a necessary distinction of the Anabaptist tradition which insists that the teachings of Jesus are neither historic relics nor dispensational ideals for a heavenly future, but that these teachings are meant to be enacted in the here and now. Similar to the modern movement of "engaged Buddhism," whereby Buddhist monks left the confines of monastic life and entered the public domain of nonviolent action,[16] the Mennonites with their emphasis on discipleship and following the teachings of Jesus have prided themselves in being the "engaged Christianity" arm of the mainline Protestant movement. It was this impulse toward 'engaged application' that provided the practical theology and necessary impetus for the more recent move of the Mennonite church into the forays of contemporary peacebuilding in the early 1990s.[17]

While open to debate, a negative aftermath of this founding myth has been the deep-rooted narrative of historical persecution that reaches back to the time of the Protestant Reformation (500–600 years ago) and that could arguably be described as having evolved into a collective *'persecution complex.'* The aftermath of this persecution complex has led to a form of insular groupthink[18] that invariably opened the Mennonite Church and its various para-church structures to the label of the "Quiet in the Land."[19] Ultimately, this withdrawal from the public square reinforces an already en-

---

15. Taken from a public presentation by Dr. Marc Gopin at the Faith-Based Peace Education Conference, Boston Theological Institute, Boston, Massachusetts, August 2010.

16. The Dali Lama Of Tibet and Vietnamese Buddhist leader Thich Nact Hanh are popular examples of leaders in "engaged Buddhism." The concept of "engaged Buddhism" captured international attention when Vietnamese Monks took to the streets and protested the Vietnam War through public immolation.

17. See Shenk, "Anonymous," 34–41, and Fager, " Rethinking Pacifism," 17–18.

18. For more information on the concept of "groupthink" see: Mandel, *Perception*, 11.

19. This notion is primarily based on a New Testament scripture from the Apostle Paul's letter to the Thessalonians which states: ". . . and to make it your ambition to lead a quiet life and attend to your own business and work with your hands, just as we commanded you . . ." (1 Thess 4:11, NASB)

grained theological conviction and deeply visceral response to any 'mixing' of church and state, the very source of Anabaptist persecution in the time of the Protestant Reformation.

The concept of a persecution complex could be compared to what social psychologist Vamik Volkan calls a chosen trauma. Volkan maintains that all nations and people groups have founded their historical memories on what he terms "chosen traumas and chosen glories."[20] The word 'chosen' is deliberately employed in this instance to refer to the guise of corporate 'selective memory' whereby nations/communities remember all that is valiant and heroic (historical glorification) and forget all that is despised and cowardly (selective amnesia) about their own past. According to Volkan, it is in the administration of this glorification of self and denigration of the Other that a nation is able to fabricate a fervent patriotism of the state and hold their citizens together in unity. Dominick LaCapra refers to the "founding trauma" that, not unlike Volkan's chosen trauma, evolves into the organizing principle around which personal and corporate identities of victim/hero are constructed.[21] In the case at hand, because of his captors' cruel and unrelenting response that ultimately led to Dirk's fateful demise at the hands of the violence system of his day, this Willems script has simultaneously become both the "chosen trauma and the chosen glory" of Mennonite nonviolence and peacebuilding.

Mennonite Peacebuilding as Subversive Engagement

The shift of the Mennonite church from the self-identified persecuted, separate "Quiet in the Land" to their entrance into the public square of peacebuilding and thereby invariably into the political realm has been deeply controversial.[22] Many people (both Mennonites and non-Mennonites) appreciate this move as a deeply profound representation of the Mennonite 'gift of peace in action' being offered for the benefit of all. However, many others are more cautious, feeling the anxiety of the potentially risky compromise of nonviolence, the insecurity of ethical complexities, and the perceived contamination to the *purity* of the Mennonite identity as repre-

---

20. Volkan, *Need*.
21. LaCapra, *Writing History*, 23.
22. One of the most salient examples of this new positioning for Mennonites is the work of Dr. Lisa Schirch, Research Professor at Eastern Mennonite University's Center for Justice and Peacebuilding. Dr. Schirch founded and leads her own nonprofit organization "3-P Human Security" in Washington DC. For more information see: http://3phumansecurity.org/site/

sented by the ideological-theological concept of the separation of "Church and State." Central to the doctrine of the separation of Church and State is the belief that as Christians, we exist in two kingdoms simultaneously—a material kingdom and a spiritual kingdom. This idea comes from injunctions recorded in John 17:14 and 18:36 where Jesus essentially says that we as his followers are to be 'in the world, but not of the world.'[23] *Interpreting what this posture looks like 2000 years later remains one of the greatest challenges facing the Mennonite church and its peace and justice witness today.*

In finding our way through this liminal space of being "in but not of" this world, we may do well to learn from those outside of our Mennonite tradition. Asian theologian, Dr. David Lim, in his excellent essay on the relationship of the church and state describes five configurations of the religious communities of Jesus' day and their relationships with the Roman occupation.[24] Firstly, there were the Sadducees who used their legal expertise to *collaborate* with the Roman Empire for personal benefit and opportunistic political gain. Secondly, the Essenes used their mystical call to *totally withdraw* in cloistered communities far removed from the hubbub of society. Thirdly, the Pharisees were known to teach and live in a bifurcated form of pious *religious segregation*. Fourthly, the Zealots represented the radical religious response by espousing *violent revolution* against Roman oppression. Finally, there was the way of Jesus and his disciples that modeled a form of prophetic service that could be aptly described as *subversive engagement* with the Roman powers. The concept of subversive engagement implies holding a critical distance while at the same time maintaining a relevant interaction with the political powers of our day. *As Mennonites venture into the forays of public peace and justice work, we would do well to articulate and develop a posture of subversive engagement as protection against cooptation and compromise.*

Another source of illumination for understanding the relationship between Mennonites and 'public powers' is from feminist thought, which avers that—when it comes to direct and structural violence—"the personal *is* political."[25] This concept is quite unsettling for a people like the Mennonites who have prided themselves in being separate from the world. Yet, as our globe continues to get smaller and technology invites multiple new forms of communication, relationship, and networking, we as Mennonites are realizing that the food we buy, the taxes we pay, the places we live, the

---

23. For an award-winning, contempory interpretation of this notion see: Kraybill, *Upside-Down Kingdom*.

24. Shenk and Stutzman, *Practicing*.

25. Carol Hanisch is a radical feminist and is best known for popularizing the phrase "The Personal Is Political" in a 1969 essay of the same name.

vehicles we drive, the way we vote, and the cross-cultural mission and humanitarian relief and development work that we do is not insulated from political consequences no matter how good intentioned. When serial rape on a Mennonite colony in Bolivia[26] is brought to the attention of the criminal justice system, or when a mentally disturbed young man shoots and kills multiple children in an Amish school in Pennsylvania before turning the gun on himself,[27] the personal becomes political. With the world's media shining a spotlight on these intimate domains, suddenly the communities involved were forced to work out their sense of betrayal, grief, shock, anger, trauma, and forgiveness in public purview.

While these examples may seem extreme, they are becoming more commonplace, especially as the Mennonite Church continues to grow and expand in the southern hemisphere (South America, Africa, and Asia).[28] It is in these regions where the direct conflicts and structural violence are unfortunately too often a part of everyday life. If the church worldwide cannot speak to the real-life issues of poverty, unemployment, homelessness, landlessness, hunger, war, disease, and forced migration, etc., it has lost its relevancy. *The challenge for the global Mennonite church is to figure out how to position itself close enough to the political realm to be relevant, but with enough distance to be able to speak prophetically and not be co-opted by the political power structures.* As the old African adage goes, "It is hard to speak to the king, if your mouth is full of his food!" The Mennonite advocacy offices in Ottawa, Canada, the United Nations in New York, and on Capital Hill in Washington, DC are a clear indication of this new era in which the Mennonite church is finding its place among the "powers that be"[29] and its unique role in subversive engagement in the public square.

Mennonite Peace Myth #2: The Russian Mennonite Persecution

> *This is a story about massacres that occurred in Southern Ukraine between 26th October and 7th December, 1919. The victims,*

---

26. See BBC coverage on this situation: http://www.bbc.co.uk/news/world-latin-america-14688458

27. See NYT coverage on this incident: http://www.nytimes.com/2006/10/03/us/03amish.html?pagewanted=all&_r=0

28. The largest Mennonite churches in membership numbers are now located in Ethiopia, Democratic Republic of Congo, and India. About two-thirds of the baptized believers in the Mennonite World Conference are African, Asian or Latin American. See: http://www.mwc-cmm.org/article/world-directory

29. Wink, *Powers that Be*.

> *avowedly-pacifist German Mennonites, included several women and elderly people; in Eichenfeld, almost one third of the village population was killed, including a 65 year-old blind woman. All the massacres occurred in the vicinity of the Makhnovist army. And then, after six weeks, they stopped.*
>
> *This is also the story of an émigré community [Mennonites] whose members invented an anarchist bogeyman to justify having betrayed their pacifist principles. It's about estate owners who earned 3000 times what they paid their labourers, landlords who conscripted soldiers to protect their wealth, and pacifists who fought for an army that killed tens of thousands of Jews. This is about myth and history, and the possibility of rapprochement between two versions of the past. Most of all, perhaps, this is a reminder that those who wish for peace tomorrow must work for equality today.*[30]

Mythmaking by its very nature is characterized by what Haitian historian Michel-Rolph Trouillot calls "silences and mentions."[31] Trouillot maintains that with every segment of historical narrative that is included (mentioned) there is an equal amount of historical narrative that is excluded (silenced): "By silence, I mean an active and transitive process: one 'silences' a fact or an individual as a silencer silences a gun. One engages in the practice of silencing. Mentions and silences are thus active, dialectical counterparts of which history is the synthesis."[32]

In his incisive essays on the Haitian Revolution against the French in 1791, Trouillot argues that this uprising was in fact the first recorded successful native revolution against colonial tyranny, but it was silenced in history because of the implications that this self-organized black resistance had on the dominant racist worldview of colonial Europe at the time. Trouillot identifies and articulates two major forms of historical silencing which he calls 'tropes' that have been employed in order to ensure that this revolution would be forgotten in the production of power in history:

> The first kind of tropes are formulas that tend to erase directly the fact of a revolution. I call them, for short, formulas of erasure. The second kind tends to empty a number of singular events of their revolutionary context so that the entire string of facts, gnawed from all sides, becomes trivialized. I call them formulas of banalization. The first kind of tropes characterizes mainly the generalists and the popularizers—textbook authors,

30. Foster, "Makhnovists."
31. Trouillot, *Silencing the Past*.
32. Ibid.

for example. The second are the favourite tropes of the specialists . . . Both are formulas of silence."[33]

Accordingly, when applying Trouillot to the narrative discourse of the Russian Mennonite persecution, it can be understood as *". . . an ambiguous blend of 'mentions' and 'silences,' whereby some peoples and their times are left out of history."*[34] Let me be clear: the Russian Mennonite persecution was and is a story of unjust massacres, rapes, and pillaging, and it even has elements of religious martyrdom/persecution especially after the Communist Red Army took over the Revolution. And in deconstructing portions of this founding Mennonite myth, I am in no way minimizing the pain and trauma of many of my Mennonite brothers and sisters of Russian descent who suffered severe tragedy and loss of life in their families. However, it is also a tale of economic conflict and injustices in power, rank, and class. For the most part, the dominant narrative of Russian Mennonite persecution often leaves the socio-economic factors out of the conflict analysis. The popular script usually takes a variation of this text that recently appeared in the book *David and Goliath* by best-selling author Malcolm Gladwell: "During the Russian Revolution and the Stalinist years, the Mennonites were persecuted—viciously and repeatedly. Entire Mennonite villages were wiped out. Hundreds of adult men were shipped off to Siberia. Their farms were looted and burned to the ground—and entire communities were forced to flee to the United States and Canada."[35]

While all this is true, for the purposes of understanding mythmaking, what is not being told is just as important. There are subjugated narratives that *also* tell a story of the Russian Mennonites being on the wrong side of a revolution. And in stating this, I believe that truth-telling requires that we reveal a narrative of the Mennonites as a foreign people who were invited to settle in a country not their own, who were given large swathes of the most fertile land by Catherine the Great, and in so doing many, though not all accumulated a great deal of wealth, elite social rank, and class prestige. All this fed an understandable feeling of resentment arising from the surrounding Russian-Ukrainian communities, primarily among the landless poor (peasant labor classes). In the words of John Rempel, "This [Makhnovist/Anarchist] army, consisting almost exclusively of Russian peasants, naturally had a strong nationalistic attitude . . . Thus a great gulf existed between these and

---

33. Ibid., 96.
34. Anderson, "Honorable Mentioning."
35. Gladwell, *David and Goliath*, 254.

the generally well-to-do Mennonite population, who had sympathized with the Germans during the occupation after 1917."[36]

Elaine Enns, a direct descendent of Russian Mennonites and a peace and justice advocate, clearly sums up the tension inherent in this "mythico-historical" narrative in the following blog entry written after making a personal pilgrimage to Ukraine in 2011:

> Lying beneath Ukrainian peasant hostility towards my Mennonite ancestors in Ukraine was a problematic wealth disparity. Moreover, there was disturbing internal economic stratification within the Mennonite colonies. Many landless Mennonites became servants on wealthy Mennonite estates, and some became so disillusioned that they joined the Communists and Anarchists to fight for a more just society. So the same social fault lines that led to the Russian revolution ran right through my grandmother's yard. In most cases, our people were not targeted because they were Mennonite, but because they were wealthy, along with Ukrainian kulaks, Jews, Baptists and Lutherans. I remember as a child asking my father why this horror had happened in Russia. He replied simply, 'We got too rich.'[37]

Another 'silenced' text from this period of history is the intentional decision to use violence by many of the Russian Mennonite communities. The motivation for the establishment of these community militia formations called *Selbstschutz* spans the spectrum from justified, reactionary self-defense on one end, to strategic, proactive protection of land, wealth, and livelihood on the other end. Whatever the case, this violent rupture in the historical Mennonite commitment to nonviolence has been hard to make sense of. "In the view of some this move saved the Molotschna villages at least from more serious damage. Others felt, however, that there were then and would be later negative consequences, and that this decision was a serious tactical error. In any case, it was hardly consistent with the traditionally pacifist Mennonite faith."[38]

In the vortex of retaliatory violence, two common narrative phenomena are unleashed—the spiral of 'enemy formation' emerges and the regenerative nature of reciprocal violence (that is, violence giving birth to violence) exacts a heavy toll. The process of enemy formation is the ultimate fruit of what is often termed "scapegoating" or "us *vs.* them" thinking. This divisive thinking is fueled by a separatist rhetoric, promoted by a sense of

36. Rempel, "Makhno."
37. Enns, "Pilgrimage."
38. Klippenstein, "Russian Revolution."

self-superiority, and finally solidified by a sub-humanization of the Other who is blamed for the violence. The focus of vengeance is then singularly channeled toward one person or people-group, while all other nuanced sources of violence are ignored or minimized in order to avoid complicating the essentialist narrative of good and evil.

In the Russian Mennonite persecution narrative, Nestor Makhno, commander of the Anarchist Army in South Russia during the Revolution of 1918–1921, became the archetypal representation of evil in monstrous and villainous proportions.[39] While historical accounts have verified that Makhno and his army were responsible for conducting a reign of terror and violence that caused untold deaths and suffering, they were not alone in this campaign. Historical record also gives account of rogue, local criminal elements who opportunistically took advantage of the conflict between Makhno and the Mennonites and led raids on Mennonite colonies in order to enrich themselves from the looting and pillaging that was transpiring.

> Local bandits united with this army [Makhnovists] to take their share in the loot of furniture, agricultural machinery, etc. What they could not take away they simply destroyed . . . It must be added, however, that the murders in the Nicolaipol settlement were committed mostly by local bands rather than the Makhno army. The Self-Defense Corps (Selbstschutz), which had been organized and drilled by German occupation army officers before the withdrawal of the German troops, was ineffectual in a military sense and only provided worse reprisals.[40]

What this and other counter-narratives like it are telling us is that the violence against the Russian Mennonite colonies was sourced in various factions inhabiting the surrounding communities, not just in Makhno's Anarchist army and that these factions apparently disliked the Mennonites enough to not only refuse to protect them in this time of war, but to go further and unleash their violent frustration on them. What is also clear is that in aligning with the German occupation of WWI and arming themselves to reciprocate violence, the Mennonites may have also incurred more violent wrath on their communities than otherwise would have occurred. A more honest and nuanced description of the Russian Mennonites of that time might read more like this:

---

39. Various undocumented accounts indicate that Makhno himself may have at one point worked for Mennonite farmers and that he had felt unjustly treated at the hands of his Mennonite employers. This long-carried personal grudge could explain an element of his vindictiveness toward the Russian Mennonite colonies.

40. Rempel, "Makhno."

> The Mennonites, too, were a mix of characters. They were landowners who earned more than whole villages. They were landless peasants, *anwohner*, who fought for the revolution. They were estate managers who whipped their workers but adored their sons. They were women who had the generosity of spirit to nurse those sick and dying Makhnovists who occupied their homes. They were bullies and thugs. They were pious Christians who resisted all military service. They were militia men who wept in church and begged forgiveness for the lives they'd taken. They were girls who lived in fear of rape. They were wealthy young adventurers who loved the smell and feel of guns. They were victims buried in mass graves. They were poor farmers in isolated villages caught in a war they didn't understand. They were proud patriarchs. They were soldiers who killed for the counter-revolution. They were pacifists.[41]

In sum, these revisionist looks at the historical myths of the Russian Mennonite persecution are not meant to glorify or vilify either the Makhnovists or the Mennonites of that time, they are an attempt to complexify the layers of destructive violence (structural or direct) that continue to overshadow this chapter of Mennonite history. *More importantly, in disclosing these counter-narratives, we are continually reminded to ask what is it that we as Mennonites can learn from this difficult history so as to not repeat it again?*

Mennonite Peacebuilding as a Paradox of Power and Vulnerability

One of the most important legacies of the Russian Mennonite persecution is the launching of the Mennonite Central Committee (MCC) in 1920 as a direct emergency relief response from North American Mennonites to the Mennonite farmers suffering from severe drought and subsequent famine that struck the Ukraine that same year. This specific relief effort opened the doors for Mennonites to begin working to address other humanitarian needs in the rest of the world, not just within their Mennonite enclaves. As Mennonites started engaging their global neighbors, especially in the global south, it meant that they needed to confront their own religious, economic, and cultural power blind spots.

Because of our historical persecution complex, we have as Mennonites tended to see possessing power as a negative asset—a socio-political commodity to be avoided—and in our emphasis on self-effacement and service,

---

41. Foster, "Makhnovists."

we have often denied having any power at all, much less misusing the power that we do have. While a good dose of humility is always commendable, the denial of personal and corporate power is a dangerous state to exist in. If the Russian Mennonite persecution has taught us anything it has been to take a serious inventory of our power. With the dawn of MCC as the official relief, development, and peacebuilding arm of the Mennonite church, we have been given ample time to come to terms with our power as Mennonites—its uses, abuses, and limits.

From the initial impulse of emergency relief, MCC moved into a decade of educational development in the 1960s. The idea was that if we could help the rest of the world get educated, material development would follow. When it became clear that education was not the only answer, we moved into strengthening agricultural, small-scale economic development programming in the 1970s. By the 1980s, the disillusionment of what appeared to be somewhat 'triumphal' neo-colonial efforts at international development cast its gloomy shadow across our work and we took on a reactionary posture of being an accompanying "presence" overseas. This observatory presence soon became redundant for our local partners and we moved into two decades of emphasis on capacitation of local partner organizations, contextual peacebuilding, and the mobilization of advocacy for social change.

It is in this place that we must continually be re-defining power through careful personal and organizational reflection and volitional transformation of our power through expressions of vulnerability. Our paradigm must cease to see power as something that is separate from us—some commodity that is in the corridors of the social elite or in the hands of those with political and economic clout. We need to acknowledge our own willingness to use 'power-over' in our dealings with others, even as Mennonites. And it would behoove us to purposefully source a different form of power—a power buttressed by vulnerability.

Vulnerability is about risks; it's about unbarring our defenseless souls before the Other and expecting God to use the Other to transform us in the process. This means living in a posture of humility as we continually realize our own impoverishment and limited horizons. Our power lies in our volitional choice to self-divest and self-disclose. So too, our witness should be one of voluntarily using power as an access point for choosing vulnerability.

We must strive to acknowledge how we have both denied and abused that power in our spheres of influence as Mennonites. We need to understand that the true power of following the 'way of Jesus' is demonstrated in our ability to generously give away (power-to) and share (power-with) in our relational interactions in order to develop our own dependency on others in the process of building 'just peace' in our world. As a global community of Mennonites, it is our responsibility to take a forensic audit of our power interactions in the following scenarios:

- *Our local partner relations*—How do we shape North-South partnerships of truly mutual exchange *and* interdependence?

- *Our inter-racial / ethnic relations*—Have we fully acknowledged our role in propagating systems of *prejudice, racism, and inequity* stemming from the unequal representation, resource distribution, and decision-making equations at a personal and corporate level?

- *Our organizational culture*—Are we truly aware on the experiential level of the tyranny of our own dominant majority (Swiss-German-Russian) Mennonite organizational culture? What do we need to take forward and what should we be leaving behind of our organizational ethos as we desire to nurture more diverse, inclusive institutional structures?

- *Peacebuilding / capacity-building endeavors*—Do we sacrificially engage with the traditionally 'powerful' *and* the 'less-powerful'? How comfortable are we with bold advocacy that could potentially and fundamentally tarnish our historical 'peaceful of the land' image?

In Matthew 10:16, Jesus instructs us to be wise as serpents (powerful) and gentle as doves (vulnerable). What does this mean in practical terms? It may mean we need to redefine 'power' as embodied in both a *tough mind* (strength) and a *tender heart* (sensitivity) in our work for peace and justice. A tough mind requires incisive thinking, realistic appraisal, and decisive judgment. A tender heart requires empathy for the pain of others and ourselves, caring compassion for those around us, and the ability to retain the unity and bond of community amidst diversity and difference. Power at its best is a creative synthesis of opposites (e.g., boldness/meekness, truth/mercy, accountability/ grace, etc.) in integrative harmony. *The challenge before us, as Mennonites, is how to align our personal lives and corporate structures of justice and peacebuilding to the values represented in these kinds of power-paradoxes.*

Mennonite Peace Myth #3: The Elmira Restorative Justice Case

> *In 1974 two youths who had been drinking and had been "talked to" by the police already, took out their frustrations on the small community of Elmira, Ontario, by doing damage to twenty-two*

different vehicles and homes. Several months later the youths pleaded guilty to the charges, and Judge Gordon McConnell in Kitchener ordered a Pre-Sentence Report. Mark Yantzi, the Mennonite Probation Officer writing up the report, discussed the case with the local Mennonite Central Committee court volunteer, Dave Worth. Both had been reading recent publications by the Law Reform Commission of Canada in which it had been stated that reconciliation played an important role in criminal justice. They also knew that reconciliation was the central concept of their Christian faith. Yantzi proposed in his Pre-Sentence Report that the youths would benefit from meeting face-to-face with their victims and making amends. Judge McConnell was intrigued by the idea, and discussed it with the probation officer. The Judge indicated that the notion had lots of merit, but it was simply not done in Western jurisprudence. He made a fateful choice nonetheless when he decided "Why not?" and put the sentencing over until Yantzi and Worth could take the youths to meet each of the victims. They did and out of that experience arose the first ever "Victim Offender Reconciliation Project (VORP)."[42]

Russ Kelly, one of the original offenders in this case and now a restorative justice practitioner and advocate himself, describes the transformative experience of meeting the persons he harmed:

> Meeting our victims was one of the hardest things I had ever done in my entire life. Accompanied by Mark Yantzi (our probation officer) and Dave Worth (a volunteer), we walked up to the victims [sic] front door to apologize, hear what the victims had to say, determine the amount of restitution, ask for forgiveness and assure the victims that they were not targeted. It was a random act of vandalism. Some victims offered forgiveness while others wanted to give us a good whipping. Nonetheless, we survived meeting the victims of our crime spree and returned a couple of months later with certified cheques to restore the amount of out-of-pocket expenses not covered by insurance. The total damage was around $2,200; my accomplice and myself each had to pay $550 restitution and each paid a $200 fine. As well, we were placed on 18 months probation. I thought that was the end of that shameful part of my life. Little did I know what would become of this judicial experiment.[43]

---

42. Northey, "Restorative Justice."
43. Kelly, *Scoundrel*.

From its inception, the burgeoning field of Restorative Justice (RJ) has been defined by its *practice*. Nowhere is this more clearly represented than in the above narrative of the original story of RJ and its employ of a simple, yet powerful justice process. It is only in recent decades that the evidence-based theory and research is finally catching up with the practice values and processes that have driven the RJ field to date. The Mennonites, especially as represented in the founding voice of Dr. Howard Zehr,[44] have played a critical role in the definition and growth of the RJ field domestically and internationally.

The magnitude of the positive legacies of this first RJ case would be hard to try to quantify. RJ has truly benefitted countless individual lives through its applications, it has been utilized to reform the whole juvenile criminal justice system in New Zealand, and it has been evoked in countless truth commissions around the world. In short, RJ has grown to have remarkable global impacts in a considerably short period of time. The adaptability and flexibility of RJ practices has encouraged creative experimentation with alternative forms of justice—experiential justice that is contextual, relational driven, community-owned, and ultimately more satisfying. The emphasis on practice has provided personal transformative justice experiences—including new levels of healing, reconciliation and repair—for affected victims, offenders, and communities. This focus on personal transformation in RJ fits well with the Mennonites, who as a religious group place strong value on individual conversion and discipleship in the 'way of Christ' for each of its members. However, a downside of this concentration on personal transformation is that RJ practices are then effectively confined to *interpersonal* interactions and the necessary critique of and engagement with corporate injustices, and the need for systemic change goes missing in the equation of justice.

Beyond the limitations of an interpersonal interpretation of RJ, the structural aftermaths of the practice-focus in RJ have also been problematic. The challenges of any practice-driven discipline are that it often fails to appreciate or encourage deep *reflection* (theorizing and analysis) and *research* (evidence-based practice, monitoring, and evaluation). The emphasis on 'doing' leads to RJ being defined as a technical set of skills, limited to a well-packaged professional social service that has been given legitimacy through its general application of procedural and policy protocols. The obsession with standardized bureaucratic growth causes RJ to become quite susceptible to cooption or easy assimilation into already existing institutional systems, be that in the judicial, corrections, or educational

---

44. See Zehr, *Changing Lenses*, and Zehr, *Little Book*.

arenas. Subsequently, RJ then becomes one more supplemental program that supports the widening net of social control imposed by the status quo, often dysfunctional, social systems already in existence. The 'unintended consequences' of this phenomenon are that RJ is in fact undergirding the very systems it purports to want to reform, or even transform.[45] Once again, to move out of this quagmire, we as Mennonites are going to have to look outside our own traditions and draw on the thinking and resources of others. We are going to need to enter the fray of the ongoing debate around the centrality of *personal or structural agency* as the primary force behind just social change and offer alternative bridging possibilities between these polemics. We will need to discover our voice in advocating for a 'third-way' restorative justice that addresses repression and oppression in the *private* as well as the *public* domains.

Mennonite Justice as Integrating Personal and Structural Agency

A key to balancing the RJ as an 'interpersonal, social service practice' and a 'framing paradigm for systemic change' is to understand RJ as a *social movement*. The concept of RJ as a social movement gives us an all-encompassing container in which to hold together the tensions of personal and structural agency in the process of just societal change. By borrowing from social movement theory, we can shed light on the interconnectivity between individual and collective roles and needs in establishing restorative justice. Firstly, we know that sustained social movements depend on individual and organizational alliances that are technically skilled and competent to assist in the strategic, organizational and logistical support of durable social change.[46] Secondly, we know that social movements in their essence consist of and are bolstered by complex processes of practice at all levels. The function of strong, localized practice is to provide the direction, guidance and restraint/constraint necessary for social movements to progress with equanimity. In other words, social movements and social practice have a symbiotic relationship. Thirdly, social movement theory[47] informs us that critical mass transformative "tipping points"[48] have only occurred in history when advocates of change have positioned themselves from *within*, and

---

45. For more incisive read on this topic see the important and critical work of Greene, "Repeat Performance," 359–90.
46. Pearlman, *Violence*.
47. Moyer, et al., *Doing Democracy*.
48. Gladwell, *Tipping Point*.

agents of provocation have positioned themselves from *without,* and they have worked together as individuals and organizations in collaboration to reinforce the undergoing transformative change of a whole system.

In order for RJ to span the divide of the personal verses structural agency debate, it will be mandatory that it begins to embrace the *social justice movement* (concerned with equity in the ownership, distribution, and decision-making of wealth and power in society) and the *transformative justice movement* (concerned with a radical, critical deconstruction and replacement of dominant structures of race, gender, and class in society writ-large). The theological values of the Mennonite tradition that place importance on economic simplicity, wealth stewardship, creation/environmental care, social service, and community living allow for a ease of dialogue, partnership, and network coalition building to take place with the proponents of social justice outside the Mennonite church. While at the same time, the historical experience of Mennonites (e.g. martyrdom, persecution, and marginalization) uniquely positions them to have certain empathic comprehension and understandings of the transformative justice movement and its view from the non-dominant perspective. *However, if we as Mennonites desire to genuinely engage the injustices surrounding us, we will be required to take stock of our own agency (both personal and structural) in misusing and abusing our dominant power-positions in race, gender, class, and religion resulting in the exploitation and oppression of others.*

Conclusion: An Authentic Mennonite Peace and Justice Witness

As Mennonites, we have often been tempted to use our founding historical myths as proof that somehow we as a people naturally carry the 'DNA' for peace and justice. In our Mennonite Churches and para-church institutions we are often apt to conflate the facilitation of peacebuilding and restorative justice with simply acting compassionately, patiently, and mercifully toward those who offend us. These assumptions are dangerous and intoxicatingly deceitful. The shared formative myths discussed in this chapter can be utilized as the means for nurturing solidarity and unity in and between multiple Mennonite/Brethren groups and their worldwide neighbors, and for these purposes the intergenerational transmission of these "mythico-histories" is commended.

However, if these same myths are transmitted as purity narratives—monolithic stories that are based on 'self' aggrandizement and 'other' degradation—they will lack complexity, nuance, and paradox. Left unchecked, these purity narratives will ultimately contribute to what Benedict Anderson termed *"Imagined Communities,"*[49] a pseudo sense of group affiliation based on an historical revisionist platform that glorifies one people while demonizing another. As Mennonites, our integrity in peace and justice work will depend on our willingness to be transparent with ourselves and others in order to carry a balanced narrative of our history—one checkered with failures and successes.

In summary, this chapter has argued that an authentic Mennonite peace and justice witness in the world will be characterized by at least the following critical points:

- That we acknowledging the complexity of our historical Mennonite identity;
- That we name our power and vulnerability and how we have used these assets for both constructive and destructive purposes alike;
- That we shed the appeal of our philanthropic service ideal that has a tendency to assume that good intentions[50] equal good results[51];
- That we seek to truly understand the motivations and genuinely engage the 'enemy-other' from within and from without; and
- That we engage in creative restorative justice work that integrates the personal and structural components of agency in order for transformation, healing, reparations, and reconciliation to occur on all levels of society.

And as such, we as Mennonites must strive to posture ourselves in 'subversive engagement' with the world—a kind of interactive dance that preserves the best of what it means to be distinct from the world's power systems while at the same time maintaining a relevant advocacy voice and willing service presence that calls forth genuine transformation through our peace and justice actions.

---

49. Anderson, *Imagined Communities*.
50. Illich, "To Hell," 314–20.
51 Anderson, *Do No Harm*.

8

Mennonites and Contemporary Human Rights

LOWELL EWERT

Introduction

TIMOTHY WICHERT, THE AUTHOR of "A Mennonite Human Rights Paradigm?" expressed a profound understatement when he wrote, "Mennonites are uneasy about human rights."[1] Paul Heidebrecht, Director of the Mennonite Central Committee Ottawa office, echoed this same sentiment some 6 years later in 2011 when he wrote that human rights language "is still uncomfortable for many both within and beyond MCC."[2] If the truth be told, I think it is fairer to state that contemporary Mennonite peace theology (if there is such a thing) cannot be reconciled with the contemporary global human rights regime. While publicly supporting initiatives that advance "human rights," few Mennonite authors or peace practitioners demonstrate a deep understanding of international or domestic human rights law and how it impacts each of us every day.

When referenced at all, human rights principles are usually critiqued for their weaknesses, lack of consistent or hypocritical enforcement, or its role in justifying the privilege of the powerful and serving the interests of the strong against the weak. Although international law can provide the

---

1. Wichert, "Human Rights Paradigm?" 331.
2. Heidebrecht, "Human Rights," 1.

weak with a protective shield against abusive power, it is often its role as a sword forcing compliance that is most noted. A perspective such as this that emphasizes the weakness and perceived violence of law in my view undermines its positive potential and makes the Mennonite peace witness far less effective.

The purpose of this chapter is to explore the role that contemporary human rights regimes have in preserving and restoring peace and why this state-centered system makes Mennonites uncomfortable. Rather than abdicating interest in human rights, however, Mennonites have turned their social focus to breathing life into the ultimate long-term objectives of human rights, despite their ambivalence towards the system itself. In this way, Mennonites have tended to advance the goals of human rights even while ignoring the system itself.

Humanitarian and Human Rights System: Summary Overview

Humanitarian and human rights standards are at the heart of the legal regime that operates to protect individuals under international law. Before one can examine Mennonite practice concerning protection of human rights, it is first necessary to identify the sources of human rights standards that are subject to this field of inquiry. The protection of civilians is primarily guaranteed by four areas of law[3]—three of which are internationally based and the fourth rooted in domestic practice—that are often subsumed in an expansive use of the term "protection of human rights." These areas of law are distinct, yet have many complementary and overlapping features. Each includes an "enforcement" regime, though international enforcement is manifested in a very different manner than is the enforcement of domestic civil or criminal law. For the purposes of this chapter, only the three international human rights mechanisms will be discussed below.

International Humanitarian Law

The first of these bodies of law, International Humanitarian Law (IHL) or the laws of war, were established to regulate warfare and minimize killing and destruction to that which is necessary to accomplish military objectives. The goal of this regulation is to make the restoration of peace more likely someday. IHL assumes that war is temporary and not a permanent

---

3. Ratner and Abrams, *Beyond Nuremberg*, 9.

condition. If a particular war will someday end, and peace will be restored, it is logical, IHL would posit, to limit the killing and destruction in order to foster and facilitate full peace once the sounds of war cease. To some extent, IHL operates as an economic or ecological limitation, mandating that only the death and destruction that is truly "necessary" is allowable.

To this end, IHL defines what Mennonite peace theology would find repugnant—addressing the issue of who can be killed, when they can be killed, and how they can be killed. IHL also provides guidance on what can be destroyed, when it can be destroyed, and how it can be destroyed. When the rules are followed, killing and destruction is permitted and is not indictable as a morally prohibited or criminal act. Additionally, unlimited warfare, once commonly accepted, is now absolutely prohibited.[4] Deliberate and widespread killing of the enemy, even of enemy combatants, is forbidden unless there is a valid military objective. IHL is primarily applicable when normal national legal mechanisms break down, i.e., during war or armed conflict when normal rule of law protecting individuals is generally absent.[5] IHL can never be derogated or suspended and essentially serves as the last chance for individuals trapped in war to claim protection under law.

The four Geneva Conventions that comprise the bulk of IHL have been adopted or accepted by every nation on earth.[6] Additional Protocols to the four Geneva Conventions are generally mostly considered binding on nations whether or not ratified, as many provisions from the Protocols are now considered to be customary international law and therefore applicable to all nations. Therefore, one can safely assume that in every situation of armed conflict, the Geneva Conventions and their Protocols are generally applicable. Without going into specific details because that would require a treatise far beyond the scope of this chapter, it is generally fair to simplistically summarize that the impact of IHL on individuals who are not actively engaged in a military conflict is to mandate that they can never be the specific object of military attack and that the civilian infrastructure (food, health systems, electrical grid, sanitation systems, etc.) must also be safeguarded.

In adhering to the rules prescribed by IHL, nations must teach the basic protections contained in IHL to their soldiers, punish those combatants

---

4. This notion explains why many believe that the use of nuclear weapons should always be prohibited as the impact of a nuclear bomb cannot be limited to a specific geographic area and it will have a ripple effect on the environment and community health that could last for hundreds of years. The use of nuclear weapons therefore fails the "war is a temporary" condition test.

5. Bouchet-Saulnier, *Humanitarian Law*, 8.

6. "Development," *International Committee of the Red Cross*.

under their control who violate the rules, and exercise universal jurisdiction over war criminals.⁷ The bottom line is that IHL, if followed, will greatly reduce death and destruction, as it is designed to minimize killing and destruction so that peace can be more easily restored. In an odd sort of way, by regulating war, the law of war is designed to promote peace and especially protect noncombatants from harm.

International Human Rights

Second, in contrast to IHL that seeks to limit armed conflict so that peace can more easily be restored, the modern international human rights system that emerged following the adoption of the Universal Declaration of Human Rights on December 10, 1948 is designed to create conditions that will preserve peace and make war less likely. In other words, human rights and IHL function at different moments in the spectrum between peace and war but are not inconsistent with each other as both "bodies of rules are concerned with the protection of the individual."⁸

Recall that the drafters of the modern legal framework for international human rights had a very practical and concrete reason for advancing the rights paradigm that they did. War could be avoided, the drafters of the Universal Declaration of Human Rights claimed in 1948, if human rights were protected. This moral and pragmatic idealism was evident in the Preamble to the Universal Declaration which boldly proclaimed that "the inherent dignity and of the equal and inalienable rights of all members of the human family is the foundation of freedom, justice and peace in the world," and further that "if man is not to be compelled to have recourse, as a last resort, to rebellion against tyranny and oppression, that human rights should be protected by the rule of law."⁹

---

7. "Under these instruments, it remains the responsibility of States to bring to justice those who commit serious violations of IHL. In some instances, States may be unable and unwilling to prosecute their citizens or other individuals who committed such crimes on their territory or under their jurisdiction. State practice has shown that in these instances, where international courts are unable to act, the exercise of universal jurisdiction by other States can be effective in overcoming this impunity gap. Numerous States have given effect to their obligations in domestic legislation. The exercise of universal jurisdiction may take the form either of the enactment of domestic laws or the investigation and trial of alleged offenders. More than 100 States have vested their domestic courts with universal jurisdiction over serious violations of IHL." "The Scope and Application," *International Committee of the Red Cross*.

8. Greenwood, "Historical Development," 9.

9. "Preamble, Universal Declaration of Human Rights, 1948," 21.

In other words, one of the most significant objectives of the Declaration was to prevent the recurrence of war, which by the mid 1940's had twice in 30 years devastated parts of the world.[10] It is therefore not illogical to conclude that the Declaration represents the clearest and most succinct political statement ever created by the world political community on the conditions that form the necessary foundation for peace. Respect for human rights was seen to be the vaccine against war.

The results of the development of this vaccine speak for themselves. Contrary to expectations, the Universal Declaration, which lacked a formal enforcement mechanism, unleashed a yearning for human rights that has not yet abated. The Declaration's seemingly toothless unenforceable character has influenced over 1,000 treaties, declarations, multinational accords, or other standards that have created more specific expectations or obligations.[11] If this outcome defines toothless impact—the common critique of the human rights system—bring on the figurative dental extractions! I challenge you to find one other international legal document that has had this same broad ripple effect as it pertains to the protection of individuals under law.

Those instruments that have become human rights treaties create explicit legal duties and responsibilities that have fundamentally redefined a nation's relationship to its citizenry. These treaties set standards for almost every area of life today—pertaining to children, economic relations, the free practice of religion, women's rights, the rights of persons with disabilities, and migrant workers, just to name a few.[12] Through these documents, the limitation of state power through human rights instruments now impacts political affairs, economic relations, and social and cultural practices. And all this happened since 1948. The speed of this change in unleashing the

---

10. Morsink, *Human Rights*, 36.

11. Taken from the course description of "United Nations Human Rights System," taught by Michael O'Flaherty and Sarah Joseph, American University, Washington College of Law, Washington, D.C. http://www.wcl.american.edu/hracademy/courses.cfm#UN. Also, see the UN online data base of 750 documents and peace agreements at http://peacemaker.un.org/.

12. To name a few specific treaties that illustrate the diversity of the expansion of the human rights movement, see Convention on the Rights of the Child; Covenant on Economic, Social and Cultural Rights; Covenant on Civil and Political Rights; Convention on the Elimination of All Forms of Religious Discrimination; Convention on the Elimination of All Forms of Discrimination Against Women; Convention Against Torture and Other Cruel, Inhumane or Degrading Treatment or Punishment; Convention on the Protection of the Rights of All Migrant Workers; Convention on the Rights of Persons with Disabilities; Convention for the Protection of All Persons From Enforced Disappearance.

yearning for human rights is breathtaking especially since the shortcomings of human rights are so well known and so often emphasized.

What this dramatic appeal of human rights has shown is that the perceived Achilles heel of the Universal Declaration—its vague and non-specific and apparently unenforceable language—has in retrospect turned out to be it most notable strength. As the Holocaust survivor and former member of the International Court of Justice Thomas Buergenthal has noted:

> The great irony here is that the Universal Declaration was drafted in hortatory language designed to emphasize its non-binding character because many member states of the United Nations did not want a binding legal document. Their governments no doubt believed that 'mere words' could do no harm, provided they did not impose legal obligations. How wrong they were! It is precisely the Declaration's language—at once eloquent, expansive and simple—that allowed it to express unequivocal universal truths in words human beings all over the world could understand and wanted to hear. No formal legal instrument could have achieved that result and had quite the same inspirational impact on the human rights movement.[13]

It is because of this flexibility and fluidity that the "Universal Declaration of Human Rights has become the most important legal document in the history of the world,"[14] as the Catholic law professor Father Robert Drinan once put it. This vagueness has allowed the Declaration to become a living and breathing instrument, not one that is static and locked into one historical moment. It can, and has, adapted with the times, resulting in new expressions of rights that no one had originally anticipated.

The "peace" impact of human rights is mind-boggling. If we take a historical view of what human rights have accomplished, we can see that how individuals are viewed in international human rights law has changed more in the last 65 years than probably in the previous 800 years since the Magna Carta. Before the Nuremberg War Crimes Tribunal and the adoption of the Universal Declaration of Human Rights in 1948, the prevailing view of international law was that the rule of a king was mostly absolute—a king not only had a divine right to rule, but also had a right to behave monstrously toward his subjects should he so chose. This notion has been forever discredited. The dignity of all is now front and center of all legal international political discourse.

---

13. Buergenthal, "Human Rights Revolution," 91.
14. Drinan, *Mobilization*, 9.

International Criminal Prosecution

Third, international criminal prosecution was initiated for the purpose of "building peace through accountability."[15] The first international criminal courts established to prosecute the gravest crimes committed during the specific circumstances of the Rwanda Genocide, the mass killings in the former Yugoslavia, and in Sierra Leone, eventually led to the creation of a more permanent body in 2002, the International Criminal Court (ICC) that had broader and ongoing jurisdiction. Rather than being limited in scope, time, and place to the above three circumstances, the ICC was given general jurisdiction over matters pertaining to treaty members. It should be noted that the ICC is a court of last resort, only acting if local authorities are unwilling or unable to act.[16]

It is clear from the language used by the United Nations in debating the establishment of the above courts that criminal accountability was not seen as a mechanism for revenge, but rather as one for peacebuilding. In the case of the International Tribunal for the Former Yugoslavia (ICTY), the UN Security Council stated that "a credible system of justice and accountability for the very serious crimes committed there would end impunity and would contribute to the process of national reconciliation and to the restoration and maintenance of peace . . ."[17]

Others have also recognized the same and explored additional benefits of international criminal prosecution in promoting peace:

> Among the many reasons given for the ability of international criminal courts to assist in building peace is that they contribute to a process of national reconciliation by substituting individual guilt for collective guilt, provide justice for victim communities, re-establish the legal order in post-conflict environments, provide a forum for truth-telling that creates an authoritative and shared record of history, deter future crimes by strengthening legal enforcement procedures, and raise the normative level of acceptable behaviour. Also, the reasoning continues, punishment of criminal actions contributes to establishing 'real peace'

---

15. Brubacher, "Striking a Balance," 9.

16. "The ICC is a court of last resort. It will not act if a case is investigated or prosecuted by a national judicial system unless the national proceedings are not genuine, for example if formal proceedings were undertaken solely to shield a person from criminal responsibility. In addition, the ICC only tries those accused of the gravest crimes. "ICC at a glance," *International Criminal Court.*

17. SC Res. 1315, UN SCOR, 4186th mtg., UN Doc. S/RES/1315 (2000).

by aiding the national transition process and restoring social equilibrium through the ability to impose the rule of law.[18]

As one can see from the above rationale for establishing the various international courts, restoring peace has been a significant goal of international prosecution. While skeptics may claim that international prosecution is too far removed in time and distance to have a deterrent effect, it is worth noting the statement by Louise Arbour, then Chief Prosecutor of the International Court for the Former Yugoslavia, that the actions of Serbian President Slobodan Milosevic indicted by the ICTY confirm the power of international criminal prosecution. In referring to Milosevic's defiance and unwillingness to respect the rights of Kosovars in the face of intense NATO bombing, Arbour noted that "after 80 days of bombing, he was still defiant; after eight days of the indictment he capitulated."[19]

The Human Rights and Humanitarian Law Dilemma for Mennonites

Despite its focus on protecting individuals from harm, the international legal regime described above has not been enthusiastically embraced by Mennonites. The stories of the Mennonite experience told in other chapters of this book help to explain why this may be. From their earliest encounters with state, our religious ancestors experienced a state that was willing to do anything to protect its power. The state was not an institution that could be trusted to live up to its commitments or that concerned itself primarily with safeguarding the dignity of the masses. This indictment of the state was as true for Anabaptists in the late 1500s in Europe as it was in Russia in the early 1900s. As a result, the world in which Mennonite pacifist theology emerged and has grown was not one that was conducive to the development of a positive view of law or the state. It therefore makes sense why Mennonites may be uneasy, uncomfortable, or ambivalent about human rights and IHL.

The advent of the modern international legal system has not successfully broken through this Mennonite resistance to understanding law as a substantial source of peace despite the fact that the modern-day legal system rests on a very different foundation than that which our forbearers encountered. When we compare the notion of the state when Mennonite

---

18. Brubacher, "Striking a Balance," 9–10. The specific sources documenting this statement by Brubacher are not included in this footnote.

19. "Interview: Tribunal Chief," *Institute for War & Peace Reporting*.

pacifist theology was forged to that of today, we are not comparing apples and apples. We are more realistically comparing a paper airplane to a space shuttle. The complexity, cooperation, regulation, and resources needed to sustain a modern state bear no comparison to that of feudal systems. Mennonite peace principles were not forged in an environment that reflects the prevailing international legal jurisprudence of today. Thus, often Mennonite principles ignore the positive potential of international human rights and humanitarian law, or inadvertently undermine them by assuming that they have limited potential.

There are indeed significant problems with the current system but this does not mean that it holds no promise. Key obvious problems include, first, that these mechanisms are all far too slow and removed to be able to react in time to protect individuals under immediate threat. They are mechanisms of last resort. If victims trapped in circumstances of injustice or war wait for the international machinery of justice to be activated, it will be a long, lonely, and painful wait. In point in fact, "the voice of the victims usually fades long before justice can hear it."[20]

Second, all these mechanisms rely on a strong state, able and required if need be, to use coercion and force to mandate the protection of human rights. Violence is not avoided by the human rights systems, and only illegal violence is prohibited. Third, all these mechanisms assume that primary responsibility for the guarantee of human rights lies with states. States are usually the source of most violations of human rights and thus we see that states are both the source of the problem and, viewed through the lens of international law, the solution for resolving human rights issues. This seems inconsistent and prone to hypocritical manipulation.

Fourth, while IHL seeks to limit damage and killing, it does not prohibit it. Advocating that parties in conflict adhere to IHL therefore puts pacifists in the seemingly untenable position of only objecting to unlawful killing and destruction, not all killing and destruction. Lastly, the human rights system does not require that everyone have complete equality, but rather that minimal standards of rights be guaranteed. This minimal guarantee makes it more possible that the dignity of all is advanced, but it does not by itself ensure that life will be without challenges for everyone. The poor will still be with us. Human rights alone will never create a utopia, but without human rights infusing our global modern nation state system, a utopia by other complementary means is impossible. This reality of the weakness of law does not mean that human rights and humanitarian law are not essential for peace, and this is where Mennonites offer much to the

20. Bouchet-Saulnier. *Humanitarian Law*, 8.

world even while only ambivalently advocating for enforcement of human rights and IHL. Let me explain.

Although human rights were originally envisioned to offer a vaccine against war, they were never intended, in my view, to be all that matter. The illustration of a building explains why human rights are insufficient to fully ensure dignity for all. Imagine the physical characteristics of a house in a cold Canadian spring and how they may be a metaphor for law. The rigid structure of inflexible law represented by human rights provides a roof against the driving hail of persecution, the walls protect against arbitrary violence, the floor guards against the seeping damp of discrimination, the windows allow a view into the practice of others, and the door a means to explore new venues.

What the house can't do, and the minimum "floor" of law usually fails to do, is ensure that the occupants love each other, show compassion to each other, care for each other, want the best for each other, or to truly be restored to each other when harm is done.[21] One cannot legislatively mandate care, concern, or compassion. Yet these intangible attributes of caring are what truly affirms the highest level of dignity implied by respect for human rights, not just tolerance, of all. But take away the protection of the individual that the house figuratively provides, and life is indeed, as Thomas Hobbes once suggested, nasty, brutish, and short. In these circumstances, all the care, concern and compassion in the world won't displace discrimination, persecution, and victimization through arbitrary violence.

The most valuable aspect of respect for human rights is that it mandates minimal conditions that make it possible for people of conscience to work towards that goal of full dignity. This goal absolutely cannot be accomplished if individualistic, atomistic, human rights are not respected. By empowering individualism, communalism—or responsibility to each other—is enabled. As Michael Edwards has so compellingly explained by describing how communities work together as part of civil society to accomplish this objective,

> [a]t its best, civil society is the story of ordinary people living extraordinary lives through their relationships with each other, driven forward by a vision of the world that is ruled by love and compassion, non-violence and solidarity. At its worst, it is little more than a slogan, and a confusing one at that, but there is

---

21. Louis Henkin so eloquently stated this principle in relation to how human rights intersect with religion: "Religion will continue to reject human rights as a total ideology. It sees human rights—cold rights—do not provide warmth, belonging, fitting, significance, do not exclude the need for love, friendship, family, charity, sympathy, devotion, sanctity, or for expiation, atonement, forgiveness." Henkin. *Age of Rights*, 186.

no need to focus on the worst of things and leave behind the best. Warts and all, the idea of civil society remains compelling, not because it provides the tidiest of explanations but because it speaks to the best in us, and calls on the best in us to respond in kind.[22]

Mennonite Responses as an Expression of Human Rights

Now here is the odd part. Although it is my contention that Mennonites do not have a theology that embraces their involvement in advancing and enforcing human rights or humanitarian law, and they cannot reconcile these international enforcement systems with their view of peace and pacifism, Mennonites have invested an enormous amount of energy into breathing life into what was intended to be the end goal of human rights. Human rights and IHL principles were never envisioned as the end game. They were instead designed to be a means towards an end—creating conditions that lead to peace in the first place (human rights) and restoring peace if violent conflict broke out (IHL). For example, if human rights were respected, so the drafters of the Universal Declaration of Human Rights believed, there would not be war. The conditions that lead to war, as inferred in the Declaration, include, for example, lacking enough food, health care, education, leisure, work, the right to marry, and basic civil and political rights.

Peace is therefore essentially broadly "defined" by international human rights law in a way that resonates with Mennonite practice. This perspective can be illustrated by applying a theory developed by William Ury in a way that he probably never envisioned but that I think is appropriate to understanding the impact of Mennonite social engagement. Ury suggests that there are ten roles a bystander can play to *prevent* issues from growing into violence, *resolve* conflicts that may erupt if prevention is unsuccessful, or manage and *contain* conflicts that cannot be resolved.[23] Ury proposes that those who work in the preventative role can do three things. First, they can provide those essentials to persons who have unmet needs. Second, the preventer can also teach skills to those who lack skills, and, third, he or she can build bridges between estranged peoples. If the preventative role is successful, latent tensions are less likely to deteriorate into violence.

If the underlying latent tensions cannot be prevented, the next best approach is attempting to resolve them by four actions: mediating, arbitrating,

---

22. Edwards. *Civil Society*, 125.
23. Ury. *Getting to Peace*, particularly chapters 5, 6, and 7.

equalizing, or healing. If resolving doesn't work, there is still one last chance to avoid violence, that is, to contain it through three actions that act as a witness to inhibit the eruption or manifestation of violence, act as a referee to ensure that if conflict does erupt disputants still play by the rules, or lastly, act as peacekeepers and step in to attempt to break up the dispute. Ury suggests that the third party can play each of these ten roles and each can be an effective antidote that renders the outbreak of violence less likely. In other words, the bystander, who may not normally have any formal or legal responsibility, has an enormous opportunity to be impactful and prevent violence with acts that affirm dignity, which is the goal of international human rights law.

These opportunities of the third party, which need not be a state actor, are what I think round out the hard legal obligations of nation states to respect human rights. The ten roles balance, or bring practical life to, the valuable rigid role of law by suggesting duties that can be carried out through civil society by ordinary people doing extraordinary things because they work together. When civil society assumes the duty of functioning in these ten roles, it profoundly achieves the true intent of human rights principles by affirming the dignity of all people. And it does this in a way that often cannot be mandated by law.

These duties challenge an individualistic rights-centric society to think about others. And by doing so, our communities and nations are radically changed. Jean Vanier captures this idea well: "A society that encourages us to break open the shell of selfishness and self-centeredness contains the seeds of a society where people are honest, truthful and loving. A society can function well only if those within are concerned, not only with their own needs or the needs of those who immediately surround them, but by the needs of all, that is to say, by the common good and the family of nations."[24] But as stated above, it is almost impossible for civil society to fulfill this role if basic, individualistic, atomistic rights are not respected. The human rights and duties debate is not either/or. It's both/and. And interestingly, the successful achievement or enjoyment of rights and the fruits of duties is dependent on the success of the other.

To more fully apply Ury's proposed ten roles[25] to Mennonite practice, consider how:

- We play a role to prevent violence when:
    1. The frustrated needs that people desperately seek are *provided* and they have access to food, clothing, hope, opportunity, love,

24. Vanier. *Becoming Human*, 34.
25. Ury, *Getting to Peace*, 191.

acceptance, and affirmation of dignity. When we support food banks, shelters for abused women, or persons who have no homes, or encourage someone, open a door of opportunity, stand up for someone being bullied, and tell someone that they are loved, respected, and valued, we are providing an essential need. While human rights principles would affirm all of these ideals, the law is powerless to mandate many of these acts of provision.

2. *Teachers* help others learn a new way, a new language, a new skill. When we walk with new refugees learning a new way of life, teaching in our schools, mentoring someone how to navigate through a difficult patch in his or her life, we are teaching skills that will benefit them for a lifetime. Teaching involves far more than what happens in our state sponsored educational systems. Think of the educational agencies, training programs, advising and counseling services, and refugee settlement agencies, to name a few, sponsored by Mennonite agencies.

3. *Bridge-builders* introduce new people to each other, take the mystery out of new cultures and traditions, open up a window to the Other, and create a stronger community that ties us all together. We are less likely to become alienated or susceptible to factionalism when we are more fully connected to others through, for example, the work of interfaith groups, peacebuilding programs, and international development practitioners, which forges a sense of community where it did not previously exist.

- We play a role to resolve matters that if unresolved may lead to violence when:

  1. A *mediator* helps persons in conflict see a different way through it and helps disputants not just resolve conflicts, but rather to transform relationships in the process—something that no state sponsored legal system can ever be expected to do. Think of local mediation, conciliation and community justice groups in your community, or the other individuals or groups that help people find a way through conflict.

  2. The *arbiter* helps sort out the rules. Think of advocacy groups such as refugee resettlement groups that assist vulnerable newcomers to resettle in a foreign land and restart their lives. Or the dozens of groups that advocate for persons with mental health problems, Huntingtons, Alzeheimer's, Crohns, or others who have health, social, or psychological needs. The impact of this human touch on

hurting people as they are guided through the difficult iceberg-filled waters of our legal and governmental systems to acquire the resources they need cannot be underestimated.

3. The *equalizer* walks alongside the vulnerable, perhaps speaking when the voiceless cannot or the timid are too afraid, and ensures that their concerns are heard. Organizations that work with victims of crime or those who have experienced loss due to the irresponsibility of drunk drivers illustrate how equalizers enable victims to become more fully restored.

4. *Healers* support and encourage each other and counsel or assist persons who are going through a difficult patch in life.

- If conditions that, if left unchecked, may lead to violence cannot be prevented or resolved, all is not lost:

    1. The *witness* can still warn the perpetrators of injustice that someone is watching. Our newspapers, magazines, bloggers, writers who send letters to the editor, or others who we may sometime consider to be a public pest pricking our collective conscience when we would rather they be quiet and leave us alone, let the public know that someone is watching. There is nothing more powerful in limiting evil than for it to know that what they are doing is being observed, written down, and that someday, someone will use this information to hold them accountable. For evil to flourish, it needs the ability to hide or deflect responsibility. Holding the flashlight of public awareness on what evil prefers to do in the back ally and in secret dungeons often limits the harm that will be done.

    2. The *referee* can insist that all parties know what the rules are, even if the rules are being violated. Human rights groups that insist that governments live up to their obligations in times of war or peace, and often shame them into more humane practice, illustrate the power of non-governmental civil society. Fair Trade groups that attempt to challenge the dominant economic system to live up to its ideals also act as a referee.

    3. And the *peacekeeper* can try to break up the fight. While fewer civil society organizations function in this capacity, the dozens of organizations that make up the accompaniment movement, in which civil peacekeepers get in between those initiating harm and its likely victims, are saving lives and minimizing rights violations in the process.

Conclusion

What is fascinating to me is that in every single role described above, one can identify multiple Mennonite-run or -inspired entities that are fulfilling one or more of these functions. Mennonites may be uneasy, uncomfortable, or reluctant to embrace an international legal system that freely uses force or coercion to enforce peace, but there has been no reluctance or ambivalence in advancing the ideals of human rights by elevating human dignity in a way that complements the global systems and makes peace more possible and violence less likely. Food, jobs, education, advocacy, and opportunity are all more possible to marginalized peoples because of the work of Mennonites and Mennonite agencies. The world is a better and more humane place because of this work.

But it alone is insufficient. It is important to remember that only the rule of law can create global systems that create conditions in which it is possible to affirm the dignity of all. These rigid legal systems limit power, but by themselves cannot create love, acceptance and community. Imagine what life would be like—how impoverished our communities, nations, and world would be—if there were no Mennonite civil society organizations complementing and breathing life into the specific, detailed, and minimalist human rights principles.

And an interesting thing happens when Mennonites working collectively do this. In addition to these direct services described above, civil society also sends a ripple effect throughout the other two sectors of society—government and business—and starts to transform these sectors too. Through the work of civil society engaged in these roles, new ideas are tested, concepts developed, and solutions discovered to common problems.[26] Some argue that the human rights movement grew out of a demand from civil society. So too did the environmental, ethical trade, some of the corporate responsibility, fair trade, and restorative justice movements.

Once a solution is tested by civil society, its strengths proven, and weaknesses identified and corrected, these ideas can be more easily replicated elsewhere and picked up by government. Many criminal courts now routinely allow some form of restorative justice to complement or even replace their judgment. Environmental protection is now a key component of many legislative acts. Business today is also very cognizant of public

---

26. "Civil society is humanity's conscience, its early-warning system, and its laboratory. It is where the world's thoughtful, committed citizens go about the business of changing things for the better. Civil society makes a transformation to sustainability possible, because it is the place where humanity's best traits come forth, most strongly and most reliably." AtKisson. "Why Civil Society," 289.

concerns related to ethical trade, ethical investing, and their responsibilities in society. It is in these ways of testing, prodding, and advocating, that civil society has fundamentally altered government and business. Mennonites have been one of many important influences in prodding these changes.

9

Mennonite Women
Making Positive Peace

MARLENE EPP

Introduction

WAR IS BAD FOR women, as numerous scholars on gender and war have shown. But war also, ironically, can be good for women, at least in the short term when it loosens rigid gender norms and creates openings for women as community leaders, economic actors, and political citizens. This has been true for women across the time and space of history. Similarly, processes of peacemaking are largely positive for women, but this too can have mixed outcomes.[1] Within the Mennonite context historically, while women were (and are) full participants in Mennonite peace work, they have also experienced the negative impact of this involvement.

Despite the pervasiveness of the peace position in Mennonite self-understanding, at least in the era of origins and in the last half-century, analyses of this stance have rarely been gendered in any way. This chapter will explore the ways in which Mennonite women have made and built peace, historically and in the recent past. While their communal religious beliefs clearly positioned them to be advocates of peace and nonviolence as opposed to war and violence, the gender norms of that community also

---

1. For analyses of the dichotomous impact of war and peace on women, see many of the essays in Cohn, editor, *Women and Wars*.

influenced how they would live that out. I propose that, while North American Mennonite women were acting out 'positive' peacemaking through their collective work to relieve suffering caused by warfare, they also experienced the direct impact of a nonresistant stance that was limited in its scope of understanding with regard to nonviolent living. For instance, Mennonite peace teachings rarely made connections between the non-bearing of weapons and nonviolence in families and households where women and children might be victims of violence. In this sense, traditions of Anabaptist-Mennonite peacemaking—expressed mainly as nonresistance—did not serve as defining models for how women should live in the face of societal violence. Most of my examples are drawn from the Canadian context, although I have attempted to go beyond this context as well.

Positive Peacemaking: Relief to the Suffering

Through their history, when confronted with and in the midst of wars waged by states, Mennonites took their cues directly from the New Testament scriptures, believing that warfare is wrong because it is contrary to Jesus' command to love one's enemies. Historically, the most concrete expression of this belief was an unwillingness to participate in secular warfare, and thus much effort was expended in securing exemption from military service and alternate status as 'conscientious objectors' (COs) for Mennonite men. The fact that women were not conscripted into the military, however, meant that women from the historic peace church traditions have by and large been left out of the great stories of nonresistant expression. As one woman said: "Because the destiny of the Mennonites revolved around the way sons were involved in [conscientious objection] and not the way the women experienced the truth of scripture, women's contribution was not as significant."[2] In the same vein, historian M.J. Heisey offered that, "Nonresistance, then, reflected not only the goal of living in a new kingdom but also unequal power among the people pursuing it."[3]

It would seem that Mennonite women had to live by, even if they didn't help define, certain Mennonite ideologies. Magdalene Redekop expressed the dilemma in this way: "It was not women who had to think about being conscientious objectors to war. My father did not quiz prospective daughters-in-law on their attitudes to pacifism. In what sense, then, can a woman be a Mennonite?"[4] In many respects, women were historically excluded

2. Wiebe, "Images and Realities," 27.
3. Heisey, *Peace and Persistence*, 19.
4. Redekop, "Through the Mennonite," 239.

from participating, except in a gendered supportive manner, in discourse regarding possibly the primary signifier over time of what it meant to be a Mennonite.

That women wanted to construct a discourse on nonresistance and conscientious objection that included them is reflected in an article by an American Mennonite woman whose sentiments were likely shared by her Canadian sisters during the Second World War. After listing twenty different methods that women could contribute to the CO cause, she said,

> Have you ever wished that you could prove your convictions on peace and war as your boyfriend, husband, brother, or son has? . . . Girls and women of the Mennonite church groups! Our Christian responsibility, to our God, the world, the church, our boys in [alternative service] is tremendous. The challenge is before us; the projects await us; the question is, do we as girls and women want to serve?[5]

Clearly, Mennonite women wanted to give their own voice to the peace position held by their church. As they were excluded from the interrogation put to their menfolk regarding nonresistance—what the men 'would not do' during war—women turned the question around and considered what they 'would do' in the midst of conflict. What they did was offer relief—material and moral—to those who suffered from the violence of war. This positive peacemaking took different tangible forms, depending on the historic time and place. For instance, Jonathan Seiling's original research on Mennonite women in Upper Canada (present-day Ontario) during the war of 1812 revealed that they "fed and housed many different kinds of people [British, Canadian, American, First Nations] during the war. Some were potential enemies but they tried to love them as neighbours."[6]

Women from historic peace churches in Canada, including the Mennonites, experienced wartime shifts in gender roles that closely paralleled the experience of their mainstream counterparts. Indeed, women found themselves supporting the 'peace effort' in much the same way that other Canadian women were supporting the 'war effort,' by rationing, preparing care packages for civilians and soldiers overseas, and entering the waged workforce. On the one hand, wars often meant economic difficulty for women because their CO menfolk might spend significant periods of time away from the household, either to perform public service work or to spend time in prison. During both world wars, many women took responsibility for managing family farms or took the unprecedented step of entering the

---

5. Ramseyer, "Will Ye Heed the Call?" 1; quoted in Epp, "Nonconformity," 68.
6. Seiling, *Feeding*.

paid workforce. Unlike wives and mothers of soldiers, however, CO women who lived in urban settings especially, and those whose plain dress identified their religious affiliation, frequently felt public censure because their menfolk were perceived to be shirking their duty to the country. The female relatives of conscientious objectors stepped outside of traditional gender roles for a short time, yet without the kind of propagandistic or material support lent to Canadian women who supported the war effort.[7]

Within certain Mennonite subgroups, a distinct and plain dress code became a particular issue during the First World War, as women were instructed to carry the banner of nonconformity for a church that was seeking to separate itself even further from a society that was hostile to its nonparticipation in military service. In this sense, women were literally 'wearing' and embodying the Mennonite peace position through their plain cape-style dresses and mandatory head coverings.[8] In fact, historian Lucille Marr states that Mennonite women's pacifism was as "non-verbal as their required clothing illustrate[d]."[9] It was during the First World War in which Mennonite women began to ask about the parameters of their own involvement in the war effort. While they were not called up for military service—as only men faced conscription beginning in August 1917—they nevertheless wondered whether other forms of labor constituted support for the war. For instance, Mary Wismer, a Mennonite woman studying to be a dietitian in 1917, grappled with the fact that her training might draw her into service in one of the many military hospitals that were being established in Canada to care for veterans of the war; she acknowledged that such work was attractive because of the pay. She wrote about her dilemma to Mennonite Bishop S. F. Coffman who encouraged her to continue her studies but consider work that would not "restrict" her Christian faith.[10] She was not alone in wondering what types of non-weapon carrying activity nevertheless represented support for the war effort. Yet, these were questions that were not fore-fronted by Mennonites in wars of the past.

Importantly, both world wars prompted a new burst in activity of material relief for war sufferers. Mennonite women, and others from historic peace churches, expressed their nonresistance primarily by providing material relief, both to their own men in work camps for conscientious objectors at home in the Second World War and to war sufferers overseas during both

7. For a fuller discussion, see Epp, "Alternative Service," 139–58.

8. For a discussion of the dress issue as it emerged amongst Ontario Mennonites, see Epp, "Carrying the Banner," 237–57.

9. Marr, "Paying," 272.

10. Letter exchange between Mary Wismer and S. F. Coffman. 1917, S. F. Coffman Collection, Mennonite Archives of Ontario [hereafter MAO].

world wars. For instance, Mennonite women at First Mennonite Church in Kitchener, Ontario (renamed thus from Berlin Mennonite Church after the city Berlin became Kitchener in 1916) agreed to do "our bit" in response to the devastation in Europe at war's end.[11] This primarily meant knitting and rolling bandages for the Red Cross, and sewing clothing and comforters to be sent overseas. Near the war's end, Mennonites and other peace churches in Ontario decided to provide to the Canadian government a "memorial gift for war relief." This led to the creation, in 1918, of the Non-Resistant Relief Organization, which would eventually raise approximately $80,000 for the relief of war sufferers, much of which was material aid such as clothing and blankets that was sewn or gathered by women.[12]

The organizational framework was thus in place for the longer tragedy that was the Second World War. Not unlike women with men in the forces, pacifist women prepared care packages with writing paper, envelopes, socks and gloves, and home baking for their own men in CO camps. In the United States, a church-administered work program for COs called Civilian Public Service (CPS) also drew women into supportive labour as nutritionists, nurses, cooks and in other roles within the 151 CPS camps established across the country. Wives and girlfriends of COs also uprooted themselves to be nearer to their menfolk in CPS camps, and together with those employed at the camps, were seen as morale-boosters and nurturers. Those involved with CPS developed vocational aspirations and also a "sense of purpose and usefulness in time of war."[13] In her analysis of nonresistance in the history of the Brethren in Christ, a related peace church, M.J. Heisey observed that for some women, the belief was "not so much proclaimed as expressed in the massive work of nurturing those under [their] care... reflecting old and ongoing gender expectations."[14]

In Canada, the Alternative Service (AS) work program for COs was government-run and so women were not as involved in the actual program as were American women with CPS. Yet, they supported and encouraged conscientious objection in a variety of other ways. In keeping with their gendered roles of nurturing and caring, women declared a non-verbal pacifist stance by regularly sending care packages and letters to their own sons and husbands in Alternative Service camps during the Second World War. For instance, Nancy Nahrgang Snyder, an Ontario woman who "thrived on

11. Minutes, First Mennonite Church Women's Society, Apr 3/18, III-12.1.8.2 Ladies Aid Minute Book 1916–1923 /2, MAO.

12. On the history of the NRRO, see Marr, *Transforming Power*; and Epp-Tiessen, *Mennonite Central Committee*; Steiner, *In Search of Promised Lands*.

13. Goossen, *Women*, 93.

14. Heisey, *Peace and Persistence*, 136.

giving reports," corresponded regularly with men who were in AS camps and then read letters and offered reports to her home congregation as a way of maintaining awareness of the distant COs.[15] And while most of the official advocacy for military exemption came from male leaders, on occasion women spoke out on behalf of their church's peace stance. For instance, when the war broke out in 1939, Elizabeth B. Toews, who had sons of conscription age, wrote to the federal government reminding it of its promises of military exemption. Apparently her letter was returned with the request that it be written in English.[16] A 1945 women's conference, held concurrently with the Conference of Mennonites in Canada sessions, featured a "timely paper" on nonresistance by Mrs. P.P. Rempel, who stressed "that it was an issue not only for men but also for girls." Among a number of recommendations that emphasized teaching peace principles, Rempel suggested that the General Conference peace committee include at least one woman.[17] In one family, it was apparently the mother who counselled her son, not yet a church member, that his only grounds for seeking military exemption were that he was German and couldn't join the army and fight his German brothers.[18]

While Mennonite men expressed their conscientious objector status in various work commitments or else entered the military, women found expanded opportunities in the paid workforce, as was true for Canadian women generally during the Second World War. Increasing labour shortages, wartime production needs, and a massive government advertising campaign summoning women to work, meant that in 1944—the peak of wartime employment—one-third of all Canadian women over the age of fifteen were in the paid labour force.[19] Married women and women with children, in particular, represented a new working cohort. Wartime industry and labour demands definitely meant that Mennonite women, like other Canadian women, entered the urban and rural workforce as never before. Furthermore, they could be found in traditionally male sectors of labour, such as in agriculture and heavy industry.

In a style that echoed much of the propaganda surrounding women's wartime roles, a 1942 article in a Toronto newspaper featured a Mennonite-owned farm north of the city where the Wideman sisters were helping to

---

15. Roth, *Willing Service*, 168.
16. Plett, *Johann Plett*, 197.
17. Patkau, *Canadian Women*, 102.
18. Koop, compiler, and Dyck, editor, "Band Plays On," 60.
19. Prentice, *et al.*, *Canadian Women*, 311. For a detailed study of Canadian women's workforce and military participation in World War II, see Pierson, *'They're Still.'*

run the farm in the absence of male hands. Entitled "Girls Man the Farm Front," the article described how Anna alone plowed 120 acres while her sister Ella "did a man's job daily."[20] In cities like Kitchener, Ontario, with a large population of Mennonites and a significant rubber industry, it was inevitable that Mennonite women would thus find themselves working in jobs that assisted the war effort. This irony, although rarely addressed at the time, was not lost on Erma Cressman, wife of a conscientious objector, who obtained a job at B. F. Goodrich making aviation boots during the war. Erma's reasoning was that she could not live on the fifty cents a day that her husband earned as a CO, though she recalled that "there was a lot of criticism at the plant" and people asked her, "How could I work on war material when my husband was a C.O.?" To which she responded, "I had no other support and no Mennonite offered me an alternate job."[21] Her dilemma echoed that of Mary Wismer's during the previous global war: how to support oneself and one's family while also supporting the peace position of one's church.

The absence of men, performing either alternative or military service, also created vacancies in non-labour sectors that shifted normative gender roles during wartime. In educational institutions, for instance, there was a dramatic flip-flop in the sex ratio, thus creating more space and allowance for women to pursue high school and postsecondary education—an example of war's ironic benefit to women. The lack of menfolk placed other kinds of demands on women and nurtured independence regarding other skills. For instance, with fewer men in their households, women learned to drive in greater numbers. These trends were evident in the United States as well, where, as Beth Graybill has demonstrated, the war years "provided a significant watershed for women" in terms of their roles within wider spheres of activity.[22]

In entering the paid workforce, relocating themselves and their children across the country and having greater access to education and other opportunities during the Second World War, Mennonite women were departing from normative gender roles in a number of ways. They were also struggling, if not consciously, with the 'positive' impact of war that such gender deconstruction could mean for women. Scenarios that saw their church leaders and menfolk focused on exemption from military service, while not considering that other non-conscripted activity was arguably a contribution to the war effort, put women in the contradictory position of responding to the exigencies of the day by taking up new opportunities to

---

20. "Girls Man the Farm Front," *Star Weekly*, 14 August 1943.
21. Harder, *Risk and Endurance*, 103.
22. Graybill, "Writing Women," 240.

exercise their skills and abilities, even if that meant participation in the war effort.

Women's nonresistant activity during the two world wars was displayed most prominently in their relief efforts on behalf of war sufferers. During both global conflicts, but especially during the Second World War, many Canadian women left the confines of home and threw their hearts and hands into voluntary organizations such as the Red Cross, International Order of the Daughters of the Empire, the Salvation Army, and Women's Institutes across the country. Whether it was to campaign for Victory Bond contributions, to organize blood banks for the Red Cross, to coordinate the collection of waste products for wartime recycling, or to individually sew and knit for relief of soldiers and civilians, the volunteer effort of Canadian women was perhaps their greatest contribution to the country during wartime. Mennonite women's organizations also received a boost during the wars as women gathered to prepare clothing, bandages, and other relief goods to be sent directly overseas, or they held sales and other events to raise money to support the activities of Mennonite organizations engaged in wartime relief.

For many Mennonite women, collecting used and sewing new clothing and quilts and knitting socks and bandages became their unique contribution to their country. In 1939 women in Ontario organized local sewing circles as part of the Nonresistant Relief Sewing Organization, an indication that they themselves viewed their material labour in the context of a faith principle. In describing the material assistance and moral support given to conscientious objectors in camps and war sufferers overseas, Clara Snider, the secretary of this organization said: "We are representing a common cause and stand for the same principles . . . United we stand, divided we fall."[23] Even while standing for a common cause, men and women expressed their peace position in differing ways. As historian Lucille Marr argues, "In marked contrast to Mennonite men, women could serve their country in socially acceptable ways, all the while upholding their convictions."[24]

Between the years 1941 and 1944, approximately $71,000 worth of clothing was sent under the auspices of Mennonite Central Committee from Canada to England, the main destination for relief supplies during the actual war years. Mennonite relief workers in England suggested that women in North America adopt the slogan "Non-Resistant Needles Knitting for the Needy" to underscore the "magnificent opportunity" that their

---

23. Clara Snider to Workers of the Nonresistant Relief Organization, 16 December 1942. John Coffman letters, MAO.

24. Marr, *Transforming Power*, 42.

work represented.[25] A 1940 report on Mennonite Central Committee's relief clothing program for war sufferers in Europe described the relationship between relief and peace thus: "In the face of war's havoc there is need for a positive testimony of peace, love, and compassion toward the suffering."[26]

The positive peacemaking was literally 'embodied' as numerous young women went overseas themselves, during and after the war, to work in orphanages, distribute food and clothing, and work at refugee centres operated by government and church agencies. Arlene Sitler of Ontario was one woman who took up this opportunity: she affirmed the material relief provided by Canadian Mennonite women, suggesting that through their giving, "the bonds of peace and Christian fellowship may become stronger throughout the world."[27] Edna Ruth Byler, an American wartime relief worker, later translated her practise of peace through material aid to the creation of what would become Ten Thousand Villages and has been described as the founder of "the entire fair trade movement."[28]

Women who volunteered for overseas postwar relief work, or who offered material assistance to conscientious objectors and war sufferers, continued to exercise 'positive peace' in the decades after the Second World War. Indeed, if notions of Mennonite nonresistance, as expressed by a male church leaders, shifted from a passive to an active pacifism in the latter part of the twentieth century,[29] it could be argued that women had already been doing exactly that. Initiatives such as Mennonite relief sales, held across North America, were described as acts of 'piecemaking'—the double reference to the many quilts auctioned at the sales and also the idea of relief work as peacemaking.[30] A history of the New Hamburg, Ontario Mennonite Relief Sale chronicles the many world conflicts happening in 1967, and goes on to describe the first sale held in May: "one small effort to bring peace to [a] world of political unrest, war, famine, and injustice."[31] Beyond the actual funds for relief raised by selling quilts, it has been proposed that quilts themselves function as "visual parables" and visual, embodied rhetorical tools that "constitute a compelling, rational story for the cause of peace."[32] Quilt-

---

25. *Missionary News and Notes*, April 1941, 61. In MAO.
26. Quoted in Marr, *Transforming Power*, 41.
27. Sitler, "Challenge," 1–3.
28. Graybill, "Writing Women," 242.
29. For analyses of this shift, see for instance, Regehr, *Mennonites in Canada*; Marr, *Transforming Power*; Neufeld, "Varieties," 243–57.
30. Knowles, editor, *Piecemakers*.
31. Ibid., 43.
32. McLaughlin, "Engendering," 6–7.

making, while not exclusively a female activity, has nevertheless functioned as a powerful symbol and concrete activity of Mennonite women. The positive peace exercised by Mennonite women also appears in such projects as the three 'world community cookbooks' that had political purposes beyond what is generally assumed to be the agenda of recipe collections. Most well-known is Doris Janzen Longacre's *More with Less* cookbook, published in 1976, with the prophetic call to eat less meat and more grains as a way of equalizing global food resources.

While wartime circumstances, in numerous contexts, have generated settings in which women exercised positive peace while their menfolk practiced withdrawal from military service, outside of wartime conflict, the Mennonite peace position could hold different meaning in women's personal lives.

A Gap in Mennonite Peacemaking: Violence against Women

As shown above, historically women did not participate in official expressions of conscientious objection, but nevertheless acted out a positive peace stance through relief to war sufferers. But while Mennonite peace thinking motived women towards relief and mutual aid, it also had negative repercussions on women when it failed to address interpersonal violence. In short, Mennonite expressions of their historic peace position rarely spoke against violence towards women. Feminist analyses of Mennonite nonresistant or pacifist beliefs have drawn attention to the ways in which notions of peace and nonviolence, espoused as key markers of Mennonites past and present, overlapped with gendered character traits such as submission, humility, and service. In an analysis of proverbs and sayings embroidered on a quilt made by young Mennonite women working as domestics in Vancouver, Ruth Derksen Siemens proposes that sayings like "Strive to live at peace with everyone," "Submit to those in authority over you," and "Love seeks no evil against another," were understood in a very gender specific manner. While for Mennonite men, such phrases meant "refusing military service [and] not provoking any violent physical attack or invasion," for the quilt-makers and domestic servants, the proverbs "were experienced as a passive response to any aggressive act . . ." and an "unquestioning acceptance of a parent's, matron's or church elder's authority."[33]

Concepts of submission and self-denial, adopted by the early Anabaptist believers to enable them to bear suffering and martyrdom when faced

---

33. Siemens, "Quilt as Text," 126–27.

with arrest, torture, and execution by religious and state authorities, become highly gendered when a model Christian-Mennonite demeanor was interpreted to be one of humility, submission, yieldedness, and readiness to suffer. In 1999, Mennonite theologian Carol Penner provocatively argued that the uplifting of suffering and submission and an ungendered emphasis on nonresistance reinforced women's inability and their community's unwillingness to speak out against domestic violence.[34] One Mennonite woman commented that Mennonite ideals absorbed during her upbringing taught her "to not speak out, to always be nice, to turn the other cheek, to carry my cross. I was socialized into powerlessness."[35] As some Mennonite women have argued, the *gelassenheit* (yieldedness) and passivity that characterized the Mennonite worldview and disposition has been reinforced by gendered characteristics of obedience and subordination.

The peace stance of Mennonites at times led to the assumption that Mennonites rejected violence in both public and private realms. Condemnation of violence in Mennonite prescriptive literature has prompted the incorrect conclusion that, as a result, violence was not tolerated in communities and households. However, violence did occur within households where patriarchal family relations were combined with literal interpretations of biblical commands that women submit to their husbands and children to their parents.[36] Such violence took the form of severe corporal punishment towards children, wife-battering, incest, and sexual abuse. Few historic sources offer evidence or reflection on personal experiences of violence within households. Yet, various studies in the 1990s confirmed the presence of violence in Mennonite households, and proposed that Mennonite beliefs and behaviours "contribute to family violence," specifically "beliefs about separation from the world, denying the existence of certain emotions like anger and sexual feelings, adhering to a hierarchy moving from God to Christ to man to woman to child, and upholding a discipleship/perfectionism model."[37] The collective incredulity amongst many Mennonites over numerous rapes committed 'within' a separated Mennonite community in 2009 only points to a lack of intentional thought to address the disconnect between theology and behaviour with regard to violence, sexuality, patriarchy, and gender relations.[38]

34. Penner, "Mennonite Silences."
35. Nickel, "In the Name," 5.
36. For evidence of violence against women within Mennonite families, see for instance, Martin, "Presence of Violence"; Block, *Assault*. See also Hildebrand, "Domestic Violence," 73–80.
37. Martin, "Presence of Violence," 23. Block, *Assault*, 80.
38. Friedman-Rudovsky, "Ghost Rapes of Bolivia."

Carol Penner argued that Mennonite perspectives on the concepts of forgiveness, obedience, and suffering have been interpreted with very gender-specific meanings for women dealing with violence in their lives.[39] In this interpretation, biblically-mandated submission became a Christian-Mennonite woman's highest virtue, even while her husband's exertion of power was an abuse of Scripture. While all Christian denominations experienced interpersonal violence as an abuse of (mostly male) power over women and children, the absolute inconsistency between theology and practice was most obvious in the 'peace' churches.

The work of Mennonite feminists—theologians, pastors, and others—to deconstruct Mennonite peace thinking towards addressing violence and abuse against women and children was prompted in large part by the women's movement of the 1960s forward. So that, in this case, Mennonite women's peacebuilding did not arise so much from historic Anabaptist-Mennonite beliefs, as it did from a social movement denouncing violence that was hidden and implicitly denied if not sanctioned. Various initiatives coming from the 'women's concerns' desk of Mennonite Central Committee in the 1970s, 80s, and beyond brought the issues of violence against women and children to the attention and action of Mennonites themselves, and thus broke through the "silence and skepticism."[40]

Feminist explorations of peace emerged in such projects as *Piecework: a women's peace theology*, when seven Canadian Mennonite women conversed about peace theology over a two-year period in the late 1990s. Among other things, they reflected on the connections between peacemaking and mothering and proposed that "working for peace is a part of the everyday, the ordinary, the mundane."[41] They also agreed that the church (presumably Mennonite) did not respond adequately to violence against women, suggesting that traditional articulations of nonresistance did not equal peace, since, in their experience of personalized violence, sometimes resistance was a good option.[42] In the early 21st century, Elizabeth Soto Albrecht has been an important voice bringing her biblical interpretation to the issue of family violence. Among other writings and addresses, Soto Albrecht's important 2008 book, *Family Violence: Reclaiming a Theology of Nonviolence*, begins with the premise that the biblical teachings at the core of a Mennonite theology of nonviolence "have not really been drawn on to bring peace to the family." More pointedly, she says that while Men-

---

39. Penner, "Mennonite Silences," 1.
40. Graybill, "Writing Women," 248.
41. Bender, et al., *Piecework*, 27.
42. Ibid., 53–56.

nonites have been good at applying their peace theology to "issues of war and injustice in local and international settings," they have been reluctant to address the "'wars' in homes."[43] Just by analyzing, writing, and teaching about this issue, feminists like Soto Albrecht are engaged in path-breaking peacebuilding that is directed both inwardly towards the Mennonite church community and outwardly towards society more broadly.

The inconsistency, indeed contradiction, between Mennonite peace ideals and realities was also manifest in churches and organizations where harassment and sexual abuse—a form of gender-based violence—was identified as a long-term problem and named as "sin." It was Mennonite women from numerous contexts who pushed their churches to address violence against women, children, and LGBTQ persons as a systemic issue, not as an individual aberration. The increasing number of personal stories testifying to violence in the home or sexual abuse by Mennonite men—including some high profile cases—were poignant and political in rejecting silence and humility as the appropriate response for Mennonite women. This storytelling is ongoing.[44] The positive peace embodied by women in their relief to war sufferers needs to extend also to official statements against interpersonal violence and education to prevent it.

The Mennonite peace position will only be fully realized when theorists and practitioners account for the connections between inter-state/inter-group violence and inter-personal violence, especially that which harms women and children. Mennonite women living in places of conflict understand that link best and are working to bring their church's peace position to bear on violence in their specific contexts. Sandra Baez Garcia, pastor of a Mennonite Brethren church in Bogota, Colombia, points out that, while people think violence in her country is related to guerrilla warfare and drugs, the primary problem with violence is in the home. She emphasizes the connections that exist between the micro-level of relationships within the household and the macro-level conflicts that characterize violence in Colombia. Conflict at both levels is driven by the desire for power.[45] Similarly, a Congolese Mennonite woman once told me, "We encourage our

---

43. Albrecht, *Family Violence*, 7, 15.

44. See, for instance, the personal stories and analysis in the special issue on sexual violence, "Lighting the Dark," *Timbrel*, the publication of Mennonite Women USA (Spring 2014). See, for instance, the personal stories and analysis in the special issue on sexual violence, "Lighting the Dark," *Timbrel*, the publication of Mennonite Women USA (Spring 2014). Also see the special issue devoted to the theme of sexual abuse in *Mennonite Quarterly Review*, 89, no. 1 (January 2015).

45. Garcia, "Conversations."

people to start peace in our families. Children need to be raised in a very peaceful family."[46]

In the Democratic Republic of Congo, where gender-based and sexual violence has been described as "epidemic" in the near twenty-year war in the eastern part of that country, Mennonite women are speaking out and taking action. Driven by the teachings of their church tradition on peace and nonviolence, they are raising awareness and educating against violence within their own communities, but also reaching out to victims of sexual violence in the war zones of their country. For instance, pastor Fifi Pombo Madikela, and four other Congolese Mennonite women participated in the World March of Women in October 2010, which took place in Bukavu in eastern Congo. Madikela, already an activist and researcher on violence against women, observed, "We talked with many women who have been raped, beaten, forced to flee their homes. We visited a hospital where their terrible injuries are treated. We heard firsthand stories of massacres and terrible murders. We know we must work hard now to teach peace to children and young people so that this vicious form of war will end."[47] Similarly, Sidonie Swana, a pastor, chaplain, and teacher in Kinshasa, is among a network of Congolese Mennonite women developing seminars and workshops to address the problem of violence and abuse.[48] Some of these women travel long distances, often by foot and through unsafe terrain, to bring education to women in small outlying villages. This they do with difficulty; as one woman remarked, "As Congolese women, the situation of the country affects us in all areas. We don't have financial resources to organize meetings and seminars for awareness building in the name of peace. Nor can we afford to organize trips and excursions for peace campaigns. However, we try hard at our churches to educate our people and local communities about peace, especially during sermons."[49]

Conclusion

While this chapter has been about women's gendered identities and peacemaking, much more work needs to be done to analyze the role that masculinity plays in shaping Mennonite men's expressions of their church's

---

46. Author's interview with Mennonite women in Tshikapa, DR Congo, July 2012.

47. Will, "Congolese Women."

48. For a brief profile of Sidonie Swana, see Charles and Robinson, "Putting," 16–17. My perspectives are also based on personal conversations with Mennonite women in DR Congo in summer 2012.

49. Author's interview with Mennonite women in Tshikapa, DR Congo, July 2012.

peace position. For instance, Mennonite men, whose lives have rarely been analyzed through a gender lens, also dealt with crises of male identity when they spurned the hyper-masculinized service in the military.[50] Or, alternately, they acted out normative models of masculinity when they temporarily took up arms to defend 'their' women and children when faced with horrific violence directed at them during the civil war in post-revolutionary Russia.[51] And we have much work to do to fully understand—and undo—why peacemaking men exert violence against women.

As well, while the focus here has been on Mennonite women as peacemakers and peacebuilders, I do not want to essentialize their identities by suggesting that women are not also capable of violence—towards men, towards children, and towards each other. Yet, Mennonite women, as participants in a historic peace church, have a unique opportunity to put principles of peace and nonviolence into positive action. This chapter has presented only a sampler of how they did this in the past—when they offered relief to those who suffered the violence of war—and in the present as they offer new articulations of nonviolence that is applicable to family and gender relations. As such, Mennonite women continue to be conscientious objectors to war and violence, in their own voices and actions.

---

50. Some work on this topic has been done. See, for instance, Epp, "Heroes," 107–117; Hiebert, "Crisis of Masculinity."

51. The *Selbstschutz*, an armed Mennonite self-defence league in present-day Ukraine from the years 1918–19, has been discussed from the point of view of the Mennonite peace position, but not with respect to prevailing assumptions and expectations about masculinity.

10

Transforming the Peacebuilder
Building Trust and Local Capacity through Containment of Ego and Cultivation of the Inner Life

RON KRAYBILL

Introduction

THREE DECADES IN THE vocation of peacebuilding have taught me that management of self in relationship to others is pivotal in peacebuilding, affecting both the likelihood of "success" as well as the nature of the work that is done. In this essay, I reflect on ways the Mennonite community shaped my understandings of self-management, how these unfolded across my career, and how to do personal formation of peacebuilders that is adequate to the challenges of the calling.

While there were elements of the early Anabaptist movement that were confrontational, the Münster rebellion being perhaps the extreme example, the Mennonite tradition that emerged valued modesty, making minimal demands for personal or public space. Suffering and the willingness to endure it gladly were quite early considered marks of Christian faithfulness. Rather than destroy evil or defeat adversaries, the goal was simpler—to retain faithfulness of action and heart as individuals and community.

Such a stance reflects in part the Anabaptists' focus on the internal life of the community as the locus of God's work rather than the public sphere and their understanding that peaceful social relations are a mark of redemption. Persecution probably exacerbated these theological orientations; families fleeing for survival to the hills and hinterlands of Europe and beyond were not in a position to demand much of anyone.

For various reasons, modesty in relationship to others became a Mennonite characteristic, not only *vis-à-vis* the larger world, but also within the community itself. Generations of life on isolated farms no doubt contributed. When life is structured around hard manual labor, things go better if one avoids self-puffery; better to just hunker down and get the job done. In the pasturelands and potato fields of Lancaster County, Pennsylvania, where I grew up, a big talker who couldn't heft hay bays or potato sacks got trimmed down to size pretty quickly. We all knew the proverb, "Pride goeth before a fall."

Theron Schlabach observed in his studies of Mennonites in North America that in the eighteenth century, Mennonites made a shift in emphasis from suffering to humility as a mark of faithfulness. The memory of suffering faded as grandchildren of the Anabaptists grew comfortable in the open spaces of North America. The result was that "among Mennonites and Amish throughout much of the nineteen century the emphasis on humility, intertwined with nonresistance, was the hallmark of the Christian life—both in practical ethics and in spirituality."[1]

By the start of the twentieth century, the picture had gotten more complex, Schlabach found, with American Revivalism influencing certain Mennonite leaders and publications towards a generally more individualistic and aggressive spirit and greater emphasis on mission effort.[2] Nevertheless,

---

1. In personal correspondence with the author in February, 2014, Schlabach wrote "in North America these Anabaptist-derived peoples had become quite comfortable and the memory of suffering was fading. Another part was influence from classical Pietism, although compared to that of Pietists the outlook of Mennonites and Amish in North America was probably more focused on communal life as compared to individual experience, and somewhat more toward rules of living and ethics in this world as compared to inner experience and hope for heaven."

2. In Schlabach's words in a personal communication with the author in February, 2014: "From about the 1880s onward (and here and there somewhat earlier), Mennonites and Amish were growing more skilled in English and more in touch with American Revivalism. As that happened the relatively progressive among them began to take cues from Revivalism's mission emphasis, its greater individualism, and its more aggressive spirit. Revivals and the revivalistic style and soteriology more and more displaced the non-aggressive humility theology. As the twentieth century opened another generation of leaders continued to fuse the newer approach with traditional Amish and Mennonite nonresistance and other distinctive doctrines, but very often they did so with influences from Protestant Fundamentalism that left their ethics and spirituality more codified and rigid. Despite that generation's emphasis on "distinctives," those leaders retained the more evangelical-Protestant soteriology, with a strong tendency to

humility theology remained deeply rooted in Mennonite communities. My experience growing up in Lancaster county in the 1950s and 1960s was that humility was still the norm and assertiveness was atypical.[3]

Schlabach admits that a sociologist "might say that Mennonite and Amish leaders used humility for boundary maintenance and social control" and notes that "calls to humility were often calls to obey and be subordinate to the group." Still, Schlabach finds humility theology a relatively constructive influence, a welcome counterweight to the aggressive individualism and self-centeredness that characterized American frontier culture and much that followed.

The sources and historical variations of a modest Mennonite footprint could be debated. But across the decades of my career, I have come to respect its value in the realm of peacebuilding, or for that matter, any vocation in which change and human development are a goal. Whether we call it servant leadership, humility theology, or plain old modesty, I have come to see dedication to advancing the well-being of others that is equal to or greater than dedication to self as a huge asset in peacebuilding.

Letting Go as Requirement of Peacebuilders

Early in my work with the Mennonite Conciliation Service, I met with John A. Lapp, the incoming executive secretary of Mennonite Central Committee. "Your goal should always be to work yourself out of a job," he commented

---

keep salvation and ethics in different realms and on different tracks. Meanwhile Old Order groups—those who had resisted progressivism and acculturation—kept a strong emphasis on humility, albeit in many cases with their own legalisms and rigidities." Schlabach, *ibid,* considers the most concise statements of his findings to be his essays, Schlabach, "Reveille," 213–26 and Schlabach, "Humble," 113–26. See also Schlabach, "Humility."

3. For example, the youth group of my home congregation, Bosslers Mennonite Church, near Elizabethtown, PA, drove ten miles from our farming community to Wrightsville, a working class community, once a month in the 1960s to distribute "The Way," an evangelical tract. Church leaders encouraged this revivalist outreach, but rarely participated themselves. As teenagers and young adults in an alien environment, we were so uncomfortable with encountering people in this rather bold activity that we simply quietly slipped tracts under doors and moved on to the next house. I pondered how to reply if someone ever asked me why I was doing this. To my relief I never had to say more than "Good morning, here's something to read" before beating a hasty retreat to the street. This seems to me anecdotal evidence that although revivalist concepts like "leading souls to Christ" had by the 1960s permeated the rhetoric and theology of Lancaster County Mennonites, emotionally and behaviorally, the mood in the largest and most influential Mennonite conference remained closer to the humility of Pietism that Schlabach finds dominant throughout the 19th century.

thoughtfully at some point. I had only inklings of its full implications then, but over time I have come to understand it as an apt encapsulation of decades of experience by a veteran Mennonite peacebuilder and development worker. Like a zen koan, it provided me with layers of insight about vocation and the requirements of peacebuilding.

I understood Lapp at the time to mean that mediators should seek timely withdrawal from conflict situations so as to encourage parties to develop their own means of working out differences. It seemed like good advice and I sought to follow it as a young peace worker with few mentors available.[4]

However, as requests for mediation increased, I sensed a call for deeper forfeiture than I had first understood. Increasingly, I understood that I should relinquish the goal of becoming the mediator and instead aim to mobilize others as mediators. Thus I shifted my priority to training mediators.

But as demand for MCS workshops increased, it became apparent that a still deeper level of relinquishment was called for. My calendar couldn't accommodate all the promising possibilities to lead training workshops. Rather than training mediators, I ought to be training trainers. I began pulling away from doing training workshops myself and sought to focus my priorities around developing others as trainers and bringing them into MCS workshops as co-leaders and leaders.

Even this focus eventually proved too narrow. The greatest requirement of peacebuilding in our world is for more than training skills; it is for a broad and courageous *vision* of possibilities widely dismissed as utopian, backed by the capacity to mobilize practically with others in living out that

---

[4] "Few mentors" for a young Mennonite peace worker merits, perhaps, some explanation. What Mennonites considered peacemaking was, until the 1980s, primarily oppositional in character. Courageous witness had been made against war by generations of young men who entered alternative service rather than accept induction into the military. The Peace Section of Mennonite Central Committee coordinated witness and lobbying against U.S. militarism. A small number of Mennonites had participated in the Civil Rights movement of the 1960s, supporting confrontation of racism. The establishment of the Mennonite Conciliation Service in 1979 marked a new era for Mennonite peace efforts, directing commitment to peace into active intermediary roles. As founding director, 1979–1988, I felt tremendous support and encouragement on every hand from church leaders, lay people, and most peace activists, who shared a consensus that a more engaged, positive outreach on behalf of reconciliation was long overdue for Mennonites. But in the early years, I also felt nearly alone in the *practice* of this new approach. Virtually no Mennonites had enough experience with mediation or facilitation to have written even anecdotally about it, let alone develop methodologies or training materials. I benefited from a mediation manual from the Quakers, the books of church conflict consultant Speed Leas, and Fisher and Ury's *Getting to Yes*, but found practical experience the richest tutor.

vision. So the "job," as I have come to understand it in recent years, is to be an ally to those with a vision for healing who are present in every society and situation of conflict, supporting them in finding ways to bring their dreams for creating institutions and networks of peacebuilders into reality.

At the root of these evolving understandings of peacebuilding lie understandings of self, relationships to others, and calling that could be stated quite explicitly: you are not in this work just for yourself, to build a great career; you are to be deeply guided by the needs of those you seek to serve. Your role is transitory; do not expect or seek permanency. In fact, success is defined in part by your ability to precipitate transition wisely, in the service of others. This will probably require relinquishment, letting go of tasks and roles that may be quite rewarding. But that is as it should be, because you have a calling higher than any one job or role; let that higher calling define your role.

Containing the Ego in Peacebuilding

To do this requires a conscious commitment to the empowerment of others and a rather substantial personal capacity to contain the ego, as the peacebuilder scales back from established roles that are often quite gratifying in order to support others who are stepping into these roles. This is easier said than done.

A critical requirement is an "ego container," as the pioneering Methodist layman and early proponent of the US Institute for Peace, Dr. James Laue, used to call it. A series of experiences early in my career brought this home clearly to me. I came to know a veteran peacebuilder in an overseas setting near the end of his career. The man had labored courageously for decades in a hostile environment and had gotten little recognition for it. Now, with the nation finally turning towards peace in his later years, he appeared determined to grasp for recognition at every opportunity. I saw firsthand how hunger for recognition blocked him and his institution, not only from doing good work, but also from getting even the recognition that was deserved.

On numerous occasions, I witnessed my acquaintance spending the first half hour talking about himself when entertaining visitors to his organization. Thirty years ago he had taken this pioneering step for peace, twenty years ago he had led the first delegations in dialogue, and these days, by the way, he sometimes hosted this or that famous personage. By the time his tribute to self was finished, most visitors had lost interest and politely moved to wrap up the conversation.

The impact was not only personal, in relationships blocked and opportunities lost, it was institutional. His organization had a reputation among related agencies for arrogance and monopolizing the field. Partnering with other organizations was difficult for his center because no one wanted to be associated with him. I vowed I would never repeat that mistake, and memories of it instilled lifelong caution against self-promotional stories of peacebuilder heroics.

But I soon discovered that I too had the capacity to offend with a lack of sensitivity to the space of others. Through a chance connection, I was invited to go to a city hundreds of miles away to explore setting up the mediation of a dispute between two factions of a prominent ethnic group. I knew several experienced mediators not far from where I was going, but I neglected to pay them a courtesy call. Weeks later, they expressed to me their unhappiness that I had come to their region to try to mediate in a conflict they and others had watched and fretted about for a long time without consulting them.

I was initially less than repentant. They were not at this time involved in this conflict. I had legitimately acquired an invitation to go. What explanation or consultation did I owe anyone?

But time brought me to see an aspect of peacebuilding I had not initially contemplated. The late Ray Shonholtz, founder of the San Francisco Community Boards program in the 1970s, often pointed out that whoever mediates gains power. His observation helps understand the ugly and poorly acknowledged reality of competition between would-be mediators in high visibility conflicts. To be seen to be the person or organization with the wisdom, skill, and connections to successfully mediate an important conflict is quite empowering to a mediator. "Blessed are the peacemakers," yes. But in fact, mediation is rarely the simple altruism it is often thought to be. Mediators may do good, but if they are successful, they usually also do well, enjoying increased credibility, honor, prestige, and enhanced CVs for future employment. Consciously or not, I think most mediators intuit this, hence the competition for the job.[5]

---

5. At one point, I worked in an institution that was fielding an active mediation unit in a highly visible public transportation conflict. Only after several months did it become apparent that there were actually two mediation efforts taking place, both sponsored by the same organization. Unbeknownst to the first team, a pair of ambitious junior mediators had begun their own quiet initiative with leaders of both sides also trying to mediate. Confronted with their irresponsible actions, the two left the organization, moved across the country, and established their own mediation center, which grew into one of the largest in the region. Mistrust between the individuals involved, now senior peacebuilders in the region, continues to this day, affecting numerous institutions as well.

In holding the mediation role tightly to myself as I traveled far from home to mediate in another region without consulting or even informing other mediators in the region, I telegraphed a message I had not intended: expanding my base of power, influence, or fame mattered more to me than accountability to others who knew the situation much better than I or giving the best shot for peace. At a minimum, I should have consulted and requested advice on this complex conflict with many layers of history. I should also probably have sought to *involve* locals as partners in the mediation effort.

I apologized, and in a long conversation that followed, developed with one of these mediators a good working relationship that supported several years of collegiality. She told me later that my willingness to admit mistakes was the single most important thing I had done to win her trust. In retrospect, I see that although I had failed, the values of self-examination and containment of self infused in me by my community enabled me to recognize a misstep, take appropriate steps to repair the damage, and to actually raise my standing with colleagues through the conversation that had resulted.

Some years after the above experiences, I made a decision that across the years stands out to me as one of the best of my career. As Director of Training at the Centre for Conflict Resolution in Cape Town, the instincts engrained in me from my early years of work at Mennonite Central Committee gave me an uneasy conscience. I could see that virtually all that I was doing could now be adequately handled by a South African trainer whom I had hired and trained. What did working myself out of a job mean now? Eventually, I initiated conversation with the head of our Centre that led to a transition. My supervisee took my place as Director of Training. I reported to him for training purposes and in addition I now picked up other special projects.

Let's be honest—no great sacrifice was involved. My salary stayed the same. Someone else had to worry about things I used to worry about. I was freed up to work on cutting edge innovations. I won a lifetime of appreciation from my astonished colleague. Truthfully, I gained more than I lost.

But that was not my motivation, nor was it apparent when I offered the move that everything would work out so well. I credit here the influence of the Mennonite community that formed me—and which through Mennonite Central Committee provided financial support to go to South Africa—for giving me the values, the modeling, and the courage required to prioritize the needs and empowerment of others, even at possible risk to my own interests. Such values are not widely found in professional guilds and training schools.

In recent years, I have worked in international settings in peacebuilding initiatives sponsored by powerful, heavily resourced international bodies. While I see the need for these initiatives and the bodies that sponsor them, I have been repeatedly let down by the ham-handedness and inconsistency of principle of many of these efforts. Often this is due, in my assessment, to the fact that the people staffing them have no doctrine of self-containment to guide them. They are as hungry for recognition, power, and control as the politicians and warlords among whom they mediate.

All too often the unspoken question that seems to guide peacebuilders in these settings is not, "What steps would best serve the needs of the people in conflict?" but rather, "What steps would best assist me and/or my organization to be seen to be an important player in peacebuilding and help position us for funding?"

I find it impossible to operate in this environment without inward turmoil and occasional confrontations with others. When should I go along with self-serving organizational agendas in order to maintain my status and position in my organization? When must I speak out on the basis of principle to do the right thing by the lights of best peacebuilding practice? When others manipulate, deceive, or take advantage of efforts for collaboration and openness in order to advance themselves or their organizations, how should I respond?

Often the answers to such questions are murky. Nevertheless, I have come to see a light footprint and disciplined restraint of ego to be essential to survival here. The competition and drives for power are high, the provocations numerous; anyone quick to defend turf and territory would spend more time in battles with colleagues and partner organizations than in peacebuilding. A path of modesty, generosity towards others, and willingness to ignore personal provocation has on several occasions taken me and the mission of peace much farther than I could have gone with a strategy of fighting, even had I fought and won. When people see that a peacebuilder operates at high levels of principle, even under provocation, trust and respect tend to follow. A light footprint is one of the few things capable of turning adversity into advantage.

The Formation of Peacebuilders

It is probably safe to say that Mennonites have earned a global reputation as peacebuilders over the last several decades. If there is a signature Mennonite *modus operandi*, at its functional core lies an expectation that peacebuilders contain themselves, in particular, their egos and claims for credit and power, and support others to rise to their fullest potential in the quest for peace.

We might take as an index of this the writings of John Paul Lederach, who has popularized Mennonite approaches to peacebuilding, conveying them to a global audience eager for something meatier than tips on "getting to yes." My sense, from conversations with practitioners and students in many places, is that the concepts from Lederach's writings that have gained widest retention are his "elicitive" approach to training, a "middle out" approach to peacebuilding strategy, and his creative strategies for inviting people in conflict situations into fresh ways of thinking and acting.

To be effective in practice, each of these concepts requires, I suggest, the presence of a certain kind of human being. To adopt an "elicitive" stance—what Mennonite Central Committee development workers in the 1970s called "a listening/learning approach"—requires bracketing the peacebuilder's understandings of wisdom and insight and bringing those of others to center stage.

A middle out approach in mediation, also a strategy of change honed by generations of Mennonite development workers, is a non-coercive, other-centered, invitational approach that recognizes that power to change is built through quiet engagement at multiple levels, not only the top; indeed, a bit of distance from the top is often beneficial. This strategy too works best in the presence of a facilitator who is skilled at leading in ways that create spaces for others. Facilitators preoccupied with projecting their power or stoking personal reputations flounder in a middle out strategy. The same is true for facilitation processes to engage the moral imagination; creativity wilts in the presence of control and struggles for power.

Clearly, many are inspired by these ideas. Well and good for the cause of peacebuilding. But how to develop and prepare the kind of human beings required to facilitate these strategies? How to inspire the personal formation required to *become* such a person?

The vocation of peacebuilding, I have come to believe, is in fact spiritually formative for those willing to reflect deeply and honestly on the work that we do. Time spent in that strange junction of alienation and hope where peacebuilders spend our years is capable of calling forth qualities of the light footprint described earlier. So perhaps there is no need to pontificate on the kind of person required for the approaches we follow: let peacebuilding do its redemptive work in transforming the peacebuilders.

But I think we could do more to encourage and assist those who are drawn to this path to reflect on and be deeply formed by it. The reflection a book such as this present volume facilitates could be foundational to such an endeavor. But to go deep, such reflection needs structure, persistence, companionship, and anchors or at least reference points in tradition. Ideally, these would be available in regular conversation with others who have walked the same path and know the opportunities and pitfalls.

The Seeker's Fellowship, a small "non-Mennonite" church in the Washington, DC area with distinctly Anabaptist leanings, in the group of churches associated with the late Gordon Cosby, has provided me with such a structure for the last several years. They made me a "missioner" of the church and appointed a small group to serve as a special support group to me. When I email prayer requests or a summary of events in my life every month or two, invariably I get several replies. On the rare occasions when I visit, they organize an update for all interested. They pray weekly for me; they supplied a bridge loan between assignments. In difficult times, I have found their support remarkably meaningful given the physical distance.

I wonder about the possibilities for an order of peacebuilders who commit to supporting each other on a journey of reflection and growth in trios or quartets for, say, a year at a time, *via* email or Skype.[6] I also wonder about the creation of an "examen for peacebuilders," a set of guiding questions formulated to facilitate regular reflection on the issues most likely to be present in the life and work of peacebuilders. The mobile, transitory lifestyle of many peacebuilders makes physical participation in support groups difficult, so at least we could create written materials and establish practices drawing upon the astonishing communications technologies of our times to facilitate engagement in a community of spirit.

Finally, I wonder about how to make mentoring a routine resource in the preparation of young peacebuilders. Voluntary service once played a huge factor in the nurturing of young people to embrace lives of service in Mennonite communities. Mennonites are unlikely ever to return to the days when so many young people spent years in service supported by the larger church. But we could certainly find ways to offer young people interested in peacebuilding careers the opportunity to have regular conversations with

---

6. I knew of one such order, perhaps still extant, made up of mostly Mennonite peace activists in the American mid-West, in the 1980 and 90s. At that time, its members were almost all nonviolent change activists, whose struggles against unpeaceful practices of governments and corporations reminded them often of the need for support. People in the more recent field of peacebuilding, in my experience, are less oriented towards prophetic approaches and not as quick to recognize the need for personal formation and support, tending perhaps to be more conventional and more individualistic than the old-line peace activists. They are perhaps more "buttoned down" and more "professional" by conventional standards, but I suspect also less resourceful than past generations about creating ongoing structures for personal support and growth and less aware of how professional structures tend to shape the worldviews and values of individuals in them towards acceptance of the status quo.

elder peacebuilders about their work and the challenges for personal and spiritual growth they encounter there.

For myself, as I suspect for many others, this would require a large tent, a non-creedal approach, to work. Critical philosophies of knowledge, like modern-day enforcers of hermeneutical modesty, have desacralized the power of dogma. For many of us, it is no longer possible to frame spirituality around the simple givens that once structured Mennonite communities and the formation of individuals in the past.

In my view, a non-creedal approach would in fact faithfully continue our tradition and beliefs. Certainly Jesus and Menno Simons displayed considerably more interest in discerning and honoring God's unfolding work in the present than in doctrinal formulations of the past. The instinct they shared to see human relationships as the realm of redemption rather than structures of piety gives us precedent. Let deep reflection, conversation, and prayer about lived experience provide the central focus of spiritual formation, with doctrine and creed as secondary reference points, rather than *vice versa*.

The stable, principled formation that I received in my family and Mennonite community gave me the inner foundations required to walk lightly in the midst of trampling herds. But the simple, structured Mennonite communities many of us grew up in are mostly gone, ravaged by malls, SUVs, Sunday football games, and tablet computers. We won't be going back to the farms. If we are to continue to form and sustain people adequate to the peacebuilding challenges of our times, we must also now update our practices and disciplines of personal formation.

11

Called to Be Snakebirds
Mennonite Historical Conditions as Inspiration for Peace Work[1]

VIRGIL WIEBE

Introduction

"SEE, I AM SENDING you out like sheep into the midst of wolves; so be wise as serpents and innocent as doves" (Matt. 10:16).

How do Mennonite communities produce and sustain human rights activism? I have been asked to reflect on how being a Mennonite has influenced a career of teaching and activism around refugee rights and arms control. Jesus' words in Matt. 10:16 have guided my reflections, leading me to a sort of "ornitheology"—how to be doves in a harsh world.

My Uncle Ted and Aunt Nettie, along with my parents, had a great influence on me. I spent summers working with Ted and Nettie on the family farm located on Mennonite Road, outside Garden City, Kansas. Ted was my dad's brother. The Mennonite Brethren had arrived in Kansas from the Ukraine in the 1874 migration. My Aunt Nettie Rempel had ended up in Kansas by way of Winnipeg, Manitoba, having been amongst the

---

1. This chapter builds on a keynote address given at the University of Winnipeg, "Conference Program: Mennonites and Human Rights," Mennonite Studies, University of Winnipeg, October 18–20, 2012, http://mennonitestudies.uwinnipeg.ca/events/human_rights_2012/ConferenceProgram.php.

post-World War II Mennonite migrants to Canada who fled the same area of the Ukraine.

Upon Uncle Ted's passing, I discovered his military draft cards tucked away in a little pamphlet entitled "Why I am a C.O."[2] The pamphlet is nothing more or less than a selection of Bible verses, and verse #5 is Matt. 10:16: "Behold I send you forth as sheep in the midst of wolves; be ye therefore wise as serpents, and harmless as doves." The serpent/dove imagery led me to the Snakebird, of the genus Anhinga.[3] The wolves/sheep metaphor also resonated. Presumably a people of peace, how have Mennonites at times been prey, predators, and even protectors when it comes to human rights?[4] When, why, and how does a history of persecution drive a people to mercy, compassion, and courage, and how can it also produce the fruits of indifference or persecution?

Peacemaker Characteristics of the Serpent Dove

I was astonished to discover the many differing and contradictory meanings one can pull out of a single verse! Here is my categorization of the different translations of the terms "serpent" and "dove" in Matt. 10:16.[5]

---

2. Wenger, *Why I am a C.O.* Of some interest, the categories listed in the cards gave Ted a farm exemption, rather than C.O status.

3. Virgil Wiebe, Called to Be Snakebirds: Mennonites, Human Rights, and State Power, Oct. 18, 2012 http://prezi.com/n_meqwio3evu/snakebirds-mennonites-human-rights-state-power/.

4. "I am the good shepherd. The good shepherd lays down his life for the sheep. The hired hand, who is not the shepherd and does not own the sheep, sees the wolf coming and leaves the sheep and runs away—and the wolf snatches and scatters them." John 10:11–12.

5. I used Bible Gateway, with a base of over 160 different translations. All of the following translations come from that source: http://www.biblegateway.com/.

Serpents/Snakes[A]	Doves
Heart Smart: Wise,[B] Prudent[C]	**Blameless:** Innocent,[D] Faultless,[E] Without Falsity[F]
Head Smart: Smart,[G] Intelligence,[H] *Astutos*[I]	**Peace-filled:** Gentle,[J] *Humildes*,[K] *Sencillos*,[L] Simple,[M] Guileless,[N] Inoffensive[O]
Street Smart: Sly,[P] Cunning,[Q] Shrewd,[R] Clever[S]	**Peaceful:** Harmless,[T] "Don't Hurt Anyone"[U]
Survival Smart: Wary,[V] Cautious,[W] *Atentos*,[X] *Listos*[Y]	

A. Translations of Matt. 10:16 use not only the word "serpents" but also "snakes." Cf. New International Version; New Life Version; Contemporary English Version.

B. New Revised Standard Version; King James Version; World English Bible; Amplified Bible; New Life Version.

C. Darby Translation; Complete Jewish Bible.

D. New Revised Standard Version; New International Version; New American Standard Bible; New Century Version.

E. Orthodox Jewish Bible.

F. Amplified Bible.

G. Easy-to-Read Version.

H. Orthodox Jewish Bible.

I. La Biblia de las Américas.

J. Good News Translation; New Life Version.

K. Traducción en lenguaje actual.

L. Dios Habla Hoy.

M. Wycliffe Bible.

N. Darby Translation; Amplified Bible.

O. The Message.

P. Wycliffe Bible.

Q. Expanded Bible; GOD'S WORD Translation; The Message.

R. New International Version; Holman Christian Standard Bible; New American Standard Bible.

S. Expanded Bible; New Century Version.

T. King James Version; World English Bible; Holman Christian Standard Bible; Complete Jewish Bible; Amplified Bible.

U. Easy-to-Read Version.

V. Amplified Bible; Living Bible.

W. Good News Translation.

X. Traducción en lenguaje actual. *Atentos* is Spanish for "attentive." Wordreference.com

Y. Traducción en lenguaje actual. *Listos* is Spanish for ready or "clever." Wordreference.com

The serpent characteristics are often in direct contrast to those of the dove. At our best as Christians, we are called to be "serpent doves"—sly, cunning, and harmless all at the same time. In Mennonite history, we find instances in which the survival smarts have led to flight and caution, and other moments when street smarts have overwhelmed the call to act peacefully.

Meet Nature's Real Serpent Dove

> "Anhinga" means devil bird or snake bird in the Brazilian Tupi language. The dark-feathered fish-eater has a very long neck, and often swims with only the neck above water, which has earned it the name, Snakebird. Kettles of Snakebird are known to migrate with other birds.[6]

The beautiful Snakebird provides analogies for the calling we have to be "serpent doves." Snakebirds find secluded roosting areas for protection and can be fiercely territorial, but also migrate with other birds. Snakebirds congregate in kettles of up to several hundred. Because of their firm attachment to safety and to place, they can fall prey to wily hunters. They migrate thousands of miles, and different varieties of the Snakebird can be found on five continents. Fearsome hunters, they live off of fish and other small creatures. They lovingly force feed their young through regurgitation. The Snakebird is both a predator and prey.

Our Favorite Mennonite Ice Fisherman: Dirk Willems

Taking up ice fishing in Minnesota has led to a new appreciation of the iconic Mennonite martyr, Dirk Willems. While we now have ice rescue teams,[7] none were on hand in 1569 in Asperen, Holland when Dirk Willems escaped from prison where he was being held on heresy charges and fled across a frozen lake. When his hefty pursuer broke through the ice, only Dirk was there to save him.[8]

Jan Luyken's image of Dirk reaching for the thief catcher proves the enduring value of an image.[9] Not only is Dirk a sheep among the wolves,

---

6. "Snakebird: Introduction," *Planetwildlife*, http://www.planetwildlife.com/information/species/snakebird-1.

7. Tesla Rodriguez, "Dive Team Set for Ice Rescues," *Winona Daily News*, January 8, 2012, http://www.winonadailynews.com/news/local/article_14302014-39ac-11e1-8e66-001871e3ce6c.html.

8. Van Braght, *Martyrs' Mirror*, 741–42.

9. Ibid., 741.

but he also models the good shepherd. You can almost see the crooked shepherd's staff in his hands, reaching out to save the drowning, freezing helpless soul. And like Jesus, this shepherd meets an ignoble end: "The thief-catcher wanted to let him go, but the burgomaster, very sternly called to him to consider his oath, and thus he was again seized by the thief-catcher, and, at said place, after severe imprisonment and great trials proceeding from the deceitful papists, put to death at a lingering fire by these bloodthirsty, ravening wolves."[10]

Martyr and savior, that bundle of Mennonite complexes neatly packaged in the life of a mortal. Dirk proved that a mere mortal could walk in the footsteps of Jesus. And Uncle Ted's "Why I am a C.O." pamphlet of verses from the 1940s carries the theme forward. Its language arcane to the postmodern ear makes me pay more attention: Matt. 5:41—"And whoever shall compel thee to go a mile go with him twain;" Matt. 5:44–45: "But I say to you, Love your enemies, bless them that curse you, do good to them that hate you, and pray for them which despitefully use you and persecute you; That ye may be the children of your father in heaven."[11] But appropriately appropriating Dirk's story is tricky. Having worked with survivors of torture for over two decades, I can say without hesitation I do not want to be a martyr. But playing the hero is also dangerous—"look at me, the human rights activist."

All We like Sheep: Learning Mennonite Martyrdom and Victimhood

> True believing Christians are sheep among the wolves . . . They must be baptized in anguish and tribulation, persecution and suffering, and death, tried in fire. —Conrad Grebel, 1524[12]

> I remained until I saw the beautiful [Snake]bird alight and gaze around to see if all was right. Alas! It was not aware of its danger, but, after a few moments, during which I noted its curious motions, it fell dead into the water . . . In this manner, in the course of one day I procured fourteen of these birds, and wounded several others. —John J. Audubon, c. 1840[13]

---

10. Ibid.
11. Wenger, *Why I am a C.O.*
12. Harder, editor, *Swiss Anabaptism*, cited in Roth, "Forgiveness," 579.
13. Audubon, *The Birds of America*, vol. 6, 445.

Persecution stories run through Mennonite history. Such stories provide great inspiration, but John Roth points out the dangers: martyr stories can blur into naive sentimentalism, a sense of self-righteousness and arrogance, and reduce complex history to morality tales of good and evil.[14]

Productive remembrance requires effort. In the words of Roth, "Keeping these stories alive is an affirmation that those who relinquished their lives did not do so in vain; . . . Remembering those who died for the principle of nonresistance testifies to the Christian conviction that the resurrection will ultimately triumph over the cross." Roth suggest three elements of "right remembering": historical accuracy, commitment to seeing the issues through the eyes of the Other with an empathic spirit, and linking remembrance to Christian discipleship.[15] These suggestions become easier the older the stories are—historical accuracy and dialogue in the midst of persecution is a tall order for those closest to the suffering. With Roth's cautions as a guide, I will look at the 1874 migration of Ukrainian Russian Mennonites to the Great Plains (my uncle Ted's family), and the persecutions of Mennonites in the Ukraine by the Soviet Communists in the 1920s and 30s (my Aunt Nettie's family).

The Great Migration of 1874: Anna Barkman and the Story of Turkey Red Winter Wheat

I am a product of the Russian Mennonite migration of the 1870s to the U.S. and Canada. My dad (and uncle Ted) descend from the Mennonite Brethren (MB) that migrated to Kansas; my mother is from the General Conference Mennonites. Family genealogies produced in the 1970s sit on my shelf.[16]

The family mythology has the Mennonites fleeing Russia because their religious freedom had been stripped away, most notably the loss of exemption from military service.[17] Upon arrival in the U.S., the story goes, Mennonites transformed American agriculture by introducing Turkey red winter wheat. These stories hit me with the greatest force at age ten in 1974, the one-hundredth anniversary of the migration. My family made pilgrim-

---

14. Roth, "Forgiveness," 581.
15. Ibid., 582–85.
16. Wiebe, Wiebe, and Wiebe, *Groening-Wiebe Family*; Voth, *Cornelius*.
17. P. S. Loewen, "Preface," In Wiebe, Wiebe, and Wiebe, *Groening-Wiebe Family* ties the migration in spirit to the Pilgrims: "They all came here to find a new home, in which they could serve God according to the dictates of their belief and their conscience. They believed in 'None-Resistance' [sic] and were willing to make sacrifices for this belief to the utmost . . . All of these families settled on the unending prairies, where the American Indian had roamed and hunted very few years previous."

ages to tour the site of Gnadenau village (the first communal site in Kansas for the Mennonite immigrants with their distinctive triangular huts) and the museums in Goessel and Hillsboro.

My most enduring memory of the anniversary was a play about Anna Barkman, the little eight year old girl who had been tasked in Russia with selecting only the finest pump grains of wheat to provide seed for the New World. Our family saw the performance at Tabor College, and my dreamy twelve year old cousin Jill played the lead role. The story recounted the reasons for their flight from Russia as well as the challenges facing the new refugees upon arrival.[18]

The Communist Purges of 1938: Aunt Nettie and the Man in the Black Uniform

My Aunt Nettie told stories of life under Soviet Communism. Born in 1924 in Einlage, Ukraine,[19] she grew up on a collective farm. In a videotaped presentation to a high school history class in Garden City, Kansas in 1983, Nettie recounted the day in 1938 when her father was taken away by the Soviet secret police:

> Well, when I had just started the seventh grade, it had been in October. We were on our way home one evening. We had just entered our own village. I lived at the far opposite end of where we entered. We met a man in black uniform. We all knew that people that wore black uniforms were members of the NKVD, or the KGB as they call them today, the secret police. And we realized that someone would be arrested. When we passed the office of the local Soviet, there was a truck parked there and we feared that not only one person would be arrested but probably several would be arrested. I think most of the students had reached home by the time I noticed that three men were approaching me in single file on the sidewalk. The first one was a man from our village. The second one was my father. And the

---

18. A coloring book also conveyed the story: *The Story of Wheat Coloring Book: Featuring the Anna Barkman Story as Played by the Anna Barkman Road Company* (Hillsboro, Kansas: TC-AV Productions, 1974). Memoirist Rhoda Janzen has much funnier recollections of the story in Janzen, *Mennonite*, 24–25.

19. See Willi Vogt, "Mennonitische Geschichte und Ahnenforschung, Chortitza," http://chortiza.heimat.eu/. This genealogy site includes the dates and places of birth (22 Sep 1924, Einlage, Chortitza, South Russia), marriage (21 Aug 1971 Hillsboro, Kansas) and death (23 Mar 2003, Garden City, Kansas) for my aunt Aganetha "Nettie" Wiebe. http://chortiza.heimat.eu/Kt/fam00148.htm.

third one was [pause] was a man in black uniform. I didn't think I'd get emotional about this anymore, but I still do. I realized immediately what had happened. My father just said, 'Nettie, is that you?' and I said, 'Yes.' It was dark and he said, 'Why don't you go on home.' When I got home, I broke down crying and my younger siblings had not understood what was happening with my father there. So they got upset there too and cried and by the time mother was able to calm us all down she wanted us to go and say goodbye to my father, and just as we were approaching the street where, that led to the highway, the truck left. And we later learned that seventeen men had been arrested that evening. One had been arrested during the day. So eighteen men had been arrested in our small village that day. I have never seen my father again. Neither did any of the other children.[20]

The Mennonite Encyclopedia entry on Einlage largely confirms Nettie's account, although she apparently had the event occurring in October, whereas this secondary source places it in July.[21] Einlage was part of the Chortitza Mennonite Colony, where Mennonites had migrated to in 1789 from Poland at the invitation of Catherine the Great. Einlage was located only a few kilometers from Zaporozhia, to which we will return shortly.

Nettie and I spoke on the farm about the meaning of her history. Our most meaningful conversations took place at the dining room table or out in the fields during harvest time when she brought food out to us in the wheat fields.[22] We spoke with great love but often little agreement. Ronald Reagan had a special place in Nettie's heart, in no small part due to his strident anti-Communism.

My political views had begun migrating to the left in high school. While I grew up in a staunchly Republican home, by high school in 1980, I had become our town's presidential campaign manager for the Quixotic campaign of John Anderson, the former Republican Congressman who ran a third party effort against Reagan. My high school buddy, Mike Peebles, and I organized activities as part of the nuclear freeze movement. By 1984, I

20. Nettie Wiebe, "Life Story" (guest lecture, History Class, Don Heinrichs, Garden City High School, 1983). Video on file with author.

21. Krahn, "Einlage." "The exile of Einlage Mennonites to the Far North or Siberia came to a climax on 30 July 1938, when two trucks of men were taken away, of whose destination no one ever heard. By 1941 a total of 245 Mennonites had been sent to forced labor camps."

22. At times it felt as if Nettie was destined for suffering—I witnessed her battle cancer with my uncle Ted nursing her back to health in the mid-80s. Another vivid memory is her surviving a car accident that occurred when she was bringing a meal to the fields during wheat harvest.

supported the Democratic presidential candidate, Gary Hart. University exposed me to the anti-apartheid movement and the peace movement against the U.S.-supported regimes in Central America. My oldest sister, Bev, had joined the Reba Place Church in Chicago, which had become very active in supporting Salvadorans and Guatemalans seeking refuge in the United States. So Nettie and I had plenty to talk about over pot roast and potatoes and rhubarb plotz—neither of us were shy about mixing religion and politics. What undergirded all of these exchanges was love: I knew these people who had had a hand in raising me loved me, and I hope they knew I loved them.

Nettie had come by her anti-Communism honestly, but I honestly did not see how the political disappearance of her father in 1938 could justify the political disappearance of other fathers in El Salvador in 1982 at the hands of a U.S.-backed government.

Wolves, or Wolves in Sheep's Clothing; or What Happened to the Indians and the Jews?

> Showing no mercy, the Anhinga [Snakebird] began pounding the fish's head on the log.[23]

> Both [Zaporozhia Mennonite mayors] Wiebe and Reimer responded directly to the 'Jewish Question' by compelling all remaining Jews to wear the infamous armband with the Star of David . . . Wiebe did not hesitate to report that all former Jewish properties had been confiscated by the city and would be used to meet the financial shortfall.[24]

Those stories of Mennonite persecution and martyrdom shared in the last section have basis in historical fact, but they did not tell the whole story. Challenging and re-shaping my identity, to our identity, as descendants of a persecuted religious minority is the acknowledgement that we have benefited from the persecution of others (perhaps as wolves in sheep's clothing) and that members of our community have actively engaged in genocidal acts (out-and-out wolves).

---

23. "Avian crowd pleasers at Green Cay Wetlands," *Rosyfinch Ramblings* blog, last modified March 6, 2011, http://blog.rosyfinch.com/?p=338.

24. Rempel, "Mennonites," 534.

Of Railroads and Indians: What Role Did the Mennonites Have in the American Genocide of Westward Expansion?

> The U.S. Congress passed the Kansas-Nebraska Bill in May 1854. By the fall of that year, the tide of Euro-American settlement was rolling over the prairies of eastern Kansas—displacing the native population. These emigrant tribes were, in large measure, removed to lands in the remaining Indian country, which later became Oklahoma. —*Kansas Historical Society*[25]

> And a century later they [the Mennonites] were busy in Ukraine Russia, turning immense steppes into fruitful fields and gardens and orchards. In the early seventies of the [19th] century they crossed the Atlantic in search of free homes and religious and political freedom. These Mothers and the Fathers never tired, never lost faith, never used force; but deeply trusted in an all overcoming Providence. —*The Groening-Wiebe Family 1768–1974*[26]

Never used force, so long as someone had done so already to their enduring benefit. When the Mennonites arrived in Eastern Kansas in the 1870s, they came in the wake of more than three decades of displacement of Native American peoples. Not only had there been Plains tribes (like the Kiowa) and less nomadic peoples including the Kansas, the Pawnees, and Osages, but over 20 different tribes from east of the Mississippi had been forcibly removed to Kansas after 1830, including the Cherokees and the Kiowas.[27] By the 1860s, "Native peoples land titles were put in service to the railroads and, to use the 19th c. white phrase, 'extinguished,'" with treaties being renegotiated to give railroads in the plains "special consideration."[28] Mennonites benefited from an explicitly racist policy by the railroads to recruit particular nationalities to populate potential agricultural lands swept of Indians. No French or Italians needed apply, only "Germans, Scandinavians, English,

---

25. "Kansas Territory," *Kansas Historical Society*, April 2010, last modified March 2013, http://www.kshs.org/kansapedia/kansas-territory/14701.

26. Wiebe, Wiebe, and Wiebe, "Dedication," In *Groening-Wiebe Family.*

27. "The Trail of Tears," *Cherokee Nation*, http://www.cherokee.org/AboutTheNation/History/TrailofTears.aspx; Michael J. Marchand, "The Historic Indians of Kansas," *Tales Out of School* October 1993, http://www.emporia.edu/cgps/tales/093tales.html.

28. William G. Thomas III, "How Railroads Took Native American Lands in Kansas," December 11, 2010, http://railroads.unl.edu/blog/?p=125 .

Welsh, and Scotch, as they make good farmers."²⁹ Historian Thomas Misa connects the dots:

> The classic crop of Kansas—hard red winter wheat—arrived with a large colony of Russian Mennonites that settled lands of the Atchison, Topeka & Santa Fe, whose land officer became known as "the Moses of the Mennonites." . . . [I]n most contests with native Americans the railroads proved irresistible. "The construction of the road," stated the Central Pacific's general solicitor, "virtually solved the Indian problem."³⁰

My father's people settled in Gnadenau village in 1874, near Hillsboro, Kansas in Marion County. Others joined them in 1876. While I have not been able to track down exactly what Indian treaty applied to the Marion County land in which Gnadenau was located, there are stories of Cherokee and Kiowa attacks on settlers in 1864 and 1868 before the Mennonites arrived.³¹ The Cherokee, a refugee people already displaced from Georgia to Kansas through the Trail of Tears, faced further relocation to Oklahoma to make way for European settlement.³²

Of Railroads and Jews: What Role Did Mennonites Have in the Holocaust?

> Dearly beloved, avenge not yourselves, but rather give place unto wrath; for it is written, Vengeance is mine; I will repay saith the Lord. Therefore if thine enemy hunger feed him; if he thirst give him drink; for in doing so thou shall heap burning coals of fire on his head. Be not overcome of evil, but overcome evil with good. (Rom 12:19–21)³³

These verses, too, are found in my uncle Ted's "Why I am a C.O." pamphlet. To my ears, the verse is a clarion call to a shrewd nonviolence that satisfies

---

29. Thomas J. Misa, *A Nation of Steel: The Making of Modern America, 1865–1925*, (Baltimore: Johns Hopkins University Press, 1995), available at www.tc.umn.edu/~tmisa/NOS/1.5_railroads.html.

30. Ibid.

31. Frank W. Blackma, ed., *Kansas: A Cyclopedia of State History, Embracing Events, Institutions, Industries, Counties, Cities, Towns, Prominent Persons, etc.*, Vol. 2 (Chicago: Standard Pub. Co., 1912), transcribed July 2002 by Carolyn Ward, http://skyways.lib.ks.us/genweb/archives/1912/m/marion_county.html.

32. "The Trail of Tears."

33. Wenger, *Why I Am a C.O.*

the thirst for vengeance with shovelfuls of love rather than hate.[34] But the passage has also been read to say that the state rather than the individual can act as God's agent of vengeance on earth. I recall my Aunt Nettie mentioning that when the German army marched into the Ukraine in 1941, the German speaking population all but rejoiced. Here were soldiers with crosses on their uniforms—an army of God marching against the godless Communists.[35]

In her 1983 lecture, Nettie shared about the German invasion of the Ukraine in July of 1941. The Russian state wanted to evacuate all of the ethnic Germans to the east to prevent them from falling into the hands of the Germans. Making a comparison to the U.S. internment of Japanese Americans, she said, "You did the same with the Japanese. You moved them inland, you didn't want them to be operating with the Japanese government."[36] The main difference, however, was that there was precious little evidence of Japanese American collaboration with the Japanese military, whereas ethnic Germans in Ukrainian Russia did end up aiding the German army.[37]

While Mennonites resisted being evacuated east in the face of the German advance, Nettie noted how the Jewish population had few qualms about fleeing east:

> And there were also a lot of Jewish people who knew the Germans were after them. And they were trying to get across the bridge. We were not in any great hurry to get across. We weren't [pause]. I forgot to mention that when my father was arrested I became very disillusioned with Communism. I realized there was something desperately wrong with this system to arrest an innocent man without any reasons and at this time I would have gone to anything except Communism. And that's the way all of us or most of us felt.[38]

---

34. For further reflections on vengeance, see Wiebe, "Washing Your Feet," 182–216.

35. The desire to settle scores, against actual or perceived perpetrators, began before World War II and continued after it officially ended. Cf. Keith Lowe, "The aftermath of the Second World War," *History Extra podcast* January 2, 2014, www.historyextra.com/podcasts.

36. Wiebe, "Life Story." Nettie also tells of the courage of her by then single mother, who braved death threats by the Communists to force the family to evacuate to the East with the retreating Soviet army. It was only when they threatened to take her children and leave her behind did she decide to join the evacuation.

37. "Collaboration," *Holocaust Encyclopedia*, U.S. Holocaust Memorial Museum, http://ushmm.org/wlc/en/article.php?ModuleID=10005466.

38. Wiebe, "Life Story."

In viewing the video, I noticed that when Nettie mentioned the Jews, she shifted from a detailed account of events to a metaphysical justification for Mennonite sympathy at the time for the Nazis. Gerhard Rempel quotes Anna Suderman, also from the Chortitza region, who addressed the issue more frankly: "In Germany we saw the opposite of Soviet Russia, that is to say something better. At that time we still revered Hitler. If he had decided upon such a solution of the Jewish question, than [sic] the Jews apparently were endangering the political security of Germany. In this manner I tried to justify the inhuman treatment of Jews."[39] I do not think it is too much of a stretch that many Chortitza Mennonites at the time would have read Matt. 12:19 as having the German army as God's avenging agent for the persecution they had suffered at the hands of the Communists.

Aunt Nettie goes on to say how the German advance overran the civilian evacuation, and how German troops advised their Mennonite group to return to their homes as quickly as possible (I suspect Jews fleeing the Germans did not wish to return). On the return journey, Nettie recalls hearing a whistle and seeing just a hand holding a hanky, waving from an alfalfa field. She discovered a wounded Russian solider, to whom she gave some milk from the cow the family had brought with them. They loaded him on their wagon.[40] So, in this instance, we move from a tortured reading of Matt. 12:19 to the embodiment of Matt. 12:20 in a heartbeat.

Gerhard Rempel details the level of complicity between some Mennonites and the Nazis in the identification and murder of the Jews in the Chortitza region of the Ukraine in 1941 and 1942. The Mennonite mayors of Old Zaporozhia (Heinrich Jakob Wiebe) and Novo Zaporozhia (Isaac Johann Reimer) required Jews to wear the yellow armbands. The mayors collaborated with the German Wehrmacht and oversaw the confiscation of Jewish property. Rempel also identifies Mennonite members of the local gendarmerie, gendarmeries that were used by the Nazi SS to kill Jews.[41] Rempel describes how specialized SS units exterminated the Jews in the Chortitza by simply marching them to the outskirts of their villages in plain sight, and then killing them en masse.[42]

While Aunt Nettie, to my knowledge, was not involved in the persecution of Jews directly, she talked of working as a translator for a German

---

39. Sudermann, *Lebenserinnerungen*, 349–52, quoted in Rempel, "Mennonites," 529–30.

40. Wiebe, "Life Story." The soldier survived but lost his leg to amputation.

41. Rempel, "Mennonites," 525–35.

42. Ibid.

railroad engineer, until the Russians forced the Germans out two years later.[43] Another Rempel, Alexander Rempel (whose father had been a prominent Mennonite bishop who had been taken away by the Communists in 1938), also found work later during the war translating for the German army. Alexander Rempel witnessed celebrations by Mennonites who had participated in the Massacre of Zaporozhia.[44] When the tide of the war turned in 1943, the German Army evacuated willing Mennonites from that region of the Ukraine, including Aunt Nettie and her family. After the war, Nettie made it to Canada, while her mother and sister were among those repatriated to Russia and forced for a time into internal exile and hard labor.[45]

Why do sheep become wolves, the victims into victimizers? Several factors seem to be at play: a very recent history of persecution; an accompanying desire for vengeance; access to power to carry out the vengeance; and a sense of being called, being the elect, being special.

Good Shepherds, and Bad

> Alexander D. Alvarez of Atmore, Ala., pleaded guilty in federal court today to violating the Lacey Act and the Migratory Bird Treaty Act (MBTA) for illegally selling and possessing the feathers of anhingas and other migratory birds protected under the MBTA . . . This case resulted from an investigation by the U.S. Fish and Wildlife Service's Office of Law Enforcement. —U.S. Department of Justice Press Release 2011[46]

My Mennonite Voluntary Service assignment in Harlingen, Texas from 1989–91 placed me with the Overground Railroad (ORR), a church based network working to assist some of the thousands of Central American refugees fleeing persecution by oppressive U.S.-backed regimes to reach the more refugee-friendly Canada.[47] We joined with Catholic nuns and priests,

43. Wiebe, "Life Story."
44. Rempel, "Mennonites," 530–31.
45. Wiebe, "Life Story."

46. Office of Public Affairs, "Alabama Man Pleads Guilty to Selling Anhinga Feathers," *US Department of Justice*, February 15, 2011, http://www.justice.gov/opa/pr/2012/February/12-enrd-220.html.

47. Gavin R. Betzelberger, "Off the Beaten Track, On the Overground Railroad: Central American Refugees and the Organizations that Helped Them," *Legacy* 11 (2011) 17, http://opensiuc.lib.siu.edu/legacy/vol11/iss1/3. "Because the U.S. government was reluctant to grant asylum to Central Americans [in the 1980s], the Overground Railroad helped refugees secure asylum in Canada through primarily legal avenues via an extensive network of churches and volunteer communities. Other 'tracks' of

Methodist ministers and Mormon laypeople, imported secular radicals and local peace activists to fight for human rights against what we saw as Ronald Reagan's hubristic and clandestine support for oppressive abusers.

As part of my introduction to the work, ORR workers Richard and Ruth Ann Friesen put Philip Hallie's *Lest Innocent Blood Be Shed* into my hands.[48] Richard and Ruth Ann were members of the Reba Place Church in Chicago, and I had learned about the Overground Railroad from my sister, Bev, who belonged to that community. ORR took its shepherding inspiration in part from communities like Le Chambon. In his book, Hallie recounts the story of Le Chambon, France, a village whose inhabitants under the leadership of Pastor Andre Trocme hid Jewish refugees under the noses of the Germans and smuggled them out of occupied France to safety. For their efforts, the village was later recognized by Yad Vashem as being Righteous among the Nations, an honor bestowed upon groups and individuals who defended the Jews during the Holocaust:

> The people of Chambon acted on their conviction that it was their duty to help their 'neighbors' in need. Many factors joined in the creation of this spirit: the Protestant history of persecution as a religious minority in Catholic France; empathy for Jews as the people of the Old Testament and a shared biblical heritage; and last but not least, the powerful leadership and example of their pastor and his wife, Andre and Magda Trocme.[49]

Trocme's children also participated in the effort, showing that age need not be an excuse for failing to do good under extreme conditions.[50]

The Overground Railroad grew in large part out of the Reba Place Fellowship, founded by Mennonite theologians who had written critiques of the failure of churches before and during World War II to confront injustice.[51]

---

the Railroad focused on delaying the deportation process as long as legally possible. Though not openly defiant like some refugee advocacy organizations in this period, the Overground Railroad successfully delivered thousands of war-torn refugees to safety."

48. Philip Hallie, *Lest Innocent Blood be Shed* (New York: Harper & Row, 1979).

49. "The Village of Le Chambon-sur-Lignon: André & Magda Trocmé, Daniel Trocmé, France," *Yad Vashem, The Righteous among the Nations*, http://www1.yadvashem.org/yv/en/righteous/stories/trocme.asp

50. Rachel Resin, "Interview of Nelly Hewett (Trocme), Righteous Gentile, Le Chambon (France)," *Holocaust Memorial Center*, November 1, 1986, http://www.holocaustcenter.org/page.aspx?pid=590.

51. Gavin R. Betzelberger, "Off the Beaten Track, On the Overground Railroad: Central American Refugees and the Organizations that Helped Them," *Legacy* 11 (2011), 23, http://opensiuc.lib.siu.edu/legacy/vol11/iss1/3.

The Protestant Huguenot village of Le Chambon of 1941[52] provides a stark contrast to the Mennonite Chortitza of 1941—courageous resistance by a persecuted religious minority to assist another persecuted minority versus cowed corporate silence in the face of the mass murder of Jews and even individual complicity in those genocidal acts.

The contexts of the two stories were different, however: Vichy France was not on the moving frontlines as was the Ukraine, and the memory of 17th-century persecutions by Catholics was not nearly so fresh as losses at the hands of Communists less than a decade old. But the two stories complement one another in the following way: How can we be more like the people of Le Chambon and less like those of Chortitza? How can we be more like shepherds, even when being sheep led to the slaughter?

At the same time, the shepherd metaphor brings with it inherent Messianic dangers. I recall Lisa Brodyaga, a living legal legend from San Benito, Texas who has advocated on behalf of refugees and immigrants for decades and who was one of the co-founders of Proyecto Libertad, a close partner of the Overground Railroad. She would occasionally chastise the rotating cast of northern civil rights attorneys and paralegals that would come to the Rio Grande. There can be a narcissistic air of civil rights tourism in which clients become objects to be saved rather than subjects to accompany on their journeys.[53] Mennonite Stephanie Krehbiel rejects many aspects of martyrdom in favor of another metaphor, the warrior, surprisingly choosing Buffy the Vampire Slayer as a role model:

> [A] vampire sizes her up. "You have a superiority complex, and you have an inferiority complex about it," he concludes. The only way to make that dialogue pithier, from a Mennonite perspective, would be to tell Buffy she had an inferiority complex, and a superiority complex about it. Either way, I recognize that tangle of humility and hubris, alienation and obligation, in the world but not of the world—what a relief to see it onscreen, shown for

---

52. Soul Han, "French Christians save Jews from Nazi Holocaust, Le Chambon, 1940–1944," *Global Nonviolent Action Database*, September 12, 2012, http://nvdatabase.swarthmore.edu/content/french-christians-save-jews-nazi-holocaust-le-chambon-1940-1944.

53. And while Lisa speaks her mind, she continues to mentor aspiring attorneys who visit the Rio Grande Valley. See, for example, Priya Patel, "A Student's Reflection: Sanctuary in the Rio Grande," *Harvard Immigration & Refugee Clinic*, July 9, 2013, http://harvardimmigrationclinic.wordpress.com/2013/07/09/a-students-reflection-a-sanctuary-in-the-rio-grande/. "Lisa very kindly opened up her home to me, allowing me to stay in a spare bedroom and work out of an office adjacent to hers."

Becoming More like Shepherds Than Sheep: Peacemaker Characteristics of the Snakebird

How have we as a Mennonite people made sense of such a bundle of contradictions? At our best, even in the midst of conflict, Mennonites have lived out the ideal of peace. In difficult times, we have fled. In some shameful times, some numbered among us have inflicted great harm.

Care for and Protection of our Young

> From birth [Snakebirds] are fed by regurgitation, which one might suppose an irksome task to the parent birds, as during the act they open their wings and raise their tails.[55]

Anhingas force feed their young by essentially swallowing the heads of their young charges, who then sup on the contents of their parent's stomach. It's a rather touching sight.[56] Mennonites have taken great pride and care in the raising of their children: "Bring up a child in the way he should go and he will not depart from it." For lack of a better word, religious indoctrination plays a central role in that upbringing, sometimes to the lasting consternation of the offspring. Strictness sometimes breeds dissent and rebellion. It also breeds discipline and indelible lessons. As a child in a Mennonite Brethren household in southwest Kansas, my spiritual community had been heavily influenced both by Anabaptism and Pietism, with generous helpings of American Fundamentalism.

Sunday school and Sunday morning worship were just the beginning. Sunday evening prayer services followed, as did Wednesday or Thursday night prayer meetings and youth services, including Boys' Brigade (the Christian version of Boy Scouts), later in the week. And Saturday mornings were hosted by the Bible Memory Association (BMA). And that was a normal week; hang on to your hats for special mission weeks, which included

---

54. Krehbiel, "Staying Alive," http://archive.bethelks.edu/ml/issue/vol-61-no-4/article/staying-alive-how-martyrdom-made-me-a-warrior/

55. Audubon, *Birds of America*.

56. A photo by Richard Fortune shows a parent feeding a fluffy young bird. Another photo by John Calvert is even more impressive—a parent feeds two chicks simultaneously. Wiebe, *Called to be Snakebirds*, slide 23.

Billy Graham movies at the local theater. Off to school we went with fistfuls of free tickets for the movies to give to our friends—"Two a Penny" and "The Cross and the Switchblade" come immediately to mind.

As early as nine or ten years old, I began noticing a split in our church between what I would call the evangelical Mennonite camp and the more fundamentalist camp. Both conservative to the point of scriptural inerrancy, but one quietly committed to a form of nonresistant pacifism and the other most definitely not. I greatly appreciated the respect with which children were regarded; apologetics were to be practiced constantly through witness to one's faith, and where better to practice for the real world than in church. I recall one Saturday evening reenactment of an Old Testament story in the fellowship hall. The story involved bloodshed of some sort, and there were voices calling for battle. Raising my little ten year old body to its full height, "The Sixth Commandment: Thou shalt not kill!" I shouted out, an outburst I recollect quieted the hall and slowed the march to battle, at least for ten seconds or so. The dynamic irony in which I was raised posited rock hard truth on the one hand, but every grain of which was open to rigorous debate.

Membership class and baptism came around the same time, a rigorous process with homework and tests. The Mennonite Brethren confession of faith really came alive in the hands of Pastor Ken Gardner, the second Baptist minister our little church on the prairie had called since my birth.

"You shall know the truth and the truth shall set you free." Little did we realize that, in the words of Flannery O'Connor, it also really did make us odd. And being willing to be odd can be an asset. Protesting the first Gulf War in 1990 while in Voluntary Service in Harlingen, Texas elicited both sympathetic shrugs of despair, as well as scorn and derision by passersby. A band of a dozen or so of us marched up and down the sidewalk outside of the Post Office, the most prominent federal building in town. "You all ought to be taken to the nearest wall and shot," spat one man on his way to mail a letter. I think the experience of handing out Billy Graham film crusade tickets at school prepared me for handling the bemusement, rejection, or threats of those post office patrons.

Force-feeding doctrine and scripture often has driven people away from the church. But a failure to rigorously pass on the faith to one's children and new converts is also a recipe for failure. The drive to be head smart and heart smart of Matt. 10:16 (intelligent and wise) is an extension of the care the Mennonite community has for its young. Far too complicated to sort out here are Anabaptist views and traditions related to education, but in the U.S. and Canada, Mennonites have created an array of institutions of secondary and higher education. The expectation in our household of six children was not whether one would go on to some form of higher education, but what college. And Tabor College, the Mennonite Brethren institution in Hillsboro, Kansas founded in 1908, was highest on the list of options.[57] As the expectation of higher education was also explicitly coupled with an expectation that each child would largely be responsible for personally funding such education, I ended up deciding on Kansas State University. I found nurture and mentoring at Manhattan Mennonite Fellowship (MMF) (a congregation affiliated with the Old Mennonite Church, the General Conference Mennonite Church, and the Mennonite Brethren Church). MMF had a lively commitment to peace activism.

Congregating in Kettles: Why Faith Community Matters

> The [Snakebird] may be considered as indefinitely gregarious; by which I mean that you may see eight or more together at times, during winter especially, or only two, as in the breeding season. On a few occasions, whilst in the interior of the southernmost parts of Florida, I saw about thirty individuals on the same lake . . . I sometimes saw several hundreds together.[58]

Faith community matters. So-called 'ethnic' Mennonites (usually meaning those of Dutch-Russian, German, or Swiss heritage) are sometimes criticized for playing the "Mennonite game" in which two people meeting for the first time (say, at a denominational convention) expend effort figuring out if and how they are related. But such exercises knit us together as a people that extend beyond place and time. And it is not limited to one race or ethnicity. A dear friend from the Democratic Republic of the Congo hails from a region where my parents and another uncle and aunt were Mennonite Brethren missionaries in the 1950s and 1960s. We were both raised in Mennonite Brethren communities on different continents and were immediately able to connect across continental and racial divides.

Congregational support for international peacemaking efforts is critical as well. Congregations become involved through direct action, advocacy efforts, prayer support and encouragement. Congregations provide places of rest and safety as well. The Snakebird provides an example that recollects the survival smarts (wariness, being cautious, attentiveness, readiness) of many early Anabaptist congregations forced underground by persecution: "The

---

57. My dad and all three of his siblings attended Tabor College, as did my two sisters and a brother. Bethel College, my mother's alma mater, was on my list, but for some reason was not in high favor in my home community (likely because it was deemed too "liberal" as a General Conference Mennonite school).

58. Audubon, *Birds of America*.

more retired and secluded the spot, the more willingly does the Snake-bird remain about it. Sometimes indeed I have suddenly come on some in such small ponds, which I discovered by mere accident, and in parts of woods so very secluded, that I was taken by surprise on seeing them."[59]

Ethiopian and Eritrean Mennonites whose families maintained the faith in house churches during the time of the Dergue and later migrated to Minnesota show the realities of other 20th-century persecution by Communist-inspired regimes. While migration in the face of persecution has often been the route of Mennonites, in Ethiopia the flight was inward into homes, when churches and institutions were confiscated but house churches provided refuge.[60]

Commingle with Others Committed to Peace and Justice

> Kettles of anhingas often migrate with other birds . . . Anhingas commonly nest in loose colonies of several to hundreds of pairs—sometimes together with egrets, herons and other water birds.[61]

What do principles mean in the larger world of political action and compromise? It is simple enough to disagree with one's political opponents on moral and practical grounds, but more difficult when the disagreements are with fellow pursuers of peace and justice. John Roth has written on engaging in ecumenical dialogue that "remembers rightly" with a "conversational posture that is committed to rethinking our particular histories and our theological commitments from the perspective of the other; that is, being ready to consider deeply held positions with an 'empathetic' spirit."[62] Such a conversational posture is required not only in considering the past, but in acting in effective consort with allies in the pursuit of justice.

---

59. Audubon, *Birds of America*.

60. "Even during its darkest days of Marxist persecution [in the 1980s] when all those institutions were lost, secret home cell churches were nourished by carefully prepared lesson guides to their Bible study activities," "Ethiopians Seek Faster Growth," *Mennonite World Review*, January 10, 2011, http://www.mennoworld.org/archived/2011/1/10/ethiopians-seek-faster-growth/?page=2.

61. "Anhingas aka Snakebirds, Darters, American Darters or Water Turkeys," *Beauty of Birds*, http://beautyofbirds.com/anhingas.html

62. Roth, "Forgiveness," 583–84.

Called to Conversion

> A raspy croaking... Grunting... Harsh rattling scream.
> —Description of the calls of the Snakebird[63]

Calls to conversion are not always welcome or pleasant sounds to those at whom they are directed. In order to fit the bill of the dove of Matt. 10:16 to be innocent, guileless, and faultless, we must be constantly engaged in self-examination and support one another. In order to be heard by those in power, our calls might at times be sound harsh.

Self-care and Care of Colleagues as Constant Conversion

As a lawyer, I am part of a self-destructive community. The legal profession has high rates of alcoholism, drug abuse, and other self-harming behaviors. Unlike other caring professions, lawyers receive little training in dealing with stress in healthy ways. As an advocate and lawyer who has been working with victims of torture and trauma for nearly twenty five years, a constant challenge has been coping with the secondary trauma, burnout and compassion fatigue that comes with such work. Such work can take not only a personal toll, but also one on family and friends. Along with my colleagues at the Interprofessional Center for Counseling and Legal Services, we try to inculcate practices of self-reflection, burden sharing, and healthy practices to develop skills of coping with such challenges over the long haul.[64]

Our communal religious practices provide the basis for such self-care as well. Small group settings can be a place of mutual support for caregivers and the traumatized. Individual prayer and meditation time can heal and gird the psyche. Individual pastoral or professional counseling can salve the soul as well as provide avenues out of self-destructive behavior.[65] In

---

63. "Anhinga: Sounds," *The Cornell Lab of Orinthology*, http://www.allaboutbirds.org/guide/anhinga/sounds.

64. For instance, we require students to read and reflect on Rebecca Napier and Sharmin DeMoss, *The Caregiver's Guide to Secondary Traumatic Stress: A Manual for Those who Work with Survivors of Torture and Severe Trauma* (Dallas: Center for Survivors of Torture, 2004). We also ask them to take anonymously the proQol5 self-test, an instrument for use in work settings with high levels of compassion fatigue/secondary trauma potential. ProQol stands for Professional Quality of Life. Professional Quality of Life Elements Theory and Measurement, http://proqol.org/Home_Page.php. We encourage students to discuss the outcomes of the test and to raise with us their struggles as they learn how to work with clients in crisis.

65. The recent re-emergence and controversy surrounding the harmful behavior of John Howard Yoder should serve as a cautionary tale. See, for example, AMBS Statement on Teaching and Scholarship related to John Howard Yoder, February 27, 2012;

my Mennonite voluntary service placement mentioned earlier, our primary organizational partner in the Rio Grande Valley was Proyecto Libertad, a legal services organization "founded in 1981 to provide legal defense and advocacy for detained Central American immigrants seeking asylum in the United States."[66] As thousands of refugees headed north, the U.S. Border Patrol and U.S. Immigration and Naturalization Services did their best to stop and deport them. Our efforts as advocates were nothing short of exhilarating and exhausting. Jonathan Jones, a paralegal who worked for Proyecto, recently recalled the experience: "It was a very intense experience. Twelve-hour days, six to seven days a week with a lot of talented people who worked day and night. I interviewed people at the detention center every day and almost every night. It was energizing to see the migrants—to see their spirit to live through very hard times."[67] Such intensity could take a toll. Proyecto staff meetings could be volatile affairs, with stories of chairs being flung across the room in anger. At a weekend retreat on secondary trauma, one legal worker (the chair thrower) questioned the expense and need for such an outing. The people really in need, he said, were the refugees. Why should we be wasting our time and money on this retreat when we could be spending them on the people who really needed it?

At the home and office of ORR leaders Richard and Ruth Ann Friesen, a disciplined and austere approach to life prevailed. Honored to live with them for a time before leaving to start a Voluntary Service house, I witnessed Richard and Ruth Ann live out their faith and their search for a spirituality for the long haul. Based in the intentional Christian community of Reba Place Church in Illinois, Richard and Ruth Ann had committed their lives to peacemaking in pressure packed situations. We daily encountered refugees in detention or in community shelters.

Richard and Ruth Ann recognized that to sustain such work, there needed to be regular individual and communal spiritual work. Daily time for reflection was set aside. Volunteers submitted weekly reflections on their experiences. Regular conference calls were made with the Chicago headquarters and the Christian community Jubilee Partners in Comer, Georgia. Support from churches around the country provided financial and prayer support. We often took mental health excursions in the national wildlife refuge to see the kiskadees, wild Parrots, and boisterous chachalacas (Mexican

---

approved April 30, 2012, http://www.ambs.edu/about/documents/AMBS-statement-on-JHY.pdf

66. *Case de Proyecto Libertad*, http://proyectolibertad.net/.

67. Fernando del Valle, "Proyecto Libertad: 30 Years Making History," *Valley Morning Star*, August 29, 2001, http://www.valleymorningstar.com/news/local_news/article_e5b13ef2-6486-5ee5-9c24-40c6cffobf30.html.

pheasants). That refuge for birds sits only miles from the federal immigration detention center imprisoning people seeking refuge. Such self-care and communal support is essential to be able to speak truth to power.

Call to Conversion—Creating Institutions

> Mr. Abbott is however correct in saying that [Anhingas] "will occupy the same tree for a series of years," and I have myself known a pair to breed in the same nest three seasons, augmenting and repairing in every succeeding spring, as Cormorants and Herons are wont to do.[68]

Kwami Anthony Appiah has argued that citizens of the world have a moral obligation to seek improvements in human rights around the world as well as in their own countries. In examining largely forgotten but foreign-led human rights campaigns in the 19th and 20th centuries, he identifies three characteristics of successful efforts: (1) foreign activists genuinely understand and respect the civilization being critiqued or sought to be changed; (2) movements go beyond campaigning rhetoric to create institutions to reinforce the change sought; and (3) foreign activists work for domestic change as well as international change.[69] The Overground Railroad provided me with an example of careful institutional creation to address a specific human rights moment that sought domestic legislative and administrative changes while also seeking to end human rights abuses abroad.

Conclusion

Wise as serpents and innocent as doves. Mennonites engaged in the work of human rights need to be heart smart, head smart, survival smart, and street smart. We need to be blameless, peace-filled, and peaceful. We need to strive to be humble shepherds and guard against becoming or assisting the ravenous wolves of the world. Martyrdom should not be a calling, or a badge of honor, or something sought out. If persecution should come, we should rely on one another and the good Lord to sustain us and guide us to control the impulse to seek vengeance. The call to be snakebirds for

---

68. Audubon, *Birds of America*.

69. Kwame Anthony Appiah and Joel H. Rosenthal, "Citizenship within and across Nations," *Carnegie Council for Ethics in International Affairs*, November 13, 2013, http://www.carnegiecouncil.org/studio/multimedia/20131107/index.html.

Jesus and for humanity is quite a tall order. In our shortcomings, we should nonetheless strive to live out Matt 10:16.

PART THREE

Application of Mennonite Peacebuilding Approaches in Conflict Settings

12

Authentic Grassroots Conflict Transformation in Egypt

Interreligious Hospitality and the Gift of Pessimism in Mennonite Approaches to Peacebuilding

ANDREW P. KLAGER

Introduction

ON A RESEARCH TRIP to Egypt in December of 2012 where I studied interreligious peacebuilding between Muslims and Coptic Christians,[1] a late evening conversation as we snaked our way through Cairo after visiting the village of El-Fashn consisted of more mundane topics—the appeal of Tim Hortons donut shops, the plethora of Kit-

---

1. I want to express my profound gratitude to the Orthodox Peace Fellowship—and Jim Forest and Alex Patico in particular—and Mennonite Central Committee BC, especially Jon Nofziger and Wayne Bremner, for jointly funding and otherwise encouraging my research in Egypt, much of which is responsible for the material presented in this chapter. I also could not have asked for better hosts than Tom and Judi Snowden, Co-representatives of MCC in Egypt. And I would also like to thank the Centre for Studies in Religion and Society at the University of Victoria, and in particular the director, Paul Bramadat, for providing the space, resources, and collegial environment to more deliberately work out some of the themes and recommendations in this chapter.

Kat billboards in Cairo, and how Justin Bieber's ubiquity makes us long for *real* music again—interrupted by brief spells of silence. The contrast was palpable as we drove through a city embroiled in undulating unrest, anger, disillusionment, deep division, and sporadic violence that, on this occasion, stemmed from Mohammad Morsi's recently issued November 22nd constitutional declaration only a couple weeks earlier. Along with a friend who accompanied me on the trip, I was traveling at the time with Ayman Kerols, the Peace Program Coordinator for Mennonite Central Committee (MCC) in Egypt, and Tom Snowden, who—with his wife, Judi—was the Co-representative of MCC in Egypt at the time. Most of the periodic silence was due, no doubt, to fatigue given the packed schedule of interviews, focus groups, and meetings we had conducted that day. But the silence also signaled bouts of introspection, for as we were lodged near motionless in a sea of Cairo's infamous traffic inching towards the presidential Ittihadiya Palace, the focal point of the latest demonstrations, Ayman—exhibiting a mix a deflation and pessimism—queried to me, "Are you optimistic that things can change?" While acknowledging the intractability and severity of the current hostilities, I responded that I nevertheless was. "Well, that's good," was his reply, "because we're tired of hoping."

This despairing admission, as honest and unadorned as it was, presents a profound challenge. How can we effectively harness the legitimate pessimism of those who have lived through seemingly endless litanies of unfulfilled promises, shallow accords that produce little more than a "cold peace,"[2] and a parlous state of personal security? The answers, even if they seem at times wildly unmanageable, clunky, and unsatisfying, imply that this pessimism is not a mere challenge to peacebuilders and conflict analysts. Instead, pessimism—as the "space where selective indifference and hope meet"[3]—is a *gift* due to the unbending need to convince even the most cynical of a conflict's resolution by appreciating its complexity, bridging the gulf between remote high-level supervision and unvarnished experiences on the ground, and taking strides to ensure its authenticity. As John Paul Lederach observes,

> Their pessimism, or what we might call a well-grounded realism, suggests that the subject of post-agreement must address certain questions: How do we view desired social change in the context of long-term social and economic divisions? What do we expect from and how do we view the quality and building of the public sphere when it has been decimated by violence or, as

---

2. Sisk, "Power-sharing," 140.
3. Lederach, *Moral Imagination*, 55.

is the case in many settings, never really existed? How is trust restored in public institutions and in leaders who are supposed to serve? How exactly does a whole society move from cycles of division and violence to respectful engagement in a way that the change is experienced as genuine?[4]

Far from an immature cynicism or defeatist indifference, if those who routinely contend with the fallout of a conflict are assured of the resolution's sustainability, can take ownership of its resolution, and are confident in the authenticity of the cessation of violence—that is, if hope has been restored—this pessimism has fulfilled its purpose. In short, the pessimism of indigenous Egyptians demands serious solutions to the intractable conflict that grips their country—both the divide between secularists and Islamists and the spasmodic threat of interreligious hostilities.

The basis for the conceptual model I propose in this chapter is the data I collected during the aforementioned research trip to Egypt in December 2012. Nearly two years after the January 25th Revolution, my travels throughout Egypt to meet with various partners of Mennonite Central Committee took place in the tense period between then president Mohammed Morsi's very unpopular decision to consolidate the executive, legislative, and judicial powers in himself and the referendum on the contentious Islamist-leaning constitution. The desire to debate the constitution and whether or not to boycott the upcoming referendum filled the air in this period of discontent, anxiety about the future, and misgivings about the direction of the Revolution. The violence that resulted in several deaths during demonstrations outside of the Ittihadiya Palace in Heliopolis—the suburb of Cairo in which my flat was located—the alleged incitement of which Morsi now stands trial, occurred the day before I arrived.

This trip mainly in Cairo, Beni Suef, El-Fashn, and Wadi Natrun allowed me to interview the director of the Bishopric of Public and Ecumenical Social Services (BLESS) and former secretary of Pope Shenouda III; the Director of the Coptic Evangelical Office of Social Services (CEOSS), a prominent NGO—possibly even the largest indigenously Middle Eastern one; the Manager of the Peacebuilding and Conflict Management department of CEOSS; and Bishop Thomas of El-Qussia and Mair (in Upper Egypt where the Coptic presence is strongest), the Director of the Anafora Retreat Centre and its attendant mediation and "post"-conflict trauma healing training for Coptic clergy from various villages throughout Egypt, of which I sat in on a seminar.

---

4. Ibid., 54.

I was also briefed on the operations of CEOSS's Peacebuilding and Conflict Management department and the CEOSS-run Middle East North Africa Peacebuilding Institute (MENAPI), which is modeled after the Summer Peacebuilding Institute at Eastern Mennonite University. I was fortunate enough to also interview several members of a "peace committee" in Beni Suef, who conduct interfaith dialogues and public forums on Muslim-Christian tensions and intervene in sectarian conflicts. To get a sense of the operations of St. Mark's Language School in Beni Suef and the Evangelical Theological Seminary in Cairo, I spoke with EFL instructors whom MCC has placed in these contexts to incorporate principles and practices of peaceful coexistence between Muslims and Copts in their English language curriculum. In addition to interviewing the Co-Representatives of MCC in Egypt, Tom and Judi Snowden, I also had meaningful exchanges with the Director of the Council of Services and Development (CSD) based in Cairo; the Peace Program Coordinator of the Ekhlas Coptic Organization for Development (ECOD) in El-Fashn—one of Egypt's poorest villages that has frequently experienced sectarian strife—as well as the Director of this same organization. Here, I was also privileged enough to conduct a focus group comprised of Muslim and Coptic workers, volunteers, and participants in the ECOD Peace Program. All of these individuals and organizations are MCC partners whose deeper indigenous familiarity with the political, economic, cultural, social, and religious landscape in Egypt have been open to and are deeply appreciative of the infusion of Mennonite support and expertise—even if evolving and incomplete—in peace and justice. I have heard their sincere and enthusiastic gratitude toward Mennonites with my own ears—a testament, I think, to the strength of their partnership and mutual areas of competency and experience.

But this chapter's emphasis on, as we will soon see, interreligious hospitality draws on several historic Mennonite impulses that also find currency in the peace work of Mennonites today, from the innovative conflict analysis by a number of dedicated peace scholars to the many conflict transformation initiatives that a litany of courageous peacebuilders implement on the ground. In particular, initiatives that transform conflict through attitudinal change at a grassroots level suggest a combined emphasis on peace and justice or a 'just peace'—i.e., the conditions that encourage and increase the likelihood of peaceful coexistence—and a suspicion of governments that extends back to the origins of Anabaptism.[5] In this sense, how to transform political isolation into an advantage has become the Mennonite raison

---

5. In addition to John Derksen's chapter in this book, see the author's articles, "From Victimization" and "Mennonite Religious Values."

d'être in conflict transformation theory and practice, with applicability for many ethno-religious groups who are similarly denied access to the levers of high-level power. To this end, although there is an "up" component—i.e., high-level government officials and decision-makers—in the "ground-up" approach to peacebuilding that has come to characterize Mennonite peace work, the social change on the "ground" is nevertheless crucial to the legitimation, implementation, and actualization of high-level peace processes. This is where the distinctively Mennonite combined accent on relationship-building, trust-building, credibility, conflict transformation rather than mere resolution, and grassroots initiatives comes into play.[6]

Accepting the Gift of Pessimism through a Disposition of Hospitality

To allay the pessimism of those trapped amid the unrelenting repercussions of violent conflict, a focus on interreligious hospitality as an antidote—though certainly *not* a panacea—to interreligious rivalry is a compelling conceptual model for fashioning and refining practical peacebuilding initiatives, methods, and gestures. With the recognition that interreligious conflicts are values-based and therefore animated by underlying insular attitudes that bubble to the surface as sectarian hostilities unfold, interreligious hospitality encourages welcoming the religious Other without deteriorating into a facile syncretism that threatens the distinct religious identities of both host and guest. The concept of universality, Thomas Reynolds is quick to remind us, "means more than reducing differences to a neutral abstraction; instead, it means the cooperative *sharing* of our differences in welcoming one another."[7] In the words of Aristotle, "It is the mark of an educated mind to be able to entertain a thought without accepting it." This sentiment reflects precisely Marc Gopin's dual criteria for using religious resources as a means of resolving conflict if they (1) invite solidarity with universal humanity and the embrace of the religious Other (2) without undermining the unique religious identity of each group.[8]

This twofold standard for interreligious peacebuilding therefore exhibits a "dialogical tension between openness and identity."[9] On the one hand, "Violence, whether spiritual or physical, is a quest for identity and the

---

6. For historical antecedents of these emphases, see Klager, "From Victimization," 119–32.

7. Reynolds, "Toward a Wider Hospitality," 187.

8. Gopin, *Between Eden*, 11–12, 31–32.

9. Moyaert, "(Un-)translatability of Religions?" 341.

meaningful. The less identity, the more violence."[10] Conversely, a deliberate quarantine from the eclectic mix of alien identities fosters the dehumanization of the religious Other through a clumsy and fear-based inexperience with strangers that can only be overcome when "[b]oundaries shade into one another, guest and host mingling in the sharing of hearth and table."[11] By conflating these two considerations, "a larger mutual indebtedness emerges in which both host and guest remain distinct yet fundamentally connected, vulnerability to vulnerability."[12] Within this delicate arrangement, therefore, it is important that the host suppresses the strategic impulse to recruit the guest through the enticement of hospitality and instead embraces the "dignity of difference."[13]

As a guide for peacebuilding amid pessimism, interreligious hospitality is a helpful conceptual model that encourages welcoming the religious Other into one's sacred space and treating them with genuine respect and dignity without, however, the threat of syncretism and erosion of religious identity. However, my goal is *not* to formulate a "theology of hospitality"[14] as a prerequisite that places two conflictive groups at the "threshold to interreligious dialogue"[15] exclusively, which are topics explored in other available resources. And although literal interpersonal acts of hospitality and more overt peacebuilding initiatives such as refugee assistance and accommodation of asylum-seekers are vitally important enterprises for building peace,[16] this is also not my primary focus. Instead, channeling Jacques Derrida's belief that "ethics is in fact hospitality,"[17] I aim to present the many facets of interreligious hospitality as a model for *envisioning* and *actualizing* peaceful coexistence more concretely through its ability to shape and refine practical peacebuilding initiatives, methods, exercises, and gestures. My proposed conceptual model therefore aims to incorporate each of the abovementioned Mennonite peacebuilding foci—even if only implicitly—without, however, exploring the more practical initiatives of problem solving workshops, mediation, storytelling, roleplaying, dialogues and public forums, networking, and other examples in some of the other chapters of this book. As a theoretical framework, it is hoped that the following is adaptable enough to guide a

10. McLuhan, "Violence," 9.
11. Reynolds, "Toward a Wider Hospitality," 181.
12. Ibid., 182.
13. Valkenberg, *Sharing Lights*, xii, 5; Allard, "In the Shade," 421–22.
14. Allard, "In the Shade," 416, 421–22.
15. Valkenberg, *Sharing Lights*, 1.
16. Michel, SJ, "Where to Now?" 532–33.
17. See Turner, "New and Old Xenophobia," 65. Cf. Derrida, *Of Hospitality*.

variety of such initiatives even if I do not have the space to outline specifically how to do this here.

In this sense, my chapter is an experiment in theory-building—advancing concepts, analyzing relationships, and proposing reasons—so others can advance practical prepositions to be implemented as tested hypotheses that account for the widespread pessimism in Egypt—or elsewhere, where apropos. I therefore propose interreligious hospitality as a conceptual model with the conviction that "the praxis of hospitality holds out the promise of cultivating interfaith vistas of justice, reconciliation, and peace."[18] Examples may include storytelling that legitimizes that experience of the oppressed while welcoming the listeners as guests who are given new insight into the depth of their hardships, role-playing that offers a religious rival the opportunity to temporarily "live out" the experiences of the religious Other in order to generate empathy; impromptu apologies or formal requests for forgiveness that replicate the vulnerability of the host-guest exchange; shared actions that mimic the hospitable exchange of gifts as a way to alleviate injustice; or negotiating a sustainable resolution in face-to-face problem-solving workshops or mediation sessions that require compromise, cooperation, and the adjustment of routines. As Pim Valkenberg rightly points out, "the only successful dialogue will be a dialogue connected with the life of the participants, not a dialogue of mere words."[19]

Hospitality in Arab Culture, Islam, and Christianity

The appropriateness of interreligious hospitality as a conceptual model for building peace between Muslims and Coptic Christians in Egypt is validated by the centrality of hospitality in Arab culture, Islam, and Christianity.[20] Hospitality is "a value deeply rooted in traditional Bedouin (and pan-Mediterranean) customs of greeting the guest" and extending "a helping hand to the wayfarer (*ibn al-sabīl*)."[21] The Nile River, for instance, is a geographic feature that orients and unites Egyptians and, as a source of sustenance and economic benefit for all, is a symbol of hospitality as the oasis of "a shared space and a common history"[22] traversing an otherwise inhospitable desert terrain. In Egypt, I was able to experience this legendary Arab hospitality when I lodged and dined at the Anafora Retreat Centre

18. Reynolds, "Toward a Wider Hospitality," 186.
19. Valkenberg, *Sharing Lights*, 100.
20. See Valkenberg, *Sharing Lights*, 27.
21. Granara, "Nile Crossings," 123.
22. Ibid., 135.

near the ancient monasteries of Wadi Natrun, which operates solely on donations. I was also humbled by the unrelenting subsidization of my entire experience, including the arrangement of tourist excursions, post-interview meals, transportation between cities and villages, and accommodations at the various locales for conducting my research by MCC and their partner organizations in Egypt. Even the common Arabic greeting of *marhaba*, or "welcome," reflects their unwavering emphasis on hospitality. "The virtue," notes Miriam Schulman and Amal Barkouki-Winter, "seems an ineluctable product of the landscape . . . To refuse a man refreshment in such a place is to let him die, to threaten the openhandedness nomadic peoples must depend on to survive."[23] In such an inhospitable landscape, hospitality becomes a "social and religious duty" that is "performed without hesitation or reluctance, even for a group of unusual strangers."[24] Due to their conspicuous strangeness and unfamiliarity with the host community's social framework inherent in this nomadic context, the guest is, as Reynolds again observes, "[m]ade vulnerable by this 'lack of place,'" and "regarded as a person in need, on a par with the marginalized in the community (e.g., orphans and widows). Accordingly," Reynolds continues, "the moral obligation of gracious hosting became paramount."[25]

The entrenchment of hospitality in Arab culture—among Muslims and Copts alike—therefore renders it an intuitively performed gesture and easily grasped principle around which to conceptualize and devise practical interreligious peacebuilding methods. The story that exemplifies the contours of hospitality in both Islam and Christianity revolves around "the honoured guests of Abraham" who appeared to him near the oaks of Mamre. This encounter stirred Abraham's hospitable nature that the Qur'an describes as "gentle, compassionate, and often turning to God" (Q51:24–28; Gen 18:1–15).[26] Here, Abraham relays an immediate offer of hospitality by demanding that his guests "not pass by your servant" (Gen 18:3), even though "[t]hese seem unusual people" (Q51:25). He then "turned quickly to his household, brought out a fatted calf" (Q51:26), and made cakes out of "choice flour" which they shared together (Gen 18:6–7). As a shared account in both the Qur'an and Christian Scriptures, enriched by unique complementary details, this story offers a solid basis for the principles that govern hospitality in Islam and Christianity.

---

23. Schulman and Barkouki-Winter, "The Extra Mile."
24. Allard, "In the Shade," 417.
25. Reynolds, "Toward a Wider Hospitality," 179–80.
26. Omar, "Embracing the 'Other,'" 438–41; Michel, "Where to Now?" 533; Allard, "In the Shade," 414–24.

Reminiscent of the "law of hospitality,"[27] or *Diyafah*, which Muhammad's wife and leading figure in Islam, A'isha, lists as one of the ten pre-eminent ethical principles,[28] a *Hadith* from *Sahīh al-Bukhārī* reports that "whoever believes in Allah and the last Day must honour his guest with the required hospitality."[29] It is, in fact, the Qur'anic principle of *ta'aruf*, as the process of getting to know the Other or "embracing the stranger as an extension of yourself,"[30] that Muslims recognize as responsible for the very existence of Arabs, Islam, Judaism, and Christianity due to the hospitality shown to Hagar by the southern Semitic tribe near present-day Mecca that triggered this chain reaction (Q37:102–109).[31] Similarly, hospitality is a basic characteristic of Christianity, which Reynolds describes as having "an unconditional character that implies the infinite hospitality of God, the divine embrace reaching out to all."[32] This hospitality is exemplified by Jesus' association with sinners and tax-collectors (Mt. 11:19; Mk. 2:15) and injunction to practice hospitality towards "the poor, the crippled, the lame, and the blind" since "they cannot repay you" (Lk. 14:12–14).[33] Jesus also hosted his disciples during the Last Supper when he "made the *berakha* at table and the accompanying rites of passing around bread and wine as a symbol of the relation between him and his disciples."[34] This scene also included the ritual of foot washing as "part of the customary hospitality surrounding a meal."[35] St. Paul also enjoins the church in Rome to "practice hospitality" and "[l]ive in harmony with one another," repeating Jesus' commandment that "if your enemy is hungry, feed him; if he is thirsty, give him drink" (Rom 12:13–20).

---

27. Abu-Nimer, "Framework for Nonviolence," 236.

28. Heck, *Common Ground*, 101–2.

29. Cited in Allard, "In the Shade," 418: Cf. Bukhārī's *Al-Adab al-Mufrad,* Chapter: The Guest Must not Stay so Long as to Trouble His Host, *Hadīth* no. 741.

30. Omar, "Embracing the 'Other,'" 440.

31. Akpinar, "Hospitality in Islam," 25; Reynolds, "Toward a Wider Hospitality," 185.

32. Reynolds, "Toward a Wider Hospitality," 184.

33. Valkenberg, *Sharing Lights*, 21–22.

34. Ibid., 21.

35. Alikin, *Earliest History*, 266. Cf. 266–68.

The Gift of Pessimism and Interreligious Hospitality in Egypt

Complexity and the Sustainability of Peace

According to Lederach, those who are pessimistic about the resolution of deep-rooted conflict "locate themselves and change and gauge authenticity within an expansive view of time and an intuitive sense of complexity."[36] Those whose pessimism is a "gift for survival" and a welcome challenge for peacebuilders and conflict analysts require "serious engagement with the complexity of the situation and a long-term view."[37] For, as Lederach again remarks, satisfying the most pessimistic means that the "birth of constructive change develops in the womb of engaging complex historical relationships, not avoiding them."[38] Pessimism, therefore, is a call to mobilization. In this sense, an appreciation for complexity implies serious engagement with the root and precipitating causes of violence and attentiveness to the constituent parts of the elaborate matrix of conditions that foment a sustainable coexistence and peace, i.e., a *'just peace'* and the *transformation* of conflict.

Complexity is a challenge first in the cognitive ecologies—or "multidimensional contexts in which we remember, feel, think, sense, communicate, imagine, and act, often collaboratively, on the fly, and in rich ongoing interaction with our environments"[39]—that shape and justify the noxious attitudes that erode interreligious harmony. Given this complexity, therefore, implementing a model of interreligious hospitality "invites disruption into household order and routine"[40] by entertaining the possibility that religious rituals, memory, narratives, myths, teachings, and values may need to be adjusted or properly nuanced in dialogues, homilies, and training sessions to emphasize the dignity of the religious Other.[41] This disruption to one's religious routine may require a sacrificial de-emphasis on texts, hymns, and prayers that dehumanize the religious Other. Or it may entail a more comprehensive (re-)education program that promotes passages from the Qur'an and Christian Scriptures, *Hadiths* and patristic wisdom that underscore the ineluctability of religious diversity and promote interreligious coexistence as the only realistic way to peacefully navigate this diversity.

36. Lederach, *Moral Imagination*, 54.
37. Ibid., 55.
38. Ibid.
39. Tribble and Sutton, "Cognitive Ecologies," 94.
40. Reynolds, "Toward a Wider Hospitality," 182.
41. See Omar, "Embracing the 'Other,'" 435.

In the spirit of interreligious hospitality, however, a genuine invitation of the religious Other into one's sacred space and "liminal zone of mutuality and sharing"[42] must nevertheless strengthen the religious identities of both host and guest. The sacrificial disruption of one's religious routine will therefore jettison the archaic narrow-minded provisional cultural or political accretions that undermine the spiritual core of a faith tradition valuing compassion, love, mercy, temperance, and humility above all else. What's more, as "the biggest obstacle to interreligious harmony is not the 'issue of the moment' but the burden of history that we all carry with us,"[43] this disruption to one's religious routine simultaneously legitimizes the guest's historical experiences of injustice, suffering, and marginalization that the erstwhile intolerant rituals previously affirmed.

More tangible, however, is the creation of just systems, institutions, and conditions through long-term development and peacebuilding that actualize the civilizing effect of hospitality. This is accomplished by untangling the Gordian Knot of entwined physical injustices that animate needs-based conflicts and breed frustration and despair.[44] The conceptual model of interreligious hospitality can therefore guide peacebuilding initiatives by *meeting the physical needs* of the religious Other in a repetitional exchange between host and guest that subverts institutionalized discrimination. By coordinating the placatory function of justice with the relational aspect of peace, hospitality therein reflects the elusive balance of peace and justice. Interreligious hospitality therefore stokes the flames of hope to re-energize even the most pessimistic by implementing an "economy of compassionate reciprocity that welcomes and provides for the vulnerable stranger."[45] This leads "to a perpetual cycle of exchanges that engage persons in permanent commitments,"[46] where "[w]elcome leads to welcome"[47] to safeguard the sustainability of peace through prolonged cooperation between host and guest. This perpetual reciprocity will further reduce the need for infrequent reconciliation meetings by addressing our "failing in the more elementary matter of day-to-day conversation with our neighbors of other faiths."[48] As Marc Gopin observes,

42. Reynolds, "Toward a Wider Hospitality," 182.
43. Michel, "Where to Now?" 536–37.
44. Reynolds, "Toward a Wider Hospitality," 186.
45. Ibid., 180.
46. Granara, "Nile Crossings," 124.
47. Reynolds, "Toward a Wider Hospitality," 183.
48. Cited in Valkenberg, *Sharing Lights*, 5; Cf. Droogers, et al., *Stereotypering Voorbij*, 183.

To take an example, it would take repeated and extensive gestures of Israelis working in Arab and Palestinian villages to build good, permanent homes before it became clear that there were Israelis who understood the Palestinian demand for justice and were serious about their desire for reconciliation and coexistence. It would take repeated gestures of religious Israelis making donations to the upkeep of mosques before it would sink in that there were many religious Israelis who did not see all Muslims as enemies. It would take repeated Palestinian offers of condolences, visits, and gestures of comfort toward Israeli victims of bombs for it to sink in that not all Arabs wanted those bombs to go off. It would take many Islamic gestures of hospitality to make religious Jews believe that they are finally welcome back to the Middle East as permanent residents. These bilateral gestures, over time, could create a far greater moderate middle than exists currently in Israel and the West Bank. This, in turn, would shift the population matrix undergirding the rejectionism of various political parties.[49]

To properly address the intricate details of these cognitive ecologies and unjust institutions, it is absolutely necessary to engage in face-to-face encounters that epitomize interreligious hospitality. Here, one is reminded of Abraham sharing a meal with his unexpected guests as a model of "mutual vulnerability and generosity that sustains the hospitable relationship."[50] This deeper and more meaningful encounter is meant to replace the artificial pious platitudes that breed pessimism and acknowledges that "hostility and enmity are constructed by human beings and thus can be unmade by human beings."[51] "It is the encounter with the other," Valkenberg suggests, "that gives rise to the fundamental importance of alterity, since the face of the other appears to me as a basic question that uproots my existence."[52] Moreover, the same unyielding assault of discouraging events that generate pessimism also requires a "selective indifference" so that these "particular events that are out of my control will not restrict or destroy my life," which staves off the internalization of maltreatment and therefore renders these events or actions forgivable in the future through face-to-face encounters.[53]

---

49. Gopin, *Between Eden*, 186–87.
50. Allard, "In the Shade," 418.
51. Omar, "Embracing the 'Other,'" 435.
52. Valkenberg, *Sharing Lights*, 13.
53. Lederach, *Moral Imagination*, 55.

Direct Involvement and the Challenge of 'Proxemics'

Lederach also notices that those who are pessimistic about the resolution of conflict in Egypt want to witness social change and a sustainable peace that is "ultimately tested in real-life relationships at the level where people have the greatest access and where they perceive they are most directly affected: in their respective communities."[54] To bridge the gap between vague high-level promises and the unpredictability of ground-level events, Lederach introduces the concept of *proxemics*. This sub-field of anthropology studies "the actual physical space that people view as necessary to set between themselves and others in order to feel comfortable."[55] In this sense, reducing the "distance between people and the processes of change" allows them to "feel directly connected to it."[56] The figurative and literal mechanism for satisfying the challenge of proxemics is *voice*, which "constitutes a social geography mapped and measured by the distance needed to create a sense of engagement." Voice, then, animates meaningful discussion and recoups power, suggesting "mutuality, understanding, and accessibility" to raise assurances "that the conversation makes a difference."[57]

The conceptual model of interreligious hospitality can meet the challenge of widespread pessimism by encouraging direct involvement in familiar settings, empowerment of locals whose cooperation mimics the exchange between host and guest, and hope-building through seizing direct personal control of—and therefore responsibility for—peacebuilding operations. As an example of the "depth of these protesters' anger, but also of its elusive outcome" after the second anniversary of Egypt's January 25th Revolution, a demonstrator who participated in a chaotic scene by stopping traffic on the Qasr al-Nil Bridge in Cairo voiced his impatience with the previous Morsi regime—now since replaced by president Abdul Fattah al-Sisi after the June 30th, 2013 mass demonstrations—by remarking, "We want to show him [the president] that we can disrupt the country." The rapid multiplication of this type of reaction is not unexpected according to analyst Amr Abdelrahman, who avers, "There is a complete rejection of institutions. No one trusts the government, the opposition, the judiciary or the police."[58] And yet, while "[p]essimism born of cynicism is a luxurious avoidance of engagement,"[59]

---

54. Ibid., 56.
55. Ibid.
56. Ibid.
57. Ibid.
58. Heba Afify, "The Politics of Violence," *Egypt Independent*, article published February 1, 2013, http://www.egyptindependent.com/news/politics-violence.
59. Lederach, *Moral Imagination*, 55.

pessimism born of exhaustion can provide the motivation for coordinating low-level, middle range, and high-level process to meet the challenge of proxemics.[60] This is accomplished by translating grassroots dissatisfaction into middle range initiatives such as problem-solving workshops, awareness and skills training, and formation of peace commissions in conflict hotspots.[61] Interreligious hospitality therefore teaches that conflict cannot be sustainably transformed unilaterally, but instead requires collaboration, cooperation, consultation, and coordination for it to be durable through "ready-at-hand" processes that can be manipulated in an *ad hoc* manner, on the fly, using a heuristic approach.

The Coptic emphasis on *citizenship* to inculcate equality—religious or otherwise—for all Egyptians presents opportunities for interreligious peacebuilding from the ground up. As Silas Allard remarks, "citizenship creates the structural space for hospitality to flourish and hospitality allows the possibilities of cooperation and coexistence latent in citizenship to emerge."[62] It is therefore important to recognize that "every dialogue takes place within a constellation of power relations,"[63] which often override the principle of citizenship and directly influence the types of grassroots initiatives, what injustices/needs/harms they address, and who takes on what role in the hospitable encounter in order to restore a balanced and just reciprocity. Exploiting the channels that connect all three levels of authority becomes paramount: if Egyptians function as equal citizens on the ground by exhibiting interreligious hospitality in practical ways, policymakers can render this phenomenon normative in the collective Egyptian conscience by enshrining it in legislation that grants equal opportunity in government, education, and worship to Muslims and Christians alike. By entertaining the hands-on alternatives to the temptation of withdrawal and self-isolation, Copts—"who are in a minority position [and] do not tolerate the majority but try to tip the balance"[64]—can use the gift of pessimism to their advantage by taking matters into their own hands instead of relying on governmental ineptitude and apathy—even direct collusion in sectarianism under the Mubarak regime—that bred their pessimism in the first place.

To this end, implementing restorative justice models to address the ugly aftermath of sectarian hostilities promotes direct involvement and a hands-on approach through community-based mediation, post-conflict

60. Lederach, *Building Peace*, 38–43.
61. Lederach, *Building Peace*, 52.
62. Allard, "In the Shade," 421.
63. Valkenberg, *Sharing Lights*, 97.
64. Ibid., 99.

trauma healing, and nonviolent alternatives to retribution. Christopher Marshall invokes the Parable of the Prodigal Son as a "parable of restorative justice" that offers

> a challenge to contemplate not only the restoration and reintegration of offenders, as an outworking of the Christian discipline of forgiveness, but also to display toward them an openhanded hospitality, a readiness to share with them what the parable calls our 'living' *(bios)* and 'substance' *(ousia)*, so that they may again participate as equals in the social and economic life of society.[65]

Such a model not only opens the opportunity for direct involvement on the ground and undermines the retributive cycle of violence, but such a hospitable "generous gesture is a great beacon of hope at this time of distress."[66] This example, and others like it that welcome direct involvement, therefore neutralizes pessimism by cultivating genuine *hope*. "In all our peacemaking efforts as in our interreligious encounters," Thomas Michel maintains, "we work with hope," not necessarily expecting "to see the results of our activities in our own lifetime" but becoming "gratified when we are permitted glimpses that our work is not in vain."[67] Compared to the unreliability of remote assurances hobbled by bureaucratic red tape, hidden ulterior motives, competing ideologies and infighting, and the paralyzing politicization of "solutions," seizing direct control over the myriad subtleties of the host-guest exchange within a familiar and immediate setting helps to kindle the hope of genuine change.

The challenge of proxemics that contributes to widespread pessimism also invites empowerment through relationship-building, which epitomizes the host-guest encounter in hospitality settings. The profoundly relational core of peace—and therefore interreligious coexistence—portends the descent of conflict into protracted violence if estrangement becomes the norm: "If we cannot treat guests with hospitality, they will become aliens. If they are aliens, we have no particular responsibility towards them, because they are not fully rights-bearing individuals. If we have no social responsibility for them, they remain outsiders. Our relationship is one of estrangement."[68]

To build relationships and enact "a praxis that risks relation with the other as loved by God,"[69] is to therefore entwine religious communities so they become mutually responsible for each other's well-being. This intercon-

65. Marshall, "Offending, Restoration," 24.
66. Omar, "Embracing the 'Other,'" 441.
67. Michel, "Where to Now?" 537.
68. Turner, "New and Old Xenophobia," 66. Cf. Derrida, *Of Hospitality*.
69. Reynolds, "Toward a Wider Hospitality," 184.

nectedness recalls the Qur'anic principle of *ta'aruf* described above, wherein diversity—or mutual strangeness in the host-guest encounter—elicits the attraction of curiosity that welcomes "intimate knowledge, and not mere toleration"[70] of the religious Other: "O Humankind! We have created you of a male and a female, and fashioned you into nations and tribes, so that you may know each other/recognize each other [*ta'aruf*] (not despise each other)" (Q49:13).[71] Indeed, the prefix *inter-* in interreligious hospitality implies both otherness and connectedness, reminiscent of the description of Abraham's visitors as both "unusual guests" and "honoured guests" in the Qur'an (Q51:24–28). But the equal weight on these two facets suggests that interfacing religious communities can be "related in such a manner that they influence one another. The prefix 'inter-,'" Valkenberg continues, "therefore conveys the notion of mutuality and partnership."[72]

It is, however, the humanization of the religious Other and empowerment through *vulnerability* that quintessentially underscore the importance of relationship-building: "Seeking hospitality is an act of vulnerability by the guest; the invitation to the table is an act of vulnerability by the host."[73] Derrida makes much of the dual definition of the Latin *hostis*—from which we get the words hospitality, host, and hostile—as either guest or enemy, and both as stranger.[74] As a deeper familiarization with the religious Other through deliberate relationship-building might mean treating one's enemy—real, potential, or imagined—with dignity and respect in a hospitable exchange between host and guest, the trepidation about fulfilling this obligation to a potential threat is empowering in the way that it leaves the decision to humanize the guest (or enemy) to the host.[75] What's more, the seemingly dominant position of the host nevertheless "marks the humble recognition that one has been gifted with something to give."[76] Conversely, as a guest can be perceived as the enemy of the host, so must the host be the enemy—real, potential, or imagined—of the guest. In this sense, the vulnerability of the guests to depend on the host to meet their needs is an intentional decision to accept rather than reject the host's hospitality and is therefore equally as empowering. Further, this hospitality "implies a radical

---

70. Omar, "Embracing the 'Other,'" 440.
71. Cited in Ibid.
72. Valkenberg, *Sharing Lights*, 11.
73. Allard, "In the Shade," 419.
74. Derrida, *Of Hospitality*, 39–45. Cf. Granara, "Nile Crossings," 122; Valkenberg, *Sharing Lights*, 12–13; Turner, "New and Old Xenophobia," 65–66.
75. Valkenberg, *Sharing Lights*, 14.
76. Reynolds, "Toward a Wider Hospitality," 181.

kenosis in which the host becomes subordinate to the wishes [and scrutiny] of the guests, and admits the possibility that they are right in their claims."[77] The empowering decision to let oneself feel this mutual vulnerability for the greater good requires the humanization of the religious Other to cope with and attenuate this ostensible threat by underscoring the "need to recognize our common humanity and see others as a reflection of ourselves."[78]

'Walking the Talk' and a Desire for Authenticity

Lederach describes the third lesson of pessimism as "what we might call the ultimate litmus test of authenticity: Did behavior actually change?"[79] Pessimism is born from an endless string of unfulfilled promises and pious platitudes that exhibit a marked disconnect from ground-level experiences. Trust-building then becomes the key to authentic change that Egyptian citizens can sense, experience, and taste in their day-to-day lives. As Abraham washed the feet of his unexpected guests, sought out "a calf, tender and good," and fed them curds and milk and cakes made with "choice flour"—repaid by one of the three guests (understood in the Christian tradition as the Triune Godhead) in a future visit that allowed Sarah to conceive a son (Gen. 18:1–10)[80]—genuine action cultivates genuine satisfaction. Hospitality's practicality therefore exhibits this authenticity: "hospitality is only hospitality when it is reciprocal between guest and host—when there is one to feed and one to eat."[81] It is, therefore, this "shared ethic of reciprocity" within the hospitable encounter between host and guest that authentic change can fulfill the challenge of pessimism and build a sustainable peace.[82] Indeed, the practical peacebuilding initiatives and attendant development priorities that the conceptual model of interreligious hospitality presides over "begin with individual agency but become collective actions, reciprocal, negotiable, and accountable, with wide social ramifications."[83] Through practical shared actions that alleviate injustices that are particular to a conflict and problem-solving workshops that address needs and interests in the spirit of interreligious hospitality, the praxis of hospitality amid an inhospitable terrain increases the likelihood of authentic change.

77. Valkenberg, *Sharing Lights*, 14–15.
78. Omar, "Embracing the 'Other,'" 441.
79. Lederach, *Moral Imagination*, 57.
80. Allard, "In the Shade," 418.
81. Ibid., 419. Cf. Béthune, "Interreligious Dialogue," 15.
82. Reynolds, "Toward a Wider Hospitality," 175.
83. Granara, "Nile Crossings," 135.

The authenticity of interreligious coexistence is further assured by the *voluntary* nature of the hospitable exchange between host and guest, as exhibited in the mutual vulnerability inherent in this exchange that we outlined above. The non-coercive encounter complies with Gopin's dual criteria in hospitality's openness and invitation without assimilation as a precondition. It therefore safeguards the authenticity of peace because the relationship is forged without arm-twisting, prohibiting the distinction between religious identities to encumber the humanization process, empathetic listening, and meeting the needs of the religious Other. "To be hospitable," Allard remarks, "an exchange must avoid both commodification and assimilation; the exchange must be freely given, freely shared."[84] As an addendum, Reynolds provides the following caveat: "If hospitality is conditioned by the intent to receive something back from the guest in return, the home becomes more a hostel or hotel, a place for paid lodging. Or worse, it can hold another hostage to the gift with excessive indebtedness, even treating the guest with suspicion or hostility until exchange value is secured."[85] One is reminded of Jesus' instructions already mentioned above, "But when you give a feast, invite the poor, the maimed, the lame, the blind, and you will be blessed, because they cannot repay you" (Lk. 14:14).[86] The authenticity of peace must therefore be reflected in the authenticity of the willing participants, cultivating a relationship that truly desires the well-being of both host and guest rather than relying on a messy contractual agreement spoiled by suspicion and obligation.

Trust-building between host and guest and among partners in peacebuilding helps to overcome the threat of suspicion and ensures the authenticity of interreligious coexistence. The vulnerability that marks the hospitable encounter requires both responsibility and dependency. These two elements form the basis of trust-building as expressed in the conceptual model of interreligious hospitality:

> Out of a sense of abundance, the host simply welcomes another, trusting that—on the basis of a shared sense of vulnerable humanity—there is a good at hand. And such trust places one in the hands of another, dependent on their good will. For once the stranger is invited in, the host yields total stability and control, adjusting the household to accommodate and attend to the unique needs of the guest as they became apparent.[87]

---

84. Allard, "In the Shade," 420.
85. Reynolds, "Toward a Wider Hospitality," 181.
86. See Ibid., 183.
87. Ibid., 181–82.

Such trust is crucial, for the invitation into one's sacred space must include the guarantee that attending to the needs of one's guest will not provide an opening for proselytization or otherwise distort one's religious identity. Trust born out of a "relational praxis"[88] also provides the motivation to mutually tend to each other's needs and interests, that cooperation is sincere and the exerted effort will achieve genuine change.

Conclusion

Interreligious hospitality as a noncompulsory act of mutual trust is a fitting response to the gift of pessimism. Even recognizing the pessimism as a *gift* requires a hospitable—and therefore empathetic and sincere—receipt of this gift as truly instructive and motivational. Both voluntarism and trust, however, require authentic *transformation*—internal and external. Regardless of the religious otherness that distinguishes host and guest, humanization transforms each hospitable encounter into an opportunity to fulfill each other's practical needs by weaving a web of conditions that cultivate a sustainable peace and interreligious harmony. As social change and substantive peace are themselves transformations that betray authenticity, religious extremists require an *inner* "attitudinal change"[89] and "quiet revolution in religious thought, both individually and collectively"[90] to capacitate them for a new mandate of interreligious peacemaking that is naturally intuitive rather than grudgingly imitative. "[S]ince a visit by a stranger, be he friend or foe, offers an opportunity to transform rancor and anger,"[91] interfacing religious communities can be transformed by overlapping their sacred spaces through shared values, teachings, myths, narratives, and their practical applications. This reflects the criteria of interreligious hospitality by strengthening both religious identities and fostering universal humanization of the religious Other simultaneously. However, the external setting within which hospitality takes place is transformed as well: "The home is made different, even strange, vis-à-vis the presence of the stranger. The familiar is de-familiarized. Things do not remain intact as they were, for the centre of gravity shifts."[92]

For peace to be authentic, then, both the actors and causes—the anthro-ontology of the religious adherent and external conditions for a sustainable

88. Reynolds, "Toward a Wider Hospitality," 183.
89. Abu-Nimer, "Conflict Resolution," 687, 689–90.
90. Gopin, *Between Eden*, 63.
91. Akpinar, "Hospitality in Islam," 24.
92. Reynolds, "Toward a Wider Hospitality," 182.

peace—must be transformed: humanization and justice go hand-in-hand. The transformation of host and guest therefore leads to the transformation of their *perception* of each other by "giving hospitality and loving-kindness to strangers, who are always to be seen as children of God, even the presence of God,"[93] which further leads to the transformation of their mutual environment through a newfound willingness to cooperate in interreligious unison. The emphasis in Mennonite peacebuilding on relationship building, trust-building, face-to-face encounters, authenticity through credibility, and grassroots transformation through development and justice expressed together in shared actions and partnerships—all of which exhibit hospitable impulses—therefore hold the potential to answer the tough questions that pessimism poses amidst sectarian conflict in Egypt.

---

93. Omar, "Embracing the 'Other,'" 439.

13

Communities of Hope
Colombian Anabaptist Churches Bridging the Abyss of Suffering with Faith

BONNIE KLASSEN

Introduction

When a paramilitary commander demanded a meeting with Mennonite Brethren church leaders in Chocó, a remote rainforest region of Colombia, they went to the appointed location with fear but also with profound clarity. Weapon in hand, the illegal armed group's commander insisted that the church's rice processing plant pay them a "war tax." José Rutilio Rivas, Mennonite Brethren Regional President, responded resolutely, "The Mennonite church has been committed to peace-building for centuries. We will not support any armed group. If you force us, we will close down our community programs. But we will not support you, even if it costs us our lives." Surprised by such boldness, the commander promised respect for their position of non-collaboration.

A couple of decades earlier, in the late 1980s, army troops threatened to kill Ricardo Esquivia, a lawyer who had been advising landless farmers. He stood facing their guns, with his wife and four children behind him, when the army commander drove up and he exclaimed, "Coronel, I am to so glad to see you. I was waiting for someone like you who would uphold the law . . ." After years of searching for a viable response to injustice, Esquivia had recently returned to his childhood Anabaptist roots, and this legacy inspired his creative, nonviolent reaction. The commander had intended to direct the execution, but the disarming words, reminding him of his constitutional role, challenged him to change his plans. Instead of death, the family faced orders to leave.

BY CONNECTING THEIR UNDERSTANDING of faith to their current context, Colombian Anabaptists,[1] like these two men, have found the audacity to act for 'just peace' and to envision the church as a healing community. This kind of action has not primarily risen out of classroom reflection. Rather, their context has driven them to dig back in history to find theological brothers and sisters that can help make sense of the actions they feel called to carry out today. As Esquivia asserted, "We change by our own work, by getting our feet wet and seeing miracles arise. We change our theology and theory based on our practice and experience."[2]

This paper seeks to describe and reflect on the conceptual and practical journey of the Colombian Anabaptist churches during the last twenty years, broadening from an emphasis on conscientious objection to military service during the late 1980s to the current holistic accompaniment of victims of the armed and social conflict across the country.

Context

Mirroring every other time and place in history when and where people have lived in the shadow of empires and their client-ruling classes, Colombians have suffered centuries of crushing violence. "Since the European invasion of what is now Colombia, many people have been killed and many seeds of hate, revenge, violence, and injustice have been sown."[3] Ricardo Esquivia's description of modern Colombia paraphrases Old Testament prophets like Hosea: "There is only cursing, lying and murder . . . bloodshed follows bloodshed. Because of this the land mourns" (Hos. 4:3). The Romans and the client religious ruling class in Judea used crucifixion as an unquestioned institution to preserve "peace and security," just as the Colom-

---

1. I use the term "Colombian Anabaptists" to refer to all three Mennonite World Conference denominations in Colombia as a group. I use this term not out of any particular academic stance, but simply because this is the term they use to collectively refer to themselves.

2. Ricardo Esquivia, interview with the author, November 28, 2001.

3. Ricardo Esquivia, interview with the author, November 13, 2001.

bian oligarchy, aided by billions of dollars in military aid from the United States, has benefited from massacres and selective assassinations to eliminate thousands of potential "obstacles" to their ambitions. Large landowners absorbed the land lost by indebted and coerced subsistence farmers during Jesus' time and during the early Anabaptist movement. Similarly, more than 5 million Colombians have been forced off their land due to violent pressures. Some of the landless farmers from the first century became bandits or revolutionaries; so too countless Colombians with no education, land, or employment have joined horrifically violent insurgent armed groups or urban gangs for lack of other viable options.[4]

In this Colombian context, there is a small but persistent network of approximately eighty Anabaptist congregations, grouped in three denominations: Mennonite Brethren, Mennonite, and Brethren in Christ. Similar to their theological predecessors from the sixteenth century, most Colombian Anabaptists live in precarious socio-economic conditions. When the first Mennonite Brethren and Mennonite missionaries arrived in 1945, they concentrated their work in remote rural regions with marginalized cultural minorities, forcibly displaced, and other ostracized communities. Urban churches, which are now the majority, sprouted up as Colombians moved to the cities en masse starting in the 1960s.

These Colombian Anabaptist denominations all tend to have small congregations in contrast to the "mega-church" movements in Colombia. The church leaders all emphasize being Christ-centered, biblically-based churches, but real differences exist between them over how the Bible is understood and applied. Not everyone agrees on how the church is called to engage the social, economic, and political realities of society. Those churches that intensely embrace a very public, socio-political role often passionately practice a wide range of charismatic spiritual practices as well, breaking stereotypical categories of "peace and justice" vs. "evangelical" churches. In all these ways, they are not dissimilar from their sixteenth century predecessors.[5]

It is important to keep in mind that these churches are not filled with saints, but instead people shaped by their context and full of all kinds of human flaws. However, this paper is written to highlight the movement of the churches deeper into the suffering of the Colombian context, not to pick apart the failings and incoherencies of specific leaders. Taking all of this into account, when a leader like Esquivia proposes "We must plant seeds of

---

4. Douglas, *Nonviolent*, 8, 92. See also Grupo de Memoria Historica, *¡Basta Ya! Colombia*, 31–42.

5. Goertz, "Introduction," 16.

hope, life, and justice so that trees of justice will grow up and crowd out the plants of hate,"[6] he is not a lone voice in the desert. The three Anabaptist denominations have met together multiple times to discern their mission, and, as noted in the "Being Salt and Light" report, they have concluded that a) the church must have an impact on society, which has political implications; b) the church's political impact comes out of radical obedience to Jesus, not political party interests; and c) the church's social ministry must arise out of clear context analysis and connection with others.[7] At least this has been the stated theory. What have their actions looked like during the past 20 years?

Nonviolence

During the late 1970s and the 1980s, the Colombian Anabaptist churches began to explore the implications of their Anabaptist roots more intentionally. It is not that the early missionaries taught nothing of Mennonite history and theology, but in the face of Catholic domination, connections with other Protestant denominations facing similar obstacles took precedence over specific denominational identities. Supported by Mennonite Central Committee (MCC) and initially also by Mennonite Economic Development Associates (MEDA), the Colombian Mennonite Brethren and Mennonite churches started the Colombian Mennonite Development Foundation (Mencoldes) in 1978. Then, impacted primarily by a context of intensifying violence, but also by the voices of theologians like John Driver[8] and by the Mennonite-based movements for conscientious objection in Honduras and Nicaragua during the 1980s, Colombian Mennonite leaders initiated the Center for Justice, Peace and Nonviolent Action (Justapaz) in 1990. This emerging institution channeled its energies into gaining legal recognition for the right to conscientious objection. As a result, Article 18 of the new 1991 Constitution guaranteed the freedom of conscience, but the Constitutional Court did not recognize the application of this right to conscientious objection to military service until 2009.

It took years for the Colombian Mennonites to find a solid circle of allies, as they were surrounded by multiple legal and illegal armed groups

---

6. Ricardo Esquivia, interview with author, November 13, 2001.

7. Comunidad, *Siendo Sal y Luz*, 5.

8. John Driver facilitated courses and workshops multiple times with all of the Anabaptist groups in Colombia between 1986 and 2008. He is perhaps one of the few speakers that all three denominations invited back and/or viewed as a reference point throughout these two decades.

sworn to military solutions and a civil society peace and human rights movement that was not at all convinced about nonviolence.[9] Now, the Mennonite church stance for nonviolence and conscientious objection is not so unusual. The civilian movements that had previous viewed war, like Emil Brunner, as "an instrument which, although brutal, could be used to resolve intolerable . . . tension . . ." realized that "it cannot be controlled, it has lost even this shred of utility . . ."[10] These movements took more radical positions against violence with the intensification of U.S. military support to Colombia in 2000. Noting the historical differences, one business sector leader who favoured the military aid stated that "only the Mennonites can ethically stand against Plan Colombia on the basis of nonviolence because the rest of the groups are not coherent in their stance for nonviolence."[11]

Throughout these years, the Colombian Mennonite Church has embraced nonviolence as an unchangeable principle, never deliberately violating this stance. In the late 1990s, the Colombian government increased the use of bodyguards and armoured vehicles in response to international pressure decrying the assassination of thousands of community and social movement leaders. Mennonites have hosted civil society meetings with a dozen security cars parked outside, but the Mennonite leaders have refused to receive this "security mechanism" themselves, even when facing death threats. Echoing Conrad Grebel's position that "the gospel and those who accept it are not to be protected with the sword" they have sought to delegitimize violence, regardless of its causes and conditions.[12] According to former Colombian Mennonite Church President, Peter Stucky, every nonviolent act is God's new order breaking through.[13]

As such, the Colombian Anabaptist churches share much in common with Anabaptist resistance to militarism from other times and places, undoubtedly because they have grown from the same roots and continue to influence each other.[14] Yet, in Colombia, the position of submission to suffering without violent resistance has generated significant personal questioning and collective debate. Numerous Colombian Anabaptist leaders

---

9. Nelson Berrío, interview with the author, March 11, 2007. Nelson Berrío has been a significant national leader in the Colombian peace movement since the 1980s.

10. As cited in Yoder, *Nevertheless*, 22.

11. Mario Gómez, interview with the author, September 20 and November 14, 2001. Mario Gomez was the representative for the Colombian commercial business sector in the Permanent Assembly of Civil Society for Peace.

12. Fast, "Conrad Grebel," 124.

13. Stucky, "Peace Churches."

14. Among other examples, see Peachy and Peachy, *Seeking Peace*, 5, 9, 12, 14, 28, 151, 155, 157.

have at some point considered joining an armed group. In an oppressive context, it has been difficult for some to swallow the word "submission." Over time, the discernment around the church's call to conscientious objection and advocacy did contribute to a clearer understanding of "submission to authorities," as recognizing worldly authorities, while at the same time declaring ultimate obedience to God, exercising the church's independent moral discernment, and expressing willingness to suffer the consequences of civil disobedience.[15] So, like the sixteenth-century Anabaptists, concrete dilemmas in the face of violence led to a more radical commitment to nonviolence.[16]

It would be completely inaccurate to state that no Colombian Anabaptist male has completed obligatory military service. Many have. If the church leadership has struggled with this issue, the broader church membership has experienced even greater dilemmas or confusion. Denominational institutions like Justapaz, and then later the Mennonite Brethren Peace Office in Cali (Edupaz) and Bible institutes in Bogotá and Chocó have dedicated significant energy towards encouraging a biblical position for nonviolence among their youth and their pastors. Education about nonviolence has not been primarily geared towards the general population, but instead towards the church itself, as it is immersed in the pressures and assumptions of society.

Despite the internal contradictions, the Colombian Mennonite Church's growing public stance promoting conscientious objection to military service did not go unnoticed by power-holders who felt that their interests were at risk. Ricardo Esquivia, Justapaz' founding Director, went into exile for several months in 1993, at risk of being arrested under false accusations. The Mennonite Seminary, which hosted Justapaz' "peacemakers program" for conscientious objectors, was formally shut down in 1997 by the national government once the program's enrollment grew to over 180 youth. Concentrated international pressure helped re-open the program. Perhaps the Mennonite experience of political persecution then deepened a commitment of solidarity towards others who suffered from political and armed pressure, just as the levels of forced internal displacement in Colombia began to peak.

---

15. Comunidad, *Siendo Sal y Luz*, 25.
16. Haas, "Michael Sattler," 137.

Sanctuary for Peace Churches

"If we choose to see systemic evil, it will open an abyss that can only be bridged by faith."[17]

The Colombian Mennonite and Mennonite Brethren churches are founding members of the Colombian Evangelical Council of Churches (CEDECOL). This federation of Protestant churches began in 1950 during a civil war referred to as "La Violencia," as an alliance to face intense legal and religious persecution directed towards non-Catholic groups. During the early 1990s, the Colombian Mennonite Church led workshops introducing conscientious objection to CEDECOL member denominations, with very sparse participation. However, as the armed conflict in Colombia intensified, an increasing number of pastors from hard-hit regions looked to the Mennonite church for orientation. In 1997, Justapaz led the creation of CEDECOL's Human Rights and Peace Commission with 11 initial members.[18] To mitigate resistance from other denominational leaders to such "political" topics, the Mennonites began to talk about human dignity instead of human rights, and emphasized the biblical concept of Shalom, understood as justice, respect, salvation, economic well-being, an end to militarism, and no more fear.[19]

Dramatic stories of massacres and forced displacement told by pastors of other denominations moved certain Mennonite leaders from workshops to new kinds of action. Initially, the response to victims focused on church-based projects with displaced families in Urabá Antioqueña, in Tolima and then in Bogotá.

Action then turned the Mennonite leaders back to theological and conceptual reflection. Thousands of people were being killed and displaced across the country. How should the church discern its involvement? Why should the church take additional risks in this context? Colombian Mennonite church leaders found inspiration in John Driver's book *El Evangelio de Paz* during the birthing of the "Sanctuary for Peace Church" vision in the late 1990s. This well-respected Anabaptist theologian accompanied the validation of this conceptual framework with church leaders from across the country in 2001. He shared how early Anabaptists created houses of refuge for victims of the Inquisition and other forms of violence. Looking further back in history, Anabaptists based many of their practices and values on

---

17. Douglas, *Nonviolent*, 69.

18. After a few years, this Commission was referred to as the Commission for Restoration, Life and Peace.

19. Driver, *Pueblo*, 17, 86, 96.

the early church, particularly with regards to anti-militarism, love for enemies, protection for people in danger, and the importance of community.[20] Although Driver continuously referred to sixteenth-century Anabaptists in his teachings, he also made clear that Mennonites have no monopoly over this perspective. It is the patrimony of any radical Christ-follower.[21]

Broader than the sanctuary movement in the United States during the 1980s, the Colombian Sanctuary for Peace Church vision embraced a wide variety of responses to violence. The unifying framework consisted of understanding church as a people, a message, and a place.

A People

> *We are a people that, full of the Holy Spirit and exercising our gifts, talents and ministries, embrace people affected by the material and spiritual war in this country, affirming the peace-making gospel of our Lord Jesus Christ and seeking their recuperation. . . . We are a people that models shalom, God's holistic salvation—personal, familiar, spiritual and social recuperations whereby people regain dignity and society is built based on nonviolence as a lifestyle.*[22]

The decision to be a Sanctuary for Peace Church necessarily happens in community. Community discernment allows for flexibility in action while still anchoring individual efforts to a collective identity that guides the work.[23] In this case, some Colombian Anabaptists have embraced their identity as a visible community of shalom, a gathered church conscious of the world's opposing reality—an identity very similar to sixteenth-century Anabaptists.[24]

The primitive church was also a healing community for many individuals of the Greco-Roman age who were displaced, allowing them to recuperate their humanity. Jesus himself formed a new reconciled community out

---

20. John Driver, "Ciudades de Refugio" (lecture, Bogotá, Colombia, November 1, 2001), "Hacia una Espiritualidad de Paz" (lecture, Bogotá, Colombia, November 8, 2001), and "Llegando a Ser Iglesia de Paz: Cultivando la Tradición de Jesús" (lecture, Bogotá, Colombia, November 9, 2001).

21. John Driver, "Sanctuary for Peace Encounter" (lecture, Cachipay, Colombia, November 1–2, 2001).

22. Justapaz, *Construyendo la Paz*, 7.

23. Steele, "Front Lines," 139.

24. Gross, "Jakob Hutter," 163.

of very diverse people, even mutual enemies. Sanctuary for Peace churches reaffirm this biblical community-based hope.²⁵

This kind of hope empowers believers for action. Like their faith ancestors, a renewed sense of community has enabled churches to face their fears. Ricardo Esquivia reaffirmed that "we gain energy from the community of faith, and that reduces our fears and gives us confidence to act as we should. When we act in the name of the church, a coherent church, we gain respect even from the different armed groups."²⁶

A Message

> *We offer a message of nonviolence . . . a call for repentance and training for people to live pacific, reconciled lives through nonviolent conflict transformation.*²⁷

Actions may speak louder than words, but in a politically polarized context, actions are easily misinterpreted. The Colombian Mennonite Church identified an urgent need to make their conceptual and theological framework known, with tactics ranging from unofficial meetings with illegal armed groups to formal dialogue with government and military officials and the use of mass media. Conversations with power-holders happened when the opportunity arose and during times of crises. Colombian Anabaptists only used mass media in response to very specific contextual changes because of the expense involved.

When the United States government pressed towards approving Plan Colombia in 2000, Colombian Mennonite leaders Peter Stucky and Ricardo Esquivia sent an open letter to Mennonite churches in the United States urging them to oppose their country's multibillion-dollar military aid program because it would be "like throwing oil on fire." A couple of years later, the new Colombian President, Alvaro Uribe Velez, announced his "Democratic Security Policy," placing expectations on everyone to actively take sides with the Colombian Armed Forces, thus ignoring the civilian population's right to neutrality. Leaders from the Mennonite, Mennonite Brethren, and Brethren in Christ churches published a ten-point statement for nonviolence in the Sunday edition of the national newspaper El Tiempo.²⁸ The newspaper advertisement coincided with the first "Pan y Paz—Bread and Peace" public

---

25. Driver, *Pueblo*, 120, 127, 132, 138
26. Ricardo Esquivia, interview with author, November 28, 2001.
27. Justapaz, *Construyendo*, 8.
28. *El Tiempo*, September 22, 2001.

vigil in recognition of September 21st as the International Day for Nonviolence and Ceasefire. Pan y Paz celebrations have been replicated by dozens of churches across Colombia on a yearly basis since then.

Although the message has varied in form and specific content, there has been a consistent practice of what John Driver calls "announcing both judgement and hope."[29] Certain church leaders have embraced a prophetic role, warning people that they are headed towards catastrophe. Like the biblical prophets, the warnings are not deterministic, but rather invitational towards alternatives.[30] The church has, at least sometimes, been a sign of the new creation that God is bringing forth. It has offered prophetic hope.[31]

For some, the Sanctuary for Peace message has been "too political." However, as suggested earlier, when the church interacts intentionally with society (with the "polis"—the people), its actions are inevitably political. There is abundant evidence that the Colombian Anabaptist leaders root their public message in the Bible, as shown through their multiple publications. This is not the place to provide an exhaustive list of biblical themes shaping their message. A small sample includes the following: a) a vision of God's Kingdom already existent here and now (Luke 17:21; Jer. 29:7); b) a vision for the church as a safe place (Deut. 19:7–10); c) the value of all creation (Genesis 1–2) and the restoration of human dignity as a constant theme in the prophetic books;[32] d) nonviolence as a sign of Christian discipleship (Matt 5:39–44; 26:52; Luke 9:51–56; Rom 12:14–21); and e) peace as the fruit of justice (Hos 2:18, 19).

> Alongside fundamental biblical texts, the most influential factor in the development of the Colombian Anabaptist church's message is sixteenth-century Anabaptist theology.[33] Anabaptist roots have provided them with a theological alternative in response to their tumultuous context, rejecting both violent action/discourse (promoted by a few Colombian religious revolutionaries) and indifference (held by many Evangelical churches).[34]

---

29. Driver, *Pueblo*, 109.
30. Douglas, *Nonviolent*, 2–3.
31. Driver, *Pueblo*, 172,173,185.
32. Driver, "La Vivencia."
33. Ricardo Esquivia, interview with author, November 28, 2001.
34. Written declaration given by the Evangelical Council of Churches in Colombia, May 2001.

A Place

> We become physical places for peace, opening our doors to facilitate: face-to-face encounters between opponents, public discussion, time for prayer and reflection where everyone can feel safe, and refuge for those who are persecuted due to their convictions or affected by violence and injustice, in a place protected by the community of faith.[35]

Like some sixteenth-century Anabaptists, the bridge of faith in response to the abyss of injustice led several churches to open up church property for providing psycho-social refuge and healing.[36] Victims of different kinds of violence—armed violence, urban violence, domestic violence—and affected by all sides of the armed and social conflict, have been able to come together and re-encounter dignity. While many other organizations have essentially cared for victims of "their own kind" or within their own interests, Sanctuaries for Peace have offered restoration and even physical protection for all kinds of people.[37] This approach fits with other Mennonite peacemakers around the world who have worked with all sides of a given conflict, helping those in need without showing preferential treatment.[38]

The Sanctuaries for Peace vision gave churches in regions of intense violence a framework within which to understand the acts of risky compassion that they chose when faced with massive displacement, assassinations, or kidnappings in their own communities. Urban middle or upper class churches could often distance themselves from violence and they raised many more "buts and what ifs." That said, all churches named doubts and fears. During the Sanctuary for Peace Encounter in November 2001, churches identified three main concerns:

1. Leaders expressed intense fear for safety, due to a lack of legal protection and a lack of formal recognition from armed groups for the church's role. There was considerable debate over whether or not to make public declarations of a church's "Sanctuary for Peace" identity.

2. Some noted concerns about distorting the mission of the church, becoming "just another social organization." This concern, together with the security risks, generated additional anxieties about losing

---

35. Justapaz, *Construyendo*, 8.
36. Klaassen, "Michael Gaismair," 92.
37. Nelson Berrío, interview with author, November 12, 2001.
38. See Peachy and Peachy, *Seeking Peace*, 63, 104, 151,190; and Gopin, "Religious Component," 234.

traditional church members for whom the potential hazards outweighed their commitment to a particular congregation.

3. Churches felt overwhelmed by the potential avalanche of complex dilemmas that this vision generates. Would victims of violence expect too much of the church? Where would the church draw limits? How would they gather enough information to analyze the implications of a particular action? Where would the necessary resources come from?

Reconciliation and Accompaniment of Victims

As churches embraced the Sanctuary for Peace vision, but also wrestled with the challenges of this framework, several complementary initiatives arose. In 2001, at the height of a series of massacres directly affecting communities with a strong presence of Protestant-Evangelical churches, Ricardo Esquivia began to write simple reports retelling these horrors to the international community. Advocacy organizations in Colombia and Washington, DC, welcomed these reports as very useful tools. By 2006, Justapaz, then directed by Jenny Neme, and the CEDECOL Commission for Restoration, Life and Peace, developed a systematic documentation system, with regional coordinators recording cases and feeding carefully analyzed information into an annual report about human rights violations affecting Protestant-Evangelical church members. Greater connection with hundreds of victims of the armed conflict underscored the need to provide more holistic support for people suffering in so many ways.

In the meantime, Anabaptist peacebuilding and victim-accompaniment work began to decentralize or develop significantly outside of Bogotá, Colombia´s capital city where most institutional growth had happened since the 1980s. Mennonite congregations started sustainable humanitarian and education projects with internally displaced people in Soacha and Ibagué. The Mennonite Brethren denomination began peace and community development ministries in Cali and Chocó. Ricardo Esquivia moved back to his natal Caribbean region in 2004, and founded the inter-Evangelical community development and peace organization, Sembrandopaz.

After a series of workshops between 2002–2005 with dozens of church leaders involved in the above-mentioned initiatives, Colombian Anabaptists started the inter-denominational program called the "Church Coordination for Psycho-social Action" (CEAS). With this increase in action across the country—all associated with Mennonites—the need to coordinate and pool resources also increased. How else could these small-scale church-based efforts maximize very limited resources to respond to overwhelming need?

How else could they try to maintain a relatively coherent message in what their actions projected to society about "the Mennonites"?

The RAV Project

When the leaders of several of these projects approached Mennonite Central Committee for additional support, the Colombia Representative encouraged the creation of a mechanism for coordination between these initiatives. As a result, the Reconciliation and Accompaniment of Victims Project emerged, commonly referred to as "RAV." Arguably, we can note parallels to Mennonite Central Committee's own creation as a single relief effort amongst members of a fractured Anabaptist family in response to compelling need. Although connections between different Anabaptist churches and projects in Colombia existed in 2008, the relationships between projects were fragile when the RAV Project began. RAV did not actually become one single project, but rather a coalition of separate efforts. However, monthly meetings between member entities—Justapaz, Mencoldes, CEAS, Sembrandopaz, the Colombian Mennonite Church, and the Colombian Mennonite Brethren Church—did contribute to greater coordination and to a common conceptual/action framework. The four institutions and two denominations have passed through many challenges, even serious tensions, in this process but it has also been an opportunity to work through their inconsistencies.[39]

Early in this process, the participating leaders named reconciliation as the ultimate horizon for these efforts. They embraced the idea of reconciliation as a paradigm, an objective, and a process, just as Hizkias Assefa had introduced to them a decade earlier during workshops organized by Justapaz in Bogotá.[40] This paradigm seemed bold in a context where most other organizations and public figures either distorted or rejected the idea of reconciliation. It led to many hours of discussion clarifying what they meant by "reconciliation." Working towards reconciliation in the middle of the atrocities of an armed conflict is a messy, confusing endeavor.[41] What were they proposing, beyond rejecting the distortions projected by others?

These Colombian Anabaptist leaders affirmed that reconciliation is both personal and political, and always spiritual. "*Reconciliation is a long-term process through which people and communities separated by violence*

---

39. Reconciliation Project notes, Mennonite Central Committee, Colombia Plan-Win Database, Feb. 10, 2009; October 7, 2009; July 26, 2011.

40. Assefa. *Peace and Reconciliation*, 10.

41. Reconciliation Project notes, Mennonite Central Committee, Colombia Plan-Win Database, Sept. 9, 2010.

and injustice learn to repair and transform their relationship, nonviolently, in order to live together with dignity, truth, justice and love."[42] It necessarily involves conflict transformation, truth, justice, repentance, holistic reparation, and forgiveness. Churches play a unique role in the relatively religious Colombian society, accompanying the personal component of reconciliation. Both victims and victimizers require personal transformation to break cycles of violence. By this time, numerous Anabaptist churches had years of experience accompanying victims of violence, but only sporadic involvement with victimizers. The conceptual discernment process highlighted the need to also accompany victimizers and foster the rational, emotional, and spiritual components of repentance and reparation among those who have caused violence. This idea broke new ground. In the broader peace/human rights movements in Colombia, the focus on justice and reparations had not contemplated the possibility of real repentance.

The churches' involvement in political components of reconciliation generated much greater debate, particularly in the broader Anabaptist church. However, as mentioned previously, general church leadership did recognize that personal transformation takes place in specific social-economic-political contexts that either facilitate or inhibit these changes. They agreed that broader structures, "powers and principalities" (Eph. 6:12–18), have a real role in perpetuating injustice and violence, and these need to be addressed. Local churches can foster restorative practices on a community level that hopefully gain structural legitimacy and legality in Colombia someday. "If it exists, no one can say it's impossible."[43]

The RAV Project leaders cautioned participating churches against excessive naiveté in their ministries, so as to not become "useful idiots" manipulated by other entities with a specific political agenda. When personal transformation manifests itself through repentance, forgiveness, or other concrete actions by victims or victimizers, what is personal quickly becomes political, and has the potential to be used by others.

The RAV Project loosely focused its work around four broad objectives, as stated in the written documents in Mennonite Central Committee files. RAV members had been carrying out work in these areas for some time already, but they had not put about all of the pieces together before. The objectives are as follows:

1. Facilitate spaces for dialogue, trust-building, analysis, and solution-building with churches, diverse sectors of civil society, and all of the

---

42. Reconciliation Project document, Mennonite Central Committee, Colombia PlanWin Database, document, Sept 2009.

43. This is a common saying of Ricardo Esquivia

armed groups involved in the conflict about the complex process towards reconciliation;

2. Support and organize programs based in local congregations to offer holistic accompaniment (humanitarian assistance, re-establishment support, and protection mechanisms) for victims of the armed conflict and to work towards the restoration of victimizers;

3. Through local, regional, and national church programs, promote and help create conditions for truth, justice, and reparation with the victims of the armed conflict as well as victimizers;

4. Build up the potential of the churches' contribution to institutionality and public policies towards reconciliation.

Peace: Dialogue and Connecting

The Colombian government, particularly since 2002, has insisted that dialogue or peacebuilding with any of the other parties in the armed conflict is exclusively their prerogative. The Colombian Mennonite Church and many other civil society groups believe otherwise. Peacebuilding in societies affected by protracted conflict is a dynamic social process in which everyone has a level of responsibility. As John Paul Lederach affirmed during a workshop that he facilitated for Colombian Sanctuary for Peace churches, "[T]he creation of social change is the art of seeing and building networks—strategic networks infused with imagination."[44]

In polarized Colombian communities, churches are often one of the few respected social actors with the capacity to mediate between divergent groups.[45] Churches can reduce distrust and fear because they are perceived as trustworthy.[46] Perhaps this seems like an unlikely role for Anabaptist churches to fulfill, with their historic tradition as "the quiet in the land." However, the diverse Anabaptist-related movements of the sixteenth century don't leave their theological progenies without precedent.[47] Precisely in line with history, as small churches, unaligned with societal power-holders, other groups perceive the Colombian Anabaptists with less suspicion of pushing hidden agendas. Consequently they have often gained significant

---

44. Zapata, *Transformación*, 24, 29, 106.

45. Ibid., 38.

46. This was the conclusion that essentially all of the authors reached in Johnston and Sampson, eds., *Religion*. See 17, 27, 47, 66, 74, 92–95, 106, 133, 216–18, 222, 227, 233, 261, 332.

47. Goertz, "Thomas Muntzer," 38.

space as a "bridge-builder" or "dialogue-facilitator" on local and national levels.

The Colombian Mennonites in Bogotá, Sembrandopaz on the Atlantic Coast, and the Mennonite Brethren leaders in Chocó and Valle have gained respect primarily because of their attitude of service rather than domination, and their theological rather than ideological approach.[48] They have offered themselves for all kinds of logistical and organizational tasks, and, as churches, they have had the infrastructure and networks (local, national, and international) to follow through on their commitments.[49] As a result, diverse social actors—not only communities that suffer from violence, but also oil companies, municipal governments, Afro-colombian community councils, among others—have sought these Anabaptist entities to facilitate social dialogue.[50] In the Atlantic Coast Region and in Arauca, Anabaptist leaders have been catalysts and accompaniers for the Citizen Commissions for Reconciliation. One Mennonite congregation in the capital city helped create the "Territories for Peace" in Teusaquillo and Soacha. These have all been opportunities for Colombian Anabaptists to inject their key values.[51]

Within this role of bridge-building, the process becomes more important than events, in contrast with many peace initiatives that focus their energy on the latter.[52] However, many possibilities for action arise out of these processes. A multitude of relationships have led some Colombian Anabaptist leaders to become involved in too many simultaneous activities to the point of exhaustion and strain on many levels. Over time, they have noted the importance of balancing diverse connections with the need to focus on more selective, strategic relationships. They live a continual tension, without resolution, between the efficiency of going deeper with small networks of organizations that share common priorities and values and the drive to connect with "the Other," bridging very diverse perspectives.[53]

Another challenge of bridge-building has been connecting with the "enemy" that others seek to eliminate. Instead of annihilation, the Anabaptist churches seek to transform those who have done terrible harm, seeking

---

48. Nelson Berrío, interview with author, November 12, 2001.

49. Esquivia with Stucky, "Building Peace," 258.

50. Reconciliation Project notes, Mennonite Central Committee, Colombia Plan-Win Database, January 23, 2012; April 25, 2012; September 5, 2012; February 17, 2010.

51. Ibid., January 23, 2012.

52. Camilo González, as stated in a meeting of the Comité de Enlace in Bogotá, November 26, 2001.

53. Reconciliation Project notes, Mennonite Central Committee, Colombia Plan-Win Database, September 13, 2011; January 23, 2012.

redemption for the oppressor and the oppressed.[54] All of the armed groups, legal and illegal, have inflicted horrific violence on their fellow Colombians, including churches. Colombian Mennonite church leaders have gone to talk with all of them—asking them to respect life and to consider nonviolent means to achieve their ends. Although many Colombians have informally talked with the illegal armed actors (paramilitary and guerrilla), these talks often happen either by force or out of some level of conceptual or practical affinity. Few have the vision and credibility to talk with all sides of the armed conflict, by choice, and without "taking sides." By focusing on their theological agenda, Anabaptist leaders have downplayed political considerations and invited genuine change. The risks have always been high—risks of betrayal, imprisonment, or death. But the commitment to dialogue has taken priority over fear and the encounters with enemies have released the leaders from their fears.

Mercy: Holistic Accompaniment of Victims and Response to Victimizers

As previous chapters of this book already affirmed, Anabaptist churches hold a long tradition of compassion for those who suffer. Colombian Anabaptists have embraced marginalized people with generous hospitality as an expression of Christ's love and as a demonstration of coherence with their commitment to nonviolence.[55] Similar to the experiences in early Anabaptist circles, victims of the Colombian armed conflict have found acceptance and regained their sense of self-worth in healing church communities, while being ostracized everywhere else in society. For these victims, Sanctuary for Peace churches have become one of the few places where they can share their pain and rebuild their lives. As one woman shared about her experience at a Mennonite church, "When I come to church, I like to volunteer in the kitchen. It's a beautiful thing to be able to do things for others again. It makes me see my life in a different light. I am not so afraid."[56]

Holistic accompaniment for victims has included emergency assistance, psycho-social and pastoral support, non-formal education programs for children and youth at risk of recruitment into armed groups, help in finding sustainable income alternatives, and basic protection mechanisms. Faced with overwhelming need, the RAV project leadership quickly agreed that they would prioritize resources for victims. The government was

54. Friesen, *Christian Peacemaking*, 68, 94.
55. Roth, *Choosing against War*, 25, 228.
56. Deckert, "Persecution to Hope," 298.

providing greater support for ex-combatants than for victims, while a restorative justice approach highlights victims' needs first. At the same time, the project leaders felt theologically called to extend their hands to victimizers as a demonstration of love for enemies and as a statement of faith in transformation. In regions of direct armed conflict, victimizers have come to the church seeking counsel and a path towards change; the church knows that closing their doors is not an option.[57] That said, work with victimizers has remained much less structured than work with victims.

Throughout this time, basic human security has been a recurring challenge. In a context where defenders of the status quo continue to literally eliminate those seeking change, community leaders and even leaders of the RAV member organizations have needed physical protection, and protection from despair.[58] The January 2012 project report records "none of the leaders we worked with were assassinated this last year" as an accomplishment.[59] Tragically, the RAV leaders have also had to share accounts of massive displacements and brutal murders affecting the very communities they accompany.[60] Turning to the government for protection does not help, since its response—armed cars and bodyguards—heightens insecurity and creates divisions in communities.[61] Instead, security has come from local, national, and international support networks.[62] Directly addressing risks has enabled local churches to accompany others who suffer instead of reacting with fear.[63] CEAS has responded to the need for psycho-social resilience through caregiver-care workshops, identified as vital to prevent burnout.[64]

Truth and Justice

The Documentation Project based in Justapaz has focused on truth-telling about the human costs of war. In addition, Justapaz, Mencoldes, and

57. Reconciliation Project notes, Mennonite Central Committee, Colombia Plan-Win Database, February 17, 2010.

58. Ibid., Oct 7, 2009; October 8, 2010; January 24, 2012.

59. Ibid., January 23, 2012.

60. Ibid., September 16, 2009, August 24 and October 8, 2010.

61. In one case, the government offered armoured cars to a community that could only be reached by donkey. As one RAV committee member commented, "Armoured cars make no sense . . . and armoured donkeys would just be silly," Ibid., January 23, 2012.

62. Ibid., September 13, 2011.

63. Ibid., notes July 26, 2011; January 23, 2012.

64. Ibid., January 23, 2012; January 28, 2013.

Sembrandopaz have all been increasingly involved in legal accompaniment for victimized communities. These actions have connected directly with loose networks of Protestant-Evangelical churches around the country and across the continent. In Colombia, many churches are located in marginalized communities, that have been hardest hit by violence. By telling their stories together, Justapaz has made broad patterns evident, debunking the myth that specific violations are isolated cases. At the same time, Protestant-Evangelical churches across the Americas have received the stories as their own, as affecting their "own people." By persistently sharing the "Prophetic Call" reports, Justapaz has encouraged wider sensitivity to the suffering and greater dialogue about the call to action. The RAV member organizations have also hosted dozens of international fact-finding or solidarity visits to communities affected by the armed conflict as another strategy for illuminating truth.[65] In some cases, "sister-church" relations developed as well.

The insistence on truth has sometimes raised concerns. How does re-telling stories of suffering contribute to the biblical mandate of forgiveness? The churches have had to develop a more complex understanding of forgiveness, and gradually more churches embraced the connection between memory, repentance, and forgiveness: "[R]emember and transform instead of forgive and forget."[66] While Mennonites in Canada annually proclaim, "To remember is to work for peace," these Colombian Mennonites complement this aphorism with the observation that "to work for peace is to remember," Truth is part of healing the oppressed and confronting the oppressor, for the salvation of both. Churches easily affirmed salvation, repentance, and forgiveness, and they gradually recognized the necessary role of truth in this process.

The RAV project's conceptual framework underscored the need for truth and justice:

> *Truth means bringing to light the actions and direct/indirect harm done within the context of the armed conflict, and the people, groups, structures and interests responsible . . . We can't allow ourselves to fall under the prophet Jeremiah's words, "They dress the wound of my people as though it were not serious. 'Peace, peace,' they say, when there is no peace" (6:14). Lies and concealment have imprisoned us and blinded us to the true web of people and interests that perpetuate the armed conflict. Truth is essential so that those responsible can confront what they have done and move towards repentance, undoing harm and putting things right*

---

65. Ibid., February 17 and October 8, 2010; September 13, 2011; January 23, 2012
66. Zapata, *Transformación*, 49, 61.

> ... The confession of responsibility, by commission or omission, for perpetuating violence and suffering could be the opportunity for profound healing in our society.
>
> We understand that there are different kinds of justice: justice that comes from laws, and socio-economic/cultural justice that comes out of just relationships and respect for the dignity of all people. Colombia needs both to overcome the current conflict . . . It is up to victims to define what recognition, restitution of their rights and reparation of harm means to them . . . Restorative justice is a process that contributes to the humanization of both victims and victimizers . . . Justice also has to connect to institutionality. It has to lead to the dismantling of the economic-political-military apparatus that has been used to sow violence and terror in our country, and to the building of just, alternative socio-economic and political structures.[67]

The community of Mampuján, comprised of around 1,200 Afro-Colombian people displaced from their land by paramilitary forces on March 11, 2000, exemplifies the efforts for truth, justice, and reconciliation. Sembrandopaz accompanied the community with humanitarian assistance, legal support, and psycho-social activities after the community members re-settled into their current location. A Mennonite Central Committee worker, Teresa Geiser, introduced the idea of "sewing their story" to women in the community who worked through many sessions of doing precisely that. Through the process, they found healing and also created numerous wall hangings depicting oppression and violence that later toured the country telling their truth. When this community was then called to testify at Colombia's first public audience for justice and reparations, they had already reflected on their experience and were able to speak truth boldly, but also extend forgiveness to the very men that they named responsible for their displacement.

Another woman whose husband was killed by the Colombian Armed Forces tells about facing her husband's assassin in court. Although she was still living with pain and fear, she was also able to publically confront and then forgive this man. She talks about the role of the church in her process: "The church has helped me immensely, spiritually and economically. I feel the presence of God when I am here. God has given me strength to think

---

67. Reconciliation Project document, Mennonite Central Committee, Colombia PlanWin Database, document, September 2009.

about forgiveness. I cannot forget what has happened to my husband, but I can pray for those who tortured and killed him."[68]

However, these high points of evident effectiveness have been contrasted by long periods of tedious persistence to generate change through legal means. The risks, as well as the cost of drawn-out advocacy campaigns, have made broad networks of national and international supporters indispensable.[69] Even the relatively "successful" case of reparations in Mampuján required years of judicial action, dialogue with local, regional, and national government officials, and a 76-kilometer nonviolent march undertaken by five hundred community members under the hot Caribbean sun. Victimized communities have valued this persistence and can see change even when barriers abound. One Mampuján woman reflected, "This march is reminiscent of our displacement, but this time we march with hope."[70]

Transformation: Advocacy and Social Change

All of the Colombian Anabaptist churches have agreed—even those who rarely engage social action directly[71]—that Anabaptist theology, historically, has shaken the foundations of society and transformed human relations. Despite uneasiness about going beyond a "spiritual agenda," the churches have affirmed the role of some Colombian Anabaptists in direct advocacy for change to public policy and societal practices.

This core group of leaders has taken communities' needs and rights before the Colombian State and the governments of other nations seeking justice and social change. At the same time, they have built genuine relationships with powerful functionaries on a regional and national level. This strategy risks compromise. It means relating without glossing over differences or permitting manipulation.[72] Special care has been taken to distance

---

68. Deckert, "Persecution to Hope," 300–301.

69. Reconciliation Project notes, Mennonite Central Committee, Colombia Plan-Win Database, September 16 and October 7, 2009, January 24, 2012, September 5, 2012.

70. Ibid., January 23, 2012.

71. In practice, it has been very difficult for local churches to move from talking about the importance of accompanying victims or working at peacebuilding to actually doing so. (RAV notes October 7, 2009) The actual percentage of local Anabaptist churches permanently and consistently carrying out "social ministries" of some sort with victims is estimated at less than half, although no rigorous studies have been done on this phenomenon.

72. Esquivia with Stucky, "Building Peace," 138.

church action from party politics.[73] They have embraced an understanding of Romans 13 that implies supporting the governance of the state, while also playing a prophetic role toward the state.[74] This means neither accepting nor rejecting the state, but discerning what is correct according to values and loyalties that transcend the State. Although this approach may differ greatly from some Anabaptists, others have also believed that Christians are not separate from the world; they are responsible for the world as both Christians and as citizens.[75]

This dialogue with power has happened without compromising the separation of church and state and without forsaking the ideal of creating alternative communities, counter-culture to a society founded on coercive power.[76] Believing that alternative communities transcend national borders, Colombian Anabaptists have tirelessly invited their faith brothers and sisters from other countries to share in their struggle for policy change and social transformation. They have boldly engaged a "reverse mission" back to those nations, like Canada, the United States, and various European countries, that formerly shaped the Colombian churches' faith predecessors.[77] The goal of transformation has been especially directed towards the church.

Conclusion: Not Getting Easier but Maybe Getting Clearer

Despite the many twists and turns in this journey, the dilemmas that Sanctuary for Peace churches identified in the November 2001 Encounter have not disappeared. At best, churches have moved from trying to sprint, to running a marathon; they have also learned to develop social ministries with broader vision and greater realism and that are more integrated into the rest of the life of the church.[78] In a context of violence and stark economic inequality, the urgent needs in communities around and within the church will always overwhelm the capacity of the church to respond.[79] Yet, when a community of displaced people evaluated the work of Colombian Anabaptist church entities by saying, "You haven't just accompanied us, you loved us," somehow

---

73. Reconciliation Project notes, Mennonite Central Committee, Colombia Plan-Win Database, July 26 and September 13, 2011.

74. Friesen, *Christian Peacemaking*, 76, 93.

75. Windhorst, "Balthasar Hubmaier," 151–152, 155.

76. Driver, *Pueblo*, 25, 39.

77. Chupp, "Creating Space," 108.

78. Reconciliation Project notes, Mennonite Central Committee, Colombia Plan-Win Database, January 23, 2012.

79. Ibid., September 16, 2009; October 7, 2009.

they measured up to Jesus' model.[80] The abyss was bridged by faith—faith that is not so much believing the incredible, but doing the impossible.[81]

---

80. Ibid., January 24, 2012.
81. Driver, *Pueblo*, 29.

14

Religious Violence, Peacebuilding, and Mennonites
The Case of Indonesia

SUMANTO AL QURTUBY

Introduction

THIS CHAPTER DISCUSSES THE phenomena of religious violence and attempts at peacebuilding in contemporary Indonesia. It also examines the contributions of Mennonite belief and actors in building global 'just peace,' religious harmony, and nonviolent actions and how this faith and these activities have in turn influenced Indonesian Muslim and non-Mennonite Christian peace advocates, interfaith dialogue activists, humanitarian workers, and conflict resolution practitioners. Finally, this chapter provides an overview of my encounter and engagement with Mennonite communities, both in the United States and my home country of Indonesia, which have deepened and shaped my thoughts, work, and practices on pacification, nonviolence, and conflict transformation.

My unvarnished initial sense or impression regarding Mennonites is that they are a conservative, "God-minded," and "illiberal" Christian community that preserves "old-fashioned," strict religious traditions and fundamental theological belief and faith. However, interestingly, this group also has a strong principle, vision, and spirit of humanity, forgiveness, nonviolence, justice and pacifism that go beyond ethnicities, religions, and cultures. For me, Mennonite theological standpoints are unique as well as inspiring partly because conservative religious groups usually do not pay much attention to world-human-related issues since their energy and passion are totally devoted to God and the afterlife through the passionate performance of rituals and religious ceremonies. This, among other features, is why Mennonites have astonished me. Mennonites teach me that religion can be used productively for boosting global just-peacebuilding rather than as a source of abhorrence, injustice, and violence.

To begin this chapter, let me clarify the term "religious violence" as it has occurred in Indonesia since the collapse of Suharto's dictatorial regime in 1998. John Sidel defines religious violence as "collective physical attacks on persons or property launched in avowed defense or promotion of religious beliefs, boundaries, institutions, traditions, or values, and behind religious symbols and slogans."[1] This article, however, classifies religious violence simply as violence that is inspired or influenced by certain religious teachings, doctrines, discourses, practices, or symbols, and is committed by religious individuals or groupings whose objectives are either religious or secular or both. In other words, it is not the "end" that determines violence's religious dimensions (in fact it is insignificant whether or not religious actors—both elites and ordinary masses—fight for religious or secular purposes such as political power, access to bureaucracy, land ownership, economic interests, etc.), but more if it is a source of inspiration for actors engaged in the violence. As long as those involved in conflict utilize religious sources of both doctrine and social capital, I will term it "religious violence."

The Indonesian case reminds us that those involved in violence, intolerance, and hostility were not all motivated by secular interests and rationales as many, if not most, liberal scholars and outside observers have argued. Even scholars who admit the religious nature of violence, such as John Sidel, view religion as a surrogate for bigger political and economic interests and overlook other ways that religion influenced people's actions. Some academics also fail to notice the significance that participants placed on religion and religious identity in the conflict settings. However, unlike the claims of (some) academics that tend to dismiss religious framing of violence and see religion simply as an instrument that religious elites utilized to mobilize religious masses and networks and manipulate religious symbols for attaining political and economic aims, many actors—both Muslims and Christians—engaged in fighting particularly in areas where inter-/ intra-religious groups involved in collective conflict and communal riots such

1. Sidel, *Riots*, 7.

as Central Sulawesi, Maluku, North Maluku, and some areas of Java Island, were essentially driven by and for religion and "otherworldly matters."

As Christopher Duncan rightly points out, the religious militias that are engaged in violence have been motivated by, among other factors, the desire to pursue "true religious goals" such as the annihilation of a particular religious community, dissemination of or conversion to a particular faith, and purification of a particular religious belief and thought, among others. For these militias, Duncan has argued, political elites have camouflaged the religious nature of the violence in favor of political and economic issues.[2] Research findings of the Indonesian Institute for Social and Religious Studies, for instance, also show that perpetrators of acts of religious violence and prejudice in some parts of Java were motivated or driven by the desire to purify some religious groupings, including local sects, which they dubbed "irreligious" and "deviant"[3] (Indonesian: "*sesat*"). Religious desecration therefore becomes one among many motives of those involved in religious conflict and bigotry.

Aside from being a source of violence in Indonesia and other countries besieged by communal strife, religion has been one among several significant elements for intergroup reconciliation and peacebuilding.[4] The Indonesian case thus suggests that scholars, practitioners, and policymakers need to go beyond a well-established liberal framework of violence and peace alike that tend to set aside the importance of religion in both conflict and peacebuilding, and then begin to rethink the religious significance in both discord and concord. One of the main challenges of scholars of peace and conflict studies is how to explain the role or the power of religion, including beliefs, identities, social networks, material culture, and the use of particular texts or imagery in conflict and post-violence settings, whether for instigating violence or supporting peace without trying to essentialize it.

The Nature of Contemporary Sectarian Violence

As with many other countries, Indonesia—the world's largest Muslim nation, with 88.7% of the total population of 240 million self-identifying as

---

2. See Duncan, *Violence and Vengeance*, 1–21. Cf. Wilson, *Ethno-Religious Violence*, 1–26. Although these two books address the same issue, namely the Christian-Muslim violence in North Maluku, both end up with somewhat different conclusions. While Wilson considers the religious issue as peripheral, Duncan takes it as a central point for those engaged in the fighting.

3. See reports on Religious Freedom of the Institute for Social and Religious Studies at http://elsaonline.com.

4. See, for example, Philpott, *Just*.

Muslims—is not immune from tensions, conflict, and violence. Before and after independence in 1945, this nation has been colored by numerous complex incidents of inter-/intra-group tensions, clashes, oppression, and intolerance. The perpetrators of these tensions included not only government officials or state apparatuses, including the security forces (the military or police), but also actors in society, the ordinary masses, and paramilitary groups. The victims, moreover, were not only non-Muslims but also Muslims, various ethnic groups, separatist groupings, and followers of local beliefs and sects.

It is important to notice that forms of violence in the aftermath of the New Order differ significantly from the previous ones; therefore, it is misleading to examine the post-New Order's violence and hostility by using outdated frameworks and analyses that place emphasis on the role of the state while neglecting society's role. During the Sukarno's Old Order rule (1945–1966) and the Suharto's New Order dictatorial reign (1966–1998), violence occurred mostly between the state (government officials and security forces) as the main actors and society (e.g., separatist organizations, communist members and sympathizers, street hoodlums, paramilitary groups, etc.) as the primary casualties. This has therefore been identified as "state violence" because it was driven mainly by political dictatorships and economic deprivations.

By the end of the New Order and its aftermath, however, this type of violence began to change from a relatively homogenous state violence to a more complex heterogeneous collective violence characterized by multiple factors, roots, agencies, and motives. In the final decade of the twentieth century, Indonesia witnessed a series of violent conflicts that differed significantly in its nature, forms, patterns, and causes from previous types of violence that broke out across the country from Aceh to Papua. The deadly violent conflicts in Aceh, Papua, and East Timor (now Timor-Leste) were, for example, deeply rooted in the prolonged issues of regionalism, sociopolitical injustice, economic discrimination, state-sponsored exploitation, and Jakarta-controlled developmentalism.

However, the sequence of violent conflicts that emerged since the mid-1990s—from social riots in Pekalongan of Central Java in 1995 and interreligious wars in Poso of Central Sulawesi and Ambon of Maluku from 1999–2003 to the bombing in Bali in 2002 and other places in Indonesia in the early twenty-first century—are truly multifaceted events that cannot be explained simply under the rubric of "ethnic conflict" or "Islamic terrorism."[5] In addition, this later form of violence has specificity, changing

5. For a discussion on the root causes and dynamics of Indonesia's post-colonial

patterns from one sort of violence to another in terms of its modalities, and is deeply entrenched in socio-historical contexts of Indonesian politics. As well, unlike violence in Aceh or Papua, which is far away from religious issues, violence occurred in the final years of Suharto's government and its aftermath has a religious dimension.[6]

Of all the forms of communal conflict in the post-Suharto rule, ethno-religious violence has been the most striking. This type of violence, in particular, occurs in the regions of "outer Java" such as Sampit, Sambas, Poso, Ambon, North Maluku, West Nusa Tenggara (especially Lombok Island), and South Sulawesi. It also takes place in urban areas of Java Island, especially West Java and some parts of East and Central Java, where hard-line Muslim groups have a strong base. In these particular regions, inter-ethnic violence (as in Sambas of West Kalimantan and Sampit of Central Kalimantan), religiously-inspired anti-pluralist actions, violations of religious freedom, incidents of religious intolerance, vigilante attacks, and Islamist extremism have been taking place particularly since the fall of the Suharto government in May of 1998.

These violent cases have included, but are not limited to, attacks against particular ethnic groups (e.g., Madurese and Dayaks), some churches belonging to particular Christian congregations, a synagogue in Surabaya, several Sufi groups, followers of Ahmadiyah (Ahmadis), local religious sects, and minority Shiite Muslims, among others. This is nevertheless not to suggest that these religious minority groups—whether Muslims or non-Muslims—have always been targeted by Islamist militant groups and mainstream Muslims. In many areas of the country, these minority groups have been living tolerantly and peacefully with majority Sunni Muslims. These majority Sunni Muslims even protect the minority groups from insults and assaults by Muslim hardliners, which for the most part come from outside regions.

Accordingly, Martin van Bruinessen's claim that post-Suharto Indonesia is dubbed an era of conservatism and radicalism, typified by the growth of radical Islamic organizations and hardline Muslim groups,[7] is only a half-truth in part because this observation tends to neglect the increase of pluralist-tolerant Islam and the contributions of peace activists, democracy advocates, and religious moderates. It is nonetheless accurate to say

---

violence see, for example, the following books: Columbijn and Lindblad, *Roots*, 3–32; Nordholt and Van Klinken, *Renegotiating Boundaries*, 1–38; Van Klinken, *Communal Violence*, 2–33; Kingsbury *Violence in Between*, 1–22.

6. See Sidel, *Riots*, 18–43. See also Pringle, *Understanding Islam*, particularly chapters 1–4.

7. See Van Bruinessen, *Contemporary Developments*, 1–58.

that since the Islamic boom of the early 1990s, the number of Indonesian Muslims identifying as religiously observant has increased significantly. Once home to one of the Muslim world's largest communities of heterodox and/or secular Muslims,[8] recent studies indicate that Indonesia today is marked by some of the highest levels of religious observance among Muslims.[9]

Interestingly, Indonesia's deepening Islamization and "religious militantization" has not increased the electoral fortunes of Islamist/Islamic political parties. As piety has surged, particularly in urban areas, the popularity of Islamist parties has sharply declined, some even failing to gain the electoral threshold; therefore, they were not allowed to compete in elections, whereas nationalist-secular ones have won the hearts of the Muslim majority. Notwithstanding the moderation that the Muslim electorate has demonstrated since 1999, outbreaks of communal riots and intolerant acts against religious minorities have indeed increased dramatically since the country's democratic opening.

As for cases of religious violence and bigotry in present-day Indonesia, a number of research and advocacy centers such as the Setara Institute for Peace and Democracy (Jakarta) and the Institute for Social and Religious Studies (Semarang) have documented these issues extensively.[10] The data from these centers show that the Muslim hardliners targeted not only Christians and other religious minorities, but also members of local sects and other Muslims groups. Unfortunately, the central government, for the most part, rarely acts firmly against those who commit violence or human rights violations, and they don't work effectively enough to prevent discrimination or the fomentation of religious hatred. Worse yet, this lack of government action and the absence of a security apparatus have bolstered sectarian religious groupings. This has also contributed to a growing use of the country's blasphemy law to put local sects, beliefs, or religious groups on trial that they recklessly and erroneously label deviant. Indonesia's "Blasphemy Law" (i.e., the Presidential Instruction of 1965 that inserted Article 156A into the nation's Criminal Code) provides further "legal legitimacy" for the vigilante actions of some Muslim extremist groupings. As Melissa Crouch has observed, this law casts a bleak outlook for "deviant" groups, "leaving religious

---

8. See Geertz, *Religion of Java*, 1–112; Hefner, *Hindu Javanese*, 3–43; Hefner, *Civil Islam*, 38–58.

9. See Noorhaidi, *Laskar Jihad*, 1–53.

10. See the reports of the two institutes on issues around anti-pluralist acts and religious intolerance at http://www.setara-institute.org and http://elsaonline.com.

minorities vulnerable to convictions for blasphemy and the risk of violence in the future."[11]

Looking at the complexity of violence and diversity of actors engaged in conflict and violence in contemporary Indonesia, it is inappropriate to solely blame the New Order or state apparatuses as the main actors and primary causes of the post-Suharto's communal conflicts. Instead, scholars and observers of the post-New Order's politics and violence need to pay attention to the local dynamics, plural factors, and shifting models of collective violence rather than—or not only—simply pay attention to the legacy of the New Order's political grievances and economic disparities, since the post-Suharto communal violence is truly a complex phenomenon and a complicated social drama.[12] The greatest portion of the anti-religious minority violence has been perpetrated not by terrorist-extremist groups but by Islamist "anti-vice" (Indonesian: "*anti maksiat*") paramilitary groupings, most notably the Islamic Defenders Front(*Front Pembela Islam*, led by Habib Rizieq Shihab), the Islamic Union Forum (*Forum Umat Islam*, led by Muhammad al-Khaththath), and the Association of Indonesian Muslim Brotherhood (*Jamaah Ikhwanul Muslimin Indonesia*, headed by Habib Husain al-Habsyi) to promote their own vision of public morality, one premised on a decidedly anti-pluralistic model of religious freedom, social tolerance, and civic pluralism.

In so doing, these "anti-vice" hardline Muslim groups are not hesitant to take over local mosques that moderate Islamic organizations had previously controlled, and then build *madrasah* (Islamic schools) and *pesantren* (Java-type Islamic seminaries) to disseminate and propagate their intolerant and strict views of Islam. Some Islamist groups are branches of or influenced by transnational Islamic organizations (e.g., HizbutTahrir, Muslim Brotherhood, TablighiJamaat, Deobandi movements, etc.), while others such as JamaahIslamiyah (founded by Abdullah Sunkar) and Majelis Mujahidin Indonesia (established by Abu Bakar Ba'asyir) are purely local, emerging from and shaped by Indonesia's unpleasant local political history and socio-economic grievances.

The outbursts of ethno-religious violence, some of which showed the telltale signs of old regime provocation, and the escalation of Islamist-militant groups have no doubt slowed the political-cultural-economic reform movement mentored by progressive Muslim intellectuals and human rights activists. This has also put the Muslim community's pluralist experiment

---

11. Crouch, "Indonesia's Blasphemy Law," 1–4.

12. The complex phenomena of the "social drama" of the post-New Order violence can be read in, for example, Columbijn and Lindblad, *Roots*.

and democratic Muslim politics into question. The problem becomes more complicated, since the Indonesian government mostly did not show a firm attitude or take resolute steps against the perpetrators of communal violence and anti-religious minority campaigns. The central government seems hesitant to protect the religious freedom of its citizens. This hesitancy can be seen in the hands-off way that the state has dealt with these cases. Indeed, they have arrested "terrorist syndicates" who blew up the Bali hotels, the Marriot hotel, and the Australian embassy. Additionally, the government has captured those who are suspected by the CIA as having an "al-Qa'ida linkage." However, they generally did not prevent attacks that Muslim hardliners have committed against certain targeted groups (e.g., Ahmadiyah, Shi'a, and other local sects).

Some scholars such as the late Abdurrahman Wahid and Greg Barton argue that the state apparatus' reluctance to perform effective measures to prevent violent actions is in part because the security personnel (especially the police) have so often been part of the law violators and the human rights transgressors.[13] Additionally, some politicians and government officials cannot fix this mess in national security partly because they themselves have violated human rights. Ironically, some provincial and district governments have even issued decrees banning particular Islamic organizations, religious sects, or cults dubbed "un-Islamic."

The above facts have made the government and the security reluctant to punish hardline Muslim groups. It is correct that some governments have on occasion cracked down on terrorists and Islamist militias. However, the political establishment as a whole has been slow to respond. The government's hesitancy reflects the fact that a small but influential wing within the coalition governments that have ruled Indonesia since 1999 subscribes to an anti-liberal and anti-pluralist model of religious liberty and pluralism.[14] In brief, once celebrated in the Western media for its moderation and tolerance, Indonesia is torn today by serious and occasionally violent disputes over religion and religious policy that those concerned with the future of Indonesian democracy, religious tolerance, and civic pluralism need to carefully examine and properly resolve.

Attempts at Peacemaking and Reconciliation

It is worth noting that numerous actors—from high-ranking government officials, political leaders, and civil society groupings to grassroots activists,

---

13. See Wahid, "Right Islam," and Barton, *Indonesia's Struggle*, 8–43.
14. Hefner, "Study of Religious," 18–27.

religious elites, and ordinary people—have tried to establish civil peace and tolerance. Despite religious violence and intolerance by a small fringe of Islamist paramilitary groups, endeavors of intergroup peacebuilding and tolerance have continued to persist even in "fragile areas" or "conflict zones" such as Sambas, Sampit, Poso, Ambon, and North Maluku. As in many other countries,[15] Indonesia has several religious groups that engage in some of the most destabilizing violence confronting other ethno-religious communities. But many believers in this archipelagic state creatively also integrate their spiritual-religious tradition and peacemaking practices.

Despite some scary occurrences of mass violence in contemporary Indonesia, there are several indications of hope for religious peacebuilding and civil coexistence, including compelling facts that underscore the Muslim majority's persisting pluralist, tolerant, and anti-violent attitude. A survey by Indo Barometer, a Jakarta-based leading research center, shows that 88.8% of respondents disagree with the use of violence to battle "immoral behavior," and only 7.4% support it. The results also indicate that 96.2% of the respondents reject the use of violence toward other religious followers (i.e., non-Muslims) and only 1.3% agree with it. Another significant finding of the survey was that 95.4% of respondents confirmed that tolerance between all religions is vital, with only 3.5% regarding it as unimportant. In addition, most respondents rejected the imposition of religious bylaws (63.3%), while 27.9% accepted this.[16]

Equally as important is the prolific application of cross-cultural/religious programs developed by the country's education institutions—Islamic and secular alike—that share common commitment to interfaith dialogue and the promotion of peace. Cross-cultural/religious education and learning are among the key words that promote the respect to others' thoughts and religious beliefs and the foundation of a culture of tolerance and pluralism. Education has a greater democratic benefit particularly when it conveys a spirit of intellectual bridging rather than exclusive bonding. More importantly, cross-cultural, understanding-based education and learning have been able to open the minds of students about the importance and meaning of heterogeneity or plurality of cultures and societies. This teaches them

---

15. For examples of the link between religion and violence, see for instance, Gopin, *Between Eden*, 35–86, and Appleby, *Ambivalence*, 57–120.

16. The survey was distributed in 33 provinces using multi-stage random sampling and face-to-face interviews with 1,200 respondents of all religions. Respondents were selected to reflect as closely as possible Central Statistics Agency demographic data. Pollster Indo Barometer conducted the survey in May 2007, to determine Indonesian Muslims opinions on terrorism and religious tolerance in their own country. See the summary of the survey's reports in *The Jakarta Post*, June 22, 2007.

to respect and appreciate other religions, Islamic sects, and local beliefs and traditions as part of God's gifts and universal wisdom. Inter-religious education encourages respect and tolerance for people of other faiths and prepares students to cast aside barriers of prejudice and intolerance.

Another reason for hope is the flourishing of civic organizations (Non-governmental organizations or NGOs and civil society associations or CSOs), moderate Muslim groups, feminist communities, pluralistic institutions, intercultural and religious groupings, grassroots peace activists, charismatic religious leaders, community elders, and tribal chiefs, among others, all of which have been vital agents of peacebuilding and reconciliation in their own respected societies across the country. There are indeed many instances of non-state peacebuilding across the nation,[17] notwithstanding the lack of scholarship, policy reports, and media coverage on this issue. Examples of peaceful civil coexistence, religious harmony, and grassroots peacebuilding abound, and many local actors and communities in this archipelago have been able to manage their tensions and differences in fruitful ways.

Furthermore, there are numerous instances of interreligious groupings and coalitions for reconciliation and peacemaking in some previously "trouble areas" such as Ambon, Central Sulawesi, and North Maluku. These initiatives promoted dialogue between people from neighboring villages whose Christian or Muslim members had fled during the upheavals following Suharto's overthrow in 1998. As I have explained elsewhere,[18] these interreligious dialogues were chiefly designed to get local Muslims and Christians talking candidly about whether they wanted to live together again or preferred to live in a new settlement with their co-religionists. Facilitators of these dialogues also taught mediation skills and encouraged people from divided groups to take the first steps towards reunification. They also established interfaith reconciliation teams at the local level, often at the instigation or with the backing of the military and local government.

These teams, usually comprising equal numbers of religious, *adat* (custom), community, and youth leaders from both sides of the conflict, aim to facilitate dialogue and the reconciliation process on the local level and to promote the return of internally displaced persons. For the most part, however, interestingly, their endeavors in the reconciliation process were genuine and purely local, initiated by actual people who were affected by the turmoil. In many cases, there were no large-scale peacebuilding

---

17. See, for example, Brauchler, *Reconciling Indonesia*, 24–230; Pariela, "Survival Strategy."

18. Qurtuby, "Peacebuilding in Indonesia"; Qurtuby, "Religious Women."

initiatives such as those supported by international agencies like the United Nations, nongovernmental organizations, or foreign governments. All of these instances have no doubt challenged the "conventional wisdom" that contemporary Indonesia is seething with religious intolerance, communal strife, and Islamist radicalism.[19]

The following are just a few examples of how local communities in some parts of Indonesia have transformed their tensions, conflicts, and discrepancies into productive ways of encouraging civil cooperation. On the Moluccan islands, where Christians and Muslims had previously engaged in bitter violence from 1999 to 2004, many local people, community leaders, and ordinary adherents of Christianity and Islam have long initiated peace and reconciliation efforts.[20] Local groups such as the Baku Bae movement, 20 Team of Wayame, Concerned Women Movement, Genuine Ambassadors for Peace, Young Ambassadors for Peace, and most notably Peace Provocateurs, are just some examples of the religiously-inspired grassroots agencies for peace that played a tremendous role in efforts of reconciliation during and after the mayhem in the Moluccas.

The interfaith alliance, Peace Provocateurs—comprising a diverse network of daring activists, students, journalists, academics, and religious leaders, both Christian and Muslim—has two specific goals: defusing religious tensions and urging calm by dispelling rumors that have the potential to incite rioting among the local populations. To achieve these aims, this group uses multiple instruments, including print and electronic media (newspapers, TVs, cellular phones), social media and online communication (Twitter, Facebook, emails), and friendship relations.

Co-founder of the Peace Provocateurs, Rev. Jacky Manuputty, has said that in Ambon city and Maluku in general, strong and close interreligious friendship can be used as an effective medium of Christian-Muslim peacemaking and reconciliation. Local religious leaders and activists such as Rev. Jacky Manuputty, Rev. John Ruhulessin, Bishop Mandagi, Sr. Brigitta Renyaan, Rev. John Sahalessy, Baihajar Tualika, Helena Rijoly-Matakupan, Thamrin Ely, Abidin Wakano, Hasbullah Toisuta, Abdurrachman Marasabessy, to name but a few, have been among the main advocates of local peacebuilding and reconciliation efforts. Their actions include leading several peace civic institutions and interfaith collaborations and running various programs and activities concerned with building interreligious trust

---

19. The contributions of "grassroots peacemakers" in keeping the peace in their areas can be seen, among others, at http://edsus.tempo.co/Perekat-republik.

20. Brauchler, *Reconciling Indonesia*, 97–99.

and harmony and developing conditions that could possibly sustain peace in the future.

Most, if not all, of these peace workers—both Muslims and Christians—were previously the victims of mass violence, many of whom lost their homes, properties, and families during the communal violence. While some of these peace activists were formerly involved in fighting for vengeance and other motives before shifting to become peacebuilding agents, others participated in reconciliation and peacebuilding work since the initial collective conflicts broke out in their regions.[21] There are many reasons for their decision to become "ambassadors of peace," some of which included their willingness to build a better future for their beloved towns and villages in terms of economy, education, cultural development, interfaith/ethnic relations, and the like. Most religious, public, and government facilities (e.g., schools, markets, offices, churches, mosques, hospitals, etc.) were damaged during the riots, making it difficult for the local population to carry out their daily activities.

They realized that violence was ultimately not the best and wise solution for resolving their complex problems, negative societal dynamics, conflicts, and differences. Some peace workers, moreover, began to shift to peacemaking activities since they witnessed brutalities committed by militias and angry masses against innocent people and the weak: children, elders, and women. Still, other peace activists started engaging in peace activities and nonviolent actions because they were aware that some interested political and religious elites misused and abused political and religious structures for political and economic gains, while manipulating the ordinary masses for supporting their hidden primordial agenda.

Stories of how local societies manage their "destabilizing conflict" to become a "stabilizing peace" can also be found in many places on Java Island. Whereas in some areas of the country such as, among others, Sampang (on Madura Island of East Java), Bogor (West Java), Banten, and Lombok (on West Nusa Tenggara), Shiites have been routine targets of violence and hostilities by, mostly if not all, Sunni militias and hardliners, in the Jepara regency of Central Java, the two religious groups have long maintained good relationships. Conversions from Sunni to Shia do not arouse sectarian rage in the region. As elsewhere in Indonesia, Sunni Muslims, most of them members of Nahdlatul Ulama, the country's largest Islamic organization, have been the dominant group in Jepara, widely known as a woodcarving town.

---

21. I discussed this particular issue in my doctoral thesis: Qurtuby, "Interreligious Violence."

Although only a few hundred Shiites live in this region, they feel safe enough to practice their beliefs and traditions publically. In fact, they have built a Java-type Islamic seminary, Pesantren Darut Taqrib, in the village of Banjaran. The leader of this pesantren, Miqdad Turkan, said, "We have a good friendship between Sunni and Shia followers. We respect each other regardless of our beliefs. We also frequently arrange social activities such as blood drives, helping disaster victims, etc."[22] Sunni and Shii leaders in the region such as Achmad Zaelani and Abdul Qadir Bafaqih attest that people in Jepara have understood plurality not only as a unique feature of this area but also as a *rahmah*, a blessing from God, that everyone needs to esteem and safeguard.

It is important to note that not only have locally-based non-state actors and peace activists carried out peacebuilding and reconciliation initiatives, but so have state actors, including high-ranking bureaucrats and government officials. Some respected political leaders such as the late Abdurrahman Wahid (former Indonesian President), Muhammad Jusuf Kalla (now an elected Vice President of Indonesia), Karel Albert Ralahalu (former Governor of Maluku), Sultan Hamengkubowono X (Governor of Yogyakarta), Mardiyanto (former Governor of Central Java), Joko Widodo (Governor of Jakarta), Abdul Kholiq Arif (Regent of Wonosobo in the southern highland of Central Java), Sinyo Sarundajang (Governor of North Sulawesi), F. X. HadiRudyatmo (Mayor of Solo), to name but a few, provide a great example of how political leaders have contributed greatly to the decrease of communal tensions and violence and the increase of intergroup respect, trust, and understanding that have become the backbone of genuine peacebuilding in their societies. Whereas Governor Sarundajang has been able to preserve peace and religious harmony in North Sulawesi, which is one of Indonesia's less violent areas, former Governor Ralahalu has been widely praised for his tremendous efforts in transforming Maluku from a "violent province" to a relatively stable area. Intense interreligious conflicts between Christians and Muslims broke out for several years in some areas of Maluku from 1999 to 2004, but now, surprisingly, this region has no record of deadly collective violence and religious intolerance.

Mennonite-Muslim Peacebuilding

Mennonite communities in Indonesia have contributed greatly to local peace efforts and social harmony. Also, some Mennonite pastors and

22. See the Sunni-Shii harmonious relations in Jepara at: http://khabarsoutheastasia.com/en_GB/articles/apwi/articles/features/2012/11/28/feature-03.

religious leaders in the country have become a source of inspiration for, not only peacebuilding work and activities related to religious tolerance and interfaith dialogue, but also peace studies. Moreover, there are a number of non-Mennonite, including Muslim, peace activists and scholars in the country who have been shaped, reshaped, and influenced by the work of Mennonite peacemakers and their peace histories, teachings, and traditions. It is undeniable that the influence of Anabaptist-Mennonite theologies, identities, and practices with regard to peace, nonviolence, and forgiveness are far-reaching. The ability of Mennonites to transform their bitter historical experiences into productive peace and nonviolence actions have been widely applauded by those concerned with the creation of global and local peace.[23]

Furthermore, the Mennonite idea—and precept—of service in particular has constituted a distinctive paradigm of relief, development, and humanization within Mennonite communities, emphasizing a sincere commitment to humanitarian work and human flourishing. Many non-Mennonite groups in Indonesia and other countries alike have admired and been influenced by this paradigm. However, while the Anabaptist-Mennonite faith is enormously vital and influential in shaping their work on the ground, actual practice in Indonesia involves collaborations with a range of actors—both secular and religious—who are of different professions, ethnicities, and religions.[24] Both Mennonite and non-Mennonite peace activists have benefited from their shared experiences in peacebuilding teams, and they have learned from each other as a result.

The Mennonite-Muslim peacebuilding narrative and collaboration between Mennonites and Muslims for cultivating civic peace, religious tolerance, and humanitarian services—some of which Mennonite Central Committee and the country's Mennonite Church congregations have supported—is evident in many areas of the country including Aceh, Nias, North Sumatra, Central Java, Yogyakarta, Central Sulawesi, Maluku, and Papua, among others. In Central Java, particularly in the districts of Pekoso and Tempur in the Jepara regency, for instance, Mennonites and Muslims have worked together for years, not only in mundane activities but also in religious ones such as the shared celebration of religious holidays (e.g., Christmas and Eid al-Fitr).

These regions, widely known as models of religious harmony, are home to Javanese Muslims and Christians linked to the Gereja Injili Tanah Jawa (GITJ), a Javanese Mennonite Church. Situated in the highlands of Muria,

---

23. See, for example, Roth, *Beliefs*.
24. See Fountain, "Translating Service," 1–20.

this region became well-known because of the GITJ church's fitting location in front of the Asyuhada mosque. Mennonites and Muslims built both the church and mosque together. During Christmas, Muslims, including village officials and religious figures, attend church, greet their fellow Mennonites, and help cook for the Christmas celebration. Mennonites have done the same during the Eid al-Fitr, an important religious holiday for Muslims that marks the end of Ramadan, the Islamic holy month of fasting.

Moreover, interestingly, Mennonites freely go to the mosque to attend prayer sessions while Muslims freely attend church services. To avoid time conflicts in religious services and prayer sessions, church and mosque officials always discuss schedules of worships and religious activities. Fascinatingly, more than just visiting and helping each other in everyday life and during the holidays, residents have been able to freely convert (either to Islam or Christianity) without fear—a situation which sharply contrasts with that of some religiously strict areas in West Java, Banten, or Lombok. For example, a local village leader once said, "Converting to another religion is a common thing at the moment here. Muslims can convert to Christians, Christians can convert to Muslims. No one will attack them. We believe in the principle of 'be to you your religion and be to me my religion.'"[25] As an outcome of free conversion, some families consist of Christians and Muslims. The village chief, Sutoyo, a Muslim, said that keeping the peace and harmony, which he believes as a sanctioned mandate from the village's ancestors, is much more important and beneficial than becoming involved in discord and violence.

The interreligious peace in these regions definitely does not drop out of the sky or heaven without the tireless effort of local religious and political leaders—both Mennonites and Muslims. Those who have contributed to peace and harmony included Giran, an Islamic teacher and mosque imam, as well as local Mennonite church leaders and teachers, namely Poniyah and her husband, Suwadi, who is a Giran's youngest brother and former devotee of Islam. Since 1977, Poniyah, a religious teacher from Yogyakarta, has been serving local villagers and pioneering initiatives that help them become tolerant peaceful religious communities. At first, it was uneasy for both Muslim and Mennonite groups to reconcile and live peacefully and tolerantly in part due to the local Muslims who considered the "new comers" of Christian Mennonites as perilous to the existence and continuity of Islamic belief in these villages. In the beginning, tensions and conflict—even

---

25. See how Jepara's Muslims and Christians overcome their tensions and disagreements in order to maintain peace and harmony in Camelia Pasandaran, "Central Java Village Shows that Unity in Diversity is Possible," *Jakarta Globe*, http://www.thejakartaglobe.com/news/central-java-village-shows-that-unity-in-diversity-is-possible.

if they did not turn violent—were driven by local Muslim conversions to Christianity (Mennonite).

As a result of this religious conversion, the arrival and spread of the "new" Mennonites had indeed outraged some Muslim elites. So, Mennonite church leaders—especially Poniyah and Suwadi—made clarifications, stating that they had only preached Christianity and Mennonite beliefs to villagers, and did not intend convert anyone to Christianity. Embracing Christianity, according to these two Mennonite church leaders, is part of God's work and not achieved by human effort. In front of village officials and Muslim leaders, the two Mennonite leaders said that the decision to convert to Christianity came from the Muslim villagers. After hearing their statements, added with intense dialogue between the two religious groups, the village's officials and Muslim leaders apologized for the misunderstanding. A local Muslim leader, Giran, stated that since conversions to Christianity were the local people's own choices and not forced on them by the Mennonite pastors and religious elites, he later decided to accept the conversions. In this regard, Giran remarked, "The most important thing is to maintain harmony."[26] After they came to understand each other, the situation changed. It took almost ten years before the relationship between the two religious communities returned to normal and the tensions turned into mutual benevolence.

Solo in Central Java is another area where Mennonites and Muslims have worked together for peace, harmony, and mutual humanization. Previously known as a "city of violence and terrorism" due to widespread communal riots and a number of active Islamist militia groups—some of which were linked to Jamaah Islamiyah and Majelis Mujahidin Indonesia, two Islamic organizations responsible for several terrorist acts in the country—Solo now enjoys reputation as a regional center for arts and culture. There are indeed many actors—both state and societal—who contributed to the transformation of Solo from a crime-ridden city into a relatively tolerant and stable area and who pioneered new peacebuilding initiatives in this complex and pluralistic city. However, a few actors deserve mention here for their tremendous contributions and role in shifting Solo from a violent city to a peaceful one. These include former Mayor of Solo, Joko Widodo (now Indonesia's elected president after the recent presidential election, and who was named the world's third best mayor by the World Mayor Project in early 2013), F. X. Hadi Rudyatmo (the Catholic Mayor of Solo), G. P. H. Dipo Kusumo (a prince of Surakarta palace), K. H. Muhammad Dian Nafi

---

26. See Pasandaran, "Central Java Village."

(a Muslim cleric), and Rev. Paulus Hartono (a Mennonite pastor), to name but a few.

In particular, Muhammad Dian Nafi and Paulus Hartono, two courageous religious leaders and peace activists, have long established solid friendships and collaboration in humanitarian efforts, interreligious dialogue, and peacemaking activities not only in Solo and the surrounding regions but also throughout the country, particularly in areas plagued by political, religious, and collective violence. While Hartono is the director of Mennonite Diakonia Service and a respected Mennonite pastor, Nafi—dubbed the Islamic cleric of reconciliation—is the leader of a *pesantren* (an Islamic boarding school) called Al-Muayyad Windan (established in 1996) in Kartasura and is deputy supreme leader of Central Java's provincial branch of Nahdlatul Ulama (Indonesia's largest Islamic organization).

Like Hartono, Nafi has long worked for interfaith dialogue, peace, and reconciliation not only in his area in Java but also in Aceh, Sampit, Sambas, Poso, North Maluku, Ambon, and Papua. A recipient of numerous awards for his peacebuilding work, Nafi also used his Pesantren Al-Muayyad as a learning center to train its students to become peacemakers and Islamic scholars of peace and nonviolence. For Nafi, Islam is a "peace builder" that teaches Muslims to live in harmony and tolerance by engaging other religions and ethnicities and by acknowledging their spiritual beliefs, cultures, and traditions. He has said that the Qur'anic injunction of "*ta'arruf*" (lit. "knowing each other") demands all Muslims to be pluralistic and tolerant towards all people regardless of their faith, race, and ethnicity.[27] He also calls for establishing contact with "extremist" or hardline individuals or groups in order to achieve constructive peace in the future.

Hartono and Nafi cofounded the Forum for Peace across Religions and Groups and the Solo Peace Institute as a cultural medium for interfaith gatherings aiming at transforming destructive conflict into productive peace. Both have broken down barriers to effective interfaith communication and developed a peacebuilding model that transforms conflicts into positive interactions. Interestingly, these two Mennonite and Islamic leaders have worked towards peace and harmony by also collaborating with and befriending some members of Hizbullah—a Solo-based Islamist paramilitary group not related to Lebanon's Shiite Hezbollah—including its commander Yani Rusmanto. Previously involved in various sectarian conflicts, many members of this group are now peace activists and humanitarian workers.

---

27. See KH M Dian Nafi's interview with Koran Sindo at http://www.koran-sindo.com/node/322647.

Besides working with Hizbullah and other Islamist paramilitary groups in Solo, Nafi and Hartono have worked with members and activists of Nahdlatul Ulama, non-Mennonite Christians, and other elements of local society to engage in various humanitarian services, post-disaster relief, interreligious dialogue, and peacemaking activities. Nafi and Hartono made every effort to change people's perspectives by highlighting the commonalities rather than the differences among different faiths, such as the fundamental values of peace, mercy, love, and compassion that Christianity and Islam share.[28] Through these efforts, Nafi and Hartono successfully broke the communication deadlock between radical Muslims and Christians in Solo. Both leaders proved that with shared compassion and humanity, a peaceful relationship based on mutual understanding is possible between two different religious groups.

Whereas Hartono admits Nafi's contributions in introducing Islamic concepts and practices of peacebuilding to him, Nafi—who attended peace and conflict studies training session at Eastern Mennonite University's Summer Peacebuilding Institute—acknowledges the contributions and influences of the Anabaptist-Mennonite peace tradition and emphasis on nonviolence in his peacebuilding work alongside Islamic teachings and the paragons of the Prophet Muhammad and early Muslim Sufis and pacifists. In particular, Nafi has praised Mennonites for their conviction and commitment to working in and advocating for global and local peace through various collaborative efforts, programs, and activities.

It is imperative to note that Paulus Hartono is not the only Mennonite peacemaker in the country. Rev. Paulus Sugeng Wijaya, former director of the Center for the Study and Development of Peace at the Duta Wacana Christian University in Yogyakarta, is another Mennonite peacemaker who has contributed greatly to the advancement of both peace studies and peacebuilding practices. As well, Nafi is definitely not alone among non-Mennonite peacebuilders in this regard. There are a number of non-Mennonite peace activists and scholars in Indonesia, including myself, who have been shaped and influenced by, among other factors, Anabaptist-Mennonite beliefs, traditions, and practices in peace, nonviolence, compassion, and forgiveness.

My Encounter with Mennonites

The year 2000 was the first time I got to know and interact with a Mennonite. That year, I was a Sociology of Religion graduate student at the SatyaWacana

---

28. See http://www.commongroundnews.org/article.php?id=32798&lan=en.

Christian University (UKSW) in Salatiga, Central Java, and one of my academic and thesis advisors was a Mennonite-Chinese professor named Mesach Krisetya.[29] A graduate of Anabaptist Mennonite Biblical Seminary in Elkhart, Indiana,[30] and former president of Mennonite World Conference, Mesach Krisetya supervised my MA thesis on the role of Chinese Muslims in the spread of Islam in Indonesia before the European colonial era.

At first, I knew Mesach Krisetya—whom I usually call Pak Mesach—as little more than a humorous, humble, friendly, and committed Christian teacher. At the beginning I did not know that he is a Mennonite. In fact, at that time, I did not know what a Mennonite was. As for Christianity, I knew only of Protestantism and Catholicism. Pak Mesach also hardly ever struggled to locate grants in support of my thesis research and writing, which I highly appreciated in part because I am a Muslim. To me, Pak Mesach is more than a mentor and teacher, but a close friend who shares anything from insights on academic issues to everyday stories. Pak Mesach also visited my home village, and I often visited his house for intellectual discussions or light chats.

It was Pak Mesach too who introduced me to some American Mennonites, including most notably Lawrence Yoder (Professor Emeritus at Eastern Mennonite Seminary) and his wife Shirlee Yoder, Dan and Jeanne Janzti (formerly co-directors of Mennonite Central Committee in Indonesia), and Edward Martin (former Asia Director of MCC and now Director of the Center for Interfaith Engagement at Eastern Mennonite University). It was through their helpful collaborations, added by the support of the Rector of UKSW, John Titaley, I was finally able to come to Eastern Mennonite University to attend a conference and workshop on peace and conflict studies, take an English course, and pursue a master's degree in conflict transformation at the University's Center for Justice and Peacebuilding.

During my studies at Eastern Mennonite University from 2005 to 2007, I was fortunate to have so many Mennonite friends and colleagues who had shared their incredible inspiring stories. I not only studied theories of human conflict and peace, I was also privileged enough to live with Mennonite families (first with Andrew and Lisa Eggman's family, and then with Lawrence and Shirlee Yoder) enabled me to interact more deeply with American Mennonites, witness their everyday lives, discuss issues surrounding Christian pacifism, and learn their spiritual beliefs, religious practices, and everyday activities.

---

29. Since 2011, Mesach Krisetya has been Dean of Liberal Arts at the Universitas Pelita Harapan in the city of Surabaya in East Java.

30. Formerly called Associated Mennonite Biblical Seminary.

During my stay in Harrisonburg, I and my Mennonite landlords and families visited numerous churches either to attend worship services and Sunday school, listen to sermons, or share my knowledge of Islam and Indonesia with the church attendees. Lawrence Yoder, in particular, had shared with me the deep histories of persecution, sorrow, injustice, and discrimination that had occurred among Anabaptist-Mennonites, and how they responded peacefully, rather than violently, to these bitter sagas. Yoder also informally discussed issues of Mennonite faith, theology, and spirituality numerous times with me.

At the same time, I shared with him the Islamic concepts of 'just peace,' nonviolence, and tolerance. He also lent me several books on the history, theology, and practices of Anabaptist-Mennonites, which I read eagerly. The Mennonite books that particularly interested me include *The Politics of Jesus* (John Howard Yoder), *Journeys of the Muslim Nation and the Christian Church* and *Global Gods* (David W. Shenk), *Beliefs: Mennonite Faith and Practice* (John D. Roth), *A Muslim and a Christian in Dialogue* (Badru Kateregga and David W. Shenk), *Anabaptists Meeting Muslims* (editors: James Krabill, David Shenk, and Linford Stutzman), and *Menno Simons: A Reappraisal* (editor: Gerald R. Brunk), among others.

At the Center for Justice and Peacebuilding, moreover, I learned a lot from a number of great peace scholars and practitioners—Mennonite or not—including Lisa Schirch, Ron Kraybill, Jayne Docherty, Barry Hart, David Brubaker, Earl Zimmerman, Howard Zehr, Nancy Sider, Pat Martin, and Roy Hange, among others. Each of these professors have shaped and strengthened my knowledge and understandings of peacebuilding and nonviolent practices. In 2010, I wrote a book (in Indonesian), titled *Among the Believers: an Indonesian Muslim Experience of Living with American Mennonites*, based on my stories of interaction, dialogue, and engagement with American Mennonites. This book has been reprinted several times and was recommended by the Ministry of Religious Affairs of the Republic of Indonesia for use as a textbook in interreligious understandings.

Although I befriended Pak Mesach long before I came to EMU, it was the Mennonite communities in Harrisonburg and, more specifically, at the University that has shaped, inspired, influenced, enriched, and strengthened my academic work, thoughts, and activities on conflict transformation, peacebuilding, and nonviolent methods. Stirred by my studies at the Center for Justice and Peacebuilding, I later wrote a doctoral thesis in the Department of Anthropology at Boston University on Christian-Muslim violence and peacebuilding in the conflict zone of the Moluccas. During my doctoral research and fieldwork in the Moluccas, once again, I engaged with and learned from number of local peace workers and scholars—both Muslims and Christians—including Jacky Manuputty, Elifas Maspaitella, Sr. Brigitta Renyaan, John Ruhulessin, and Abidin Wakano, to name but a few. Like my engagement with Mennonites, my daily interaction and conversations with peacemakers, conflict resolution practitioners, and interfaith dialogue activists in the Moluccas have augment my knowledge and understanding of peacebuilding and nonviolent practices.

Similar to the events and contours of Mennonite history, my own family has also experienced suffering, intimidation, and marginalization. The "Mennonite story" is also my story. As a Muslim who believes in, practices, and advocates for interreligious peace, civil tolerance, and religious freedom, I have been a routine target of black campaigns and insults from hardline Muslim groups and Islamist leaders who reject religious pluralism, civil liberty, and equal citizenship and who defend Islamic superiority in the process. Moreover, members of my family have long been subjects of coercion, rudeness, and disdain from my village's "aristocrats," wealthy people, and government officials—all of whom are "nominal Muslims"—due to my father's strong commitment to good and clean governance, civic peace, religious harmony, and civil tolerance.

As is typical in Indonesia, I was born and raised in a Muslim family. My father, who died in January 2011 at the age of 85, was a rural *modin* (a religious official in a village), a modest imam (a prayer leader), and a poor farmer in a small and isolated village in the highlands of Central Java. He was the first person to introduce Islam in the village and taught basic Islamic teachings to the villagers, which I later continued upon my return from an Islamic boarding school (*pesantren*).

My father was no zealot. In fact, my father befriended a foreign Catholic elementary school teacher named Sumanto who lived with him and his family for years in my parents' modest house during his time of service as a teacher in the village. Throughout the years, my father told me, they both shared many things—food, jokes, stories, culture, and so forth—while still respecting each other's faith and tradition. When Muslims celebrated Eid al-Fitr, Sumanto would give my father a present—usually a *sarung*, *peci*, or other articles of clothing—and wished him a happy holiday. And when Christmas came, my father always gave Sumanto a small gift and wished him a Merry Christmas. Perhaps due to their close friendship, and as a sign of respect, my father later named me, his youngest son, Sumanto. "I wish you someday will become a good person like him," my father once told me before God took his soul.

Despite suffering regular insults and torture by the village's political elites (my father was once stabbed with a sword in his neck that almost killed him), my father never took revenge and never suggested that his children should do so either. Instead, he always advised us to follow an old Javanese saying: *"menang tanpo ngasorake"* ("winning without defeating [the "enemies"]") by loving and forgiving them, asking God to help them open their minds and hearts, showing respect and hospitality, and pursuing knowledge and education in the sciences. My father believed that vengeance and violence are not the best way to undermine our village's "darkness."

Having had a strong spirit of religious tolerance, my father has indeed influenced my journey in life. Upon finishing my studies at Islamic schools in Central Java, I have befriended many non-Muslims, from Chinese Buddhists and Javanese Hindus to Protestants, Catholics, and Mennonites, hoping to learn from many different cultures and religions. As my father taught me, it is impossible to comprehend the depth and beauty of Islam without understanding the spiritual essence of other faiths.

My father was not the only target of violence in my family; my maternal grandparents were also victims of a brutal murder. More specifically, they were among the casualties of the 1965–66 anti-Communist pogroms in Indonesia that resulted in millions of deaths, whereas millions of others lost their valued properties: land, houses, livestock, and so forth. According to my mother, my grandparents were cruelly killed by an angry mob. She also told me that many of those who had been murdered, including her parents, were not actually communists. They were killed, she said, simply because they sang "Genjer-Genjer," a popular song composed by Muhammad Arief of Banyuwangi (East Java) in 1942 that was also commonly sung by members of the Indonesian Communist Party (PKI). Traumatized, my mother and her older brother fled to a faraway district and hid in the middle of a wild jungle with nothing but the clothes they wore.

My mother's story does not stand alone. Many people killed during this period actually had nothing to do with Communism or the PKI, much less with atheism, as the New Order regime propagandized. Ordinary people, including my grandparents (who were mostly, if not all, illiterate), did not understand what Communism meant, much less Marxism-Leninism. Membership of the PKI in the 1960s reached more than three million people, making it the largest Communist Party outside the Soviet Union and China, but most people sympathized with the party simply because they admired its pro-people agenda.

Although the anti-Communist murder is behind us, we still have to deal with these dark episodes from our past. For me in particular, responding to the killings is dilemmatic. On one hand, my own family has been directly affected by the bloodbaths. But I am also a functionary of Nahdlatul Ulama, an Islamic organization, many of whose young activists were involved in the campaigns. However, for the sake of the nation's future, there is nothing we—including the government—can do but promote forgiveness and reconciliation. I believe that there can be reconciliation and a decrease in anti-communist sentiment in Indonesia only if there is a sincere willingness to forgive. I believe that while revenge will produce a vicious cycle of violence, pardon will generate a web of friendship and solidarity across ideological, ethnic, and religious divides.

Concluding Remarks

As a concluding remark, let me share what Islam means to me. To me, Islam, as the Qur'an has stated, is *rahmatanlil 'alamin*—a "blessing and a source of love and compassion for all humanity"; therefore, it is the "theological duty" of all Muslims in this world to ensure that this message is embodied on earth. It is imperative to notice that Prophet Muhammad PBUH also befriended and built contacts with people from diverse ethno-religious backgrounds, including Jews and Christians, as outlined by early biographers of the prophet such as Ibn Ishaq, Ibn Hisham, Baladhuri, and Tabari.

As a result of Christian-Muslim contacts, for example, some spiritual and moral values of Eastern Christianity (e.g., Syrian Orthodox beliefs)—which had entered the Arab world and Middle East since the time of St. Paul—have influenced and shaped some foundations of Islamic teachings. When the Prophet Muhammad PBUH said, "I felt the Holy Spirit (*nafs al-rahman*) from Yemen," he was referring to Jesus Christ. The Qur'an also mentions [Sura Al-Ma'ida (5), verse 82, for example] the community of Christian priests, which it depicts as "learned, humble, and not arrogant." Civil peaceful coexistence between Christians and Muslims was apparent in the early history of Islam.[31] This history is a source of inspiration for me in establishing dialogue across ethno-religious lines, building mutual trust and respect with people of other faiths, and establishing genuine peace and tolerance.

Although my peacebuilding work has been inspired and shaped by multiple sources (Islamic and non-Islamic), roots (personal, family, and social histories), and agencies (Muslim and non-Muslim peacemakers), my profound engagement and dialogue with Mennonite communities—in the United States and Indonesia—have indeed deepened and reinforced my understanding and knowledge of peacemaking and nonviolent practices, partly because Mennonites were the first non-Muslim religious people whom I encountered that have strong pacifist convictions and vision. And, to be

---

31. See Goddard, *Christian-Muslim Relations*.

honest, American Mennonites were the first Christians to help me better understand the complexity and plurality of Christianity in the United States.

Before arriving in the United States in 2005, I assumed and thought that all American Christians were "Islamic/Muslim haters" and strong supporters of George W. Bush's "War on Terror." American Mennonites—although some of them whom I knew did endorse the war on "Islamic terrorism"—have indeed changed my perceptions and stereotypes of American/Western Christianity. The community of Eastern Mennonite University's Center for Justice and Peacebuilding—and, added to this, other historic peace churches such as the Quakers, Brethren in Christ, and the Amish—had particularly opened my mind to another side of Western Christianity. And for this reason, I owe them a thousand thanks.

15

Remembering a Perforated Land
Strategies of Peacebuilding in Palestine-Israel

ALAIN EPP WEAVER

Introduction

TO TRAVEL TO THE Gaza Strip—assuming that one manages to secure permission from the Israeli military to enter—is to pass into a territory cordoned off from the world and under surveillance from all sides and to be confronted by Israeli spatial practices of exclusion and containment of Palestinians in their most extreme form.[1] Go today to the Shejaiyeh neighborhood of Gaza City (or to Beit Hanoun, or Khuza'a), and one encounters a topography of desolation and destruction, a haunted landscape of twisted rebar and shattered concrete, the aftermath of fifty days of bombardment of Gaza by the Israeli military in the summer of 2014 that uprooted hundreds of thousands of Palestinians, the majority of them already refugees. Mennonite work in Palestine-Israel began within a similar geography of devastation in 1949, with Mennonite Central Committee (MCC) sending Titus Lehman to work as a nurse in the camps of the Gaza Strip that had just been created to shelter the hundreds of thousands of Palestinian refugees driven from their homes during what the State of Israel calls the War of Independence and what Palestinians call the *nakba*, or catastrophe.

---

1. See, for example, Strand, "Tightening the Noose," 6–23; Tawil-Souri, "Digital Occupation," 27–43; and Li, "Gaza Strip," 38–55.

Then as now, the Gaza Strip bore witness to the violence wrought by Zionist cartographies that imagine "a land without a people for a people without a land."

Mennonites have often understood themselves as an exilic people, a people whose own permanent homeland is in God. Some Mennonite theologians have linked this exilic narration of Mennonite identity to a theological mandate for peacebuilding for "seeking the peace of the city" (Jer. 29:7) in which God's people finds itself exiled. For Palestinians and Israeli Jews, exile has also been central to their narrations of identity, albeit in different ways. For Zionism, exile is a state of being to be negated through the return to the land and (for mainstream Zionists) the establishment of a Jewish state. But in practice, this Zionist attempt to overcome exile created new exiles, with the uprooting of hundreds of thousands of Palestinians in 1948 and the ongoing dispossession of Palestinians inside Israel, the Occupied Territories, and the diaspora. What might memories from exile contribute to the search for peace, understood as Palestinians and Israeli Jews alike being able to live securely under vine and fig tree? Too many peacebuilding efforts in Israel-Palestine, I contend, have proceeded in a despatialized manner, ignoring the territorial realities within which Palestinians and Israelis live. Effective peacebuilding, in contrast, must attend to the ongoing geographies of dispossession created by the State of Israel and link memory work to embodied mappings of new forms of life in the land.

This essay thus focuses on peacebuilding practices carried out by Israelis and Palestinians that map alternative geographies to those created by the violent exclusions of the nation-state, peacebuilding as counter-cartographic practice animated by alternative forms of remembering. I begin with a brief overview of Mennonite work in Israel-Palestine, followed by an examination of Mennonite theological accounts of memory, exile, and peacebuilding, asking what good news, if any, the experience of exile might have for people facing ongoing dispossession. To help answer that question, I then turn to a discussion of Israeli-Palestinian peacebuilding efforts, critiquing initiatives that approach the conflict in a deracinated fashion. I then explore the efforts of one Mennonite-supported Israeli organization, Zochrot, to take seriously the geographies of dispossession created by Zionism and to engage in mapping practices that perforate Zionism's imagined landscapes and reveal alternative possibilities for mutuality within the land for both Palestinians and Israelis.

Mennonites, Exile, and Peacebuilding

Mennonites have worked among and alongside Palestinians and Israelis for over sixty years. As noted above, MCC, as the relief, development, and peacebuilding agency of Mennonite and Brethren in Christ churches in Canada and the United States, began its presence in the area in 1949, responding to the needs of Palestinian refugees, first with a worker in the Gaza Strip and then later opening up a unit in the camps around Jericho.[2] Shortly afterwards, Mennonite mission agencies started work inside the new State of Israel, with an emphasis on support for Messianic Jewish congregations.[3] More recently, for nearly a quarter century Christian Peacemaker Teams (founded and supported by Mennonites, among others) has maintained a presence in the Hebron district in the south of the Occupied West Bank, experimenting with different forms of nonviolent direct action to counter the Israeli occupation and looking for ways to support Palestinian efforts at nonviolent resistance.[4] All three agencies would describe "peacebuilding" as being an essential dimension of their work, even as their understanding of what is meant by peacebuilding has varied widely and has shifted over time. This understanding ranges from spiritual reconciliation within the body of Christ between Messianic Jews and Palestinian evangelicals and governmental advocacy in support of Palestinian farmers planting their fields so that they are protected from confiscation to the accompaniment of Palestinian schoolchildren to prevent them from being harassed by Israeli settler-colonists.

No single theological vision has animated these Mennonite peacebuilding efforts over the past decades. Yet the fact that long-time CPT worker Kathleen Kern gave the title *As Resident Aliens* to her history of CPT's efforts in the West Bank suggests that at least some Mennonite peacebuilders in Palestine-Israel have conceived of their work as taking place within the context of an exilic or diasporic missiology where the church lives as a community in exile amidst the nations of the world and works for the well-being of its neighbors. John Howard Yoder, arguably the most prominent Mennonite theologian of the twentieth century, gave the most sustained articulation of this exilic missiology, building on God's call to the Israelite exiles in Babylon to seek the peace of the city to which God has sent them.

---

2. For a history of MCC's first 50 years of work with Palestinians and Israelis, see Weaver and Weaver, *Salt and Sign*.

3. Marie Shenk offers an account of Mennonite mission efforts among Messianic Jews in Shenk, *Mennonite Encounter*.

4. Veteran CPT worker Kathleen Kern surveys and analyzes CPT's first decade in Palestine in Kern, *As Resident Aliens*.

The people of Israel, in Yoder's account, are called to embody a paradigmatic existence of radical reliance upon God alone in order to bear witness to God's wisdom and righteousness, and this calling is borne by the church as well. The arc of the biblical narrative, from Abraham to Jesus, bears witness to this vocation. "What begins in Abraham, and crests in Jesus," Yoder insisted, "is not merely a different set of ideas about the world or about morality: it is a new definition of God. A God enters into relations with people who does not fit into the designs of human communities and their rules."[5] The connective thread running throughout the Old Testament witness is the calling to trust in God alone for one's protection and salvation and to embody a communal politics of "not being in charge" commensurate with that trust. Yoder explained that this trust in God "opens the door to his saving intervention. It is the opposite of making one's own political/military arrangements. Jeremiah's abandoning statehood for the future is thus not so much forsaking an earlier hope as it is returning to the original trust in JHWH [sic]."[6] Israelite kingship (or, to be anachronistic, "statehood") was, in this telling of the biblical narrative, something of an anomaly, subject to critique from within the scriptural witness that points back to Israel's reliance on God.[7] The exile in Babylon thus represented not a disruption in God's plans for his people, but rather an opportunity to return to radical dependence on God. "The move to Babylon was not a two-generation parenthesis, after which the Davidic or Solomonic project was supposed to take up again where it had left off. It was rather the beginning, under a firm fresh prophetic mandate, of a new phase of the Mosaic project."[8] The people of Israel's exile is a sending out into mission, a point Yoder drove home in his paraphrase of the injunction in Jer. 29:7 as "Seek the salvation of the culture to which God has sent you."[9] On this account, then, Christians (including Mennonites) are called to engage in peacebuilding as part of their exilic vocation.

---

5. Yoder, *Jewish-Christian Schism*, 243.

6. Ibid., 71.

7. Yoder noted that "both in doctrine and in sociology the king is relativized. He is at best the servant of divine righteousness, not its origin."—Ibid., 73. For Yoder, the Israelite temptation to kingship prefigures the Christian temptation of Constantinianism.

8. Ibid., 184. Or also: "To be scattered is not a hiatus, after which normality will resume" (p. 183).

9. Ibid., 202, n. 60.

Exile, Zionism, and Palestinian Identity

That Mennonites of European descent—with their histories of migration and at times forced displacement—would gravitate to an exilic missiology is perhaps no surprise. Less obvious is whether or not an understanding of exile as mission might provide a compelling vision for other peoples marked by histories of exile like the Palestinians. Yoder himself pondered this question, asking if there is something about this "vision of the dignity and ministry of the scattered peoples of God which might be echoed or replicated by other migrant peoples? Might there even be something helpful in this memory which would speak by a more distant analogy to the condition of peoples overwhelmed by imperial immigration, like the original Americans or Australians, or the Ainu or the Maori?"[10] Put another way: how might a Mennonite peacebuilding vision that emerges from an exilic missiology resonate with Palestinians and Israeli Jews?

Israeli political theorists and historians of Zionism have demonstrated that in the Zionist narration of Jewish history and identity, exile is fundamentally a distorted and abnormal condition, a condition not only to be overcome, but even negated. As Amnon Raz-Krakotzkin has convincingly argued, the interrelated notions of the negation of the diaspora, the "return to the land" (*ha-shiva le-eretz yisrael*), and the "return to history" (*ha-shiva la-historia*), function as central concepts in the conception of history and in the collective memory of the Israeli political imagination, forming a "national colonial theology."[11] As Raz-Krakotzkin observes,

> With the concepts of the negation of exile and the return to history, the Jewish Zionist implantation in Palestine comes to be considered as the restoration of Jewish sovereignty, the return of the Jewish people to a land presented as its own (and supposedly empty), and as the success of Jewish history, the fulfillment of millenarian aspirations. The return to history is presented as the return to national and political sovereignty which the Jews had known in biblical antiquity and in the Second Temple period.[12]

Jewish life in exile, from the perspective of mainstream Zionism, is negated as abnormal or even diseased, a problematic condition to be remedied through aliyah, or ascent, to the land of Israel and the "return" of the Jewish

---

10. Yoder, *For the Nations*, 82.

11. My discussion of the Zionist motifs of "the negation of exile" and "the return to history" has been primarily informed by Raz-Krakotzkin, *Exil et Souveraineté*. All translations from the original French are mine. See also, Piterberg, *Returns of Zionism*, especially chapter 3 and Raz-Krakotzkin, "National Colonial Theology," 312–26.

12. Raz-Krakotzkin, *Exil et Souveraineté*, 27.

people to the history of nation-states. Zionism presents exile as "a defective existence, incomplete or abnormal, a situation in which 'the spirit of the nation' could not fully express itself": the Jewish nation could only find its fulfillment in its own land and with its own state.[13]

Raz-Krakotzkin proceeds to argue that negating exile goes hand in hand with justifying the history of the victors, a history that erases the past of the conquered. The negation of exile shapes a "Zionist conscience" that rests on "effacing and repression," on the erasure not only of Jewish life in diaspora but also of Palestine's history prior to the Zionist return.[14] Mainstream Zionist imagination conceptually erases Palestinians from view, heralding the settlement of a land without a people for a people without a land, and such conceptual erasure proves a perilously short distance from actual practices and policies of the forcible dispossession and displacement of Palestinians.[15] Just as the exiled Jewish people lived outside of history, according to the Zionist historical schema, so too was the land of Israel presented as "empty," "condemned to exile as long as there was no Jewish sovereignty over it: it lacked any meaningful or authentic history, awaiting its own redemption with the return of the Jews."[16] However, because the land was, of course, not literally empty, Zionist return to history and the land would be inevitably and inextricably bound to practices and policies of uprooting and dispossession, with returning Jewish exiles in turn creating new exiles. The negation of exile thus did not eliminate exile, but instead simply transferred it onto Palestinians.

In order to counter Zionist practices of dispossession, Raz-Krakotzkin joins other prominent Jewish thinkers like Daniel Boyarin and Judith Butler in calling for a recovery of resources from Jewish life in the diaspora to point forward to new ways of living in the land.[17] A recovery of exile as a political and theological category decenters those who live in the land, opening up a "longing for the land within the land" that might become "a new starting point of all who dwell in the land, a basis for their partnership," Raz-Krakotzkin suggests.[18] An exilic landedness, in the felicitous phrasing of Sidra DeKoven-Ezrahi, molds "citizens and sojourners" who "touch down lightly but are never quite grounded."[19] These political theorists con-

13. Ibid.
14. Ibid., 32.
15. See, for example, Raz-Krakotzkin, "Peace without Arabs," 59–76.
16. Piterberg, *Returns of Zionism*, 94.
17. See Boyarin and Boyarin, *Powers of Diaspora* and Butler, *Parting Ways*.
18. Amnon Raz-Krakotkzin, quoted in Silberstein, *Postzionism Debates*, 182.
19. DeKoven-Ezrahi, *Booking Passage*, 240.

tend that narrating Jewish identity as an exilic identity opens up visions of life in the land not bound to the violent politics of the nation-state. These visions perforate the flat, homogeneous space of nationalist cartographies, and instead produce mappings of place that accept and embrace the fundamentally heterogeneous character of the landscape.

This narrative recovery by Raz-Krakotzkin, Butler, the Boyarins and others of exile and diaspora as a resource for mapping alternative Palestinian-Israeli futures beyond the ongoing and intensifying violence of partition and practices of dispossession finds a counterpart in the reflections of the late Palestinian-American critic, Edward Said, on exile as a material condition and as a critical stance. Said stressed the materiality of exile and warned against the dangers of romanticizing or aestheticizing exile. Exile, he underscored, is "the fundamental condition of Palestinian life," from the mass dispossessions during the *nakba* of 1948 up until the present day.[20] Because of his attention to the real deprivations of exile, Said argued that respect for Palestinian refugee rights, including the right of return, was essential to durable peacebuilding.[21]

Yet even as Said insisted on the devastation of exile, he also argued that exile should be conceived of as the proper place of the critic.[22] Exile teaches the practices of standing apart, of not making uncritical alliances with state or other entrenched forms of power, of what Said called, following Paul Virilio, "counter-habitation," that is, alternative forms of living that contest the violent politics of state power. Only exilic counter-habitation, Said suggested, will be adequate to resist colonial forms of geography that leave no room for heterogeneous places.[23]

Given his embrace of exile as a critical stance, Said had an uneasy relationship to Palestinian nationalism. On the one hand, Said affirmed the Palestinian struggle for a recognized, secure existence in the land from which or within which Palestinians have been displaced. On the other hand, Said claimed a preference for "restless nomadic activity over the settlements of held territory."[24] To learn the positive lessons of exile, Said argued, is to learn that ultimately "[h]omecoming is out of the question. You learn to transform the mechanics of loss into a constantly postponed metaphysics of return."[25]

20. Said, *After the Last Sky*, 5.
21. See, for example, Said, "Introduction," 1–6.
22. Said makes this case extensively throughout his study, *Representations of the Intellectual*.
23. Said, *Culture and Imperialism*, 402. See also Virilio, *L'Insécurité*, 88ff.
24. Said, *After the Last Sky*, 150.
25. Ibid., 50.

Exile thus for Said cultivates an opposition to homogeneous mappings of space that make exclusive connections between nation and territory and an appreciation for the heterogeneity of actual places, an appreciation for how particular places in Palestine-Israel have a mixed character and cannot be reductively coded as exclusively Palestinian or Israel.

Exile, Place, and Peacebuilding Practice

How might recoveries of exile as a critical stance like those undertaken by Raz-Krakotzkin and Said shape Israeli-Palestinian peacebuilding efforts? I would suggest that such recoveries point to the need for peacebuilding efforts that are simultaneously rooted within the violent terrain of partition and exclusion and capable of mapping alternative visions for co-presence and mutuality from within that terrain.

Such peacebuilding efforts must go beyond the most prominent type of peacebuilding initiatives, those receiving substantial funding from Western donor governments, namely "contact" initiatives that focus on bringing Israelis and Palestinians together for different types of encounters, encounters that one Palestinian peacebuilder has, with some degree of cynicism, described to me as "let's eat hummus together" events. These types of peacebuilding initiatives, animated by "contact theory," build on the work of sociologist Gordon Allport and the assumption that addressing prejudicial views held at the cognitive level is key to addressing discrimination.[26] These planned encounters aim at reducing inter-group hostility and building common understanding. Significant diversity exists among such planned encounters. Ifat Maoz has distinguished among the following: efforts aimed at fostering coexistence; initiatives that involve working on joint projects; encounters where Palestinians and Israelis confront one another, but in a controlled setting; and projects that focus on narrative story-telling emerging from each group's respective experiences.[27]

Peace researchers have begun to raise critical questions about how effective such peacebuilding initiatives are at simply initiating inter-group contact between Palestinians and Israelis, let alone motivating solidarity or activism to oppose discrimination and occupation.[28] An additional critique of such initiatives, however, would be that they tend to be despatialized and deracinated in at least two ways. First, such contact encounters are

---

26. Allport, *Nature of Prejudice*. See, for example, Blagojevich, "Peacebuilding," 555–562 and Gawerc, "Peace-Building," 435–78.
27. Maoz, "Does Contact Work," 115–25.
28. See, for example, Maoz, "Is There Contact," 185–97.

despatialized in that they tend to unfold in places that are constructed and presented as neutral, yet the material, territorial realities that have shaped how participants travelled to the encounter are effaced. So, for example, these encounters might take place in the conference room of a hotel in Jerusalem, or in tents in the Negev/Naqab desert, or Cyprus, or a camp setting in the United States. The seemingly neutral spatial location of these encounters effaces the fact that Palestinian participants from the Occupied West Bank or the Gaza Strip will have had to obtain permits from the Israeli military government to travel and will have had to navigate through various checkpoints, roadblocks, and security controls in order to attend. The location of these encounters outside of the Occupied Territories also erases from view how the Israeli government actively prevents and forbids its citizens from entering Area A in the West Bank (the main population centers) and almost completely prevents access to the Gaza Strip for Israelis. Israelis participating in planned contact events do not see the realities of spatial control and repression within which Palestinians exist on a daily basis, and these contact events, taking place either within space coded as Israeli or outside Israel-Palestine, do little to confront Israeli participants with these spatial realities. Second, these encounters tend to be deracinated to the extent that the focus on attitudes and prejudices precludes serious conversation on and action to oppose how the geography and architecture of occupation constraints, controls, and chokes off Palestinian economic, social, and political life. These contact encounters might create space over time for sharing individual and group narratives—but to the extent that the narratives are shared as reflections of inner, subjective states, rather than as also bound up with material, spatial practices of military occupation, the usefulness of such contact initiatives in motivating action to dismantle structures of occupation is dubious.

Fortunately, not all peacebuilding initiatives that bring together Palestinians and Israeli Jews in intergroup encounter succumb to the pitfalls of despatialization and deracination. Ta'ayush ("coexistence" in Arabic), for examples, brings together Palestinians and Israeli Jews for joint solidarity actions in order, in its own words, "to end the occupation and to achieve full civil equality through daily non-violent direct action."[29] Another organization whose peacebuilding practices take seriously the geography of displacement and dispossession within which Palestinian-Israeli Jewish intergroup encounters unfold is Zochrot, an organization whose Hebrew name means "remembering" or "the ones who remember." Zochrot is dedicated, in its

---

29. For an overview of Ta'ayush's activities, see its website, http://www.taayush.org. See also, Shulman, *Dark Hope*.

own words, to "remembering the *nakba* in Hebrew."[30] For Zochrot, the memory of Palestinian towns and villages before 1948 and the Israeli role in their destruction need not be feared as a curse but can instead be embraced as a sign of hope. Zochrot was founded in 2002 by a small group of Israeli Jews with the mission "to commemorate, witness, acknowledge, and repair" by making the *nakba* part of Israeli Jewish discourse and memory; several Palestinians with Israeli citizenship soon joined them in the endeavor. Its main activity consists of organizing return visits to the sites of destroyed Palestinian villages (now often covered over by Israeli national parks or forests) and then posting signs in Arabic and Hebrew marking the ruins and former sites of village structures. Through these return visits and a variety of other actions, Zochrot re-members the landscape, narrating memory of particular places (i.e., destroyed Palestinian villages) in order to project a vision of Palestinian and Israeli Jewish mutuality and co-presence, in which Palestinian memory and presence are no longer viewed as threats to be contained and policed but rather as integral dimensions to Israeli Jewish life in the land.[31] By situating its actions within places of exile amidst a Zionist space predicated upon the negation of exile, Zochrot's activities perforate and challenge the empty, homogeneous space of the Zionist imagination and performatively map new landscapes of possible future mutuality and co-presence.

Conclusion

In the midst of the Israeli bombardment of the Gaza Strip in the summer of 2014, Palestinian playwright Amir Nizar Zuabi penned a meditation on the tunnels dug by Gazans, tunnels depicted by the Israeli media as "terror tunnels," tunnels that from a Palestinian perspective have served military purposes but have also functioned as desperate attempts to circumvent the military and economic blockade of the Strip. Reflecting on the underground nature of Gaza's economy and resistance, Zuabi imagined a different geography for Palestine-Israel, one not captive to the homogeneous, flat spaces of the nationalist imagination: "we start to hope that if we keep on digging, all the way to the core, if we don't stop, if we perforate the land like a honeycomb, if we make it as flimsy as silk, maybe it will suddenly collapse in on itself." With such a collapse, "the upper part and the lower part will blend" and "the rules will change." No longer will "Israeli" and "Palestinian"

---

30. For the organization's trilingual website, see, http://www.zochrot.org.

31. For discussions of Zochrot's work, see, Shah, "'Different Kind,'" 34–37 and Bronstein, "*Nakba* in Hebrew," 214–41.

be tightly cordoned off identities, kept strictly separate from one another, with Palestinian spaces walled off and policed. Rather,

> we'll be able to say with a sigh of relief: Here is a piece of sky mixed with a cracked piece of sea; here is Shujaiyeh mixed with Sderot [an Israeli town near the Gaza Strip where some Palestinian rockets fell]; here is Zeitoun [a neighborhood in Gaza] mixed with the Mount of Olives; here is compassion mixed with relief; here is one human being mixed with another. And we'll know that we were saved from the living death in which we are trapped, and now we'll join the life of above, and with them build a new land.[32]

As Zionist practice demonstrates, memory work fueled by the nationalist imagination creates maps depicting the land as a unified whole, an empty container within which the project of nation-building might unfold. Such memory work threatens to turn the complex, textured places of the land into a flat, homogeneous space. Actual places, in contrast to such abstract space, are always already heterogeneous and perforated, home to a diversity that nationalisms cannot account for and seek to wall off as a threat. A key task for peacebuilding in Palestine-Israel, then, is to remember identity and its tie to place in a different way, a way that embraces the perforated character of the land and the presence of the Other as a blessing rather than a curse. In the face of the devastation wrought by the nationalist imagination in Palestine-Israel, the alternative memory work and mappings carried out by groups like Zochrot seem undeniably fragile. Yet within the fragility of such witness lies the powerful promise of a coming, future landscape not defined by the violence of partition, containment, and control but by co-presence and mutuality.

---

32. Zuabi, "Underground."

16

The Mennonite Peacebuilding Response to Interethnic Division in the Democratic Republic of the Congo

Fidele Ayu Lumeya

Introduction

Designing a peacebuilding scheme for countries with a history as convoluted and complicated as that of the Democratic Republic of the Congo (DRC) and Angola, where Mennonites have had a remarkable presence through the work of Mennonite Central Committee (MCC), is no mean feat. One is unsure where the history pertinent to the conflict begins, which then complicates analysis and has ramifications for designing an intervention strategy. What does emerge unequivocally as one begins the process of unpacking the conflict, identifying actors and motives and the like, is the interconnected nature of these factors. Any peacebuilding design must therefore somehow systematically address these issues if it is to eventually produce a sustainable peace.

Before presenting a brief analysis of the conflict in the Democratic Republic of the Congo and Angola and the Mennonite peacebuilding efforts, it is necessary to briefly convey the operational definition of peacebuilding as it is understood and used within the confines of this chapter. Luc Reychler defines peacebuilding as "efforts required on the way to the creation of a sustainable peace zone: imaging a peaceful future, conducting overall needs assessments, developing a coherent peace plan, and designing an effective implementation of the plan."[1] Reychler further observes, "[T]he overall aim of peacebuilding is to transform conflicts constructively and to create a sustainable peace environment."[2] Elsewhere, Reychler contends, "[P]eacebuilding requires a peace architecture: a clear and compelling vision of the peace one wants to create; a comprehensive assessment of what is needed to realize this peace; a coherent plan; and an effective implementation of this plan."[3]

In addition to the more material dimensions, Lewis Rasmussen inserts a critical distinction by adding the relational and symbolic aspects of peacebuilding. For Rasmussen, peacebuilding "depends on the ability to transform the conflict situation from one of potential or actual mass violence to one of cooperative, peaceful relationships capable of fostering reconciliation, reconstruction, and long term economic and social development."[4] Thus one can see that for the purposes of this chapter, peacebuilding is understood to be an interlocking series of initiatives aimed at addressing both the root causes of issues and grievances while at the same time attempting to improve patterns of relating and the overall quality of life of the parties.

Having delineated this definition, we can now give an encapsulated overview of the history of nations now referred to as the Democratic Republic of the Congo and Angola and analyze the conflict that happened along its Eastern border (Bukavu, South Kivu) in relation to the 1994 Rwandan Genocide and the Mennonite peacebuilding effort.

A Burdensome History

Mapping the conflict in the Democratic Republic of the Congo seems to be a task of almost Sisyphean proportions. Where does one begin to tell the story? At what point can one begin a conflict analysis of such a complex and complicated history? How much detail will be sufficient to explain and corroborate the peacebuilding design to follow? Not wanting to devote the entire chapter to an in-depth analysis of the conflict, what follows here is a compromise of sorts—a very abbreviated exploration of colonial and independence periods of Congo's history, with a more developed exploration of the most current conflict and peacebuilding efforts.

1. Reychler, "Conceptual Framework," 12.
2. Ibid.
3. Ibid., 93.
4. Rasmussen, "Peacemaking," 41.

The nation that constitutes the current day Democratic Republic of the Congo was originally occupied by Negrito peoples, more commonly referred to as "pygmies." They were pushed into the mountains and forests by encroaching Bantu and Nilotic settlers and now represent a mere 1% of the population of the Great Lakes sub-region.[5] In the thirteenth century, the empire of the Kongo rose to prevalence, spanning a geographic area covering the northern portion of Angola, as well as the west and central portions of the Congo. Through successive interaction with Portuguese, British, Dutch, and French merchants engaged in the slave trade, the Kongo Empire lost relative power. In 1879, the Belgian King Leopold II set up a private venture to colonize this portion of Africa, and the Conference of Berlin in 1885 formally recognized his "Congo Free State."[6] Leopold's agents committed horrific atrocities to conquer and dominate Congolese ethnic groups, including the maiming of indentured servants in the rubber industry.[7] Accusations of this became an international cause célèbre and drew massive demonstrations, forcing the Belgian state to annex the Congo as an official colony.[8] Thus, the Congo Free State became the Belgian Congo.

The Belgians proved to be less than benevolent colonizers, installing a system of institutionalized discrimination whereby the advancement of Congolese through the ranks of civil service and local administration required an abandonment of Congolese culture in favor of adopting a more European, "civilized," "evolved" worldview and manner of being. As the winds of change swept through Africa and surrounding countries gained independence from their colonial masters, the Congolese began to militate for independence as well. While in 1955 Belgium had drafted a 30-year transitional plan for granting this colony its independence, by 1959 it was forced to withdraw in the face of massive nationalist riots in Leopoldville (now Kinshasa).[9] On June 30, 1960, Congo became an independent nation with Patrice Lumumba as Prime Minister and Joseph Kasavubu as President. There were only three Congolese university graduates at this point in time.

The transition to independence was not trouble-free, however, and only a month after the official ceremony the Congolese army mutinied and the mineral-rich province of Katanga seceded. Belgian troops returned to the Congo, ostensibly to protect Belgian interests and citizens. The United

5. "Country Profile: Democratic Republic of the Congo."
6. Ibid.
7. Hochschild, *King Leopold's Ghost*.
8. Ibid.
9. "Country Profile: Democratic Republic of the Congo."

Nations sent in its first peacekeeping mission to the Congo with the mandate to restore order, but not to put down the secession or otherwise tamper in Congo's internal affairs. In frustration, Lumumba turned to the Soviet Union for support, earning himself the antipathy and suspicion of the European and North American capitalist nations. By early 1961 the nascent Congolese political scene was in tatters as Lumumba was arrested and murdered and power struggles among the early nationalists dominated the transition period. In August 1961, UN troops began disarming the Katangese militias and by 1963, Tshombe, the self-declared President of Katanga, agreed to end the secession.[10]

In 1965, a young army colonel, Joseph Mobutu, perpetrated a coup and declared himself president, beginning his 32-year reign as Congo's all-powerful supreme leader. He quickly abolished the office of Prime Minister and the multiparty system. He engaged in an ill-fated program of "African Authentication" or "Zaïrianization," in which the name of the country was changed from Congo to Zaïre, and all foreign businesses were nationalized and redistributed to cronies. He changed his name to Mobutu Sese Seko and "encouraged" his citizens to likewise adopt African names. In 1970, he held Presidential elections for which he was the only candidate; Mobutu won a 7-year term as President. He then centralized the administration of the nation and effectively put in place a political and economic system of patronage and clientelism. He ran the country much as Leopold had done, as if it was his own corrupt fiefdom. State structures and a reciprocal, transparent political culture were never allowed to evolve under Mobutu. Given his strategic geopolitical placement in the center of Africa and his avowed aversion to communism, Mobutu created his own system of international patronage with the powerful capitalist countries.

Copper prices fell during the course of the 1970s, provoking a recession and resulting social crises. Students and the military began to riot and revolt and there were periodic coup attempts throughout 1978–1979. By the early 1980s opposition groups such as the unarmed Union pour la Democratie et le Progres Social (UDPS) had formed, and international support for Mobutu and his excesses was waning.[11] In 1989, Zaïre defaulted on a loan from Belgium, resulting in the cancellation of development projects, thus further exacerbating the economic deterioration of the nation. Civil unrest grew.

In 1990, perhaps reading the writing on the wall, Mobutu declared the end of the single-party state and created a transitional government, though

---

10. Ibid.
11. "Background Notes: Congo."

retaining the position of head of state and all the powers there invested.[12] Riots by unpaid soldiers in 1991 (which required the intervention of 2,000 French and Belgian paratroopers to contain) forced Mobutu to agree to a coalition government with opposition leaders.[13] In 1992, the long-awaited Sovereign National Conference was convened, with 2,000 delegates from various political parties participating. This body accorded itself legislative powers and recognized Catholic Archbishop Laurent Monsengwo as its chairperson with UDPS front man, Etienne Tshisekedi, as Prime Minister.[14] By the year's end, Mobutu had created a shadow administration complete with a rival Prime Minister. In 1994, after a process of negotiation, the two administrations were folded into one: the High Council of the Republic Parliament of Transition (HCR-PT). Mobutu remained as head of state and the compromise candidate, Kengo Wa Dondo, was named Prime Minister. Presidential and Parliamentary elections were repeatedly scheduled over the next two years but were never actually held.

A major destabilizing factor at this time was the 1994 Genocide in Rwanda. This event had a catastrophic spillover effect that ultimately led to the downfall of Mobutu. Over a million predominantly Hutu Rwandan refugees sought asylum in Zaïre, some of whom were directly implicated in the Genocide. For two years these refugees lived in camps closer than the prescribed 150 kms from the Rwandan border; former Hutu military and extremist militias such as the Interahamwe staged repeated incursions and attacks into Rwanda. The government of Rwanda grew tired of the lack of international attention or action and took matters into their own hands by recruiting the former Lumumbist rebel Laurent Kabila to front an insurgent uprising starting in the east of the country. Long-time ally Uganda joined Rwanda to unseat Mobutu and install a friendlier regime. Refugee camps were attacked and disbanded, (the first such incident in the United Nations High Commission for Refugee's history), the Interahamwe was destabilized and driven deeper into Zaïre, and Mobutu's seemingly iron-fisted hold over the country was shaken. The demoralized Zaïrian army quickly ceded territory to the advancing rebels, and Kabila's coalition quickly took control of Zaïre. Mobutu's 32-year reign was over.

Kabila declared himself President of the renamed Democratic Republic of the Congo on May 17, 1997.[15] An outsider in the Kinshasa political circles, Kabila had to rely on his Rwandan patrons and members of his

12. "Country Profile: Democratic Republic of the Congo."
13. "Background Notes: Congo."
14. Ibid.
15. Ibid.

Baluba-Kat ethnic group for support and guidance. Initially, the "liberation" of Congo was greeted with much hope, but this sentiment quickly turned to suspicion as Kabila failed to implement his promised reforms. Cognizant of his lack of a Congolese constituency, Kabila banned political opposition and became increasingly repressive, cracking down on journalists and the like. Popular opinion began to demand the ousting of foreign troops and political advisors. Kabila capitulated and asked his Rwandan and Ugandan backers to leave Congo.

On August 2, 1998, Rwandan and Ugandan troops revolted against their forced departure, and fresh troops invaded the Congo. Rwandan troops hijacked a plane from the east and captured a military base in the west less than 400 kms from the capital. Rwandan troops would have captured Kinshasa had it not been for the intervention of Angolan and Zimbabwean troops.[16] Rwandan troops retreated back to the east of Congo, where they allied themselves with nascent armed opposition groups. Rwanda eventually backed the Rassemblement Congolais pour la Democratie (RCD), predominantly comprised of Congolese ethnic Tutsi, while Uganda backed the Mouvement pour la Liberation du Congo (MLC), comprised of many former Mobutists. Initially united by a common desire to oust their former protegé Kabila, the partnership between Uganda and Rwanda frayed and devolved into proxy warfare between the RCD and MLC, finally resulting in two separate instances of combat between Rwandan and Ugandan troops in the eastern city of Kisangani. Supporting the Kabila regime and fighting on his behalf were the nations of Angola, Zimbabwe, Chad, and Namibia.[17] All parties involved in the war that has become "Africa's first world war" were benefiting from their presence by extracting natural resources such as diamonds, gold, and coltan, a mineral used in the fabrication of micro-chips and cell phones found only in the eastern portion of the DRC. At that point, Congo was effectively divided into three segments, with the parties having arrived at a military deadlock.[18]

After intense negotiation, a cease-fire was declared and the Lusaka protocol was signed in August 1999.[19] This arrangement, consistently praised by Congo-watchers as being an inherently workable agreement, had four basic components: a comprehensive and inclusive cease-fire; the deployment of a UN peacekeeping operation, MONUC; the withdrawal of all foreign troops; and an "Inter-Congolese Dialogue" to form a transitional

16. Ibid.
17. International Crisis Group. *Scramble for the Congo.*
18. "Background Notes: Congo."
19. Ibid.

government leading to elections.[20] The six African nations involved in the fighting in the DRC signed the accord, with the MLC and RCD rebel groups signing a month later. The United Nation's Security Council authorized a 5,500-strong peacekeeping force (MONUC) to monitor the cease-fire in February 2000, but continued violations and fighting between the belligerents effectively blocked the rapid deployment of MONUC.[21] Once deployed, MONUC's mission was not facilitated by Kabila's administration, which it accused of continuing to hamper its movements.

In January 2001, Kabila was assassinated by his own bodyguard, and his son, Joseph Kabila, was named his successor. Laurent-Désiré's son proved to be more amenable to the peace process and facilitated the full and unrestricted deployment of MONUC. In October 2001, the Inter-Congolese dialogue—intended as a forum for discussing the future political dispensation of the Congolese government—was convened in Addis Ababa, Ethiopia, mediated by former Botswanan President, Ketumile Masire.[22] These meetings produced little of substantive value and were subsequently adjourned. In February 2002, the dialogue was reconvened in South Africa and was attended by representatives of the government, the unarmed political opposition, the armed opposition, civil society, and the Mai-Mai (traditional local militias of the east). This series of talks resulted in an agreement signed by several of the parties, but most notably not by the major armed and unarmed opposition groups, thus making it an agreement that was incapable of being implemented.

Consultation again reconvened in October 2002, and this series of talks, referred to colloquially as the Sun City talks, resulted in an all-inclusive power-sharing accord, formally ratified by all parties in April, 2003.[23] A transitional government was created, with Kabila remaining as President with four Vice Presidents, one coming from each of the major rebel groups. Each rebel group received seven ministries in the interim government as well.[24] General elections, the first since Congo took its independence from Belgium, were scheduled for June 2005.

Simultaneously, progress was made with external forces. By the end of 2002 all Namibian, Zimbabwean and Angolan troops had withdrawn from Congolese territory. The Rwandan and Congolese governments met in Pretoria, South Africa, to normalize relations, after which Rwandan troops

20. Ibid.
21. "Country Profile: Democratic Republic of the Congo."
22. "Background Notes: Congo."
23. Ibid.
24. "Country Profile: Democratic Republic of the Congo."

also withdrew from the Congo. The Kinshasa government agreed to disarm the Hutu rebel extremists who continued to operate from their territory. Ugandan troops formally withdrew in May 2003.[25]

While progress was made to re-establish peace in the DRC, difficulties remained. In April 2003, ethnic fighting unrelated to the recent war in Congo erupted in the Ituri region, requiring the deployment of a UN-sponsored French force to protect local civilians. In actuality, the government of Kinshasa had been unable to establish complete and uncontested control over a large swathe of its territory, mostly in the east. In the first half of 2004, there were two unsuccessful coup attempts, and the integration of all armed forces into a unified army had proven largely futile. In June 2004, former rebel troops mutinied and occupied the eastern town of Bukavu for weeks.[26] Similar forces rebelled again in December 2004. In March 2005, nine Bangladeshi soldiers serving with MONUC were killed in skirmishes in the still-troublesome northeast.[27] Throughout this period, Congo had accused Rwanda of repeatedly disrespecting its territorial integrity by staging incursions back into Congo.

In short, while progress was made, much work remained to be done in terms of peacebuilding if a return to conflict in the DRC was to be avoided. There were clearly both *endogenous* domestic factors and very tangible *exogenous* factors which were impinging upon and influencing the progression, escalation, and prolongation of the conflict in the DRC. These internal and external factors needed to be considered and addressed through specific, intentional interventions, for if they were neglected, it would be highly unlikely that the DRC would be able to experience a just and sustainable peace. I will in the following pages analyze the peacebuilding framework designed by the Congolese Mennonite Churches to address endogenous and exogenous factors and the strategies used.

Peacebuilding Strategies to Address Endogenous Factors: Connecting and Networking from within the Church of Christ in Congo (ECC)

Clearly throughout the DRC's convoluted and troubled history, competition over perceived scarce resources, including access to power and decision-making, has played a crucial role in the internal, domestic component of the

---

25. Ibid.
26. Ibid.
27. Ibid.

conflict. There is a saying in Congo that "one finger cannot wash somebodies face; you rather need many fingers." The Mennonite Church understood that a small denomination such as theirs could not by itself be an agent of change in the Congo. They took advantage of their membership in the Congolese church network—known as ECC—to join their voices with other members in order to address the endogenous factors. Together with the Council of Churches, they designed a peacebuilding framework that took into account the following sectors:

Political Development

Elizabeth Cousens argues that addressing the fundamental, political issues must be the cornerstone of a peacebuilding design. The original purpose of peacebuilding, according to Cousens, is "consolidating whatever degree of peace has been achieved in the short-term and, in the longer-term, increasing the likelihood that future conflict can be managed without resorting to violence."[28] The essential priority of peacebuilding for Cousens is "the construction or strengthening of authoritative and, eventually, legitimate mechanisms to resolve internal conflict without violence."[29] Self-enforcing peace should be the end goal. This is understood as the ability "to cultivate political processes and institutions that can manage group conflict without violence but with authority and, eventually, legitimacy. If war is a continuation of politics by other means," Cousens continues, "peacebuilding can be seen as an opportunity to channel 'war' into manageable forms of competition or to support what I. William Zartman and others characterize as the *reinstitution of political life*."[30]

In the 1960s, Mennonite congregations—mainly those established in the western province of Bandundu and the two Kasai provinces in the southwest—saw themselves more as victims of post-independence wars and didn't play key roles at the national level. In the 1990s, they became more involved, partially due to the influence of Congolese Mennonite lay people who had the opportunity of further education, and understood that their faith without actions is dead. The country needed their knowledge on issues of peace and justice. This group of young Mennonite intellectuals—mainly those with law degrees and with other non-theological degrees—were sent as delegates to the political platform of the National Council of Protestants to bring a Mennonite voice to the national debate.

28. Cousens, "Introduction," 4.
29. Ibid.
30. Ibid., 12.

Peace, Justice, and Development: A Congolese Peacebuilding Framework

The Congolese Mennonite Churches view peacebuilding as a tool with three legs. The first leg is *peace*, the second is *justice*, and the third is *development*. In 2003, they were given the opportunity to participate, for the first time, in the national dialogue in Sun City (South Africa) that was held to draft a peace agreement to end the war that had started in 1998. They clearly expressed the need for peace through power sharing, justice for the victims, and long-term development as a lasting solution. They understood that the solution was a double-edged sword—there could not be peace in a country without development, and a country cannot expect to have development without peace and justice. Peace, justice, and development go hand-in-hand.

The view that the Congolese Mennonite delegates presented at the national debate is shared by Kumar, who writes that "peace agreements are launching points . . . that need to evolve in the long run into successful politics and economies."[31]

Lessons Learned

The 2003 Inter-Congolese National Debate that gave a voice to all Congolese to express their views on the future of the country concluded with the formation of a transitional system of government. This eventually led to a more inclusive, democratically-elected, reciprocal form of long-term governance.

Furthermore, the Inter-Congolese Dialogue has proven to be an excellent starting point for negotiating Congo's future political dispensation. Domestic actors in the conflict, specifically the armed and unarmed opposition groups, were encouraged to respect the power-sharing arrangements they themselves negotiated and ratified in the Pretoria Peace Agreement.

Best Practices

Congo, as with many other African countries, has experienced many peace agreements that led to nowhere except another war. This time all delegates, including the Mennonites, decided to create a partnership agreement with the diplomatic community that was living in the Congo and with the United Nations mission in the Congo. The diplomatic community was assigned to encourage the Congolese government to initiate a series of

---

31. Kumar, "Conclusion," 197.

confidence-building measures in which various parties and constituencies were given specific portfolios and tasks during the transition.

The other example of best practices of the Inter-Congolese Dialogue (2003) was the decision that in order to accomplish a lasting peace in Congo, it would be necessary to build and support the capacity within the ethnic militias and opposition groups early on as they transition into viable political parties capable of fielding candidates, formulating public policy, and governing.

For that reason delegates were asked to contribute human resources with knowledge and the capacity to train the entire Congolese society in peacebuilding and democracy, rules of law, good governance, and election monitoring. Through the Mennonite World Conference, the Mennonite Central Committee, and the Mennonite personal network of connections, skilled Mennonites came forward to share their knowledge and to train fellow Mennonites as well as members of the Church of Christ in Congo (ECC).

Training in democratization, civil society capacity-building, policy formation, and the like should be undertaken fairly early in the peacebuilding process, as the skills imparted will be of critical importance in further stages of the peacebuilding scheme. NGOs such as the Center for Democracy, CIVITAS International, the National Democratic Institute for International Affairs, and the National Endowment for Democracy[32] and Mennonite universities (such as Eastern Mennonite University's Center for Justice and Peacebuilding) could be contracted to deliver such trainings—funded by USAID grants, which are traditionally intended for democratization efforts.

It is said that the end justifies the means. A transitional government structure was created as a result of the negotiations and peace process, and elections scheduled to follow a two-year- transitional period were held. The Congolese civil society, including the Church of Christ of Congo (ECC), was reluctant to consider the postponement of these elections. This was understandable given the historical antecedents of Mobutu routinely scheduling elections but never holding them. Unlike that of South Africa and other transitional situations where there existed national registers and voter registration systems, there had not been an official census in the DRC since Independence. Given the degree of deterioration of the physical infrastructure of the roads, transportation system, and the like, conducting a national census would not be an easy or quick task.

Lessons learned included the knowledge that without a valid and systematized census that would lead to the establishment of voter eligibility,

---

32. Aall, *et al, Guide to IGOs*, 157–167.

the likelihood of accusations of voter fraud and the contestation of election results would be almost certain. This would not in any way solidify or enhance the larger peace process as observed elsewhere in countries transitioning from war to peace. Confronted by such a reality, the contribution that the international community made during the transition period created a success story of peacebuilding in the Congo (2003–05). Specifically, the donor nations most involved in the DRC peace process (CIAT—discussed in-depth later in this chapter) helped the transitional government plan by organizing and implementing a national census and establishing voter eligibility requirements. Once again, the transitional government of Congo called on the churches to make a positive contribution. Mennonite Churches of Congo used their administration books in which members' names are recorded when planning to go home to register and conduct a census. Qualified voters were issued photo identification and assigned to a specific voting district.

Finally and relatedly, the government of Congo set forth unequivocal legislation resolving the status of minority groups, especially those of Rwandan origin.[33] The legislation stated that all individuals who could demonstrate residency in the DRC prior to June 30, 1960 would be recognized as Congolese citizens, guaranteeing all the inherent rights and responsibilities. The legislation included measures of protection and guarantees of non-discriminatory treatment, thereby reducing the potential influence of ethnic entrepreneurs. This legislation was promulgated in 2006 and represented one of the fundamental, nation-building statements of the transitional government. Resolving the national identity issue of contested ethnic groups allowed them to participate in the national census, and to become registered voters and engaged citizens.

The Mennonite delegates were in agreement with the national dialogue—justice in the DRC required taking into account the root causes of war. The issues of the endogenous people—such as the status of the ethnic minority of people of Rwandan origin, also known as Banyamulenge—had to be resolved before peace would prevail.

Disarmament, Demobilization, and Reintegration (DDR): The Military Conversion and Contributions of Congolese Mennonites

As with many countries seeking to pull out of civil war, the DRC decided to effectively demobilize and disarm all combatants operating within the Congo. A young Mennonite was given the leadership of this complex

---

33. For a discussion on a related experience, see Sokalski, *Ounce of Prevention*, 74.

department and was assigned the rank of minister. Unfortunately, the ill-planned and underfinanced Disarmament, Demobilization, and Reintegration (DDR) Program did not offer former combatants the opportunity to transition from warriors to members of civilian life. The success of the DDR lies mainly in providing former combatants with the educational, vocational, and financial resources needed for reentry into civil society. "Supporting a demobilization process is not just a technical military issue. It is a complex operation that has political, security, humanitarian, and development dimensions as well."[34] The same author goes on to warn, "if one aspect of this pentagram is neglected, the entire fragile peace process may unravel."[35] DDR programs should have run parallel to, but not compete with, larger social development programs. The DRR was lacking key ingredients, starting with the Mennonite lack of interest, resources, and willingness to call upon their brothers and sisters as they did with other peace process components as mentioned above. The missing ingredients in this key process of the transition included the demobilized former soldier's lack of access to credit and start-up funds for small income-generating schemes, materials for housing, access to training, and vocational assistance. Though on paper all sounded good, in reality funding was diverted from programs specifically designed to meet their needs, and the coordinating body that reported to the transitional government was controlled by thousands of corrupted individuals. As elsewhere, the flaws of past experiences in many Africans countries were repeated. The young Mennonite ended by leaving in order to avoid compromising his Christian values.

Social and Economic Development: The Role of Congolese Mennonites and the Contributions of Mennonite Economic and Development Associates (MEDA)

There is a Congolese proverb that says, "An empty belly doesn't have ears." As a case in point, peace efforts have to be nurtured by well-planned and implemented food security and livelihood programs following the transition and election. Transitioning from war to peace requires that the economic, political, and social institutions and infrastructure grow exponentially in order to both support and stimulate social change. Perhaps the current greatest obstacle to the restoration of a lasting peace is the social and economic crisis of the DRC, brought about by decades of fiscal mismanagement and

---

34. Salomons, "Security," 20.
35. Ibid.

inadequate investment in social capital and physical infrastructure.[36] As the World Bank has observed, "[C]ountries affected by conflict face a two-way relationship between conflict and poverty- pervasive poverty makes societies more vulnerable to violent conflict, while conflict itself creates more poverty," so it is lived in the DRC.[37] The transition in Congo was like setting on a stool with only two legs. As one can observe all that follows—the person sitting loses their balance and falls. If the peace process and justice needs were very nearly met, the development—especially the economic development—was not. The economy of Congo had not yet been controlled by responsible fiscal programs aimed at creating employment and encouraging foreign investment in industry and production.[38]

The DRC is a predominantly subsistence agriculture-based economy with an incredibly strong informal economic system. This is especially true in the western and southwestern provinces where most Mennonites live. While reflecting an ability on the part of Congolese to survive Mobutu's predatory government, the informal economic system built on barter and buy-and-sell micro-businesses is incompatible with long-term, large-scale economic development. Efforts must focus on increased production and improved quality of life of the Congolese citizens through access to medical care, educational opportunities, and participation in governance in a safe, clean, sustainable environment.

This is an area of multi-sectorial development in the peacebuilding design that is not an area in which Non-Governmental Organizations (NGOs) can play a critical, central role. The government, financial institutions, and other development agencies such as MEDA must step forward. A plethora of NGOs are needed to address the many short term competing vital needs and concerns, but the long term belongs to the government as it has the mandate to invite investors and get loans. It is estimated that 3.8 million civilians have died due to the poverty and disease fomented by five years of war.[39] It was imperative then, as it is now, that the transitional government, as well the current elected government, create a coordinating body to evaluate the proposed programs of the operational NGOs seeking to work in the DRC. The body would grant work visas and synchronize efforts so as to ensure that there would be no unneeded duplication in certain sectors or geographic areas while other sectors or areas go underserviced. For sustainable, long-term peace, development at the national level must be equivalent

36. Mpangala, "Conflict Resolution."
37. Quoted in Junne and Verkoren, "Challenges," 1.
38. Kamphuis, "Economic Policy."
39. International Crisis Group. *Africa Briefing*, 1.

in all the regions and for all the various ethnic groups. The Mennonites of Congo would help as they did in the past, by inviting the expertise of the Mennonite Economic Development Associates (MEDA) to assist in the areas of job creation, food security, and livelihoods. In the 1970s, MEDA purchased vast farming lands and created employment in the western provinces of Congo that kept young Congolese of that province away from war. Many Congolese, however, could not understand why MEDA had been reluctant to return to Congo but rather had preferred to open offices elsewhere in Africa.

Equally important in the process of post-conflict development is the need to build social capital such as "trust, norms of reciprocity, and tolerance, and associational networks."[40] The work of NGOs such as Mennonite Central Committee and its local Mennonites NGOs again lends itself well to this task. In the 1960s, MCC in the Congo did not have other Mennonite NGOs with which to partner. Instead, MCC worked with Congolese Mennonite Churches, which at that time did not have as many skilled development actors as it does today. To its credit, MCC designed training programs that have equipped local Mennonites in Congo with skills such as designing, monitoring, and conducting evaluations of projects. Unfortunately, the past ten years of MCC programs in Congo have been dominated by a diminished budget for development to the point that the MCC-trained development actors have the capacity and experience but cannot meet the needs of their communities in terms of food security and livelihood. To close the leadership gap within the MCC office in the Congo and solve the conflict between MCC and the Congolese churches with respect to adequate Congolese representation within MCC, local Congolese staff members were promoted to the top management level and became bridge builders between MCC and its partners—the local Mennonite churches. Instead of taking development projects out of the peacebuilding context, most of MCC capacity-building in the Congo—mainly in Eastern Congo—integrated conflict transformation as a component, and programs were implemented with the explicit goal of fostering interethnic cooperation, especially in the east from 1995–1999.

Lessons Learned and Best Practices from Mennonite Development Projects in Congo

Projects that jointly benefit the various ethnic groups in the area, but that require their collaboration to succeed (such as the construction of a regional road system or provincial hospital), are to be encouraged. Thus such

40. Prendergast, *Frontline Diplomacy*, 124.

infrastructure construction and repair can have the intentional secondary effect of developing and/or repairing the social and communal infrastructure, while at the same time delivering more tangible goods and services.

Lessons learned from the Congolese Mennonite partnership with both MEDA and MCC are that regardless of what happened in their past, partners such as the three above mentioned organizations have to come together as they did in the 1970s and 1980s, with concrete programs such as the Teacher Abroad Program (TAP). TAP had an impact on Congolese education at the local and national levels, as did MEDA, by designing an industrial plant in the Congo. Education programs were among the larger initiatives in the Congo in which Mennonites participated. For example, they created jobs for some church members who were hired to work at different capacities with volunteers. Today in the Congo, chances are that at in every corner of the country, one can talk to people about the contribution of Mennonites to education and they will hear the mention of TAP. This is how Mennonites connected the teachings of peace, justice, and development in the Congo to historical Anabaptist beliefs and values as they have been expressed around the world.

Peacebuilding Strategies to Address Exogenous Factors: The Mennonite Church of Congo and Their Response to the Rwanda and Angola Crises

As stated in the beginning of this chapter, there are exogenous factors that we need to consider when deliberating over peacebuilding processes in the Congo and related Mennonite roles. Ignored, these exogenous factors make it virtually impossible to envision, let alone inaugurate, a sustainable peace in Central Africa. By area Congo is the second largest country in Africa after Algeria. Congo has nine bordering states, including Rwanda in the East and Angola in the South. It is only recently that Mennonites have churches in both Rwanda and Angola. Congo is a member of the regional network of countries known as the Great Lakes countries. Congo is also a member of the group of countries known as the Southern African Development Countries (SADC). The network of Protestant churches in the Congo known as the Church of Christ in Congo (ECC) is a member of the regional network of the council of churches of both regions—Great Lakes and Southern Africa. The Mennonite churches of Congo have their delegates in these networks. This position is the one that Mennonites of Congo use to advocate for peace, justice and conflict prevention. Building coalitions is one of the many ways Mennonites of Congo approach peace and justice.

The Need for a Complementary Peace Processes in the Great Lakes Region

Unfortunately, the Democratic Republic of the Congo is bordered on almost all sides by highly unstable countries going through their own transition periods since the end of cold war in 1990. Rwanda, Uganda, Burundi, the Central African Republic, and Sudan all currently have insurgency and rebellions. Angola is more stable after more than twenty-five years of civil war. As mentioned earlier, the spillover effect from Rwanda's 1994 genocide cannot be underestimated—the resulting war in 1996 heralded the downfall of one of Africa's most entrenched dictators, Mobutu Sese Seko. In short, the DRC currently exists in a "tough neighborhood" where endogenous factors in any of the above-listed countries could provoke events that have the potential to either complicate or complement the peace, justice, and development in the Congo.

Therefore, I will argue here that there is a need to simultaneously design and implement comparable peacebuilding processes in neighboring countries. As the DRC forms part of a much larger regional zone of conflict, it is contended here that peace in the DRC will not be sustainable as long as any of its neighbors continue to experience stress or instability. And this is true at the individual and church level, as many ethnic groups are linked, and at the political level, as mainly ethnic militias are able to kill in one country and find refuge in another. The ICG argued that "a comprehensive solution . . . is urgently needed."[41] It is not within the scope of this chapter to suggest such peacebuilding designs, but suffice it to say that the Mennonites of Congo took a systems perspective when considering the situation in the DRC. They identified the contributing regional factors and addressed them in an effort to change the regional dynamic from one of proxy warfare to one of orderliness and cooperation. Although this effort has been minimal it is a beginning, their effort represents the seeds, if not a tree. The presence of delegates from the Mennonite churches of Congo in the local, national, regional, and global church structures is the channel that Mennonites used to advocate for peace and justice.

The Seeds of Mennonite Peace: The Contributions of Congolese Mennonites to Higher Education in the Congo

After independence, talking about higher education in the Congo referred to two entities: the Catholic Church and the government of Congo.

---

41. International Crisis Group. *Africa Briefing*, 7.

Congolese who were willing to go to university had to go to Catholic-owned and government-owned universities. These limited choices were a challenge to most Protestants in the Congo, including the Mennonites. Therefore, the need to create a university that would reflect Protestant values and beliefs became an urgent need. For that reason, they asked for the Mennonites of Congo to partner with other churches to create the University of Kisangani in northern Congo. The Mennonites of Congo invited North American Mennonites to respond to the call. Young Anabaptist Mennonites from the United States and Canada responded to the call by joining other Protestants around the world to create the Protestant University of Kisangani. Today, Mennonite efforts to build a coalition to create a University in collaboration with other Protestants should be perceived as a great Mennonite contribution to peace through higher education in Congo. Most Congolese Protestant communities sent their members to Kisangani for higher education. Those who studied at Kisangani Protestant University are today leading either their church communities in top management positions or are working as public servants. One thing that is common among alumni is their pride in attending a Protestant university that reflected their values and beliefs.

Generational Thinking about Peace and Mennonite Contributions to Peacebuilding during the Angolan Civil War

The Angolan Civil War lasted twenty-seven years (1975–2002). Many Angolans left the country and were exiled in the Congo, where they were welcomed by Congolese Mennonite Brethren churches, including those of the Kinshasa, Kikwit, Kajiji, and Panzi. War in Angola divided not only politicians but also the Church of Angola in exile. Ethnicity defines where one belongs, whether church or politics or neighborhood. Membership in political parties in Angola and the Congo is ethnic-based. Aware of this ethnically divided society that was yet to be born, the new Angolan Mennonite members received teachings on peace and justice from the Congolese Mennonite leaders. In reality, the Mennonites of Congo did not have much to offer to the Angolan post-conflict reconstruction, as had the North American Mennonites to the Congo. It is said in the Congo that one can only give what (s)he knows best. So, sharing knowledge with regard to peace and social justice will be the major contribution of the Mennonites Church of Congo to the Angolan leaders and their members. Capacity-building seminars in conflict transformation aimed at equipping Angolan leaders in exile in the Congo and their members would be the area where the Mennonites of Congo will focus most. Angolan Mennonites will leave the Congo equipped with peacebuilding skills such as negotiation, dialogue, listening, and mediation to name but a few.

The importance of this modest contribution of the Congolese Mennonites has an impact on trans-generational thinking. This thinking revolves around the idea that the current generation not only prepares the next generation, but shares their knowledge with the current one and prepares it to pass on this knowledge to the many subsequent generations to come. Congolese Mennonites were unable to meet the never-ending needs of the Angolan refugees in the Congo, mainly those who became Mennonites. Therefore, Mennonite Brethren Mission Service International (MBMSI) will be invited to address some financial needs of the Angolan Mennonites. The MBMSI representative office in the Congo provided—among many other services—leadership training, substantial grants, and paid jobs, while encouraging them to start teaching their constituents the Portuguese language. Portuguese is an Angolan national language and most Angolan refugees in the Congo did not speak Portuguese. Because of the deep ethnic division among the Angolan Mennonites living in the Congo, the Congolese Mennonites and their counterparts, such as MBMSI, played the role of peace broker among the Angolan Mennonite leaders. Power struggles among the Angolan Mennonite leaders in exile in the Congo became obvious. Very often the leaders of the Congolese Mennonite churches were called in to mediate the Angolan conflicts around power sharing. Angolan Mennonite members, mainly from an ethnic majority group, preferred to have leaders who belong to their ethnic group even though the "chosen leader" did not meet the qualifications. For that reason, the three Angolan Mennonite churches currently have leaders who are not necessarily underqualified, but are nevertheless underperforming for many reasons including low education levels.

Lessons Learned and Best Practices from Responding to the Exogenous Factors in the Case of Angola

Twenty-six years later, Angola started moving from a country embroiled in war to a country in search of peace to a country that, today, has finally found peace. This environment created the opportunity for the return of all Angolan political and church leaders who were living in the Congo. The opening of the Mennonite Biblical Institute in Kikwit and in the South of Bandundu Province to train most of the Angolan Mennonite leaders was a forward thinking initiative in terms of preparing a generation of leaders to guide their society from warfare to a long-lasting peace. Leaders of the

Angolan Mennonite Church participated in seminars on reconciliation and power sharing based on the past experience of Congolese Mennonites. It was therefore hoped that these church leaders would be able to build peace in their homeland for a generation of Angolans who decide to become Mennonites in Angola rather than in exile.

Best Practices in Planting the Seeds of Peace in Angola Among Mennonite Brethren Church Leaders

The potential for economic development and multilateral cooperation to be fostered by such functional, economically feasible joint ventures is obvious. Yet, given the not-insubstantial degree of animosity remaining—principally among the MB church leaders of Angola—including an economic development structure as a component of peacebuilding, while highly promising, requires the involvement of impartial but interested third parties. Hence, a follow-up committee should also be implemented and could be enlarged to include countries such as the Congo and United States, but also various Mennonite agencies. MCC has made an effort to avoid isolating the three Angolan Mennonite churches. Thanks to MCC, these three Mennonite churches are members of the Mennonite World Conference. Such ventures offer opportunities for the churches and agencies that are involved in peacebuilding to work together on joint projects for mutual benefit, clearly exemplifying the idea of superordinate projects.

Conclusion: The Final Piece of the Puzzle—Timing

I will conclude this chapter by addressing the final piece of the peacebuilding puzzle: that of timing. John Paul Lederach has written extensively on the question of timing and timeframes as they relate to the often imprecise subject of peacebuilding. Unlike specific development and infrastructure projects found within the Mennonite efforts to build peace, sustain justice, and work on development—which are often results-oriented and time-bound—peacebuilding requires an alternative understanding of time. Lederach encourages peacebuilders to cultivate a polychronic rather than monochronic approach to time, sequencing, and reconciliation work.[42] In short, this entails the ability to work on multiple tasks, initiatives, and projects at the same time, as we have seen with the Mennonites of Congo. He advocates for a "multiplicity of activities and a simultaneity of actions . . .

---

42. Lederach, *Journey*, 78.

doing several things at the same time."⁴³ This requires a systemic rather than linear perspective regarding people, relationships, activities, and context. One must cultivate the ability to plan for the future, work in the present, and deal with the past. Therein lies the intuitive art of peacebuilding.

For a context such as that of the DRC, Lederach proposes that interveners and actors adapt a "present to future to the past" approach.⁴⁴ He stipulates that "the common need for survival has created interdependence in the present."⁴⁵ Parties must bracket the past and set it aside for the moment. They must then "develop a relationship based on their common immediate needs. The present provides the possibility of a new relationship, a new beginning."⁴⁶ By focusing on the common needs of the present, parties can "move towards and into the *emerging future*. Perhaps at a much later point, they will return to the past."⁴⁷ The witness account found in this chapter adopts this perspective by focusing on development and infrastructure projects and immediate issues of governance, the working through of which can facilitate the negotiated and mediated materialization of a more democratic, secure future. The past won't be forgotten however, and must be dealt with through storytelling and other communal efforts to foster ethnic cohabitation. The Mennonite historical infrastructure for preserving and disseminating stories of past suffering to inspire peacebuilding and development on behalf of those who suffer in the same way today fits this mold.

43. Ibid.
44. Ibid., 70.
45. Ibid., 71.
46. Ibid., 73.
47. Ibid., 75.

17

Overcoming Trauma, Grievance, and Revenge in Bosnia-Herzegovina and Kosovo

Fostering Nonviolent Reconciliation Efforts

DAVID STEELE

Introduction

ON MAY 19, 1993, the bodies of a Serb man and a Muslim woman lay in a no-man's-land between the warring sides in Sarajevo. Bosko and Admira had been promised safe passage by both sides, but the promise of a future was cut short by sniper's fire. Their attempt to escape the ravages of war had failed. But as their bodies lay in an embrace for almost a week while each side fought for possession, they became a symbol of tolerance and togetherness.[1] Their love could not overcome all the obstacles of the moment, but perhaps it could point the way to a reconciled future.

How does one begin to walk the difficult road to reconciliation when the tragedy of the Balkan wars, most notably in Bosnia-Herzegovina and Kosovo, has far surpassed the woes of Job? A complete answer to this question is certainly very complex. What follows in this chapter is a review of a specific approach to the creation of a climate for constructive,

---

1. Drakulic, *Balkan Express*, 151–56.

nonviolent resolution of conflict in these two countries. The selected project is one that aimed to foster attitude change (such as humility, open inquiry, empathy, trust, and solidarity) through the use of reconciliation practices (such as trauma healing, hospitality, apology/acknowledgment of wrongdoing, forgiveness, and restorative justice) which utilized a variety of people-to-people processes (such as storytelling and active listening, perception clarification, dialogue/conciliation, ritualization, and more formal roles like mediation and problem solving).

Although similar to Mennonite values and practices, the peacebuilding program presented here has been led primarily by other faith-based actors. Yet Mennonite values and methodology provided significant guidance in the early stages of the project in Bosnia-Herzegovina. For example, prior to initiation, the project director attended courses at the Summer Peacebuilding Institute at Eastern Mennonite University in Harrisonburg, Virginia. Also, for the first four years, periodic evaluation of the project was conducted in consultation with a steering committee composed of EMU faculty members, including conflict resolution experts, John Paul Lederach and Ron Kraybill, as well as theologian and former MCC staff person in Yugoslavia, Gerald Shenk. Finally, Barry Hart, a Mennonite practitioner who specialized in trauma healing in Croatia, was a member of the leadership team for three of the early workshops in 1995–96.

The examples in this chapter come almost exclusively from the author's own experience of directing projects on conflict resolution training primarily, but not exclusively, for religious people in the former Yugoslavia from 1993–2006. In order to contextualize these efforts, however, it is necessary to begin by examining the root and precipitating causes of the conflicts and the particular factors influencing any attempt at transformation. Finally, in order to gain significant insight into wider applicability, it is important to end the chapter by analyzing the effectiveness of any engagement, examining the degree of continuity of any ongoing programming, and evaluating the criteria used to measure success.

The Conflict Drivers

Specialists in conflict analysis have frequently been divided between those who view conflicts as caused by *substantive drivers* (such as territory, resources, economy, politics, or use of armed force) and those who emphasize *identity drivers,* (focused on group memberships such as religion, ethnicity, tribe, or race). Yet I will contend that all conflicts, including those in Kosovo and Bosna-Herzegovina, involve the interplay between both kinds of drivers. In fact, it is common to find that specific conflict drivers of both types are primary, while others in each category are secondary.

Any conflict analysis of the causes of conflict in the Balkans, whether one looks historically or at the current dynamics, must recognize the important role played by a variety of substantive drivers. For example, any examination of the catastrophic change during the 1990s must recognize the important role played by political, military, territorial, and economic factors. Signs of economic crisis began in the late 1970s with declining economic growth, rising foreign debt, considerable increases in unemployment and inflation, and fall of overall living standards. During the 1980s, the more prosperous regions/sectors of Yugoslav society became increasingly disturbed by financial losses going "down the drain" in Belgrade's central government and the need to subsidize the poorer republics. On the other hand, the poorer republics felt exploited by the richer ones and much of the society resented the amount diverted into corruption on the part of those powerful enough to use such tactics to either maintain or increase their assets at the expense of common people. The political stagnation and bureaucratic dysfunction that developed during the 1980s contributed to this economic decline and accelerated the demise of the Communist system, leading to the promotion of government decentralization and grassroots mobilization. However, similar to the aftermath of the Arab Spring a couple decades later, the result was a power vacuum. Into this vacuum came a resurgent nationalism that had been tightly restrained throughout the nearly four-decade rule reign of Josip Tito. Slobodan Milosevic, whose entire governmental career had been within the Communist party, seized the initiative by re-aligning his politics with the emerging identity driver—Serbian ethnic and sectarian nationalism.[2] Within a few years, he (and to a lesser extent his Croatian counterpart, President Franjo Tudjman) acquired dictatorial powers that precipitated political secession, to which Milosevic responded with the overpowering military force over which his government initially had almost exclusive control. Consequently, a number of critical substantive conflict drivers rose to prominence: territorial (reignited due to claims of political independence and sovereignty); armed force (which redrew borders, ethnically cleansed populations, and killed vast numbers of people—most notably in the siege of Sarajevo and the massacre at Srebrenica); and economic crisis of historic proportions on a par with Germany in the 1930s (excepting the tycoons who profited enormously from wartime corruption).[3]

---

2. Vladisavljevic, "Break-up of Yugoslavia," 143–60.
3. Bennet, *Yugoslavia's Bloody Collapse*, 187–92.

Given these developments, it is understandable that many analysts emphasize the primacy of the substantive drivers and subordinate the importance of religion and ethnicity. The former are typically much more visible than the identity drivers. The rationale for this prioritization is that identity simply gets used by the principal actors who are primarily motivated by substance rather than affiliation (e.g., politicians using ethnicity or religion to gain the real levers of power). Serbian dictator Milosevic certainly played the religion card in stoking Serbian nationalism in his quest to gain political and military control over both Bosnia-Herzegovina and Kosovo. But he could not have succeeded unless there was substantial support for this perspective within the Serbian Orthodox faith tradition and within the Serbian population. Yet many analysts still insist that it takes a substantive "trigger event" to propel even the initial escalation of conflict—like the use of violence against peaceful protestors (as happened at the beginning of the war in Sarajevo[4]) and for years against the nonviolent resistance promoted by the elected President Ibrahim Rugova of Kosovo.[5] Though such an explanation does accurately represent the spark that escalates some conflicts, religion and ethnicity can also play a significant role as triggers. When Milosevic joined the Serbian Orthodox Patriarch, German of Serbia, in celebrating the 600th anniversary of the Battle of Kosovo in 1989, he ominously referred to the need for Serbs to be engaged in battle, using the sectarian mythology surrounding this historical event to link his political ambition to religion and ethnicity, presenting himself in a messianic role as national savior.[6] Consequently, the exact roles that identity or substantive drivers played are not easy to categorize, but both are important. One must look carefully at each conflict to accurately discern the relationships between multiple drivers.

A close examination will reveal the extent to which ethno-religious identity did become one of the major drivers that fuelled the violence which tore that former nation apart in the 1990s. When community-wide fear levels grew exponentially due to discrimination, oppression, violence, and dislocation—producing a serious security threat—the parameters of identity were inevitably drawn ever more narrowly. Instead of affirming multiple layers of belonging, there was a tendency to become firmly attached to one exclusive, entrenched identification, bounded by an increasingly fixed and rigid definition. When religion and ethnicity are united as a single, fused, primary identity marker, as was the case in much of the former Yugoslavia,

---

4. Becirevic, *Genocide*, 63.
5. Spencer, "Islamic Politics," 24.
6. Gligorijevic, "Kosovo," 5.

religion is often used to legitimize the ethnic quest. This type of identity formation can exist even within largely secular societies, which much of the former Yugoslavia had become. Despite the imposition of Communism following WWII, the seeds of a "folk religion" persisted, with its collective memory, values, superstitions, half-forgotten scriptures, and customs. When societies are drawn into the brutalities of war and one's sense of self or community is denied legitimacy or respect, it is tempting for even the nominally religious to seek meaning in their primal social and sacred frames of reference. Consequently, at such a point of vulnerability, many buy into what might be called a survival alliance: "Our co-religionists are closer to us than the enemy; they speak a language the community recognizes. They understand us better, provide the only security available, and offer a framework of meaning and values when all of life is in turmoil."

Among the Albanian population in Kosovo, Yugoslav identity was never central and ethnicity became even more fixed as the primary marker. But for Kosovo Serbs, as well as Serbian Orthodox and Croatian Catholics in Bosnia-Herzegovina, the primacy of Yugoslav identity was quickly replaced by a fused and rigid ethno-religious identification in the minds of much of the population. Bosnian Muslims abandoned their Yugoslav identity during the War in Croatia in 1991, but many were left searching for a primary identification even after the war began in Bosnia. These cosmopolitan Bosniaks (a new designation adopted by many Muslims), as well as the professional elites among Croats and a few Serbs, had relished the inter-ethnic/religious relationships they had cultivated throughout their lives. As a result, they only belatedly understood the latent conflict that was enmeshed within the social, religious, and political mentality and structures of their society. Even those who resisted this total ethno-religious integration (including some minority religious groups) were often placed in these categories, and treated accordingly, by the bulk of society. As a result, even they often became caught in the inevitable conflict between the ethno-religious in-groups and out-groups—"us" vs. "them."

Religious leaders played an especially important role in these dynamics. There were denunciations accusing the leadership of all the main religious traditions of complicity—to varying degrees—in fostering ethnic/sectarian hostility. At the same time, each of the religious hierarchies issued official statements, sometimes jointly, calling for an end to the fighting, denouncing atrocities, condemning ethnic cleansing, and affirming the need to maintain basic standards of human rights including refugee return and access to humanitarian aid. Frequently, however, the atrocities listed referred exclusively to those committed against, rather than by, one's own people. Especially during the war in Bosnia-Herzegovina, the religious leaders of each community tended to deny their own culpability, while pointing an accusing finger at the other religious communities, the political nationalists, and the Communists.[7] These negative nationalist tendencies were most apparent in locations where a given tradition was dominant since it is there that the tradition sensed a threat to its "rightful place in society." Where a tradition was in the minority, it tended to be more accommodating, often out of a need for its very survival. In Kosovo, after observing the negative role religious leaders tended to play in Bosnia-Herzegovina, the religious hierarchy saw more clearly the dangers of complicity and silence. The Serbian Orthodox, Catholic, and Islamic leaders more consistently opposed the violations perpetrated by all groups, beginning prior to the outbreak of full-scale war, though not before the Albanian shift from President Ibrahim Rugova's strategy of nonviolence to the emergence of the Kosovo Liberation Army.[8] Yet in the time since the end of the wars in both countries, religious discrimination continues to exist, especially against minority communities.[9] Consequently, it is now these religious leaders who tend to voice concern and condemnation over violations committed against their communities. Such response, whether in 1992 or 2014, is understandable to some extent, given people's expectations that their leaders will advocate for the well-being and the traditions of their own communities. Moreover, it is important to recognize that all religious leaders, especially the Serbian Orthodox, have been (and still are) anxious to play a larger public role in societies searching for their traditional foundations after emerging from decades of marginalization under Communist rule.

---

7. One example is the "Memorandum of the Holy Assembly of Bishops of the Serbian Orthodox Church," issued in May 1992 that called for recognizing the human rights of everyone and condemned the war, the displacement of civilians, and the destruction of religious buildings. Yet it itemized only Orthodox Churches that had been destroyed and concentration camps where Serbs were imprisoned ("Memorandum of the Holy Assembly of Bishops of the Serbian Orthodox Church, Issued at its Regular Session Held from the 14th to the 27th of May, 1992," in Nicholas V. Trkla, "Position of the Serbian Orthodox Church Regarding the War in the Former Yugoslavia" [unpublished English language collection of Serbian Orthodox Church Statements], Chicago, September 1994). Another example is the "Statement of Croatian Bishops Regarding the Situation in Bosnia and Herzegovina," made at the Council of the Croatian Bishops' Conference on October 7, 1992 (reported in *Christian Information Service, (KIS)* AJ.12.01, Zagreb) in which the bishops noted that all the citizens of Bosnia-Herzegovina were suffering the consequences of war, but only the Croat Catholics were "going through great trial and martyrdom." Others were labeled as aggressors, but no Croats were condemned for criminal activity.

8. International Crisis Group, "Religion in Kosovo," 1–16.

9. Marusic, "Religious Tolerance."

At the same time, as in most conflict situations, we must be careful not to stereotype all members of a particular ethno-religious group. While some clerics consistently aligned themselves with ethnic/sectarian nationalism, others have taken courageous stands against this from the onset of hostilities until the present day. Specific examples, illustrating various processes and practices utilized by these domestic actors, as well as external counterparts, to facilitate constructive, nonviolent resolution of conflict, will be included in the next section of this chapter.

A Program Aimed to Foster Peaceful Conflict Transformation

The primary focus in this presentation of efforts to transform attitudes and behaviors of individuals and communities in Bosnia-Herzegovina and Kosovo will be centered around a project which the author directed on "Conflict Resolution Training for Religious People in the Former Yugoslavia" (1994–2003) based in the Program on Conflict Prevention at the Center for Strategic and International Studies (CSIS) in Washington, DC. The information contained in the rest of this chapter, therefore, will draw most heavily on the personal experience of the author, who led an international team composed, at various points, of Russian, Polish, Dutch, Palestinian, and Pakistani workshop leaders.[10] The objectives of this project, which existed in both Bosnia-Herzegovina and Kosovo, involved leading training workshops, supporting the planning and implementing of interfaith cooperation efforts, and establishing and building the capacity of indigenous organizations. At times these efforts were supported, and even co-sponsored by other organizations.[11] In addition, the author led or as-

---

10. Most of the information presented to describe in this first section will not be documented in written sources since much of it is based on unpublished reports, notes, and personal recollections by the author. However, one can find comparable or additional information in the following publications by the author: "Christianity in Bosnia-Herzegovina and Kosovo" and "Contributions of Interfaith Dialogue."

11. Partner relationships were established, at various points—sometimes for very specific events, other times for the entire project during a given time period in one country. Partner organizations included Mercy Corps, Catholic Relief Services, The Franciscan Order in Bosnia, The Islamic Community in Bosnia-Herzegovina, The Serbian Orthodox Church in Bosnia, The Academy of Sciences and Arts in Sarajevo, Sarajevo Phoenix (women's organization), The Centre for Peace, Nonviolence and Human Rights in Osijek Croatia, The Association "Abraham" in Sarajevo, Millennium Rainbow of Mostar, The Conflict Transformation Program at the Center for Justice and Peacebuilding at Eastern Mennonite University, and The Program on Negotiation at Harvard Law School, among others.

sisted in training workshops, conferences and round tables for religious and secular participants from both countries while working with a number of other institutions from 1993–2006.[12] Presented here are some of the most critical components of the preparation and implementation phases, illustrated with some informative examples.

The Preparation Phase

Two aspects of project preparation—trust-building and project design—are selected for examination here. Together, they present the foundational conception and core methodology that formed the basis of the approach utilized.

Trust-building

The first step in any conflict prevention or transformation process is to build the trust necessary to set the context for interaction. This task is both difficult and crucially important in a context where literal survival is the most pressing concern (very much the case at the point of initial involvement in both Bosnia-Herzegovina and Kosovo). Gaining this rapport began through networking and partnerships with trusted entrées. Assisting to lead a training workshop, under the auspices of Mennonite Central Committee in 1993 provided a valuable introduction to a whole range of religious leaders and influential laity within the region, most especially in Bosnia. The high regard which the Mennonites had achieved, due especially to the nine years of time invested by the project director (the former head of MCC's program in Yugoslavia), provided instant credibility that would have taken years to develop by oneself. The entrée into Kosovo (which occurred a number of years later) was enabled through the author's own extensive networking among Serbs throughout the region, though most significantly promoted

---

12. These included work with participants from both countries for the Boston Theological Institute and a couple of summer schools in the Balkans ("Renewing Our Minds" and "Summer School of Inter-Confessional Dialogue and Understanding"); work with Bosnians for Mennonite Central Committee, Conference of European Churches, and Conflict Resolution Catalyst; and work with Kosovars while working for Mercy Corps, the Organization for Security and Co-operation in Europe (OSCE), the United State Institute of Peace (USIP), and the Institute for Democracy and Ethnic Relations in Kosovo. Many of the methods employed during the CSIS workshops were also utilized in these programs. However, the preparation phase, as described in the next section, applies only to the CSIS project since the other organizations had that responsibility in those cases rather than the author.

by an advisor to the Serbian Orthodox Episkop Artemije who attended a CSIS workshop in Serbia in 1997 and subsequently secured the support of the episkop as well as numerous Kosovo Serbian political figures. On the other hand, it was a close working relationship with Mercy Corps which had established a very high level of trust and credibility with the Kosovar Albanian political leadership during the years prior to that war.

Yet establishing one's own credibility required nurturing trusting relationships with indigenous, not just international, actors. In Bosnia, the initial contacts were with Franciscan priests from Sarajevo. In particular, Father Ivo Markovic, who attended the MCC workshop in 1993, demonstrated an unusual openness, even eagerness, for relational transformation. As the training agenda moved from the sharing of traumatic experience to an invitation to reflection on personal accountability, Father Markovic demonstrated tremendous vulnerability by first sharing his experience of detention and near execution at the hands of Serbian militias, followed by his admission to Serbs in that workshop that his attitude of bitterness and resentment toward them, who had never harmed him, could not be justified. Having witnessed the creation of a safe environment which gave him both insight and courage, and his growing awareness of an entirely new field of faith-based conflict resolution methodology and practice, led him, at the end of that workshop, to extend an open invitation to assist the religious communities of Bosnia-Herzegovina to develop a constructive peacebuilding role. Father Markovic later set up meetings with religious leaders of all communities throughout the Muslim-Croat Federation, including the Franciscan director of the interfaith organization, *Zajedno*, in Sarajevo who, in turn, helped establish a relationship with the Muslim president of the Academy of Sciences and Arts who agreed to host the first CSIS workshop in Bosnia. In April 1995, Father Markovic then provided the only transportation possible into Sarajevo, as well as accommodation in a Franciscan Church, for the leadership team. Arriving in this besieged city, the workshop facilitators found a group of eager participants, representing all of Sarajevo's ethnic and religious diversity (including two Serbian Orthodox priests) gathered for training in conflict transformation and peacebuilding in the midst of constant shelling. What became apparent during this workshop, and later as the project developed, was the degree to which credibility was established simply by coming in the midst of a war zone.

The most difficult relationships to build within Bosnia, however, were not with Muslims and Catholics, but with the Serbs living in the Bosnian Serb Republic. For many of them, America was the enemy, and Protestants were viewed with suspicion. Outsiders from the West were often perceived as undermining their identity and a threat to their security, having assisted in tearing their nation apart through secession. Consequently, a decision was made to spend a number of years developing relationships by talking with episkops (bishops) and priests within this church, even inviting some to workshops held in Serbia and in the Muslim-Croat Federation, before attempting to hold the first workshop in the Bosnian Serb Republic in 1999.

Program Design

Beginning to work in a war context, then adapting to a post-war environment, resulted in the eventual development of a multi-tiered methodology. It was literally impossible at the beginning of the project to look for ways to resolve some of the most dire problems people were facing. It was a major accomplishment simply to bring together people from all the faith traditions and ethnic communities. Therefore, instead of emphasizing problem-solving—the focus of many conflict resolution models in the 1990s—a decision was made to shift to a focus on reconciling people rather than resolving issues.

Yet from the very beginning there was recognition that an effective people-to-people approach had to address more than relational difficulties. The leadership team frequently planned sessions on appreciative inquiry (eliciting positive experiences), and always included an evening party (even within besieged Sarajevo) where participants sang, told jokes, laughed, and frequently shared impromptu stories reflecting both memories of a positive past and a critique of all current leadership. The purpose was to enable a collective faith-based catharsis that touched mind, heart, and body. Eventually, a four-tiered modus operandi was established. Fulfillment of all three program objectives (training, interfaith cooperation, and indigenous capacity-building) would involve four foci: Relationship building, Identity formation, Problem solving, and Leadership development.

1. *Relationship Building:* Fostering quality relationships, which began with initial trust-building prior to sponsoring any activity, was not only the starting point, but continued to hold primary importance throughout the program. Most of the training workshops began with this focus and some were entirely devoted to it. Even when attempting to achieve other objectives, there were times when there was a need to reset working relationships among people already committed to a joint endeavor. After commitments had already been made to gradually transfer all programmatic responsibilities to a newly created indigenous NGO in Bosnia-Herzegovina, the bombing of Yugoslavia during the Kosovo War temporarily put all organizational development

and capacity-building on hold. Great effort had to be expended on rebuilding relationships between members of the advisory board and staff from both entities—the Bosnian Serb Republic and the Muslim-Croat Federation.

People-to-people encounters, similar to the processes and practices utilized in Mennonite peacebuilding, were also of central importance in Kosovo. Relationship building was prominent within most of the five CSIS workshops as well as in seven led by the author on behalf of the Organization for Security and Co-operation in Europe (OSCE). The same methodology as developed for the CSIS workshops was utilized in the OSCE trainings, which were held to enhance faith-based relationship building among Kosovars and capability to facilitate such dialogue among internationals working there. Yet, by the time workshops had started following the war in Kosovo, the methodology was adjusted to allow for a greater combination of foci within a single workshop, especially linking relationship building with identity formation and sometimes problem solving.

2. *Identity Formation:* Very early, it became clear in Bosnia-Herzegovina that healthy relationships could not be built without addressing issues of identity. Initially this topic was incorporated into workshops focused on reconciliation among mixed identity groups. Despite growing awareness on the part of each ethno-religious group regarding the dynamics surrounding self-perception among members of other groups that attended these interreligious trainings, it later became clear that the dynamics of identity formation needed to be examined within each group. A decision was made, therefore, to examine this topic in single-confessional workshops, one each for the Catholic, Serbian Orthodox, and Muslim communities. An effort was made to ensure some degree of uniformity for the sake of comparative analysis and, with permission, sharing perspectives on at least some similar issues among the faith communities. However, as representatives from each faith community were engaged in preparation of participant lists, agendas, and methodology, each workshop became unique in many respects. A significant factor contributing to the uniqueness arose due to the opportunity to address issues of concern for the given religious community. Since all participants were from the same tradition, this encouraged attendance on the part of more conservative members who had refrained from participation in interfaith events. The presence of greater intra-group diversity, combined with the focus on identity, inevitably brought to the fore tensions within each faith community since conservative and liberal factions frequently had very

divergent visions of their religion's role in Bosnian society. Yet, such events also carried the possibility for healing divisions which could undermine cooperative efforts. After the bombing of Yugoslavia during the Kosovo war, an unplanned workshop that included only Bosnian Serbs from both entities was needed in order to create significant intra-faith dialogue between divergent internal perspectives regarding issues central to Serbian Orthodox identity. Use of fellow Serbs to open new lenses on Serbian identity and perspective created enough trust for staff and advisory board members from both entities to resume efforts to establish the newly created indigenous NGO.

In Kosovo, the early combination of identity formation, relationship building, and problem solving was, in part, due to the different relationship between religion and ethnicity as well as growing competence on the part of program staff to integrate these foci. Approaches were developed to provide each tradition with the opportunity to explore its identity, yet also share that directly with participants from other traditions. Even when it was decided in one workshop to limit participation on the basis of religion, this training was designed for all Christians, each representing a rather small minority of Kosovo's population: Albanian Catholics, Albanian Protestants, and Serbian Orthodox. Consequently, identity, as well as relationship building, was examined across major ethnic divisions, yet with the opportunity to discover some areas of compatibility as Christians despite the differences inherent within the three major divisions in the church.

3. *Problem Solving:* At the beginning of the project in Bosnia-Herzegovina, the intent had been to open the initial workshop in Sarajevo with storytelling in order to build relationships that the leadership team believed were necessary prior to problem solving. Two factors, however, led to a change in plans. Difficulty in reaching Sarajevo meant the workshop started late without a guarantee that severe shelling might suddenly end the workshop prematurely. This reduced timeframe, coupled with strong participant desire to initiate interfaith action and not just talk, led to a decision to focus immediately on problem solving. However, the obstacles to accomplishing this in a war zone proved overwhelming. It was not until follow-up to the third workshop in Bosnia (after the war was over) that a working group finally was able to implement an action plan. As a result, we fashioned a model that would be replicated in many regions of Bosnia-Herzegovina and then taken to Kosovo.

In Kosovo, the last workshop held as part of the CSIS project focused exclusively on problem solving. It was also unique in that participants came from Bosnia-Herzegovina as well as Kosovo and, in addition to religious leaders, it included journalists, local government officials, community council leaders, professors, physicians, and other professionals from the various ethnic/religious groups in each country. This was not the first time, however, that a workshop had begun with problem solving. The author previously co-led one sponsored by the United States Institute of Peace (USIP) in southeastern Kosovo (the region least affected by violence and ethnic cleansing), in which various professional groups from both ethnic communities were guided through a problem solving process. In addition, the author co-led five more problem solving workshops for USIP and led six for OSCE and one for Mercy Corps. The participants and agendas varied depending on the purpose, though none were for religious groups. Most were designed for municipal government officials, some for other professional groups, and a few for minority groups attempting to negotiate for some benefits in the Final Status Talks.

4. *Leadership Development:* Leadership training and indigenous organizational capacity building were built into the CSIS project in Bosnia-Herzegovina, but not Kosovo. CSIS sponsorship of conflict transformation workshops in Kosovo ended after only two years due to an institutional decision to end the entire program in 2003. This pre-empted any possibility of creating the core nucleus of trained and committed participants essential to developing such capacity.

The impetus to develop indigenous capacity that was equipped to provide training in conflict resolution, reconciliation, and peacebuilding with the religious communities was first suggested by participants in the 2nd CSIS workshop which ended on the very last day of the Bosnian War in 1995. This workshop was hosted by the headmaster of a Franciscan school in Visoko, a Muslim-controlled community, three hundred meters from the border with the Bosnian Serb Republic and one town away from the heart of Croatian-controlled territory in Central Bosnia. Coming from a war-weary, but visionary group of Muslim, Serbian Orthodox, and Catholic Croatian participants, such a request could not be ignored.

Initially, however, the focus was on skill development in the facilitation processes essential to interfaith dialogue, reconciliation, and cooperation. Two CSIS workshops were designed for specifically this kind of leadership training. Both were held in Hungary and included participants from Croatia and Serbia as well as Bosnia-Herzegovina.

One year following this workshop, a new NGO called the Center for Religious Dialogue (CRD) was established in Bosnia-Herzegovina in 1998, and a process was initiated to enable it eventually to take over the CSIS project on conflict resolution training for religious people. Selection of a model for institutional structure was made in consultation with the leadership of all three major religious communities, and support was obtained from various international and indigenous organizations. The process of organizational development was then led by the core nucleus of local consultants and committed participants. The key role that CSIS staff played, especially the project director, was focused on individualized training in both facilitation skills and organizational development for the two Bosnian consultants, one from each entity. This onsite mentoring process was then augmented by offering relevant educational opportunities to these consultants through a number of specialized international venues.

The Implementation Phase

The focus in this section of the chapter will be on the ways in which the implementation of the four types of workshops and follow-up activities utilized processes and practices similar to those that Mennonites have developed.

Approach to Identity Issues

Given the declared focus on religious identity as a raison d'être for the project, a decision was made from the beginning to assist participants in experiencing the religion of the Other. Each day of every workshop started with a spiritual message delivered by a different faith community. This served to place the entire encounter within a spiritual dimension that was led by the faith communities themselves and enabled all present, including workshop leaders, to experience other religions "from within." Repeating this ritual of faith day after day made clear the centrality of one extremely important identity marker. Yet it was also clear that a non-threatening way was needed to handle contentious dynamics related to ethno-religious differences. This issue was frequently introduced through an exercise in which participants had to form themselves into groups without talking. Since each participant was given a colored star on his/her forehead, most people assumed that the groups had to be formed around the color of star. How groups actually formed, where tensions emerged and were resolved, and how minority and majority groups interacted (i.e., through assimilation? or exclusion?), revealed much about the identity formation process. Debriefing this exercise usually highlighted many dynamics that could readily be identified in interethnic and interreligious contexts within both Kosovo and Bosnia-Herzegovina (for example, observing how people from families of mixed heritage sometimes functioned differently). The value of this game was that these dynamics could be observed in a rather non-threatening context before being applied to the very sensitive identity issues at stake in reality.

The most common approach to the issue of identity formation involved an exercise in which participants were asked to identify various components of their identity out of a long list, including gender, profession, ethnicity, religion, citizenship, family, and other markers. Then they were asked to select, first, those most important to them; then the ones most recognized by others; and finally the ones that gave them the most trouble. Frequently, the top choices selected to describe oneself tended to be religion, ethnicity, and family, though members of the various ethnic/religious groups tended to prioritize them differently. As previously noted, among Kosovar Albanians (Catholic and Muslim) ethnicity rather than religion tended to be central; whereas for many Bosnians, religion and ethnicity were fused into a single primary identity marker. Very often, however, one's own choice of preference did not match the way one tended to be seen by the Other or what one believed was the most troubling among one's own identity markers. Recognition of these distinctions led to increased awareness that one's own perceptions of the Other may not fit how that person or group sees themselves.

It also raised the distinction between individual and group identity. By what means did they acquire their individual sense of belonging? Was it a reflection of group identity or a reaction against this? In either case, what were the sources that informed their identity formation? Was it family? School? Religious community? Media? Something else? What sources formed their perspective regarding the identity of others? What values were associated with each other's identity? Fundamental questions would frequently arise in the subsequent discussions. Who were the Serbian Orthodox people in Bosnia-Herzegovina? In Kosovo? Who were the Croatian Catholics in Bosnia-Herzegovina or the Albanian Catholics in Kosovo? Who were the Slavic Muslims in Bosnia-Herzegovina or the Albanian Muslims in Kosovo? What was the relationship between religion and ethnicity? How were they different? How were they related? What impact did group identity have on individuals? What were the obstacles to even asking these questions?

Yet inevitably such a discussion opened the door to inquiring how one might reframe one's identity or facilitate an evaluation by one's group of its identity. Three different ways to reframe identity tended to emerge:

1. *Choose a different identity as primary, even if only temporarily:* Two workshops in Bosnia-Herzegovina illustrated some fairly simple possibilities. In one case, following the workshop, Serbian and Muslim women invited neighborhood mothers to meet together for coffee. In another case, during a workshop in Bosnia-Herzegovina, two women—one Muslim, the other Catholic—found common ground sharing "grandmother stories." Family and gender (much less divisive in these situations than ethnicity or religion) had become primary and could become the basis for building relationships. A third example from Kosovo illustrates a much more conscious choice of workshop design in order to build relationships around a professional identity. In the aforementioned workshop sponsored by USIP, a group of Albanian and Serbian medical professionals donned their professional hat instead of their ethnic one, enabling a fruitful discussion of the medical needs of and resources available to various communities.

2. *Redefine one's primary identity in more flexible terms:* What does it mean to be a believer in one's faith tradition? Sometimes this resulted in participants re-evaluating why some particular component of their faith was more important than other beliefs? Or could they view a particularly troublesome aspect of it differently? For example, some Bosnian Muslims could begin to question whether their faith demanded that justice in the form of trials for war criminals was essential before they could consider cooperating on anything else. Some Serbian Orthodox believers could embrace an understanding of their faith that was not bound to the mythologies of Serbian nationalism.

3. *Affirm the identity of the other and allow it to influence how one sees oneself:* Discussion, in fact, usually culminated around the question of how one could affirm one's own sense of identity while not demeaning the identity of the other. For some Bosnians who were in mixed marriages or the children of such parents, this became extremely important. Those people could often help point others to the ways in which they could affirm one another. Ritual also has the power to accomplish this, as has been demonstrated by Father Markovic, the Franciscan priest who opened the way for this project to take root in Bosnia. As a musician, Father Markovic decided to start an interethnic and interfaith choir called Pontamina following the war. According to him, the first task was to convince each group to sing the songs of the other

group. After much dialogue to overcome resistance, the group began to coalesce, practice its music, and then bring this rich mixed heritage all over Bosnia-Herzegovina. According to Father Markovic, who is himself a Croat, the high point of his experience conducting this choir was when their concert received a standing ovation in one of the centers of Croatian Catholic nationalism in Herzegovina.

Occasionally, literature from one's own faith community was used to stretch any fixed perceptions of their identity. At the single-confessional Catholic workshop in Kiseljak, Bosnia, for example, participants read an article by a Croatian theologian that raised many provocative questions. What defined a good Croat? Did one need non-Croats in order even to understand one's own identity? Had they ever had any non-Croat friends? If so, what did this suggest about themselves? What parts of Croatian culture did they treasure and why? From which ones did they want to keep their distance and why? Discussion around these questions in small groups showed that participants were able to wrestle honestly with issues of religion and politics, reflect critically on themselves and their community, and engage constructively in dialogue between conservative elements from Herzegovina and more liberal representatives from Bosnia. Concluding this workshop with a Mass—celebrated by one of the participants, the Vicar General of the Sarajevo Diocese—provided a powerful ritualized affirmation of who they were as a common faith community.

At the single-confessional workshops for Serbian Orthodox and Bosnian Muslims, renowned figures within each of these traditions were also used to challenge any rigid identity formation. At the Serbian Orthodox workshop in Visegrad, the writings of a former Serbian Orthodox episkop of Western Europe during World War I presented the true identity of the church as non-militaristic, anti-imperialist, and a forum through which different nationalities could find commonality. At the Muslim workshop in Sarajevo, on the other hand, two Bosnian professors as well as a Muslim member of the leadership team presented the positive contributions of Islam to peacemaking. Emphasis was placed on the parts of the sacred literature and tradition that encourage diversity, affirm human dignity and equality, and espouse tolerance and openness to others.

Whatever the exact approach, the focus on identity normally led to a discussion on the role of the religious community in the society as a whole. What often helped participants to deal constructively with this issue during interfaith workshops was an exercise based on Psalm 85 developed by John Paul Lederach, the well-known Mennonite practitioner and scholar in peacebuilding. In this exercise, separate groups defined the concepts of truth, mercy, justice, and peace, followed by a facilitated dialogue among participants speaking on behalf of each element in the full vision of shalom. Informed by experiencing the psalmist's vision of the rightful place of faith communities within pluralistic societies, it became more difficult to frame one's own identity in isolation or to remain caught within prevailing exclusive nationalist mentalities. Despite the tensions that surfaced between liberal and conservative elements in each faith community, the overall outlook that prevailed within each tradition took pride in describing the positive contributions it felt that it made to the entire society.

Approach to Relationship Building

Building effective relationships requires facilitating a "learning conversation," the kind of story-telling in which each party has something to offer and each party has something to learn. It requires active and empathetic listening, handling emotions constructively, and clarifying and correcting perceptions in order to facilitate the sharing of narratives. The journey of reconciliation requires an encounter with oneself as well as with the Other. One cannot ignore all the grievances of the past, but then must shift the participants' focus to creating a better future. In a context where there has been excessive violence, the facilitator must establish trust by empathizing with the suffering of all parties, then assist hurt and victimized people to acknowledge their own prejudices, stereotypes, and misperceptions, and help all parties to overcome a revenge mentality. In order to facilitate such a reconciliation process in the first workshop with an equal numbers of participants from each Bosnian entity (in 1998), the CSIS project team began by eliciting questions from participants based on their past experiences and current expectations. The concerns expressed focused attention immediately on individual and relational healing: How can we live with our questions about the war? How can we cooperate with God in healing internal pain and division? How can we expand our understanding of each other? How can we develop cooperative working relationships? As done in previous and subsequent workshops, the leadership team then led participants through a number of specific steps, each one utilizing a combination of experiential learning and interpretive reflection that would assist participants in moving to the next step in the reconciliation process.

Step 1: Mourning: Expressing Grief and Accepting Loss

At the beginning of the work in Bosnia-Herzegovina, religious leaders were asked what they spent their time doing. Clerics from all traditions answered that they conducted funerals more than anything else. In the face of the tragedy of war, religious leaders, to whom people initially turn, become "first responders." Enabling people to experience an effective grieving process is, therefore, an essential first step in reconciliation and peacebuilding. Without a sensitive process of mourning, one that encompasses religious ritual as well as empathetic understanding, traumatized individuals and communities cannot prevent their understandable hurt and anger from developing into revenge and counter-aggression. Typically, the process began with storytelling in interethnic/religious groups of six to eight people where participants were asked to recount a difficult experience and how their faith helped them through it. When care was taken to design an environment where each group member felt safe enough to share his or her personal experience of loss and what helped them to live through the loss, then participants could be heard even by the Other. When they discovered that their hurts, whether great or comparatively small, were taken seriously by others, cross-cutting bonds began to develop. Refugees from one group began listening and even cried with refugees from a rival group as they realized the depth of their common experience. In this way, people's deep pain, rather than becoming a barrier, became a bridge. Workshop leaders then introduced the prayer of lament (used by all Abrahamic traditions) as a faith-based, communal ritual by which suffering, grievance, and the need for justice could be offered up to God for resolution, freeing the faithful from the temptation to impose their own vindication. In response, sometimes a common lament was composed, based on the collective experience shared by all faith communities; other times each faith community wrote and shared its own lament. One poignant moment occurred when a Bosnian Serb Orthodox priest declared that, for the first time since his brother's death during the war, he had been able to grieve in a way that enabled him to imagine a hopeful future. A priest who had initially come on a surveillance mission to report on a suspicious, foreign-led interfaith project heartily endorsed it as a healing process and introduced the project director to his episkop.

Step 2: Confronting Fears

Moving from grievance to fear involved helping participants turn their attention even more from the past to the future. In many cases, there was an intrinsic connection. Victims of atrocities tend to believe that the trauma they have experienced will happen again, that the perpetrator will come back. People in the midst of war, or its aftermath, are legitimately afraid of many things: threats to personal safety, social transformation, economic crisis, political manipulation, and so forth. All groups fear foreign control, indigenous threats to security, and the loss of dignity and honor.

Yet if reconciliation is to occur, people must not be controlled by fear. Consequently, it is important to help people make wise choices in handling anxieties. At times, the workshop facilitators would begin a discussion by inviting participants to speak about external fears, listing ones that people know exist within the population or within their whole religious group. In some cases, it helped to invite participants to ask about threats or dangers rather than fears. This allowed the person to objectify the fear, focusing on the outside stimulus rather than the internal emotion. As someone talked about the fears of the group or the external danger, one's own feelings became apparent, even if not self-acknowledged.

Yet there were many people who wanted to express their fears. Whether expressed directly or indirectly, there was cathartic value to this process. People were encouraged to explore the degree to which the danger was real, re-perceive the situation and one's response in light of new information, and receive support from their religious faith as well as the empathy (and perhaps shared apprehension) of others, possibly including people from the feared community.

Immediately following the war in Bosnia, a woman who, with her young children, spent time in a concentration camp, shared with other workshop participants how her faith in God helped her to control fear in the face of torture and her use as a human shield against outside attacks. Her honest recollection of the surprising strength she found when confronting past fears, as well as a realistic acknowledgment of her ongoing struggle with post-traumatic stress, helped stimulate others from each ethnic/sectarian community to express their own fears and examine best ways to respond. This kind of honest, open, and faith-oriented engagement with fear, as opposed to suppressing it, repeatedly assisted many traumatized people to avoid the descent into increasingly fixated antagonism, rage, and revenge.

Step 3: Identifying Needs and Re-humanizing the "Other"

At this point in the process of dealing with the effects of violent conflict it is important, despite one's own desperate needs, to shift attention from oneself and one's group to the Other. Therefore, the question now placed before the participants was, "Why did *they* do this to us?" Though it would be easy to be accusatory in response, participants were requested to be honestly inquisitive. Were they really willing to know who the Other is—their needs, concerns, and motivations? It was not easy to ask this question due to the existence of persistent stereotypes—distortions functioning as a group survival mechanism and often fueled by anger. Yet it was possible to recognize that the actions of one's adversary were motivated by legitimate human needs. In fact, the workshop facilitators emphasized that the only approach likely to change the adversarial dynamic was an effort to understand the Other's fears and concerns. If workshop participants had previously identified each other's fears in Step 2, they would have already recognized some needs. Fear, by definition, is related to the potential deprivation of perceived needs. While adversaries' demands may be unacceptable, it was possible to re-humanize the adversaries themselves by expressing solidarity with basic needs as well as any legitimate pursuit of them. In fact, very often participants realized that certain needs and fears were held in common by supposedly incompatible groups. Discovery of such compatibility where it was not expected helped to build bridges of understand or even empathy on many occasions.

During one of the OSCE workshops in Kosovo, the majority Albanian participants absolutely insisted on telling their stories first. After they had all shared their grief, their fears, and the priority needs of their oppressed community, they finally allowed one of the minority Serbs to speak. A Serbian woman then told of her own experience of rejection and repression by the same Serbian police and militias due to her efforts during the war to identify human rights violations against Albanians. In this case, after overcoming the shock of learning that a Kosovo Serb had acted completely contrary to any of their expectations, these Albanians made a concerted effort to understand the even greater loneliness experienced by someone who had come to their aid at the expense of exclusion from her own people.

Another poignant illustrations of re-humanizing the Other happened during the first workshop in Sarajevo. An imam, who had come to that besieged city after Serbian soldiers had overrun his own village, shared how he had asked about the needs of the Serbs who were laying siege against his Muslim people. He did this while still in his village, with his people eating grass to survive, while Serbian guns shelled his village day and night. In an honest attempt to answer the question about *Serbian* needs, he recollected times in past history when it was his Muslim people who had victimized Serbs. This was a very unusual admission for anyone in the former Yugoslavia to make at that time, especially one who had suffered as greatly as this man. The entire interfaith group of workshop participants listened carefully as he concluded that the Serbs, as a minority population in Bosnia with historical memories of their own victimization, were afraid of the same fate as his Muslim people. They all feared for their survival. This Muslim man was still upset about the terror that his people had endured. He still viewed the act of aggression against them as evil. But the aggressors were not labeled as Serbian devils, a common accusation by non-Serbs. Instead they were real people with legitimate fears and needs. As the imam finished speaking, the whole room—including Muslim, Serbian, and Croatian participants—was quiet. They had witnessed a truly remarkable act of re-humanizing an enemy group.

Step 4: Acknowledgment of Wrongdoing: Apology, Truth-Telling, and "Re-Writing History"

In a society rife with targeted violence, accountability is even more difficult to ensure than normally is the case. Yet calls for accountability were essential to any successful effort even to initiate a stable and 'just peace' in either Bosnia-Herzegovina or Kosovo. When approached with sensitivity, acknowledgment of responsibility became possible, even in the wake of endemic violence. When reconciliation began with an effective grief process that acknowledged the suffering of all groups, then everyone had to admit that, for each group afflicted, responsibility existed somewhere. When violence was pervasive throughout a society, and all workshop participants had become aware of the extent of suffering among all groups, they could not escape the conclusion that pain had also been inflicted by one's own group. To demonstrate the healing potential, rather than focusing only on blame, examples were often shared of faith communities that had experienced mutual transformation by combining prayers of lament with prayers of confession and affirmations of God's forgiveness.

Although joint contribution and responsibility are important to affirm in contexts involving mass violence, it was also important to help participants recognize some important distinctions. First, it was necessary to distinguish acknowledgment from apology. Acknowledgment involves recognizing that wrong has been done by members of one's own group, even if the person speaking has not participated in any of this activity. Apology, on the other hand, involves taking responsibility for wrongs in which the person speaking has participated. Apology implies personal liability and, if sincere, should be accompanied by contrition, sorrow, and remorse. Second, it was also important for workshop leaders to distinguish between what the Catholic Church calls sins of commission and sins of omission. The question was not only "What did you do?" but "What did you fail to do and should have done?" Third, it was important to help participants recognize that acknowledgement of, and even apology for, attitudes can be significant. The issue at stake is more than behavior; it is also about the biases, prejudices, and stereotypes that lead to bitterness and hatred. Finally, the impact of the acknowledgment or apology was sometimes affected by the context. Was it done in a quiet, private, individual manner or offered publically for many or all to hear? Was it communicated by someone in a position of authority, by many members of a group, or just a lone individual? Acknowledgement or apology by an individual is not meaningless. In fact, at times it can have great significance, and at other times it can be a steppingstone to wider acknowledgment. Any process of self-assessment and truth-telling, if done with sensitivity, saves face, protects honor, and avoids undue shame. It also has the effect of revising each group's historical record to reflect what has been learned.

One example helps to illustrate the variety of ways in which individuals and groups have begun to take responsibility for wrongs committed. The story told previously about Father Ivo Markovic, the Bosnian Franciscan held captive and almost killed by Serbian soldiers, illustrates a remarkable capacity for self-reflection and apology when he addressed all the Serbs in the workshop (none of whom came from Bosnia). He told them that he had to apologize for the fact that he had come there with a grudge against all Serbs, but quickly followed this by acknowledging that none of them had ever done him any harm and he had no right to his negative attitude toward them. As soon as Father Markovic was finished, a Serbian Orthodox priest spoke and told him that his own Serbian people had done great harm to this Franciscan brother and to many innocent Croats and Muslims in Bosnia. In the space of five minutes the entire workshop had seen examples of both an apology for an attitude and an acknowledgment of wrongs committed, not by oneself, but by one's group. The quick succession of statements demonstrated the catalytic potential of even a lone apology for an attitude.

Step 5: Choosing to Forgive

Forgiveness should never be forced on anyone. However, the approach utilized in these workshops involved helping participants to reconsider their basic understanding about what forgiveness involves. The facilitators typically began by introducing two basic perspectives—forgiveness as an interactive or unilateral practice.

1. Forgiveness is most commonly seen as an interactive process between parties, one in which they negotiate their way from violation to restoration of relationship. Offenders acknowledge their wrongdoing, express remorse, and engage in restitution or reparation as agreed and appropriate. Victims refrain from vengeance, express empathy for offenders as fellow human beings, and may release offenders from all or part of their deserved penalty.

    When presenting this perspective in traumatized societies recovering from war, like Bosnia and Kosovo, the task of separating victims from offenders (as already noted) is by no means easy. Very often, by this point in the process of relationship building, participants in these societies have come to the point of acknowledging this reality. In addition, workshop leaders might ask what they expected if an interactive process was not possible. What if one's specific adversary was dead, or inaccessible, or unwilling to communicate? In such a case, participants were asked to consider another approach to forgiveness.

2. Forgiveness can be seen as a unilateral act in which a wronged party decides, for its own sake, to set aside its anger and resentment, neither requiring nor eliminating the need for action on the part of the other party. One of the workshop leaders described this as giving up all hope of a better past and investing oneself in the future.

    A unilateral process like this is certainly difficult. Yet, workshop leaders made clear that to contain anger and hatred did not mean stifling one's emotions. Instead, the emphasis was on placing effective controls over them, finding appropriate ways to vent the hurt that underlies anger and hatred in order to eventually free oneself from their captivity. Storytelling remained an excellent way to approach this topic of forgiveness in training workshops. Participants were asked what their past experience had been, either when offering or receiving forgiveness. Or what difficulties they had encountered when experiencing either end of the process. As people began to share their experiences, many questions were raised, yet bonds were also built among groups. The experience in these workshops frequently showed that people who entered with the resolve never to even consider forgiving the other side, left believing that forgiveness was possible, even if they were not yet ready to act on that conviction. Some participants even went further than that. One of the most impressive instances occurred at one of the OSCE workshops in Kosovo. An Albanian participant spoke at length on the first day about why it was alright for him to hate Serbs. By the end of the next day, it was obvious that a major transformation had occurred in his attitude when the same man participated in discussions of wrongdoing by Albanians against Serbs and told the Serbs he had learned, for the first time, the freedom that could come from forgiving them.

Step 6: Envisioning Restorative Justice

When individuals or groups within a society have begun a mutual process of identifying needs and acknowledging wrongs vis-à-vis all significant stakeholders, as was the case in one workshop after another in both Bosnia and Kosovo, then the participants are ready to examine the question of justice. However, care was taken to identify the kind of justice that needed to be examined, one radically different from that emanating out of a revenge mentality. Workshop leaders stressed the fact that an adequate definition of justice needed to start from a different reference point than the monitoring and punishment of unjust acts. Although vitally important to the maintenance of a stable society, exposure and retribution represent only the negative side of justice. A fully adequate understanding must begin with an evaluation of the norms and values that form the foundation for a positive vision of right relationships between all units within the society (a concept of justice that actually has its roots in all three major Abrahamic faith traditions—Judaism, Christianity, and Islam).

Restorative justice programming has recently been articulated very clearly by Mennonite peacebuilder Howard Zehr from Eastern Mennonite University. His is one of the major contemporary voices that has mainstreamed this concept into the larger peacebuilding field. The CSIS experience in Bosnia and Kosovo has illustrated how the understanding of justice by traumatized people can be transformed through a relationship-building process that introduces participants to a restorative understanding of justice. Focusing on the restoration of right relationships between individuals and groups began to be addressed quite naturally as a result of progress made while addressing the previous steps already discussed. Because restorative justice focuses on harm inflicted on victims, rather than on blame and punishment of offenders, the grievances and fears shared in steps 1 and 2 provided a natural starting point in the identification of specific justice concerns. Because restorative justice requires giving attention to the needs of all parties, the mutual needs identified in Step 3 helped disparate groups to discover common and/or compatible justice concerns. Because restorative justice is concerned with identifying the obligations of each party, the acknowledgments of responsibility outlined in Step 4 provided the initial impetus toward taking corrective measures. During the whole process of helping participants to explore possibilities and then implement specific projects, the purpose was to find justice concerns that all ethnic/sectarian units within the society could affirm and to identify positive measures that could be undertaken jointly to meet those needs.

One clear example of success in altering perspectives on both forgiveness and justice occurred in the workshop in Bugojno, on the border between the regions of Bosnia and Herzegovina where Croatian Catholic and Bosnian Muslim conflict had been severe. The Croats emphasized forgiveness as an essential mindset that could alter perspectives and behaviors. The Muslims, on the other hand, insisted that justice required punishment of Croatian war criminals before cooperation on anything else could be considered. This difference, based upon very different theologies and evident in many practical approaches of each group, was at the heart of the current conflict between these two groups. Arguments over this issue were interjected into most any topic discussed. The effective use of a perception clarification exercise, however, helped the whole group to develop greater understanding of one another. In the process, each faith community began to see some aspects of the other's perspective that they could affirm. Muslims could affirm that justice involved more than prosecution of war criminals. Addressing some of the humanitarian needs expressed by both communities also constituted a just response. Catholics could affirm that despite the great need for a transformation of orientation that the call to forgiveness represents, this was not all that their faith called them to pursue. As a result, the whole group found a way to affirm the necessity for both a reorientation from past to future and an expanded vision of justice. By the end of the workshop, Muslims even talked about their failure to forgive and Catholics spoke of the lack of justice for non-Croats in Croat-controlled areas. Finally, this workshop ended with the formulation of concrete plans to address some common justice concerns. The most significant proposals included the following: (1) distributing to churches and mosques a declaration of religious tolerance that had already been published in Bosnia-Herzegovina, (2) developing more interreligious dialogue groups, and (3) encouraging the return of refugees by confronting those who are inhibiting this initiative and asking imams and priests to take an active role in welcoming all people back to their homes.

Approach to Problem Solving

The problem-solving process was frequently started at the end of many workshops following the identification of restorative justice concerns that all could affirm. However, the task of developing concrete action plans either had to be completed at a subsequent workshop or by working groups established at a workshop that were then given the task of developing action plans on their own with modest supervision by local staff. In either case, the process had to begin by formulating some kind of selection criteria by which to choose from among the various justice concerns. Meeting all the needs of any society is unrealistic. Therefore, working groups were encouraged first to select a few critically important needs, brainstorm options which could conceivably meet those needs, and then evaluate which one(s) they believe—given their resources and any obstacles—could be developed into a feasible action plan that could effectively address the needs.

At the initial Bosnian workshop in Sarajevo, following the presentation of a problem solving methodology and selection of critical issues (including minority rights, ecumenical prayers, interfaith declarations addressing religious/political/military linkage, fair and balanced media coverage, and humanitarian provision of basic survival needs), participants formed small groups that focused on each problem. Though they were able to map out, quite accurately, the important actors and constituent concerns, no group could finalize any kind of workable action plan, either during or after the workshop. However, the project director learned after the war that one individual—Dr. Seid Hukovic, the President of the Academy of Sciences and Arts, which co-sponsored the workshop—had utilized the problem-solving methodology presented at the workshop to convince the Bosnia Muslim political leadership to accept the ceasefire that led to the Dayton Accords which ended the war. Yet the leadership team had concluded that the greatest accomplishment was the establishment of relationships and cultivation of a healing process that could address the terrible suffering and oppression of war. Therefore, despite the incredible value of the insight and capability demonstrated by one person with access to top-level decision makers, relationship building had to be the essential starting point for addressing the very real problems faced by the average workshop participant.

The first time action planning by a group resulted in project implementation; however, the actual plan that was developed during the workshop also completely failed due to factors beyond the control of the religious leaders involved. What succeeded was the commitment to developing a completely different action plan without any outside assistance, which returned sixteen hundred internally displaced persons to their homes in Fojnica over the next seven years. It was clear that the effort to build deeper relationships over the course of two workshops, plus the identification and practice of steps in an action planning process, could lead to impressive results.

One example illustrates the whole process—identification of justice needs, selection of priorities, recognition of obstacles, and implementation of a plan—all within a three-day workshop held in Sipovo, in the Bosnian Serb Republic. During the second day, participants from both entities spent considerable time outlining a number of specific justice concerns facing Bosnia-Herzegovina. They selected the need for the creation of jobs and a viable economy as most important. The most formidable obstacle to meeting this need was then identified as corruption, a topic central to any progress in Bosnia-Herzegovina. After proposing a number of actions that required long-term planning and implementation, these workshop participants decided that use of the media to raise awareness of the problem with the entire population could be initiated immediately. On day three, the Bosnian Serb media were invited to interview one participant from each of the three major faith communities represented, one of whom was a Serbian Orthodox bishop. All the participants took part in preparation for this event by meeting with their designated representative to share their concerns. During the interview itself, all three representatives criticized the role played by the political and religious leadership of each group and shared the conviction that all citizens in the country shared in the responsibility for corruption. Bosnian Serb media produced an hour-long show on corruption that evening. Shorter programs on radio and television were also broadcast in the Muslim-Croat Federation. During the next couple days, workshop participants reported frequent mention of the program throughout the country. What started as simply a training workshop on interfaith reconciliation had ended with the design and implementation of a specific restorative justice project which had highlighted one of Bosnia's most pressing needs and called for universal responsibility on the part of the entire public. The problem of corruption was certainly not solved, but at least at this moment, could not be ignored.

The most significant problem solving in Kosovo was accomplished through a cooperative effort involving the CSIS director, a Mercy Corps employee who had joined the project staff (in Bosnia and Kosovo), and the advisor to the Serbian Orthodox Episkop of Kosovo who had attended a CSIS workshop in Serbia. Functioning as a back channel of communication between Yugoslav, American, and the "shadow" Kosovo Albanian governments, this team of faith-based actors initiated dialogue processes to create and evaluate ways to resolve peacefully the points of contention, thereby preventing the onset of war. After these efforts failed, however, the team continued an unofficial mediation shuttle during the war. They identified and clarified some misperceptions, thereby resolving some emotionally laden negotiating obstacles, and then conducted a series of brainstorming sessions that fed possible alternatives for settling many remaining issues into top governmental levels, including NATO. Toward the end of the war, the team was part of a larger delegation which successfully negotiated the release of three U.S. soldiers captured by the Yugoslav military. During the same stay in Belgrade, they explored a number of detailed options in consultation with a top-level Yugoslav official that could contribute toward a final peace agreement. Before departing, the team was informed that Milosevic had agreed to end the war, providing the first indication that a breakthrough was possible. They then reported the details to officials within the U.S. Department of State and the Kosovo Albanian President and his cabinet. Within six weeks, the official negotiating team finalized the peace agreement and each government acknowledged that the CSIS role had been critical to ending the war.

Approach to Leadership Development

Two basic strategies established at the beginning of the CSIS project were collaborative planning and a workshop follow-up designed to empower participants and partner organizations. The role of the local consultants, in both entities, was critical to network building, selection of participants, workshop logistics, domestic presentation of project goals and activities, resourcing of working groups to develop, and implement action plans. Over time, these consultants increasingly functioned as co-leaders in designing and leading workshops, initiating or supporting various peacebuilding efforts, and establishing an independent, indigenous Bosnian NGO focused on faith-based conflict transformation. Two examples of significant peacebuilding initiative were taken by the consultant in the Muslim-Croat Federation. Vjekoslav Saje, as a Catholic lay person, developed such great rapport with the Metropolitan of the Serbian Orthodox Church immediately following the war, that Metropolitan Nikolai relied on him for transportation on trips throughout the Muslim-Croat Federation. This created further opportunity to enhance his relationship with this important Serbian Orthodox leader. Saje then became the only indigenous member of a multi-organizational team which facilitated the creation of the Interreligious Council of Bosnia-Herzegovina, a top-level interfaith organization that still exists in 2015. The process of establishing the Council culminated with the leaders of the four largest faith communities (Muslim, Catholic, Serbian Orthodox, and Jewish) adopting a "Statement of Shared Moral Commitment" and pledging themselves to work together to facilitate reconciliation among their peoples.

As indicated previously, the initial programmatic step specifically designed by CSIS to empower local leadership involved holding two skill development workshops for local staff and key committed workshop participants from Serbia, Croatia, and Bosnia-Herzegovina. The first workshop focused on perception clarification to help create a social atmosphere in which leadership could emerge and grow. Bringing together participants from these three countries for the first time since the war initially generated intense negative dynamics based on extremely different perceptions. A careful facilitation process by the workshop leadership, however, managed to create a safe space for both expressing one's own emotions and listening for the feelings of other participants. In the end, these participants saw the value in acquiring dialogue facilitation skills that could effectively handle explosive conflict. The second leadership training workshop was used to further hone these dialogue facilitation skills, especially through the use of role play, and to coordinate the efforts of existing working groups, most notably efforts already begun on enabling refugee/IDP return by clerics and laity in both entities. Increased understanding of stages and processes in group development in a former Communist society that was unaccustomed to the presence of civil society then served to enable project consultants and the core nucleus of committed participants to take initial steps toward the establishment of indigenous organizations.

Once the Centre for Religious Dialogue (CRD) was established in 1998, a process was designed to develop the organization and transfer all programming and responsibilities from CSIS to CRD within three years. The first step involved the selection of a model for institutional structure. The decision was made to develop a freestanding institute rather than connecting this project organizationally to the Interreligious Council of Bosnia-Herzegovina or developing separate organizations to represent each religious tradition. This decision was made in consultation with leaders of each of the religious communities. Since these persons were representatives from the Interreligious Council, as well as functioning as heads of their own communities, this was deemed important in order to guarantee legitimacy and ongoing support. Various kinds of sponsorship and assistance were also offered by a variety of other sources. The local Bosnian Open Society Foundation expressed interest in providing funding, a local organization called Citizen's Initiative provided office space in Banja Luka (Bosnian Serb Republic), and Mercy Corps provided office space in Sarajevo and set up a financial account for this project within its organization. Internally, an organizing committee was established with the objective of forming an advisory board and initiating organizational development. This advisory board then began the process of setting goals, registering the institution in both entities, selecting staff, and assuming financial responsibility.

The primary role that CSIS played, in addition to keeping the program running until each segment was transferred to CRD, consisted of providing individualized training for the two project consultants who were being prepared to take over leadership roles in the new organization. This training that the project director provided included guidance at various stages of organizational development, tutoring in proposal writing, and mentoring the increasing level of leadership that these consultants performed during workshops and supervision of all subsequent working groups. To augment the educational opportunities that CSIS offered to these consultants, opportunities were made available through a number of specialized international venues: the Summer Peacebuilding Institute at the Center for Justice and Peacebuilding at Eastern Mennonite University, courses on conflict management at the Program on Negotiation at Harvard Law School, workshops run by the Center for Attitudinal Healing in Tiburon, California, and training in organizational development in the former Yugoslavia through the Centre for Peace, Nonviolence and Human Rights in Osijek, Croatia.

Even before CRD took over the entire CSIS project in Bosnia-Herzegovina in 2001, both local consultants led a workshop for Catholic Relief Services to train educators in conflict transformation. After CRD assumed full responsibility, it implemented a number of its own projects, expanding the type of programming beyond that which CSIS had provided. Some examples included (1) organizing Summer Friendship Camps in the Bosnian Serb Republic to help children, youth, and disabled veterans cope with trauma and despair by providing spiritual healing, problem solving skill development, and occupational training; (2) developing a dialogue process involving young theologians and other professionals from the various faith traditions in Mostar, the largest city in Herzegovina, which was in ruins at the end of the war; and (3) establishing a dialogue process with a community of Muslim extremists who had come to Bosnia from other countries and married local women.

Analysis of Success

This case study provides many examples of the transformation of both attitudes and behavior, from small steps to momentous turning points, within both Bosnia-Herzegovina and Kosovo. Yet one must still ask what lasting impact can be seen. The CSIS project existed for seven years in Bosnia-Herzegovina, but other than the effort to end the Kosovo war, it sponsored workshops for only three years in Kosovo. The project director continued to lead workshops under other auspices in Kosovo for another three years, but no indigenous organization was established to take over the project. CRD did continue its work until 2007, but then disbanded due to inadequate funding. Despite the discontinuation of any reconciliation efforts that were a direct outgrowth of the CSIS project, there has been lasting impact through the efforts of partner organizations and institutions that workshop participants had subsequently founded.

Some of these programs have been sponsored by international organizations. For example, Catholic Relief Services, under the direction of indigenous leadership in Bosnia-Herzegovina, continues to work on reconciliation efforts such as psycho-social training and the creation of safe space for the sharing of narratives by the various ethno-religious communities, as well as leading an effort to build a Network for Peace which enables cooperation among a wide variety of peacebuilding efforts in that country.[13] In Kosovo, the World Conference on Religion and Peace (one of the organizations that facilitated the establishment of the interreligious councils in both Bosnia and Kosovo), together with Norwegian Church Aid sponsored the first major conference for the leaders of all faith communities. This "Interfaith Conference on Peaceful Coexistence and Dialogue," hosted by the Serbian Orthodox in Pec/Peja, consisted of speeches, visits to various holy places, and a joint appeal to dialogue and unity. Although there was very little immediate follow-up to this gathering, OSCE sponsored fifteen local interfaith forums followed by a Kosovo-wide interfaith conference in 2013. The joint appeal resulting from this conference was more specific, focusing on calls for legal safeguards regarding freedom of religion. OSCE has followed up this conference primarily by providing legal advice to religious communities.[14]

More significant, however, have been the reconciliation efforts sponsored by indigenous organizations. In Kosovo, major recent efforts have

---

13. Goran Bubalo, Chief of Party, Catholic Relief Services in Bosnia-Herzegovina. Interview with author, July 25, 2014; and source for various unpublished documents describing the current work of CRS in that country.

14. OSCE Mission in Kosovo. "Role of religious leaders."

been initiated by the Kosovo Government. The Ministry of Foreign Affairs has organized two annual Weeks of Tolerance and Reconciliation in 2013 and 2014. Leaders of all religious communities, top-level government officials, as well as representatives of international governmental and religious organizations have gathered to reflect on the state of faith relations, especially in Kosovo. These event—part of the government's "Interfaith Kosovo" program—have been designed to address religious politicization, minority protection, freedom of speech and religion, countering violent extremism, and economic development. At the end of the 2014 event, a working group met to develop action plans for a Center for Interfaith Dialogue in Kosovo.[15]

The most significant outgrowth of the CSIS project, however, is the "Face to Face" Interreligious Service that the Bosnian Franciscan priest, Ivo Markovic, established in Sarajevo in 1996 and that is still operating today. The CSIS project, including the director, frequently provided encouragement as Father Markovic challenged religious leaders in all communities to detach themselves from ethno-nationalism and initiated contact with the Serbian Orthodox Church by travelling each week to the capital of the Bosnian Serb Republic for one year following the war. He also organized and directed the Pontanima Choir, conducted roundtables for theologians and religious leaders to dialogue at the local level, organized interfaith prayer broadcasts through Bosnian media, and facilitated dialogue sessions and peace projects involving a wide variety of participants from leading clerics to women's and youth groups. This kind of grassroots, indigenous programming is also exactly the kind of programming MCC chooses to support. In fact, MCC has also provided even more sustained support for Father Markovic and the "Face to Face" Interreligious Service than did CSIS.[16]

Although a complete list of reconciliation efforts in Bosnia and Kosovo would be much more extensive than can be recounted here, many analysts and local citizens still raise questions regarding this kind of programming and the lack of stable relationships as well as governmental and civil society institutions. Ethno-religious division and its political manifestation are still considered entrenched. One very recent study concludes that an evaluation of the levels of trust, deep contact, and mutual acceptance among 210

---

15. Ministry of Foreign Affairs, Republic of Kosovo. Various documents regarding the "Interfaith Kosovo" program. Retrieved on October 10, 2014 from http://www.interfaithkosovo.org/events/?lang=En.

16. Puljek-Shank, "Mennonite Experience," 132–149. One can also find numerous other examples of Mennonite support for indigenous peacebuilding organizations in the Balkans in this document, as well as two other sources: Puljek-Shank and Puljek-Shank. "Contribution of Trauma Healing, 155–184; and Mennonite Central Committee, *Peace Office Newsletter* 40, no. 3 (July–September 2010). A series of articles compiled by Amela Puljek-Shank, MCC co-representative for Southeastern Europe.

interviewees in Bosnia-Herzegovina and 57 in Kosovo reveals that deep divisions remained. In fact, contrary to the expectations of many, both from the region and outside, the study contends that the International Criminal Tribunal for the Former Yugoslavia has hardened the divisions rather than providing a vehicle for reconciliation.[17]

At the same time, another very recent study of factors affecting reconciliation in Bosnia-Herzegovina has come to a very different conclusion. After interviewing 616 people from 13 municipalities, this research discovered strong local support for reconciliation and trust-building processes. 75% of respondents in each part of the country expressed their belief that efforts to build inter-ethnic/sectarian relationships would have a positive impact on the whole society. Furthermore, respondents who were religious indicated greater willingness to support reconciliation processes that address perspectives on the past. However, the results also indicate that people thought any reconciliation process needed to be implemented country-wide and that the best facilitators would be educators, though religious leaders would be trusted by a majority, while political leaders were seen as needing to be on the receiving end of such efforts.[18]

What both of these studies indicate is that sole reliance on traditional forms of retributive justice or the reforms commonly proposed for social and political post-war reconstruction are insufficient. Reconciliation efforts are the glue that holds all the rest of post-conflict reconstruction together. Without effective dialogue and dispute resolution mechanisms that can establish good working relationships between conflicted groups, it is likely that democratic governance will become deadlocked, security will be derailed by suspicion, economic development will too often succumb to interests that appear to be competing, delivery of essential services will be obstructed, and even justice will be construed only in negative terms of guilt and punishment rather than a mutual search for the values and mores that can underpin the common good. At the same time, reconciliation cannot be the only focus. Since conflict influences the performance of each of the other components, reconciliation must interface with each of them in order to assist parties in effectively handling differences and resolving disputes that arise within each arena.

The question remains, however, as to the criteria by which one can measure the effectiveness of reconciliation processes. In evaluating the CSIS project, a decision was made to collect written evaluations from all participants at the end of each workshop and then repeat the same evaluation

---

17. Clark, *International Trials*, 113, 126, & 182.
18. Wilkes, *et al.* "Factors in Reconciliation."

process six months later in order to assess longer-term perceptions. Later in the life of the project, personal interviews conducted by local staff were added to this process. Factors assessed included the viability of emerging ideas or proposals, the degree of change in attitude or perspective on the part of participants, the utility of specific exercises or presentations, the nature or significance of personal interaction between participants, and the quality of relationships between project staff and workshop participants. This very subjective input provided very important information that enabled the leadership team to make adjustments that would both correct any misperceptions or biases on the part of the leaders and respond to the emerging shifts on the part of participants' experience, whether that be toward, or away from, tolerance and cooperation.

A relatively new process, recently introduced into the monitoring and evaluating of peacebuilding, has given a name to this kind of assessment process. "Developmental evaluation" was created to fit the changing, complex, turbulent conditions encountered when dealing with violent and post-violent societies. Rather than being tied to measurable results, the aim is to facilitate and support dynamic innovation. Rather than identifying what is provable, one is encouraged to aim beyond perceived possibilities. Instead of looking for predictable, pre-programmed outcomes, the hope is to discover unanticipated, emergent ones. Rather than assuming that fixed, standard interventions are best, one is encouraged to explore alternatives.[19]

Such an approach may actually fit better with religious faith than social science—trusting in the Almighty for justice; believing in the power of forgiveness to transform; acting out of the conviction that one's efforts will bear fruit whether or not it is apparent. If one sees oneself as part of the action of God, then one may be better able to perceive one's role as enabling, not determining. One might also be spared the negative view of failure, able instead to see it as opportunity for learning—from the dynamics inherent in situations that sometimes appear hopeless, from those with whom we serve who have been challenged and enlightened by the same God.

As I look forward and ask what needs to happen now, I keep returning to the centrality of building and rebuilding community as the crucial focal point in empowering faith-based reconcilers. This takes much more extensive investment of time, energy, and resources than most donors are willing to provide without proven, measurable results. Yet it is the strengthening of these relationships with indigenous actors, and the building of their local capacities, that must take priority if we are going to be able to see beyond

---

19. Patton. *Developmental Evaluation*.

the obvious, recognize the emergent, and be part of whatever innovation becomes necessary for effective conflict transformation in the future.

Bibliography

Aall, Pamela, Lt. Col. Daniel Miltenberger, and Thomas G. Weiss. *Guide to IGOs, NGOs, and the Military in Peace and Relief Operations.* Washington, DC: United States Institute for Peace, 2000.
Abu-Nimer, Mohammed. "Conflict Resolution, Culture, and Religion: Toward a Training Model of Interreligious Peacebuilding." *JPR* 38 (2001) 685–704.
———. "A Framework for Nonviolence and Peacebuilding in Islam." *Journal of Law and Religion* 15.1/2 (2000–2001) 217–65.
Ackerman, Peter and Jack Duvall. *A Force More Powerful: A Century of Nonviolent Conflict.* New York: Palgrave Macmillan, 2001.
Akpinar, Snjezana. "Hospitality in Islam." *Religion East & West* 7 (October 2007) 23–27.
Albrecht, Elizabeth Soto. *Family Violence: Reclaiming a Theology of Nonviolence.* Maryknoll, NY: Orbis, 2008.
Alikin, Valeriy A. *The Earliest History of the Christian Gathering: Origin, Development and Content of the Christian Gathering in the First to Third Centuries.* Texts and Studies of Early Christian Life and Language 102. Leiden: Brill, 2010.
Allard, Silas Webster. "In the Shade of the Oaks of Mamre: Hospitality as a Framework for Political Engagement between Christians and Muslims." *Political Theology* 13 (2012) 414–24.
Allport, Gordon. *The Nature of Prejudice.* 1954. Reprinted, New York: Basic Books, 1979.
Anderson, Benedict. *Imagined Communities: Reflections on the Origin and Spread of Nationalism.* Rev. ed. New York: Verso, 1991.
Anderson, Kent. "Honorable Mentioning." http://weeklywire.com/ww/07-28-97/tw_book2.html.
Anderson, Mary B. *Do No Harm: How Aid Can Support Peace—or War.* Boulder, CO: Rienner, 1999.
Appleby, R. Scott. *The Ambivalence of the Sacred: Religion, Violence, and Reconciliation.* Lanham, MD: Rowman & Littlefield, 2000.
Ash, Timothy Garton. *The Uses of Adversity: Essays on the Fate of Central Europe.* New York: Random House, 1989.
Assefa, Hizkias. *Peace and Reconciliation as a Paradigm.* Nairobi: ACIS, 1993.
Assefa, Lydette. "Creating Identity in Opposition: Relations between the Meserete Kristos Church and the Ethiopian Orthodox Church, 1960–1980." *MQR* 83 (2009) 539–70.

AtKisson, Alan. "Why Civil Society Will Save the World." In *Beyond Prince and Merchant: Citizen Participation and the Rise of Civil Society*, edited by John Burbidge, 285–92. New York: Pact Publications, 1997.
Audubon, John James. *The Birds of America*. Vol. 6. New York: Audubon, 1856.
Augsburger, David W. *Conflict Mediation across Cultures: Pathways and Patterns*. Louisville: Westminster John Knox Press, 1995.
Aurbacher, Killian. "1534." In *Anabaptism in Outline*, edited by Walter Klaassen, 293. Classics of the Radical Reformation 3. Scottdale, PA: Herald, 1981.
"Background Notes: Congo, Democratic Republic of the." *U.S. Department of State*. Last modified September 30, 2011. http://www.state.gov/outofdate/bgn/congokinshasa/187743.htm.
Bacon, Edwin. *The Gulag at War: Stalin's Forced Labour System in the Light of the Archives*. New York: New York University Press, 1994.
Barrett, Lois. "Ursula Jost and Barbara Rebstock of Strasbourg." In *Profiles of Anabaptist Women: Sixteenth-Century Reforming Pioneers*, edited by C. Arnold Snyder and Linda A. Huebert Hecht, 273–87. Waterloo, ON: Wilfrid Laurier University Press, 1996.
Barth, Karl. *Church Dogmatics*. IV, *The Doctrine of Reconciliation*. Edited by T. F. Torrance. Translated by G. W. Bromiley. Edinburgh: T. & T. Clark, 1958.
———. *Protestant Theology in the Nineteenth Century*. Grand Rapids: Eerdmans, 2002.
Bartlett, Roger P. *Human Capital: The Settlement of Foreigners in Russia, 1762–1804*. Cambridge: Cambridge University Press, 1979.
Barton, Greg. *Indonesia's Struggle: Jamaah Islamiyah and the Soul of Islam*. Sidney: University of New South Wales Press, 2004.
Baylor, Michael G., ed. and trans. *The Radical Reformation*. Cambridge Texts in the History of Political Thought. Cambridge: Cambridge University Press, 1991.
Beachy, Kristen. *Thumb Screws and Testimonies: Poems, Stories, and Essays Inspired by the Martyrs Mirror*. Scottdale, PA: Herald, 2010.
Becirevic, Edina. *Genocide on the Drina River*. New Haven: Yale University Press, 2014.
Bender, Harold S., Sam Steiner, and Richard D. Thiessen. "World Mennonite Membership Distribution." In *Global Anabaptist Mennonite Encyclopedia Online*. January 2013. http://gameo.org/index.php?title=World_Mennonite_Membership_Distribution&oldid=103542.
Bender, Rosalee, et al. *Piecework: A Women's Peace Theology*. Winnipeg, MB: Mennonite Central Committee Canada, 1997.
Benedict, Philip. *Christ's Churches Purely Reformed: A Social History of Calvinism*. New Haven, CT: Yale University Press, 2002.
Bennet, Christopher. *Yugoslavia's Bloody Collapse: Causes, Course and Consequences*. New York: New York University Press, 1995.
Berger, Peter & Thomas Luckmann. *The Social Construction of Reality: A Treatise in the Sociology of Knowledge*. Garden City, NY: Anchor Books, 1966.
Béthune, Pierre-François de. "Interreligious Dialogue and Sacred Hospitality." *Religion East & West* 1 (2007) 1–22.
Blagojevich, Bojana. "Peacebuilding in Ethnically Divided Societies." *Peace Review: A Journal of Social Justice* 19 (Winter 2007) 555–62.
Blickle, Peter. *The Revolution of 1525*. Baltimore: Johns Hopkins University Press, 1981.
Block, Isaac I. *Assault on God's Image: Domestic Abuse*. Winnipeg, MB: Windflower Communications, 1999.

Blum, Jerome. *Lord and Peasant in Russia: From the Ninth to the Nineteenth Century*. Princeton: Princeton University Press, 1971.
Botes, Johannes. "Conflict Transformation: A Debate Over Semantics or a Crucial Shift in the Theory and Practice of Peace and Conflict Studies?" *International Journal of Peace Studies* 8.2 (2003) 1–27.
Bouchet-Saulnier, Francois. *The Practical Guide to Humanitarian Law*. New York: Rowman & Littlefield, 2002.
Bourdieu, Pierre, et al. *The Logic of Practice*. Translated by Richard Nice. Stanford, CA: Stanford University Press, 1992.
Boyarin, Daniel, and Jonathan Boyarin. *Powers of Diaspora: Two Essays on the Relevance of Jewish Culture*. Minneapolis: University of Minnesota Press, 2002.
Boyd, Stephen B. *Pilgram Marpeck: His Life and Social Theology*. Durham: Duke University Press, 1992.
Brady, Thomas A., Jr. *Ruling Class, Regime and Reformation at Strasbourg, 1520–1555*. Studies in Medieval and Reformation Thought 22. Leiden: Brill, 1978.
Braght, Theilman J. van. *The Bloody Theatre or Martyr's Mirror* (1660). Translated by Joseph F. Sohm. 2nd ed. Scottdale, PA: Herald, 2002.
Brauchler, Birgit, ed. *Reconciling Indonesia: Grassroots Agency for Peace*. London: Routledge, 2009.
Brock, Peter. *Varieties of Pacifism*. 4th ed. Syracuse, NY: Syracuse University Press, 1998.
Bronstein, Eitan. "The *Nakba* in Hebrew: Israeli-Jewish Awareness of the Palestinian Catastrophe and Internal Refugees." In *Catastrophe Remembered: Palestine, Israel and the Internal Refugees*, edited by Nur Masalha, 214–41. London: Zed, 2005.
Brubacher, Matthew. "Striking a Balance: Humanitarian, Peace, and Justice Initiatives." *CGR* 28.3 (2010) 7–21.
Bruinessen, Martin van, ed. *Contemporary Developments in Indonesian Islam: Explaining the Conservative Turn*. Singapore: Institute of Southeast Asian Studies, 2013.
Brunk, Gerald R., ed. *Menno Simons: A Reappraisal*. Harrisonburg, VA: Eastern Mennonite University, 1992.
Buergenthal, Thomas. "Centerpiece of the Human Rights Revolution." In *Reflections on the Universal Declaration of Human Rights: A Fiftieth Anniversary Anthology*, edited by B. Van der Heijden and B. Tahzib-Lie, 91–94. The Hague: Nijhoff, 1998.
Burger, Edward K. "Erasmus and the Anabaptists." PhD diss., University of California, Santa Barbara, 1977.
Burton, John W. and Frank Dukes. *Conflict: Practices in Management, Settlement, and Resolution*. New York: Palgrave Macmillan, 1990.
Bush, Perry. *Two Kingdoms, Two Loyalties: Mennonites Pacifism in Modern America*. Baltimore: Johns Hopkins University Press, 1998.
Butler, Judith. *Parting Ways: Jewishness and the Critique of Zionism*. New York: Columbia University Press, 2013.
Byler, Dennis. *Los Genocidios en la Biblia: Reflexiones sobre la Violencia y la No Violencia en la Historia del Pueblo de Dios*. Barcelona: Clie, 1997.
Canadian Mennonite Board of Colonization Collection, Mennonite Heritage Centre, Winnipeg, Manitoba.
Cattepoel, Dirk. "The Mennonites of Germany, 1936–1948, and the Present Outlook." In *Fourth Mennonite World Conference Proceedings, August 3–10, 1948*, 14–22. Akron, PA: MCC, 1950.

Charles, Sylvia Shirk and Laurie Oswald Robinson. "Putting a Face On the Page." *Timbrel* (March/April 2008) 16–17.

Chatfield, Charles. "Thinking about Peace in History." In *The Pacficist Impulse in Historical Perspective*, edited by Harvey L. Dyck, 36–51. Toronto: University of Toronto Press, 1996.

Chupp, Mark. "Creating Space for Peace: The Central American Peace Portfolio." In *From the Ground Up: Mennonite Contributions to International Peacebuilding*, edited by Cynthia Sampson and John Paul Lederach, 104–21. Oxford: Oxford University Press, 2000.

Clark, Janine. *International Trials and Reconciliation: Assessing the Impact of the International Criminal Tribunal for the Former Yugoslavia*. New York: Routledge, 2014.

Coggins, James R. "Toward a Definition of the Anabaptists: Twentieth-Century Historiography of the Radical Reformers." *JMS* 4 (1986) 183–207.

Cohn, Carol, ed. *Women and Wars*. Cambridge, UK: Polity, 2013.

Cohn, Henry J. "Anticlericalism in the German Peasants' War." *Past & Present* 83 (1979) 3–31.

Coleman, Heather J. *Russian Baptists and Spiritual Revolution, 1905–1929*. Indiana-Michigan Series in Russian and East European Studies. Bloomington: Indiana University Press, 2005.

Colin, Jean-Philippe, and B. Losch. "'Touche pas à Mon Planteur': Réflexions sur les 'Encadrements' Paysans à Travers Quelques Exemples Ivoiriens." *Politique Africaine* 40 (1990): 83–99. http://horizon.documentation.ird.fr/exl-doc/pleins_textes/pleins_textes_5/b_fdi_23-25/31282.pdf.

Colombijn, Freek and J. Thomas Lindblad, eds. *Roots of Violence in Indonesia: Contemporary Violence in Historical Perspective*. Leiden: KITLV Press, 2002.

Comunidad Cristiana Hermandad en Cristo, Iglesia Menonita de Colombia and Hermanos Menonitas de Colombia. *Siendo Sal y Luz: Reflexiones Anabautistas sobre la Responsabilidad de la Iglesia frente a la Sociedad y el Estado*.

"Conversation with Pfistermeyer, 1531." In *Anabaptism in Outline*, edited by Walter Klaassen, 124. Classics of the Radical Reformation 3. Scottdale, PA: Herald, 1981.

Coser, Lewis A. *The Functions of Social Conflict: An Examination of the Concept of Social Conflict and Its Use in Empirical Sociological Research*. New York: Free Press, 1964.

"Country Profile: Democratic Republic of the Congo." *BBC News*. Last modified September 16, 2014. http://www.bbc.com/news/world-africa-13283212.

Cousens, Elizabeth M. "Introduction." In *Peacebuilding as Politics: Cultivating Peace in Fragile Societies*, edited by Elizabeth M. Cousens and Chetan Kumar, 1–20. Boulder, CO: Rienner, 2001.

Crouch, Melissa. "Indonesia's Blasphemy Law: Bleak Outlook for Minority Religions." *Asia Pacific Bulletin* 146 (January 26, 2012) 1–4.

Curle, Adam. *Tools for Transformation: A Personal Study*. Stroud, UK: Hawthorn, 1990.

Czada, Roland, Thomas Held, and Markus Weingardt, eds. *Religions and World Peace: Religious Capacities for Conflict Resolution and Peacebuilding*. Baden-Baden: Nomos, 2012.

Davis, Kenneth. *Anabaptism and Asceticism: A Study in Intellectual Origins*. Studies in Anabaptist and Mennonite History 16. Scottdale, PA: Herald, 1974.

"Decade to Overcome Violence, 2001–2010: Churches Seeking Reconciliation and Peace." http://www.overcomingviolence.org.

Deckert, Jennifer Chappel. "From Persecution to Hope: Mennonite Mothering in a Context of Violence." In *Mennonite Mothering*, edited by Rachel Epp Buller and Kerry Fast, 293–307. Bradford, ON: Demeter, 2013.

DeKoven-Ezrahi, Sidra. *Booking Passage: Exile and Homecoming in the Modern Jewish Imagination*. Berkeley, CA: University of California Press, 2000.

Denck, Hans. "Commentary on Micah, 1527." In *Anabaptism in Outline*, edited by Walter Klaassen, 292. Classics of the Radical Reformation 3. Scottdale, PA: Herald, 1981.

Deppermann, Klaus. *Melchior Hoffman*. Edinburgh: T. & T. Clark, 1987.

Derksen, John. *From Radicals to Survivors*. Bibliotheca Humanistica & Reformatorica 61. 'T Goy-Houten: Hes & de Graaf, 2002.

Derrida, Jacques. *Of Hospitality*. Translated by Rachel Bowlby. Cultural Memory in the Present. Stanford: Stanford University Press, 2000.

"Development of International Humanitarian Law." *International Committee of the Red Cross*. Last modified May 13, 2010. http://www.icrc.org/eng/who-we-are/history/since-1945/history-ihl/overview-development-modern-international-humanitarian-law.htm.

Dietrich, Wolfgang. *Elicitive Conflict Transformation and the Transrational Shift in Peace Politics*. New York: Palgrave Macmillan, 2013.

Douglas, James W. *The Nonviolent Coming of God*. Maryknoll, NY: Orbis, 1991.

Drakulic, Slavenka. *The Balkan Express: Fragments from the Other Side of War*. New York: Norton, 1993.

Driedger, Leo, and Donald B. Kraybill. *Mennonite Peacemaking: From Quietism to Activism*. Scottdale, PA: Herald, 1994.

Drinan, Robert F., SJ. *The Mobilization of Shame*. New Haven: Yale University Press, 2001.

Driver, John. "The Church: The Missional Kingdom of the Kingdom." In *Without Spot or Wrinkle: Reflecting Theologically on the Nature of the Church*, edited by Karl Koop and Mary Schertz, 122–25. Occasional Papers 20. Elkhart, IN: Institute of Mennonite Studies, 2000.

———. *Community and Commitment*. Mission Forum Series 4. Scottdale, PA: Herald, 1976.

———. *Pueblo a Imagen de Dios . . . hacia una visión bíblica*. Bogotá: Semilla-CLARA, 1991.

———. *Radical Faith: An Alternative History of the Christian Church*. Kitchener, ON: Pandora, 1999.

———. "La Vivencia de la Paz a Nivel de la Comunidad y la Familia." Lecture delivered at Ciudades de Refugio, Bogotá, Colombia, November 7, 2001.

Droogers, Andre, et al.. *De Stereotypering Voorbij: Evangelischen en Oecumenischen over Religieus Pluralisme*. Zoetermeer: Boekencentrum, 1997.

DuBois, Heather and Janna L. Hunter-Bowman. "The Intersection of Christian Theology and Peacebuilding." In *The Oxford Handbook of Religion, Conflict, and Peacebuilding*, edited by Atalia Omer, Scott Appleby, and David Little. Oxford: Oxford University Press, 2015.

Dula, Peter. "A Theology of Interfaith Bridge-Building." In *Borders and Bridges: Mennonite Witness in a Religiously Diverse World*, edited by Peter Dula and Alain Epp Weaver, 160–70. Scottdale, PA: Herald, 2007.

Duncan, Christopher. *Violence and Vengeance: Religious Conflict and Its Aftermath in Eastern Indonesia*. Ithaca, NY: Cornell University Press, 2013.
Dyck, Cornelius J. *An Introduction to Mennonite History: A Popular History of the Anabaptists and the Mennonites*. Scottdale, PA: Herald, 1993.
———. "The Life of the Spirit in Anabaptism." In *Essays in Anabaptist Theology*, edited by H. Wayne Pipkin, 111–32. Text Reader Series 5. Elkhart, IN: Institute of Mennonite Studies, 1994.
Dyck, Harvey L., "Peter Brock as a Historian of Worldwide Pacifism: An Appreciation." In *Pacifist Impulse in Historical Perspective*, edited by Harvey L. Dyck, 3–11. Toronto: University of Toronto Press, 1996.
Dyck, Isaak M. *Hinterlassene Schriften vom Aeltester Isaak M. Dyck, Blumenfeld, Mexiko*. Cuauhtémoc: Jacob Klassen Fehr, 2000.
———. "Emigration from Canada to Mexico, Year 1922." Translated by Robyn Dyck Sneath. Unpublished manuscript in possession of author Royden Loewen, 2005.
———. *Anfangs Jahre der Mennoniten in Mexiko*. Cuauhtémoc: Heinrich Dyck, 1995.
———. *Die Auswanderung der Reinlaender Mennoniten Gemeinde von Kanada nach Mexiko 1970*. Cuauhtémoc: Imprenta Colonial, 1993.
Dyck, Johann P. "A Root out of Dry Ground: Revival Patterns in the German Free churches in the USSR after World War II." *JMS* 30 (2012) 97–112.
Dyck, Peter. "A Theology of Service." *MQR* 44 (1970) 262–80.
Edwards, Michael. *Civil Society*. Cambridge, UK: Polity, 2003.
Elliot, Jane. *Using Narrative in Social Research: Qualitative and Quantitative Approaches*. London: Sage, 2005.
Enns, Elaine. "Pilgrimage to the Ukraine: Revisioning History through Restorative Justice." Last modified 2001. http://www.bcm-net.org/pilgrimage-to-the-ukraine-revisioning-history-through-restorative-justice-elaine-enns.
Enns, Fernando, Scott Holland, and Ann Riggs. *Seeking Cultures of Peace: A Peace Church Conversation*. Telford, PA: Cascadia, 2004.
Epp, Frank H. *Mennonites in Canada, 1786–1920: A History of a Separate People*. Toronto: Macmillan, 1974.
———. "One Hundred Volunteers Needed." *The Canadian Mennonite* 28 (January 1955) 2.
Epp, Marlene. "Alternative Service and Alternative Gender Roles: Conscientious Objectors in B.C. During World War II." *BC Studies* 105 & 106 (Spring/Summer 1995) 139–58.
———. "Carrying the Banner of Nonconformity: Ontario Mennonite Women and the Dress Question, 1900–1960." *CGR* 8.3 (1990) 237–57.
———. "Heroes or Yellow Bellies? Masculinity and the Conscientious Objector." *JMS* 17 (1999) 107–17.
———. *Mennonite Women in Canada: A History*. Winnipeg: University of Manitoba Press, 2008.
———. "Nonconformity and Nonresistance: What Did It Mean to Mennonite Women?" In *Changing Roles of Women within the Christian Church in Canada*, edited by Elizabeth Gillan Muir and Marilyn Färdig Whiteley, 55–74. Toronto: University of Toronto Press, 1995.
Epp, Peter. "A Brief History of the Omsk Brotherhood." *JMS* 30 (2012) 113–32.
Epp-Tiessen, Esther. *Mennonite Central Committee in Canada: A History*. Winnipeg, ON: CMU Press, 2013.

Escobar, Samuel. "Latin America and Anabaptist Theology." In *Engaging Anabaptism: Conversations with a Radical Tradition*, edited by John D. Roth, 75–88. Scottdale, PA: Herald, 2001.

Esquivia, Ricardo, with Paul Stucky, "*Building Peace from Below and Inside—The Mennonite Experience in Colombia*." In *From the Ground Up: Mennonite Contributions to International Peacebuilding*, edited by Cynthia Sampson and John Paul Lederach, 120–44. Oxford: Oxford University Press, 2000.

Fager, Chuck. "Rethinking Pacifism." *Christianity Today* 45.15 (3 December 2001) 17–18.

Fairfield, Paul. "Dialogical Education?" In *Gadamer's Hermeneutics and the Art of Conversation*, edited by Andrzej Wierciński, 553–64. Münster: Lit, 2011.

Fast, Heinold. "Conrad Grebel: The Covenant on the Cross." In *Profiles of Radical Reformers*, edited by Hans-Jürgen Goertz, 118–31. Kitchener, ON: Herald, 1982.

———. "The Dependence of the First Anabaptists on Luther, Erasmus, and Zwingli." *MQR* 30 (1956) 104–19.

Fast, Larissa A. "Frayed Edges: Exploring the Boundaries of Conflict Resolution." *Peace & Change* 27 (2002) 528–45.

Fiorenza, Francis Schüssler. "Systematic Theology: Task and Methods." In *Systematic Theology: Roman Catholic Perspectives*, edited by Francis Schüssler Fiorenza and John P. Galvin, 1–89. 2nd ed. Minneapolis: Fortress, 2011.

Fogelman, Aaron Spencer. *Hopeful Journeys: German Immigration, Settlement, and Political Culture in Colonial America, 1717–1775*. Philadelphia: University of Pennsylvania Press, 1996.

Foster, Wayne. "The Makhnovists and the Mennonites: War and Peace in the Ukrainian Revolution." Last modified May 25, 2011. http://libcom.org/history/makhnovists-mennonites-war-peace-ukrainian-civil-war.

Foucault, Michel. *Power/Knowledge: Selected Interviews and Other Writings, 1972–1977*. Edited and translated by Colin Gordon. New York: Pantheon, 1980.

Fountain, Philip Michael. "Translating Service: An Ethnography of the Mennonite Central Committee." PhD diss., Australian National University, 2011.

Freedman, Jill, and Gene Combs. *Narrative Therapy: The Social Construction of Preferred Realities*. New York: W.W. Norton Company, 1996.

Freire, Paulo and Donaldo Macedo. *Pedagogy of the Oppressed*. 30th Anniversary Edition. Translated by Myra Bergman Ramos. New York: Bloomsbury Academic, 2000.

Friedman-Rudovsky, Jean. "The Ghost Rapes of Bolivia." *VICE* 5 August 2013. http://www.vice.com/en_ca/read/the-ghost-rapes-of-bolivia-000300-v20n8.

Friesen, Aileen. "The Case of a Siberian Sect: Mennonites and the Incomplete Transformation of Russia's Religious Structure." *JMS* 30 (2012) 139–48.

Friesen, Abraham. *Erasmus, the Anabaptists, and the Great Commission*. Grand Rapids: Eerdmans, 1998.

———. *In Defense of Privilege: Russian Mennonites and the State Before and during World War I*. Winnipeg, MB: Kindred, 2006

Friesen, Duane K., ed. *Christian Peacemaking and International Conflict: A Realist Pacifist Perspective*. Scottdale, PA: Herald, 1986.

Friesen, John. "Mennonites in Poland: An Expanded Historical View." *JMS* 4 (1986) 94–108

Galtung, Johann. "Cultural Violence." *JPR* 27 (1990) 291–305.

Garcia, Sandra Baez. "Conversations with International Peacemakers." *Mennonite Global Learning Network, International Community of Mennonite Brethren*, 2013. http://icomb.org/mgln-peacejustice.

Gawerc, Michelle I. "Peace-Building: Theoretical and Concrete Perspectives." *Peace & Change: A Journal of Peace Research* 31 (2006) 435–78.

Geertz, Clifford. *The Interpretation of Cultures*. New York: Basic Books, 1973.

———. *The Religion of Java*. London: Free Press of Glencoe, 1976.

Gerber, Barbara B. "Sebastian Lotzer: An Educated Layman in the Struggle for Divine Justice." In *Profiles of Radical Reformers*, edited by Hans-Jürgen Goertz, 72–87. Kitchener, ON: Herald, 1982.

Gladwell, Malcolm. *David and Goliath: Underdogs, Misfits, and the Art of Battling Giants*. New York: Little, Brown, 2013.

———. *The Tipping Point: How little Things Can Make a Big Difference*. New York: Little, Brown, 2000.

Gligorijevic, Milo. "Kosovo Lekcije iz Istorije." *Nedeljne Informativne Novine (NIN)*, no. 2008 [special supplement] (June 25, 1989).

Goddard, Hugh. *A History of Christian-Muslim Relations*. Chicago: New Amsterdam, 2001.

Goertz, Hans-Jürgen. "Introduction." In *Profiles of Radical Reformers*, edited by Hans-Jürgen Goertz, 9–25. Kitchener, ON: Herald, 1982.

———. "Karlstadt, Müntzer and the Reformation of the Commoners, 1521–1525." In *A Companion to Anabaptism and Spiritualism, 1521–1700*, edited by John D. Roth and James M. Stayer, 1–44. Brill's Companions to the Christian Tradition 6. Leiden: Brill, 2007.

———. *Die Täufer: Geschichte und Deutung*. Munich: Beck, 1980.

———. "Thomas Muntzer: Revolutionary in a Mystical Spirit." In *Profiles of Radical Reformers*, edited by Hans-Jürgen Goertz, 29–44. Kitchener, ON: Herald, 1982.

González, Justo L. *The Story of Christianity*. Vol. 2: *The Reformation to the Present Day*. San Francisco: Harper & Row, 1984.

Goossen, Rachel Waltner. *Women against the Good War: Conscientious Objection and Gender on the American Home Front, 1941–1947*. Chapel Hill: University of North Carolina Press, 1997.

Gopin, Marc. *Between Eden and Armageddon: The Future of World Religions, Violence, and Peacemaking*. New York: Oxford University Press, 2000.

———. "The Religious Component of Mennonite Peacemaking and Its Global Implications." In *From the Ground Up: Mennonite Contributions to International Peacebuilding*, edited by Cynthia Sampson and John Paul Lederach, 233–55. Oxford: Oxford University Press, 2000.

Granara, William. "Nile Crossings: Hospitality and Revenge in Egyptian Rural Narratives." *Journal of Arabic Literature* 41 (2010) 121–35.

Graybill, Beth. "Writing Women into MCC's History." In *A Table of Sharing: Mennonite Central Committee and the Expanding Networks of Mennonite Identity*, edited by Alain Epp Weaver, 239–62. Telford, PA: Cascadia, 2011.

Grebel, Conrad. "Letter to Thomas Müntzer." In *The Radical Reformation*, edited by Michael G. Baylor, 36–48. Cambridge Texts in the History of Political Thought. Cambridge: Cambridge University Press, 1991.

Greene, Dana. "Repeat Performance: Is Restorative Justice Another Good Reform Gone Bad?" *Contemporary Justice Review: Issues in Criminal, Social, and Restorative Justice* 16 (2013) 359–90.

Greenwood, Christopher. "Historical Development and Legal Basis." In *The Handbook of Humanitarian Law in Armed Conflicts*, edited by Dieter Fleck, 1–38. Oxford: Oxford University Press, 1995.

Gregory, Brad. "Anabaptist Martyrdom: Imperatives, Experience, and Memorialization." In *A Companion to Anabaptism and Spiritualism, 1521–1700*, edited by John D. Roth and James M. Stayer, 467–506. Brill's Companions to the Christian Tradition 6. Leiden: Brill, 2007.

———. *Salvation at Stake: Christian Martyrdom in Early Modern Europe*. Cambridge, MA: Harvard University Press, 2001.

Gross, Leonard. "Jakob Hutter: A Christian Communist." In *Profiles of Radical Reformers*, edited by Hans-Jürgen Goertz, 158–67. Kitchener, ON: Herald, 1982.

Grupo de Memoria Historica. ¡Basta Ya! Colombia: Memorias de Guerra y Dignidad. Bogotá: Imprenta Nacional, 2013.

Haas, Martin. "Michael Sattler: On the Way to Anabaptist Separation." In *Profiles of Radical Reformers*, edited by Hans-Jürgen Goertz, 132–243. Kitchener, ON: Herald, 1982.

Haile, Ahmed Ali and David Shenk. *Teatime in Mogadishu: My Journey as a Peace Ambassador in the World of Islam*. Harrisonburg, VA: Herald, 2011.

Hall, Thor. "Possibilities of Erasmian Influence on Denck and Hubmaier in Their Views on the Freedom of the Will." *MQR* 35 (1961) 149–70.

Hallie, Philip. *Lest Innocent Blood be Shed*. New York: Harper & Row, 1979.

Handbook of Information on the Mennonite Central Committee. Rev. ed. Akron, OH: MCC, 1945.

Harder, Helmut. *The Biblical Way of Peace*. Strasbourg: MWC, 1982.

Harder, Laureen. *Risk and Endurance: A History of Stirling Avenue Mennonite Church*. Kitchener, ON: Stirling Avenue Mennonite Church, 2003.

Harder, Leland, ed. *The Sources of Swiss Anabaptism: The Grebel Letters and Related Documents*. Scottsdale, PA: Herald, 1985.

Harding, Vincent. *Hope and History: Why We Must Share the Story of the Movement*. 2nd ed. Maryknoll, NY: Orbis, 2009.

Hasan, Noorhaidi. *Laskar Jihad: Islam, Militancy, and the Quest of Identity in Post-New Order Indonesia*. Ithaca, NY: Cornell Southeast Asia Program Publications, 2005.

Haude, Sigrid. "Gender Roles and Perspectives among Anabaptist and Spiritualist Groups." In *A Companion to Anabaptism and Spiritualism, 1521–1700*, edited by John D. Roth and James M. Stayer, 425–66. Brill's Companions to the Christian Tradition 6. Leiden: Brill, 2007.

Hecht, Linda Huebert. "Review of the Literature on Women in the Reformation and Radical Reformation." In *Profiles of Anabaptist Women: Sixteenth-Century Reforming Pioneers*, edited by C. Arnold Snyder and Linda A. Huebert Hecht, 406–15. Waterloo, ON: Wilfrid Laurier University Press, 1996.

Heck, Paul L. *Common Ground: Islam, Christianity, and Religious Pluralism*. Washington, DC: Georgetown University Press, 2009.

Hefner, Robert W. *Civil Islam: Muslims and Democratization in Indonesia*. Princeton: Princeton University Press, 2000.

———. *Hindu Javanese*. Princeton: Princeton University Press, 1989.

———. "The Study of Religious Freedom in Indonesia." *Review of Faith and International Affairs* 11.2 (2013) 18–27.
Heidebrecht, Paul G. "Introduction." *Mennonite Central Committee Peace Office Newsletter: Human Rights and the Quest for Justice and Peace* 41.2 (2011) 1–2.
Heidebrecht, Paul G., and Jenn Wiebe. "Advocacy and Peacebuilding: Making Distinctions and Connections." *Intersections* 1.1 (2013) 9–12.
Heisey, M. J. *Peace and Persistence: Tracing the Brethren in Christ Peace Witness through Three Generations*. Kent, OH: Kent State University Press, 2003.
Heisey, Nancy R., and Daniel S. Schipani, eds. *Theological Education on Five Continents: Anabaptist Perspectives: Consultation on Theological Education on Five Continents*. Barrakpore, India: Mennonite World Conference, 1997.
Henkin, Louis. *The Age of Rights*. New York: Columbia University Press, 1990.
Hergot, Hans. "On the New Transformation of the Christian Life." In *The Radical Reformation*, edited by Michael G. Baylor, 210–25. Cambridge Texts in the History of Political Thought. Cambridge: Cambridge University Press, 1991.
Hershberger, Emily. "A Neo-Anabaptist Approach to Missions: Ralph and Genevieve Buckwalter and the Hokkaido Mennonite Church, 1949–1980." *Mennonite Quarterly Review* 78 (2004) 385–414.
Hiebert, Bruce. "A Crisis of Masculinity: North American Mennonites and World War 1, 2008." Ph.D. diss., Simon Fraser University, 2008.
Hiebert, P. C. *Feeding the Hungry: Russia Famine 1919–1925*. Scottdale, PA: Mennonite Central Committee, 1929.
Hildebrand, Mary Anne. "Domestic Violence: A Challenge to Mennonite Faith and Peace Theology." *CGR* 10.1 (1992) 73–80.
Hillerbrand, Hans J. "Anabaptism and the Reformation: Another Look." *Church History* 29 (1960) 407–18.
———. "Radicalism in the Early Reformation: Varieties of Reformation in Church and Society." In *Radical Tendencies in the Reformation: Divergent Responses*, edited by Hans J. Hillerbrand, 25–41. Kirksville, MO: Sixteenth Century Journal Publishers, 1988.
Hochschild, Adam. *King Leopold's Ghost*. Boston: Houghton Mifflin, 1998.
Hoekema, Alle. *Dutch Mennonite Mission in Indonesia. Historical Essays*. Occasional Papers Series. Elkhart, IN: Institute of Mennonite Studies, 2001.
Hoffman, Melchior. "June/July 1533." In *Anabaptism in Outline*, edited by Walter Klaassen, 59–60. Classics of the Radical Reformation 3. Scottdale, PA: Herald, 1981.
Hooker, David Anderson, and Amy Potter Czajkowski. *Transforming Historical Harms*. Harrisonburg, VA: Coming to the Table and the Center for Justice and Peacebuilding at Eastern Mennonite University, 2011. http://comingtothetable.org/wp-content/uploads/2013/10/01-Transforming_Historical_Harms.pdf.
Horst, Willis. *Mision sin Conquista: Acompanamiento de Comunidades Indigenas Autoctonas como Practice Misionera Alternative*. Buenos Aires: Kairos, 2009.
Hostetler, Beulah Stauffer. "Nonresistance and Social Responsibility: Mennonites and Mainline Peace Emphasis, ca. 1950 to 1985." *MQR* 64 (1990) 49–73.
Huber, Tim. "Upside-Down Kingdom Down Under: From Amish and Hutterites to a Diverse Network, Anabaptism Draws Scattered Followers in Australia and New Zealand." *Mennonite World Review*. April 30, 2012. http://www.mennoworld.org/archived/2012/4/30/upside-down-kingdom-down-under/.

Hubmaier, Balthasar. "On Heretics and Those Who Burn Them." In *Balthasar Hubmaier: Theologian of Anabaptism*, translated and edited by H. Wayne Pipkin and John H. Yoder, 58–66. Classics of the Radical Reformation 5. Scottdale, PA: Herald, 1989.

———. "Summa of the Entire Christian Life." In *Balthasar Hubmaier: Theologian of Anabaptism*, translated and edited by H. Wayne Pipkin and John H. Yoder, 524–62. Classics of the Radical Reformation 5. Scottdale, PA: Herald, 1989.

Huebner, Christ K. *A Precarious Peace: Yoderian Explorations on Theology, Knowledge, and Identity*. Polyglossia: Radical Reformation Theologies 1. Scottdale, PA: Herald, 2006.

Hut, Hans. "The Mystery of Baptism, 1526–27." In *Anabaptism in Outline*, edited by Walter Klaassen, 48–53. Classics of the Radical Reformation 3. Scottdale, PA: Herald, 1981.

Hutter, Jacob. "The Fourth Epistle." In *Anabaptism in Outline*, edited by Walter Klaassen, 325–26. Classics of the Radical Reformation 3. Scottdale, PA: Herald, 1981.

———. "Letter to the Prisoners at the Hohenwart, 1535." In *Anabaptism in Outline*, edited by Walter Klaassen, 91–92. Classics of the Radical Reformation 3. Scottdale, PA: Herald, 1981.

Hynd, Doug. "Anabaptism Down Under: The Anabaptist Association of Australia and New Zealand." *Anabaptism Today* 25 (2000) 21–24.

"ICC at a glance." *International Criminal Court*. http://www.icc-cpi.int/en_menus/icc/about%20the%20court/icc%20at%20a%20glance/Pages/icc%20at%20a%20glance.aspx.

Illich, Ivan. "To Hell with Good Intentions." In *Combining Service and Learning: Cross-Cultural Learning*, edited by Jane C. Kendall, 314–20. Mt. Royal, NJ: National Society for Experimental Education, 1968.

Inchausti, Robert. *The Ignorant Perfection of Ordinary People*. Suny Series in Constructive Postmodern Thought. Albany: State University of New York Press, 1991.

International Crisis Group. *Africa Briefing: Back to the Brink in the Congo*. Brussels: International Crisis Group, 2004. http://www.crisisgroup.org/~/media/Files/africa/central-africa/dr-congo/B021%20Back%20to%20the%20Brink%20in%20the%20Congo.pdf.

———. "Religion in Kosovo." *International Crisis Group Balkan Report No. 105*. Pristina/Brussels (January 3, 2001) 1–16.

———. *Scramble for the Congo: Anatomy of an Ugly War*. Brussels: International Crisis Group, 2000. http://www.crisisgroup.org/~/media/Files/africa/central-africa/dr-congo/Scramble%20for%20the%20Congo%20Anatomy%20of%20an%20Ugly%20War.pdf.

International Fellowship of Reconciliation. *Peace Is the Will of God: A Testimony to the World Council of Churches*. Geneva: Brethren Service Commission, 1953.

"Interview: Tribunal Chief Prosecutor Louise Arbour." *Institute for War & Peace Reporting*. http://iwpr.net/report-news/interview-tribunal-chief-prosecutor-louise-arbour.

Jantzi, Jeanne, and Tim Shenk. "Indonesian Mennonites and Muslims Work Together after Earthquake." *A Common Place* (October 2010) 4–6.

Janzen, Rhoda. *Mennonite in a Little Black Dress: A Memoir of Going Home*. New York: Holt, 2010.

Johnston, Douglas, and Cynthia Sampson, eds. *Religion, the Missing Dimension of Statecraft*. New York: Oxford University Press, 1994.

Juhnke, James C. "Turning Points, Broken Ice, and *Glaubensgenossen*: What Happened at Prairie Street on July 27–28, 1920?" In *A Table of Sharing: Mennonite Central Committee and the Expanding Networks of Mennonite Identity*, edited by Alain Epp Weaver, 66–83. Telford, PA: Cascadia, 2011.

———. *Vision, Doctrine, War: Mennonite Identity and Organization in America, 1890–1930*. Mennonite Experience in America 3. Scottdale, PA: Herald, 1989.

———. "War and the Mennonite Agenda in the 20th Century." In *Unity amidst Diversity: Mennonite Central Committee at 75*. Akron: MCC, 1996.

Junne, Gerd and Willemjin Verkoren. "The Challenges of Postconflict Development." In *Postconflict Development: Meeting New Challenges*, edited by Gerd Junne and Willemjin Verkoren, 1–18. Boulder, CO: Rienner, 2005.

Justapaz, *Construyendo la Paz en Ambientes Eclesiales*. Bogotá: Justapaz, 2005.

Kahle, Wilhelm. *Evangelische Christen in Russland und der Sowjetunion*. Wuppertal: Oncken, 1978.

Kamen, Henry. *The Iron Century: Social Change in Europe, 1550–1650*. London: Weidenfeld & Nicolson, 1971.

Kamphuis, Bertine. "Economic Policy for Building Peace." In *Postconflict Development: Meeting New Challenges*, edited by Gerd Junne and Willemjin Verkoren, 185–210. Boulder, CO: Rienner, 2005.

Kateregga, Badru D., and David W. Shenk. *Islam and Christianity: A Muslim and Christian in Dialogue*. Grand Rapids: Eerdmans, 1980.

———. *A Muslim and a Christian in Dialogue*. Scottdale, PA: Herald, 1997.

Kaufman, Gordon D. "Jesus as Absolute Norm?: Some Questions." In *The Limits of Perfection: A Conversation with J. Lawrence Burkhholder*, edited by Rodney J. Sawatsky and Scott Holland, 118–21. Waterloo, ON: Institute of Anabaptist-Mennonite Studies, Conrad Grebel College, 1993.

Keim, Albert. *The CPS Story: An Illustrated History of Civilian Public Service*. Intercourse, PA: Good Books, 1990.

Kelly, Russ. *From Scoundrel to Scholar . . . The Russ Kelly Story*. Self-published, 2006.

Kern, Kathleen. *As Resident Aliens: Christian Peacemaker Teams in the West Bank, 1995–2005*. Eugene, OR: Cascade Books, 2010.

Kim, Kyong-Jung. "Anabaptism in Korea." In *Churches Engage Asian Traditions*, edited by John A. Lapp and C. Arnold Snyder, 311–14. Intercourse, PA: Good Books, 2011.

King, Andre "From Sectarianism to the World's Stage: An Analysis of Mennonite and Historic Peace Church Efforts at Voicing the Validity of Pacifism in Post-WWII Europe, and its Culmination in the Puidoux Conference of 1995." Goshen College History Senior Seminar Paper, 1999. Box 10, Folder 48, Mennonite Church Historical Committee John Horsch Mennonite History Essay Contest Records, 1949–2011. Mennonite Library and Archives. Bethel College, North Newton, KS.

Kingsbury, Damien, ed. *Violence in Between: Conflict and Security in Archipelagic Southeast Asia*. Singapore: Institute of Southeast Asian Studies, 2005.

Klaassen, Walter, ed. *Anabaptism in Outline*. Classics of the Radical Reformation 3. Scottdale, PA: Herald, 1981.

———. *Anabaptism: Neither Catholic nor Protestant*. Waterloo, ON: Conrad, 1973.

———. "Michael Gaismair: An Early Proponent of Social Justice." In *Profiles of Radical Reformers*, edited by Hans-Jürgen Goertz, 88–96. Kitchener, ON: Herald, 1982.

Klager, Andrew P. "From Victimization to Empathetic Solidarity: The Historical Seeds of Interreligious Peacebuilding and Human Rights Advocacy in Anabaptist-Mennonite Origins." *JMS* 32 (2014) 119–32.

———. "Mennonite Religious Values as a Resource for Peacebuilding between Muslims and Eastern Christians." *Peace Research: The Canadian Journal of Peace and Conflict Studies* 43 (2011) 127–55.

Klassen, A. J., ed. *Alternative Service for Peace in Canada during World War II, 1941–1946*. Abbotsford, BC: Mennonite Central Committee BC, 1998.

Klassen, John M. "Women and the Family among Dutch Anabaptist Martyrs." *MQR* 60 (1986) 548–71.

Klassen, Peter J. *Mennonites in Early Modern Poland and Prussia*. Baltimore, MD: Johns Hopkins University Press, 2011.

Klinken, Gerry van. *Communal Violence and Democratization in Indonesia*. Routledge Contemporary Southeast Asia Series 15. London: Routledge, 2007.

Klippenstein, Lawrence J. "Mennonite Pacifism and State Service in Russia: A Case Study in Church-State Relations, 1789–1936." PhD diss., University of Minnesota, 1984.

———. "Russian Revolution and Civil War." *Global Anabaptist Mennonite Encyclopedia Online*. Article published 1989. http://gameo.org/index.php?title=Russian_Revolution_and_Civil_War&oldid=93426.

Knowles, Paul, ed. *Piecemakers: The Story of the Ontario Mennonite Relief Sale and Quilt Auction*. New Hamburg, ON: English Garden, 2004.

Koontz, Gayle Gerber. "Peace Theology in Transition: North American Mennonite Peace Studies and Theology, 1906–2006." *MQR* 81 (2007) 77–96.

Koontz, Ted. "Thinking Theologically about War against Iraq." *Mennonite Quarterly Review* 77, no. 1 (January 2003): 93–108.

Koop, Heidi, comp., and Helga Dyck, ed. "The Band Plays On: Mennonite Pioneers of North Kildonan Reflect." Unpublished manuscript, Mennonite Heritage Centre, Winnipeg, Manitoba, 1998.

Krabill, James R. "Evangelical and Ecumenical Dimensions of Walking with AICs." In *Evangelical, Ecumenical and Anabaptist Missiologies in Conversation*, edited by James Krabill, Walter Sawatsky, and Van Engen, 240–47. Maryknoll, NY: Orbis, 2006.

———, David W. Shenk, and Linford Stutzman, eds. *Anabaptists Meeting Muslim: A Calling for Presence in the Way of Christ*. Scottdale, PA: Herald, 2005.

Krahn, Cornelius. *Dutch Anabaptism*. 2nd ed. Scottdale, PA: Herald, 1981.

———. "Einlage (Chortitza Mennonite Settlement, Zaporizhia Oblast, Ukraine)." *Global Anabaptist Mennonite Encyclopedia Online*. Article published 1956. http://gameo.org/index.php?title=Einlage_(Chortitza_Mennonite_Settlement,_Zaporizhia_Oblast,_Ukraine)&oldid=91674.

Kraybill, Donald *The Upside-Down Kingdom*. 25th anniv. ed. Harrisonburg, VA: Herald, 2003.

Krehbiel, Stephanie. "Staying Alive: How Martyrdom Made Me a Warrior." *Mennonite Life* 61 (2006). http://ml.bethelks.edu/issue/vol-61-no-4/article/staying-alive-how-martyrdom-made-me-a-warrior/.

Kreider, Alan. "The London Mennonite Centre's First Fifty Years." *Anabaptism Today* 32 (2003) 2–11.

Kreider, Alan, Eleanor Kreider, and Paulus Widjaja. *A Culture of Peace: God's Vision for the Church*. Intercourse, PA: Good Books, 2005.

Kreider, Alan, and Stuart Murray, eds. *Coming Home: Stories of Anabaptists in Britain and Ireland*. Scottdale, PA: Herald, 2000.

Kreider, Robert S. "Anabaptism and Humanism: An Inquiry into the Relationship of Humanism to the Evangelical Anabaptists." *MQR* 26 (1952) 123–41.

———. *My Early Years: An Autobiography*. Kitchener, ON: Pandora, 2002.

Kreider, Robert, and Rachel Waltner Goossen. *Hungry, Thirsty, a Stranger: The MCC Experience*. Mennonite Central Committee Story Series 5. Scottdale, PA: Herald, 1988.

Kumar, Chetan. "Conclusion." In *Peacebuilding as Politics: Cultivating Peace in Fragile Societies*, edited by Elizabeth M. Cousens and Chetan Kumar, 183–220. Boulder, CO: Rienner, 2001.

LaCapra, Dominick. *Writing History, Writing Trauma*. Baltimore: John Hopkins University Press, 2001.

Lapp, John A. "The Peace Mission of the Mennonite Central Committee." *MQR* 44 (1970) 281–97.

Latourette, Kenneth Scott. *A History of Christianity*. Vol. 1, *Beginnings to 1500*. Rev. ed. New York: Harper & Row, 1975.

Lederach, John Paul. "Building Peace in Somalia." *Sojourners Magazine* (January 1994). http://sojo.net/magazine/1994/01/building-peace-somalia.

———. *Building Peace: Sustainable Reconciliation in Divided Societies*. Washington, DC: United States Institute of Peace, 1998.

———. Conflict Transformation in Protracted Internal Conflicts: The Case for a Comprehensive Network." In *Conflict Transformation*, edited by Kumar Rupesinghe, 201–22. New York: St. Martin's, 1995.

———. "Journey from Resolution to Transformative Peacebuilding." In *From the Ground Up: Mennonite Contributions to International Peacebuilding*, edited by Cynthia Sampson and John Paul Lederach, 45–55. Oxford: Oxford University Press, 2000.

———. *The Journey toward Reconciliation*. Scottdale, PA: Herald, 1999.

———. *The Little Book of Conflict Transformation: Clear Articulation of the Guiding Principles by a Pioneer in the Field*. Intercourse, PA: Good Books, 2003.

———. "Mennonite Central Committee Efforts in Somalia and Somaliland." In *From the Ground Up: Mennonite Contributions to International Peacebuilding*, edited by Cynthia Sampson and John Paul Lederach, 141–49. Oxford: Oxford University Press, 2000.

———. "Missionaries Facing Conflict and Violence: Problems and Prospects." *Missiology: An International Review* 20 (1992) 11–19.

———. *The Moral Imagination: The Art and Soul of Building Peace*. Oxford: Oxford University Press, 2005.

———. "Of Nets, Nails and Problemas: A Folk Vision of Conflict in Central America." Ph.D. diss., University of Colorado, 1988.

———. "Pacifism in Contemporary Conflict: A Christian Perspective." Paper commissioned by the US Institute of Peace, Washington, DC (July 20, 1993).

———. *Preparing for Peace: Conflict Transformation Across Cultures*. Syracuse, NY: Syracuse University Press, 1995.

———. *Seguir a Jesús: El Camino de la Etica Cristiana*. Mexico City: El Faro, 1993.

———, and R. Scott Appleby. "Strategic Peacebuilding: An Overview." In *Strategies of Peace: Transforming Conflict in a Violent World*, edited by Daniel Philpott and Gerard Powers, 19–44. New York: Oxford University Press, 2010.

Lederach, John Paul, and Mark Chupp. *El Conflicto y la Violencia: En Busqueda de Alternativas Creativas*. Guatemala City: Semilla, 1994.

Lederach, John Paul, and Ronald Kraybill. "Paradox of Popular Justice: A Practitioner's View." In *The Possibility of Popular Justice: A Case Study of Community Mediation in the United States*, edited by Sally Engle Merry and Neil Milner. Ann Arbor: University of Michigan Press, 1995.

Lederach, John Paul, Ron Kraybill, and Alice Price. *Conflict Transformation: The Mediation Training Manual*. Akron, PA: Mennonite Conciliation Service, 1989.

Lehman, James O. and Steven M. Nolt. *Mennonites, Amish, and the American Civil War*. Baltimore: Johns Hopkins University Press, 2007.

Lehman, M. C. *The History and Principles of Mennonite Relief Work: An Introduction*. Mennonite Relief Service 1. Akron, PA: Mennonite Central Committee, 1945.

Letkemann, Peter. "The Fate of Mennonites in the Volga-Ural Region, 1929–1941." *JMS* 26 (2008) 181–200.

Levi-Strauss, Claude. *Myth and Meaning*. New York: Schocken, 1979.

Li, Darryl. "The Gaza Strip as Laboratory: Notes in the Wake of Disengagement." *Journal of Palestine Studies* 35.2 (2006) 38–55.

Liechty, Joseph, and Cecelia Clegg. *Moving beyond Sectarianism: Religion, Conflict, and Reconciliation in Northern Ireland*. Blackrock, Co. Dublin: Columba, 2001.

Littell, Franklin H. *The Origins of Sectarian Protestantism*. New York: Macmillan, 1952.

Loewen, Helmut-Harry, and James Urry. "Protecting Mammon: Some Dilemmas of Mennonite Nonresistance in Late Imperial Russia and the Origins of the Selbstschutz." *JMS* 9 (1991) 34–53.

———. "American Nationalism and the Rural Immigrant: A Case Study of Two Midwest Communities, 1900–1925." *JMS* 12 (1994) 118–36.

———. *Family, Church, and Market: A Mennonite Community in the Old and New Worlds, 1850–1930*. Toronto: University of Toronto Press, 1993.

Loewen, Royden, and Steven M. Nolt. *Seeking Places of Peace*. Global Mennonite History Series: North America. Intercourse, PA: Good Books, 2012.

Lozano, Alix. "A 'Weak Church' Seeks Security in a Violent Land: Experiences of the Colombian Mennonite Church." In *At Peace and Unafraid: Public Order, Security, and the Wisdom of the Cross*, edited by Duane K. Friesen and Gerald W. Schlabach, 291–309. Scottdale, PA: Herald, 2005.

Lyotard, Jean-François. *The Postmodern Condition: A Report on Knowledge*. Translated by Geoff Bennington and Brian Massumi. Minneapolis: University of Minnesota Press, 1984.

MacGregor, Felipe E., SJ, and Marcial Rubio Correa. "Rejoinder to the Theory of Structural Violence." In *The Culture of Violence*, edited by Kumar Rupesinghe and Marcial Rubio Correa. New York: United Nations University Press, 1994.

MacMaster, Richard K. *Land, Piety, Peoplehood: The Establishment of Mennonite Communities in America, 1683–1790*. Mennonite Experience in America 1. Scottdale, PA: Herald, 1985.

Malkki, Liisa H. *Purity and Exile: Violence, Memory and National Cosmology among Hutu Refugees in Tanzania*. Chicago: University of Chicago Press, 1995.

Mandel, Robert. *Perception, Decision Making, and Conflict.* Washington, DC: University Press of America, 1979.

Maoz, Ifat. "Does Contact Work in Protracted Asymmetrical Conflict? Appraising 20 Years of Reconciliation-Aimed Encounters between Israeli Jews and Palestinians." *JPR* 48 (2011) 115–25.

———. "Is There Contact at All? Intergroup Interaction in Planned Contact Interventions between Jews and Arabs in Israel." *International Journal of Intercultural Relations* 26.2 (2002) 185–97.

Marr, Lucille. "Paying 'The Price of War': Canadian Women and the Churches on the Home Front." In *Canadian Churches and the First World War*, edited by Gordon L. Heath, 263–80. McMaster Divinity College Press General Series. Eugene, OR: Pickwick Publications, 2014.

———. *The Transforming Power of a Century: Mennonite Central Committee and its Evolution in Ontario.* Kitchener, ON: Pandora, 2003.

Marshall, Christopher D. "Offending, Restoration, and the Law-Abiding Community: Restorative Justice in the New Testament and in the New Zealand Experience." *Journal of the Society of Christian Ethics* 27.2 (2007) 3–30.

Martin, Steven P. "The Presence of Violence in the Mennonite Church and Family Systems." M.Th. Thesis, Waterloo Lutheran Seminary, 1990.

Marusic, Sinisa. "Religious Tolerance Patchy in Balkans, State Department Says." *Balkan Insight.* July 29, 2014. http://www.balkaninsight.com/en/article/report-minority-religious-groups-under-threat-in-balkans.

Matthews, Mark. *Smoke Jumping on the Western Fire Line: Conscientious Objectors during World War II.* Norman: University of Oklahoma Press, 2006.

Mayo, Peter. *Gramsci, Freire, and Adult Education: Possibilities for Transformative Action.* Global Perspectives on Adult Education and Training. New York: Zed, 1999.

McKenny, Gerald. *The Analogy of Grace: Karl Barth's Moral Theology.* Oxford: Oxford University Press, 2013.

McLaughlin, Elizabeth W. "Engendering the *Imago Dei*: A Rhetorical Study of Quilts and Quiltmaking as Metaphor and Visual Parable in the Anabaptist Peace Tradition." Ph.D. diss., Regent University, 2007.

McLuhan, Marshall. "The Violence of the Media." *Canadian Forum* 56.664 (1976) 9–12.

Mennonite Central Committee Canada Collection. Mennonite Heritage Centre, Winnipeg, Manitoba.

Mennonite Central Committee, Peace Section. *The Kingdom of God and the Way of Peace.* Lombard, IL: MWC, 1979.

Mennonite World Conference Records, 1923–2012. Mennonite Church USA Archives—Goshen. Goshen, Indiana.

Michel, Thomas, SJ. "Where to Now? Ways Forward for Interreligious Dialogue: Images of Abraham as Models of Interreligious Encounter." *Muslim World* 100 (2010) 530–38.

Midgley, Mary. *The Myths We Live By.* New York: Routledge, 2003.

Miller, Donald E. *Seeking Peace in Africa: Stories from African Peacemakers.* Telford, PA: Cascadia, 2007.

Miller, Donald E., Gerard Guiton, and Paulus Widjaja. *Overcoming Violence in Asia: The Role of the Church in Seeking Cultures of Peace.* Telford, PA: Cascadia, 2011.

Miller, Joseph S. "A History of the Mennonite Conciliation Service, International Conciliation Service, and Christian Peacemaker Teams." In *From the Ground Up: Mennonite Contributions to International Peacebuilding*, edited by Cynthia Sampson and John Paul Lederach, 3–29. Oxford: Oxford University Press, 2000.

Miller, Keith Graber. *Wise as Serpents, Innocent as Doves: American Mennonites Engage Washington*. Knoxville: University of Tennessee Press, 1996.

Mitchell, Christopher. "Beyond Resolution: What Does Conflict Transformation Actually Transform?" May 2002. http://www.gmu.edu/programs/icar/pcs/CM83PCS.htm.

Moch, Leslie Page. *Moving Europeans: Migration in Western Europe since 1650*. Bloomington: Indiana University Press, 1992.

Mock, Melanie Springer. *Writing Peace: The Unheard Voices of Great War Mennonite Objectors*. Studies in Anabaptist and Mennonite History 40. Telford, PA: Pandora, 2003.

Morsink, Johannes. *The Universal Declaration of Human Rights: Origins, Drafting, and Intent*. Philadelphia: University of Pennsylvania Press, 1999.

Moyaert, Marianne. "The (Un-)translatability of Religions? Ricœurs Linguistic Hospitality as Model for Inter-religious Dialogue." *Exchange* 37 (2008) 337–64.

Moyer, Bill, et al. *Doing Democracy: The MAP Model for Organizing Social Movements*. Gabriola Island, BC: New Society Publishers, 2001.

Mpangala, Gaudens P. "Conflict Resolution and Peace Building in Africa as a Process: Case Studies of Burundi and the Democratic Republic of the Congo." Paper presented at the Nyerere Week Conference, 22–23 April 2004.

Murray, Stuart. "Anabaptist Network." *Global Anabaptist Mennonite Encyclopedia Online*. In *Global Anabaptist Mennonite Encyclopedia Online*. March 2012. http://gameo.org/index.php?title=Anabaptist_Network&oldid=112117.

———. *Church after Christendom*. After Christendom. Milton Keynes, UK: Paternoster, 2004.

Nation, Mark Thiessen. *John Howard Yoder: Mennonite Patience, Evangelical Witness, Catholic Convictions*. Grand Rapids: Eerdmans, 2006.

Neufeld, Tom Yoder. "Varieties of Contemporary Mennonite Peace Witness: From Passivism to Pacifism, from Nonresistance to Resistance." *CGR* 10 (1992) 243–57.

Neufeldt, Colin P. "Reforging Mennonite *Spetspereselentsy*: The Experience of Mennonite Exiles at Siberian Special Settlements in the Omsk, Tomsk, Novosibirsk, and Narym Regions, 1930–1933." *JMS* 30 (2012) 269–315.

———. "Separating the Sheep from the Goats: The Role of Mennonites and Non-Mennonites in the Dekulakization of Khortitsa, Ukraine (1928–1930)." *MQR* 83 (2009) 221–91.

Nickel, Janis E. "In the Name of Harmony Voices Are Lost." *MCC Women's Concerns Report* 121 (July–August 1995) 5–6.

Nikol'skaia, Tat'iana. *Russkii Protestantizm I Gosudarstvennaia Vlast' V 1905–1991 Godakh*. St. Petersburg: European University Press, 2009.

Nolan, John P., ed. *The Essential Erasmus*. New York: Mentor, 1964.

Nordholt, Henk Schulte, and Gerry van Klinken, eds. *Renegotiating Boundaries: Local Politics in Post-Suharto Indonesia*. Verhandelingen van het Koninklijk Instituut voor Taal-, Land- en Volkenkunde 238. Leiden: KITLV Press, 2007.

Northey, Wayne. "Restorative Justice and Spiritual Origins." Last modified November 19, 2004. http://m2w2.com/wp/wp-content/uploads/2009/08/rj-spiritual-origins-nov-2004.pdf.

Omar, A. Rashied. "Embracing the 'Other' as an Extension of the Self: Muslim Reflections on the Epistle to the Hebrews 13:2." *Anglican Theological Review* 91 (2009) 433–41.

OSCE Mission in Kosovo. "Role of Religious Leaders Important in Fostering Respect and Understanding between Different Communities in Kosovo, OSCE Conference Participants Say." September 17, 2013. http://www.osce.org/kosovo/105027.

Oyer, John S., and Robert Kreider. *Mirror of the Martyrs: Stories of Courage, Inspiringly Retold, of 16th Century Anabaptists Who Gave Their Lives for Their Faith*. Intercourse, PA: Good Books, 1990.

Ozment, Steven. *The Age of Reform, 1250–1550*. New Haven: Yale University Press, 1980.

Packull, Werner O. *Mysticism and the Early South German-Austrian Anabaptist Movement, 1525–1531*. Studies in Anabaptist and Mennonite History 19. Scottdale, PA: Herald, 1977.

Pariela, Tonny D. "Damai Di Tengah Konflik Maluku: Preserved Social Capital sebagai Basis Survival Strategy." PhD diss., Universitas Kristen Satya Wacana, 2008.

Pater, Calvin A. *Karlstadt as the Father of the Baptist Movements: The Emergence of Lay Protestantism*. Toronto: University of Toronto Press, 1984.

Patkau, Esther. *Canadian Women in Mission, 1895–1952–2002*. Saskatoon, SK: Canadian Women in Mission, 2002.

Patton, Michael Quinn. *Developmental Evaluation*. New York: Guilford, 2010.

Peachy, Titus, and Linda Gehman Peachy. *Seeking Peace*. Intercourse, PA: Good Books, 1991.

Peachey, Urban. *The Role of the Church in Society*. Carol Stream, IL: MWC, 1988.

Pearlman, Wendy. *Violence, Nonviolence and the Palestinian National Movement*. Cambridge: Cambridge University Press, 2011.

Penner, Carol Jean. "Mennonite Silences and Feminist Voices: Peace Theology and Violence Against Women." Ph.D. diss., Toronto School of Theology, 1999.

Petroff, Elizabeth Alvilda. *Medieval Women's Visionary Literature*. New York: Oxford University Press, 1986.

Philips, Dirk. "The Church of God, 1558." In *Anabaptism in Outline*, edited by Walter Klaassen, 298–300. Classics of the Radical Reformation 3. Scottdale, PA: Herald, 1981.

———. "The True Knowledge of Jesus Christ, 1558." In *Anabaptism in Outline*, edited by Walter Klaassen, 36–39. Classics of the Radical Reformation 3. Scottdale, PA: Herald, 1981.

Philpott, Daniel. *Just and Unjust Peace: An Ethic of Political Reconciliation*. New York: Oxford University Press, 2012.

Philpott, Daniel, and Gerard Powers, eds. *Strategies of Peace: Transforming Conflict in a Violent World*. New York: Oxford University Press, 2010.

Pierson, Ruth Roach. *'They're Still Women after All': The Second World War and Canadian Womanhood*. Toronto, ON: McClelland & Stewart, 1986.

Piterberg, Gabriel. *The Returns of Zionism: Myths, Politics, and Scholarship in Israel*. London: Verso, 2008.

Plett, Delbert F. *Johann Plett: A Mennonite Family Saga*. Steinbach, MB: Crossway, 2003.

"Preamble, Universal Declaration of Human Rights, 1948." In *Basic Documents on Human Rights*. Edited by Ian Brownlie. 3rd ed. Oxford: Clarendon, 1992.

Prendergast, John. *Frontline Diplomacy: Humanitarian Aid and Conflict in Africa*. Boulder, CO: Rienner, 1996.

Prentice, Alison, et al. *Canadian Women: A History*. Toronto, ON: Harcourt Brace Jovanovich, 1988.

Pringle, Robert. *Understanding Islam in Indonesia: Politics and Diversity*. Honolulu: Hawaii University Press, 2010.

Proceedings: Witnessing to Christ in Today's World: Mennonite World Conference, Assembly 12, Winnipeg. Strasbourg, France: Mennonite World Conference, 1991.

Puljek-Shank, Randall. "Mennonite Experience with Interfaith and Ecumenical Work in Southeast Europe." In *Borders and Bridges: Mennonite Witness in a Religiously Diverse World*, edited by Peter Dula and Alain Epp Weaver, 132–49. Scottdale PA: Cascadia, 2007.

Puljek-Shank, Randall, and Amela Puljek-Shank. "The Contribution of Trauma Healing to Peacebuilding in Southeast Europe." In *Peacebuilding in Traumatized Societies*, edited by Barry Hart, 155–84. Lanham, MD: University Press of America, 2008.

Qurtuby, Sumanto Al. "Peacebuilding in Indonesia: Christian–Muslim Alliances in Ambon Island." *Islam and Christian–Muslim Relations* 24 (2013) 349–67.

———. "Religious Women for Peace and Reconciliation in Contemporary Indonesia." *International Journal on World Peace* 31 (2014) 27–58.

———. "Interreligious Violence, Civic Peace, and Citizenship: Christians and Muslims in Maluku, Eastern Indonesia." PhD diss., Boston University, 2012.

Raber, Mary. "History of MCC Programs in the Former Soviet Union." Unpublished paper, 2008, III–2.

Ramseyer, Edna. "Will Ye Heed the Call?" *Missionary News and Notes* (November 1943) 1.

Rasmussen, J. Lewis. "Peacemaking in the Twenty-First Century: New Rules, New Roles, New Actors." In *Peacemaking in International Conflict: Methods and Techniques*, edited by I. William Zartman and J. Lewis Rasmussen, 23–50. Washington, DC: United States Institute of Peace Press, 1997.

Ratner, Steven R., and Jason S. Abrams. *Accountability for Human Rights Atrocities in International Law: Beyond Nuremberg*. Oxford: Oxford University Press, 2001.

Raz-Krakotzkin, Amnon. *Exil et Souveraineté: Judaïsme, sionisme, et pensée binationale*. Paris: La Fabrique, 2007.

———. "A National Colonial Theology: Religion, Orientalism, and the Construction of the Secular in Zionist Discourse." *Tel Aviver Jahrbuch für deutsche Geschichte* 30 (2002) 312–26.

———. "A Peace without Arabs: The Discourse of Peace and the Limits of Israeli Consciousness." In *After Oslo: New Realities, Old Problems*, edited by George Giacaman and Dag Jørund Lønning, 59–76. London: Pluto, 1998.

Redekop, Calvin W. *The Pax Story: Service in the Name of Christ 1951–1976*. Telford, PA: Pandora, 2001.

Redekop, Magdalene. "Through the Mennonite Looking Glass." In *Why I Am a Mennonite: Essays on Mennonite Identity*, edited by Harry Loewen, 226–53. Kitchener, ON: Herald, 1988.

Regehr, T. D. *Mennonites in Canada*. Vol. 3, *1939–1970: A People Transformed*. Toronto: University of Toronto Press, 1996.

———. "Lost Sons: the Canadian Mennonite Soldiers of WW II." *MQR* 66 (1992) 461–80.

Reimer, John C. *75 Gedenkfeier der Mennonitischen Eindwanderung in Manitoba, Canada*. Winnipeg, MB: North Kildonan, 1949.

Reimer, William and Bruce Guenther. "Relationships, Rights, and 'Relief': Ninety Years of MCC's Integrated Response to Humanitarian Crises." In *A Table of Sharing: Mennonite Central Committee and the Expanding Networks of Mennonite Identity*, edited by Alain Epp Weaver, 353–374. Telford, PA: Cascadia, 2011.

Rempel, Gerhard. "Mennonites and the Holocaust: From Collaboration to Perpetuation." *MQR* 84 (2010) 507–49.

Rempel, John. "Makhno, Nestor (1988–1934)." In *Global Anabaptist Mennonite Encyclopedia Online*. Article published 1957. http://gameo.org/index.php?title=Makhno,_Nestor_(1888-1934)&oldid=101752.

Reychler, Luc. "From Conflict to Sustainable Peacebuilding: Concepts and Analytic Tools—Conceptual Framework." In *Peace-Building: A Field Guide*, edited by Luc Reychler and Thania Paffenholz, 3–15. Boulder, CO: Rienner, 2001.

Reynolds, Thomas E. "Toward a Wider Hospitality: Rethinking Love of Neighbour in Religions of the Book." *Irish Theological Quarterly Review* 75 (2010) 175–87.

Richards, Paul. *Fighting for the Rain Forests: War, Youth and Resources in Sierra Leone*. Oxford: Curry, 1996.

Riedeman, Peter. "Account of Our Religion, Doctrine and Faith, 1542." In *Anabaptism in Outline*, edited by Walter Klaassen, 28–31. Classics of the Radical Reformation 3. Scottdale, PA: Herald, 1981.

Roper, Lyndal. *The Holy Household: Women and Morals in Reformation Augsburg*. Oxford: Clarendon, 1989.

Roth, John D. *Beliefs: Mennonite Faith and Practice*. Scottdale, PA: Herald, 2005.

———. *Choosing against War: A Christian View*. Intercourse, PA: Good Books, 2002.

———. "Forgiveness and the Healing of Memories: An Anabaptist-Mennonite Perspective." *Journal of Ecumenical Studies* 42 (2007) 573–88.

———. "The Plight of COs Continues Today." *The Mennonite* 17.4 (2014) 9.

———. "Recent Currents in the Historiography of the Radical Reformation." *Church History* 71 (2002) 523–35.

Roth, John D., and James M. Stayer, eds. *A Companion to Anabaptism and Spiritualism, 1521–1700*. Brill's Companions to the Christian Tradition 6. Leiden: Brill, 2007.

Roth, Lorraine. *Willing Service: Stories of Ontario Mennonite Women*. Waterloo, ON: Mennonite Historical Society of Ontario, 1992.

Rott, Jean. "La Guerre des Paysans et la Ville de Strasbourg." In *Investigationes Historicae. Eglises et Société au XVI siècle*, 1:199–208. Strasbourg: Oberlin, 1986.

Rupesinghe, Kumar, ed. *Conflict Transformation*. New York: Palgrave Macmillan, 1995.

———. "Conflict Transformation." In *Conflict Transformation*, edited by Kumar Rupesinghe, 65–92. New York: Palgrave Macmillan, 1995.

Said, Edward W. *After the Last Sky: Palestinian Lives*. New York: Columbia University Press, 1999.

———. *Culture and Imperialism*. New York: Vintage, 1994.

———. "Introduction: The Right of Return at Last." In *Palestinian Refugees: The Right of Return*, edited by Naseer Aruri, 1–6. London: Pluto, 2001.

———. *Representations of the Intellectual: The 1993 Reith Lectures*. London: Vintage, 1994.

Salomons, Dirk. "Security: An Absolute Prerequisite." In *Postconflict Development: Meeting New Challenges*, edited by Gerd Junne and Willemjin Verkoren, 19–42. Boulder, CO: Rienner, 2005.

Sampson, Cynthia, and John Paul Lederach, eds. *From the Ground Up: Mennonite Contributions to International Peacebuilding*. New York: Oxford University Press, 2000.

Sattler, Michael. "Trial and Martyrdom." In *The Legacy of Michael Sattler*. Translated and edited by John H. Yoder. Scottdale, PA: Herald, 1973.

Savin, Andrei I. "'Divide and Rule': Religious Policies of the Soviet Government and Evangelical Churches in the 1920s." Translated by Walter Sawatsky. *Religion in Eastern Europe* 32 (2012) 1–18.

Sawatsky, Walter. "Changing Mentalities: Inter-Relationships between Mennonites and Slavic Evangelicals in Siberia and Central Asia." *JMS* 30 (2012) 315–63.

———. "From Russian to Soviet Mennonites 1941–1988." In *Mennonites in Russia*, edited John Friesen, 299–337. Winnipeg: CMBC Publications, 1989.

———. "Historical Roots of a Post-Gulag Theology for Russian Mennonites." *MQR* 86 (2002) 149–80.

———. "Pacifist Protestants in Soviet Russia between the Wars." In *The Long Way of Russian Pacifism (Russian)*, edited by Tatiana Pavlova, 262–84. Moscow: Russian Academy of Sciences, Institute of World History, 1997.

———. *Soviet Evangelicals since World War II*. 1981. Reprinted, Eugene, OR: Wipf & Stock, 2007.

Scharnschlager, Leopold. "Leupold Scharnschlager's Farewell to the Strasbourg Council." Translated and edited by William Klassen. *MQR* 42 (1968) 211–18.

Schlabach, Theron F. *Gospel versus Gospel: Mission and the Mennonite Church, 1863–1944*. Studies in Anabaptist and Mennonite History 21. Scottdale, PA: Herald, 1980.

———. "The Humble Become 'Aggressive Workers': Mennonites Organize for Mission, 1880–1910." *MQR* 52 (1978) 113–26.

———. "Humility." In *Global Anabaptist Mennonite Encyclopedia Online*. Published 1989. http://gameo.org/index.php?title=Humility.

———. *Peace, Faith, Nation: Mennonites and Amish in Nineteenth-Century America*. Mennonite Experience in America 2. Scottdale, PA: Herald, 1988.

———. "Reveille for *Die Stillen im Lande*: A Stir Among Mennonites in the Late Nineteenth Century." *MQR* 51 (1977) 213–26.

Schrock-Shenk, Carolyn, and Lawrence Ressler, eds. *Making Peace with Conflict*. Scottdale, PA: Herald, 1999.

———, and Jim Stutzman. *Mediation and Facilitation Training Manual: Foundations and Skills for Constructive Conflict Transformation*. 3rd ed. Akron, PA: Mennonite Conciliation Service, 1995.

Schulman, Miriam, and Amal Barkouki-Winter. "The Extra Mile." *Issues in Ethics* 11. 1. Article published Winter 2000. http://www.scu.edu/ethics/publications/iie/v11n1/hospitality.html.

"The Scope and Application of the Principle of Universal Jurisdiction: ICRC Statement to the United Nations, 2013." *International Committee of the Red Cross*. Last modified October 18, 2013. http://www.icrc.org/eng/resources/documents/statement/2013/united-nations-universal-jurisdiction-statement-2013-10-18.htm.

Scribner, Robert. *The German Reformation*. Atlantic Highlands, NJ: Humanities, 1986.

———. "Religion, Society and Culture: Reorienting the Reformation." *History Workshop* 14 (1982) 2–22.

Seiling, Jonathan. *Feeding the Neighbouring Enemy: Mennonite Women in Niagara during the War of 1918.* St. Catharines, ON: Gelassenheit, 2012.

Sensenig, Peter M. "Peace Clan: Mennonite Theology and Practice of Peacemaking in Somalia, 1953–2013." Ph.D. diss., Fuller Theological Seminary, 2013.

Shah, Meera. "'A Different Kind of Memory': An Interview with Zochrot." *Middle East Report* 244 (Fall 2007) 34–37.

Shelley, David. "Asia Conference Chooses Directions in Taiwan." *Courier* 1.3 (1986) 1–2.

Shenk, David W. *Global Gods: Exploring the Role of Religions in Modern Societies.* Scottdale, PA: Herald, 1999.

———. *Journeys of the Muslim Nation and the Christian Church: Exploring the Mission of Two Communities.* Scottdale, PA: Herald, 2003.

Shenk, David W., and Linford Stutzman, eds. *Practicing Truth: Confident Witness in Our Pluralistic World.* Scottdale, PA: Herald, 1999.

Shenk, Gerald. "Anonymous are the Peacemakers." *Christianity Today* 44.14 (4 December 2000) 31–41.

Shenk, Marie. *Mennonite Encounter with Judaism in Israel: An MBM Story of Creative Presence Spanning Four Decades, 1953–1993.* Elkhart, IN: Mennonite Mission Network, 2000.

Shenk, Wilbert, ed. *Anabaptism and Mission.* Missionary Studies 10. Scottdale, PA: Herald, 1984.

Shulman, David. *Dark Hope: Working for Peace in Israel and Palestine.* Chicago: University of Chicago Press, 2007.

Sidel, John T. *Riots, Pogroms, Jihad: Religious Violence in Indonesia.* Ithaca, NY: Cornell University Press, 2006.

Sider, Ronald. "God's People Reconciling." In *Eleventh Mennonite World Conference Proceedings, July 24–29, 1984,* 224–32. Lombard, IL: Mennonite World Conference, 1984.

Siemens, Ruth Derksen. "Quilt as Text and Text as Quilt: The Influence of Genre in the Mennonite Girls' Home of Vancouver (1930–1960)." *JMS* 17 (1999) 118–30.

Silberstein, Laurence J. *The Postzionism Debates: Knowledge and Power in Israeli Culture.* New York: Routledge, 1999.

Simons, Menno. "Confession of the Distressed Christians, 1552." In *The Complete Writings of Menno Simons,* translated by Leonard Verduin and edited by J. C. Wenger, 499–522. Scottdale, PA: Herald, 1956.

———. "Encouragement to Christian Believers, 1556." In *The Complete Writings of Menno Simons,* translated by Leonard Verduin and edited by J. C. Wenger, 1046–49. Scottdale, PA: Herald, 1956.

———. "Foundation of Christian Doctrine, c. 1537." In *The Complete Writings of Menno Simons,* translated by Leonard Verduin and edited by J. C. Wenger, 103–226. Scottdale, PA: Herald, 1956.

———. "Reply to Gellius Faber, 1554." In *The Complete Writings of Menno Simons,* translated by Leonard Verduin and edited by J.C. Wenger, 623–781. Scottdale, PA: Herald, 1956.

———. "Why I Do Not Cease Teaching and Writing, 1539." In *The Complete Writings of Menno Simons,* translated by Leonard Verduin and edited by J. C. Wenger, 289–320. Scottdale, PA: Herald, 1956.

Sine, Tom. *The Mustard Seed Conspiracy: You Can Make a Difference in Tomorrow's Troubled World.* Waco, TX: Word, 1981.

Sisk, Timothy D. "Power-sharing after Civil Wars: Matching Problems to Solutions." In *Contemporary Peacemaking: Conflict, Violence, and Peace Processes,* edited by John Darby and Roger Mac Ginty, 139–50. New York: Palgrave Macmillan, 2003.

Sitler, Arlene. "A Challenge to Mennonite Women." *Women's Activities Letter* 18 (February 1946) 1–3.

Smith, Kathleen E. *Remembering Stalin's Victims: Popular Memory and the End of the USSR.* New York: Cornell University Press, 1996.

Snyder, C. Arnold. *Anabaptist History and Theology: An Introduction.* Kitchener, ON: Pandora, 1995.

———. "Beyond Polygenesis: Recovering the Unity and Diversity of Anabaptist Theology." In *Essays in Anabaptist Theology,* edited by H. Wayne Pipkin, 1–33. Text Reader Series 5. Elkhart, IN: Institute of Mennonite Studies, 1994.

———. "Mysticism and the Shape of Anabaptist Spirituality." In *Commoners and Community,* edited by C. Arnold Snyder, 195–215. Kitchener, ON: Pandora, 2002.

———. "Swiss Anabaptism: The Beginnings." In *A Companion to Anabaptism and Spiritualism, 1521–1700,* edited by John D. Roth and James M. Stayer, 45–82. Brill's Companions to the Christian Tradition 6. Leiden: Brill, 2007

Snyder, C. Arnold, and Linda A. Huebert Hecht, eds. *Profiles of Anabaptist Women: Sixteenth-Century Reforming Pioneers.* Studies in Women and Religion/Etudes sur les femmes et la religion 3. Waterloo, ON: Wilfrid Laurier University Press, 1996.

Sokalski, Henryk J. *An Ounce of Prevention: Macedonia and the UN Experience in Preventive Diplomacy.* Washington DC: United States Institute of Peace, 2003.

Spencer, Metta. "Islamic Politics in the Balkans: A Short History." *Peace Magazine* (January–March, 2002) 24. http://peacemagazine.org/archive/v18n1p24.htm.

Sprunger, Keith L. "God's Powerful Army of the Weak: Anabaptist Women of the Radical Reformation." In *Triumph over Silence: Women in Protestant History,* edited by Richard L. Greaves, 45–74. Contributions to the Study of Religion 15. Westport, CT: Greenwood, 1985.

Stayer, James M. *Anabaptists and the Sword.* 2nd ed. Lawrence, KS: Coronado, 1976.

———. *The German Peasants' War and Anabaptist Community of Goods.* McGill-Queen's Studies in Religion 6. Montreal: McGill-Queen's University Press, 1991.

———. "Swiss-South German Anabaptism, 1526–1540." In *A Companion to Anabaptism and Spiritualism, 1521–1700,* edited by John D. Roth and James M. Stayer, 83–118. Brill's Companions to the Christian Tradition 6. Leiden: Brill, 2007.

Stayer, James M., Werner O. Packull, and Klaus Deppermann. "From Monogenesis to Polygenesis: Historical Discussion of Anabaptist Origins." *MQR* 49 (1975) 83–121.

Stauffer, G. Ethelbert. "The Anabaptist Theology of Martyrdom." In *Essays in Anabaptist Theology,* edited by H. Wayne Pipkin, 211–44. Text Reader Series 5. Elkhart, IN: Institute of Mennonite Studies, 1994.

Steele, David. "At the Front Lines of the Revolution: East Germany's Churches Give Sanctuary and Succor to the Purveyors of Change." In *Religion, the Missing Dimension of Statecraft,* edited by Douglas Johnston and Cynthia Sampson, 119–52. New York: Oxford University Press, 1994.

———. "Christianity in Bosnia-Herzegovina and Kosovo: From Ethnic Captive to Agent of Reconciliation." In *Faith-Based Diplomacy*, edited by Douglas Johnston. London: Oxford University Press, 2003.

———. "Contributions of Interfaith Dialogue to Peace-building in the Former Yugoslavia." *Interfaith Dialogue and Peace-building*, edited by David R. Smock. Washington, DC: United States Institute of Peace, 2002.

Steiner, Sam. *In Search of Promised Lands: A Religious History of Mennonites in Ontario*. Studies of Anabaptist and Mennonite History 48. Kitchener, ON: Herald, 2015.

Stjerna, Kirsi. *Women and the Reformation*. Malden, MA: Blackwell, 2009.

Stoltzfus, Duane. *Pacifists in Chains: The Persecution of Hutterites during the Great War*. Baltimore: Johns Hopkins University Press, 2013.

Strand, Trude. "Tightening the Noose: The Institutionalized Impoverishment of Gaza, 2005–2010." *Journal of Palestine Studies* 43.2 (2014) 6–23.

Stucky, Peter. "The Concept of Sanctuary for Peace Churches." Talk at Teusaquillo Mennonite Church, Bogotá, Colombia, November 5, 2001.

Stutzman, Ervin. *From Nonresistance to Justice*. Scottdale, PA: Herald Press, 2011.

Suderman, Andrew. "Friendship developed through Anabaptist Network in South Africa." Mennonite Mission Network, *Network News*, June 6, 2013, http://www.mennonitemission.net/Stories/News/Pages/FriendshipdevelopedthroughAnabaptistNetworkinSouthAfrica.aspx.

Suderman, Robert J. "Mennonite World Conference Peace Commission Peace Audit: Summary and Commentary, June 2012." Mennonite World Conference. http://www.mwc-cmm.org/sites/default/files/website_files/peace_audit_2012_en.pdf.

Sudermann, Anna. *Lebenserinnerungen: 1893–1970*. Winnipeg, MB: Mennonite Heritage Center, 1970.

Tawil-Souri, Helga. "Digital Occupation: Gaza's High-Tech Enclosure." *Journal of Palestine Studies* 42.2 (2012) 27–43.

Tissen, Fran. "News from Kazakhstan: Christians in Kazakhstan Take Position on Changes to Law on Religion." *Religion in Eastern Europe* 32.2 (2012) 25–26.

Toews, John B. *The Mennonites in Russia, 1917–1930: Selected Documents*. Winnipeg, MB: Christian Press, 1975.

Toews, Paul. *Mennonites in American Society, 1930–1970: Modernity and the Persistence of Religious Community*. Mennonite Experience in America 4. Scottdale, PA: Herald, 1996.

Touch Any Corner: A Brief History of the International Visitor Exchange Program 1950–2000. Akron, OH: MCC, 2000.

Tribble, Evelyn, and John Sutton. "Cognitive Ecologies as a Framework for Shakespearean Studies." *Shakespeare Studies* 39 (2011) 94–103.

Trothen, Tracy J. *Shattering the Illusion: Child Sexual Abuse and Canadian Religious Institutions*. Waterloo, ON: Wilfrid Laurier University Press, 2012.

Trouillot, Michel-Rolph. *Silencing the Past: Power and the Production of History*. Boston: Beacon, 1995.

Turner, Bryan S. "The New and Old Xenophobia: The Crisis of Liberal Multiculturalism." In *Islam and Political Violence: Muslim Diaspora and Radicalism in the West*, edited by Shahram Akbarzadeh and Fethi Mansouri, 65–86. New York: Tauris, 2010.

Umble, Jenifer Hiett. "Women and Choice: An Examination of the Martyrs' Mirror." *MQR* 64 (1990) 135–45.

Umlauft, Hans. "Letter of Hans Umlauft to Stephan Rauchenecker, 1539." In *Anabaptism in Outline*, edited by Walter Klaassen, 294–95. Classics of the Radical Reformation 3. Scottdale, PA: Herald, 1981.

Urry, James. *None but Saints: The Transformation of Mennonite Life in Russia, 1789-1889*. Winnipeg, MB: Hyperion, 1989.

———. *Mennonites, Politics, and Peoplehood: Europe, Russia, Canada, 1525–1980*. Winnipeg: University of Manitoba Press, 2006

Ury, William L. *Getting to Peace: Transforming Conflict at Home, at Work, and in the World*. New York: Viking, 1999.

Valkenberg, Pim. *Sharing Lights on the Way to God: Muslim-Christian Dialogue and Theology in the Context of Abrahamic Partnership*. Studies on the Contact between Christianity and Other Religions, Beliefs, and Cultures 26. Amsterdam: Rodopi, 2006.

Vanier, Jean. *Becoming Human*. 1998. Reprinted, Toronto: Anansi, 2008.

Väyrynen, Raimo, ed. *New Directions in Conflict Theory: Conflict Resolution and Conflict Transformation*. Newbury Park, CA: Sage, 1991.

Virilio, Paul. *L'Insécurité du territoire*. Paris: Stock, 1976.

Vladisavljevic, Nebojsa. "The Break-up of Yugoslavia: The Role of Popular Politics." In *New Perspectives on Yugoslavia: Key Issues and Controversies*, edited by Dejan Djokic and James Ker-Lindsay, 143–60. New York: Routledge, 2011.

Volkan, Vamik D. *The Need to Have Enemies and Allies: From Clinical Practice to International Relations*. Master Work Series. Northvale, NJ: Aronson, 1994.

Voth, Stanley. *Cornelius Voth and Helena Richert Voth*. Self-published, 1979.

Wagner, Jörg. "Wer Christo jetzt will folgen noch, 1527, *Ausbund*, 1564." In *Anabaptism in Outline*, edited by Walter Klaassen, 88. Classics of the Radical Reformation 3. Scottdale, PA: Herald, 1981.

Wahid, Abdurrahman. "Right Islam vs. Wrong Islam." *The Wall Street Journal*, December 12 (2005).

Waite, Gary K. "The Anabaptist Movement in Amsterdam and the Netherlands, 1531–1535." *Sixteenth Century Journal* 18 (1987) 249–65.

Weaver, Alain Epp. "Parables of the Kingdom and Religious Plurality: With Barth and Yoder toward a Nonresistant Public Theology." *MQR* 72 (1998) 411–40.

———, and Sonia K. Weaver. *Salt and Sign: Mennonite Central Committee in Palestine, 1949–1999*. Akron, PA: Mennonite Central Committee, 1999.

Weaver, J. Denny. *Anabaptist Theology in the Face of Postmodernity: A Proposal for the Third Millennium*. C. Henry Smith Series 2. Telford: Pandora, 2000.

———. *Becoming Anabaptist: The Origin and Significance of Sixteenth-Century Anabaptism*. 2nd ed. Scottdale, PA: Herald, 2005.

Weiss, Alexander. "The Transition of Siberian Mennonites to Baptists: Causes and Results." *JMS* 30 (2012) 133–38.

Wenger, C.D. *Why I Am a C.O.: In Two Parts*. 5th printing. Harrisonburg, VA: self-published, 1948.

Wichert. Timothy. "A Mennonite Human Rights Paradigm?" In *At Peace and Unafraid: Public Order, Security, and the Wisdom of the Cross*, edited by Duane K. Friesen and Gerald W. Schlabach, 331–47. Scottdale, PA: Herald, 2005.

Wiebe, Joel A., Vernon R. Wiebe, and Raymond F. Wiebe, *The Groening-Wiebe Family 1768-1974*. Hillsboro, KS: Mennonite Brethren Publishing House, 1974.

Wiebe, Katie Funk. "Images and Realities of the Early Years." *Mennonite Life* 36.3 (1981) 22–28.
Wiebe, Virgil. "Washing Your Feet in the Blood of the Wicked: Seeking Justice and Contending with Vengeance in an Interprofessional Setting." *University of St. Thomas Law Journal* 1 (2003) 182–216.
Wilkes, George, et al. "Factors in Reconciliation: Religion, Local Conditions, People and Trust." *Diskursi* [Special edition]. Published by the University of Edinburgh, Project on Religion and Ethics in the Making of War and Peace and the Center for Empirical Research on Religion in Bosnia and Herzegovina (May 2013).
Will, Emily. "Congolese Women Rally against Mass Rapes in War." *Mennonite World Review* 10 December 2010. http://www.mennoworld.org/archived/2010/12/13/congolese-women-rally-against-mass-rapes-war/.
Williams, George H. *The Radical Reformation*. 3rd ed. Kirksville, MO: Sixteenth Century Journal Publishers, 1988.
———. *La reforma radical*. Mexico: Fondo de Cultura Económica, 1983.
Wilson, Chris. *Ethno-Religious Violence in Indonesia: From Soil to God*. Routledge Contemporary Southeast Asia Series 18. London: Routledge, 2008.
Windhorst, Christof. "Balthasar Hubmaier: Professor, Preacher, Politician." In *Profiles of Radical Reformers: Biographical Sketches from Thomas Müntzer to Paracelsus*, edited by Hans-Jürgen Goertz and Walter Klaasen, 144–57. Kitchener, ON: Herald, 1982.
Wink, Walter. *The Powers that Be: Theology for a New Millennium*. New York: Doubleday, 1998.
Wyntjes, Sherrin Marshall. "Women and Religious Choices in the Sixteenth Century Netherlands." *Archiv für Reformationsgeschichte* 75 (1984) 276–89.
———. "Women in the Reformation Era." In *Becoming Visible: Women in European History*, edited by Renate Bridenthal and Claudia Koonz, 165–91. Boston: Houghton Mifflin, 1977.
Yoder, John Howard. *As You Go: The Old Mission in a New Day*. Focal Pamphlet 5. Scottdale, PA: Herald, 1961.
———. *For the Nations: Essays Public and Evangelical*. Grand Rapids: Eerdmans, 1997.
———. *The Jewish-Christian Schism Revisited*. Edited by Michael Cartwright and Peter Ochs. Grand Rapids: Eerdmans, 2002.
———, ed. and trans. *The Legacy of Michael Sattler*. Scottdale, PA: Herald, 1973.
———. *Nevertheless: Varieties of Religious Pacifism*. 3rd ed. Scottdale, PA: Herald, 1992.
———. *The Politics of Jesus*. Grand Rapids: Eerdmans, 1972.
Yoder, John Howard, with Joan Baez, Tom Skinner, Leo Tolstoy. *What Would You Do [If a Violent Person Threatened to Harm a Love One?]: A Serious Answer to a Standard Question*. Scottdale, PA: Herald, 1983.
Yoder, John Howard, Nélida M. de Machain, and Ernesto Suárez Vilela. *Textos escogidos de la Reforma Radical*. Buenos Aires: Federación Argentina de Iglesias Evangélicas, 2008.
Zapata, Maria Lucia. *Transformación de Conflictos y Reconciliación*. Bogotá: Justapaz, 2013.
Zehr, Howard. *Changing Lenses: A New Focus for Crime and Justice*. A Christian Peace Shelf Selection. Scottdale, PA: Herald, 1990.
———. *The Little Book of Restorative Justice*. Intercourse, PA: Good Books, 2002.

Zimmerman, Ruth and Bonnie Price Lofton. "From Dream to Reality: 10 Years of Peacebuilding." *Peacebuilder Magazine* (Summer/Fall 2005) 3–7.

Zuabi, Amir Nizar. "The Underground Ghetto City of Gaza." *Haaretz English Edition*. August 4, 2014. http://www.haaretz.com/opinion/.premium-1.608653.

Index

A

AAANZ (Anabaptist Association of Australia and New Zealand), 105
Abdelrahman, Amr, 243
Abraham, and hospitality, 238, 247
acknowledgment, 351–52
activism, *see* advocacy
advocacy
    in Colombian Anabaptist churches, 271–72
    by MCC, 68, 76–77, 82–83, 87
    by Mennonite World Conference, 103
    overview of, 107
    transition to, 147–49
aftermaths, 143
Albrecht, Elizabeth Soto, 69, 189–90
Allard, Silas, 244, 248
Allport, Gordon, 305
All-Union Council of Evangelical Christian Baptists (AUCECB), 50
Alternative Service (AS) work program, 66, 78, 182–83
American Mennonite Relief organization, 43
Anabaptism (Klassen), 68
Anabaptism Today (journal), 104, 104n37
Anabaptist Association of Australia and New Zealand (AAANZ), 105
Anabaptist Network, 104–5, 104n40
Anabaptist Network in South Africa (ANiSA), 106
Anabaptist-Mennonite
    use of term, 90n2
Anabaptists, 13–14, 21. *See also* global Anabaptist-Mennonite church; Mennonite peacebuilding, roots of; Mennonites; persecution, of Anabaptists; *specific groups and churches*
And When They Shall Ask (film), 38, 38n1
Anderson, Benedict, 161
Angola, 309, 325, 326–27, 327–28
Angolan Mennonite Church, 326–27, 327–28
ANiSA (Anabaptist Network in South Africa), 106
apocalypticism, medieval, 16, 26
apology, 351–52
Appiah, Kwami Anthony, 226
Aquila relief organization, 52
Arab hospitality, 237–39
arbitration, 174–75
Asia Mennonite Conference, 107n46
Assefa, Hizkias, 263
Ausbund (hymnbook), 34
Australia
    Anabaptist Association of Australia and New Zealand, 105
Austrian Anabaptists, 14, 16
Avignon schism, 14–15

B

Balkans, *see* Bosnia-Herzegovina and Kosovo peacebuilding project

Index

Barkman, Anna, 210
Barkouki-Winter, Amal, 238
Barth, Karl, 117, 132, 133, 134, 135–36, 139
Barton, Greg, 281
Belize, 110
Bender, Harold S., 67
Bentzen, Simon, 29
Better Angels of Our Nature (Pinker), 1
Bienenberg (European Mennonite Bible School), 95
Blough, Neil and Janie, 98
Blum, Jerome, 62
Bolivia, 55, 110, 149
Bosnia-Herzegovina and Kosovo peacebuilding project
  introduction to, 330–31, 336–37
  acknowledgment of wrongdoing, 351–52
  analysis of Balkan conflict, 332–36
  analysis of success, 361–62, 363–65
  Center for Religious Dialogue, 343, 359–60
  choosing to forgive, 353–54
  confronting fears, 349
  identity formation issues, 340–41, 343–47
  Interreligious Council of Bosnia-Herzegovina, 359
  leadership development issues, 342–43, 358–60
  mourning, 348
  problem solving issues, 341–42, 356–58
  program design phase, 339
  re-humanizing Other, 350–51
  relationship building issues, 339–40, 347–56
  restorative justice, 354–56
  studies on reconciliation in, 362–63
  trust-building phase, 337–39
Brethren of the Common Life, 17, 18
bridge-builders, 174
Brodyaga, Lisa, 219, 219n53
Brunner, Emil, 255
Buckwalter, Albert and Lois, 97
Buckwalter, Ralph and Genevieve, 97
Buddhism, engaged, 146, 146n16
Buffy the Vampire Slayer, 219–20
Burton, John W., 120n19
Byler, Dennis and Connie, 98
Byler, Edna Ruth, 186

C

Canada
  Alternative Service work program, 66, 78, 182–83
  Mennonite immigration to, 63
  military exemption and, 61, 64–65, 74
  refugee sponsorship and, 88
  See also North American Mennonites
Canadian Central Committee, 73
Canadian Mennonite Board of Colonization, 73–74, 77
Catholic Relief Services, 361
CCECB (Council of Churches of Evangelical Christian Baptists), 49, 50
CEAS (Church Coordination for Psycho-social Action), 262–63
CEDECOL (Colombian Evangelical Council of Churches), 257, 262
Center for Justice and Peacebuilding, Eastern Mennonite University, 100–101
Center for Peacemaking and Conflict Studies, Fresno Pacific University, 100
Center for Religious Dialogue (CRD), 343, 359–60
Center for Strategic and International Studies (CSIS), *see* Bosnia-Herzegovina and Kosovo peacebuilding project; Center for Religious Dialogue
Central America, and Anabaptist theology, 98–99
Chertkov, Vladimir, 41
children, 220, 221–22
China
  Mennonite Partners in China, 105
chosen trauma, 147
Christ Seul (journal), 95

Christian Humanism, 18–20, 31, 35–36
Christian Peacemakers Teams (CPT), 69, 300
Christianity
　hospitality in, 239
　and Islam, 296
Christliche Dienste (CD), 53
church, and state, 148–49
Church and Peace network, 95
Church Coordination for Psychosocial Action (CEAS), 262–63
Church of Christ in Congo (ECC), 317, 319, 324
citizenship, 244
civil society, 171–72, 173, 176–77, 176n26
Civil War (US), 62
Civilian Public Service (CPS), 66, 78, 93, 182
Coffman, S.F., 181
Cold War, 56–57, 81
collective memory, 141–42
Colombia, 190–91, 252–53, 259, 265
Colombian Anabaptists
　introduction to, 251–52, 252n1, 253–54, 272–73
　advocacy and social change, 271–72, 271n71
　conscientious objection and, 108, 256
　holistic support for victims, 267–68
　message of, 259–60
　nonviolence and, 254–56
　other nonviolence initiatives of, 262–63
　Reconciliation and Accompaniment of Victims Project (RAV), 263–65, 267–68, 269–70
　role in peacebuilding, 265–67
　Sanctuary for Peace Church vision, 257–58, 261–62, 267
　truth and justice and, 268–71
　See also Justapaz; Sembrandopaz
Colombian Evangelical Council of Churches (CEDECOL), 257, 262

Colombian Mennonite Development Foundation (Mencoldes), 254, 268–69
Conference of Historic Peace Churches (CHPC), see Historic Peace Churches
conflict analysis, 331–32
conflict resolution, 118–21, 119n12, 123, 123n29, 124–25, 129, 129n59, 138
conflict transformation
　approach of, 118–19, 121–22, 122n25
　conflict in, 118n7, 118n9
　elicitive approach to, 123–24, 130–31
　just peace and, 120
　Mennonite peacebuilding and, 115
　relationships in, 120–21
　Rupesinghe on, 119n10
　in Somalia, 130–31
　theoretical underpinnings to, 118–19, 118n8
　time horizon of, 119–20
Congo, see Democratic Republic of Congo
Congolese Mennonites
　Angolan Mennonites and, 326–27
　Church in Christ in Congo (ECC) and, 316–17, 324
　Congolese peacebuilding dialogue and, 320
　and Disarmament, Demobilization, and Reintegration (DDR) Program, 320–21
　higher education and, 326
　lessons learned from, 324
　peacebuilding approach of, 317, 318
　regional peacebuilding and, 325
　social and economic development and, 323
　See also Democratic Republic of Congo
conscience, freedom of, 19–20
conscientious objection
　Alternative Service (Canada), 66, 78, 182–83

conscientious objection *(continued)*
  basis of, 32
  Civilian Public Service (US), 66, 78, 93
  in Colombia, 254, 256
  crisis of male identity and, 192
  in Germany and Switzerland, 53, 95
  MCC and, 78
  in North America during world wars, 63–66, 74, 93
  as peace witness, 107–8
  stigma of, 67
  women and, 179–80, 180–81, 182–83
  See also military exemption
contact theory, 305–6
conversion, calls to, 224
cookbooks, 187
Coptic Christians, 233–34, 244. *See also* hospitality; interreligious hospitality
Council of Churches of Evangelical Christian Baptists (CCECB), 49, 50
Cousens, Elizabeth, 317
CPT (Christian Peacemakers Teams), 69, 300
CRD (Center for Religious Dialogue), 343, 359–60
Cressman, Erma, 184
Croat Catholic Church, 335n7
Crouch, Melissa, 279

D

decency, politics of, 56
Democratic Republic of Congo
  approach to, 309, 329
    Disarmament, Demobilization, and Reintegration (DDR) Program, 320–21
  gender-based violence in, 191
  higher education in, 325–26
  history of, 311–16
  Inter-Congolese National Debate, 318, 319
  peacebuilding definition for, 309–10
  peacebuilding process in, 318–20
  regional relations and peacebuilding, 324–25
  social and economic development, 321–23
  Teacher Abroad Program (TAP), 324
  See also Congolese Mennonites
Denck, Hans, 15, 20
Derksen, Wilma, 85
Derrida, Jacques, 236, 246
developmental evaluation, 364
Devotio Moderna, 17, 31
Dirks, Elizabeth, 29
Dordrecht Confession, 47
dramaturgical studies, 142
Driedger, Leo
  Mennonite Peacemaking, 67, 95
Driver, John, 99–100, 254, 254n8, 257, 260
Duncan, Christopher, 276
Dutch Anabaptists, 14, 15, 17, 28, 39, 47
Dyck, Peter, 82

E

Eastern Mennonite University, 100
ECC (Church of Christ in Congo), 317, 319, 324
Eckhart, Meister, 15
economics, 22, 27
economics, and Anabaptists, 28
ecumenical dialogue, 95–96, 223. *See also* interfaith initiatives; interreligious hospitality
education, 123n34, 174, 221–22
Edwards, Michael, 171–72
ego container, 197, 200
Egypt
  equal citizenship in, 244
  hospitality in, 237–39
  research trip to, 233–34
  unrest in, 232, 233, 243
  See also interreligious hospitality
Einlage, Ukraine, 210–11, 211n21
elicitive approach, 123–24, 130–31, 136n86, 201
Elmira restorative justice case, 156–57

empathetic solidarity, 2, 3, 117–18, 138. *See also* solidarity
encounters, 132
Enns, Elaine, 152
Enns, Fernando, 96
environmental protection, 176
Epp, Marlene, 67
Epp, Peter, 46
equalizers, 175
Erasmus, Desiderius, 18–19, 20, 31
Eritrean Mennonites, 223
Escobar, Samuel, 99
Esquivia, Ricardo, 251–52, 253–54, 256, 259, 262
Ethiopian Mennonites, 108, 223, 223n60
Euro-Asiatic Accrediting Association (EAAA), 53
European Mennonite Bible School (Bienenberg), 95
European Mennonite Peace Committee, 95
Evangelical Christian Baptists (Russia), 48, 49, 50–51. *See also* Russian evangelicals
exile, 299, 302–5
exilic missiology, 300–301, 302
experiential approach, 124, 124n37, 136, 136n84

F

fair trade movement, 186
faith, freedom of, 19–20
faith communities, 222–23
Family Violence (Albrecht), 189–90
Fast, Jakob, 50
Fast, Viktor, 54, 55
feminist thought, 148–49, 189–90
Fogelman, Aaron, 60
forgiveness, 353–54
founding trauma, 147
Franz, Delton, 68
freedom of conscience and faith, 19–20
Freire, Paolo, 116n3, 123, 123n34
Fresno Pacific University, 100
Fretz, John, 79
Friesen, Abraham, 38n1

Friesen, Richard and Ruth Ann, 218, 225–26
Froese, Peter, 41, 44
Funk, John F., 61

G

García, César, 103
Garcia, Sandra Baez, 190
Gaza Strip, 298–99, 307. *See also* Palestine-Israel
Geiser, Teresa, 270
gelassenheit (yieldedness), 3, 15–16, 188
Geneva Conventions, 164
Gerber, Hans Ulrich, 96
Gereja Injili Tanah Jawa (GITJ), 287–88. *See also* Indonesia
German Mennonite Peace Committee, 107
German Theology (book), 15
global Anabaptist-Mennonite church
 approach to, 92–93
 activist engagements in, 107
 challenges to peace witness of, 111–12
 conscientious objection and, 107–8
 demographic shift of, 91, 103, 149n28
 interfaith initiatives and, 108–9, 111
 Mennonite colonies as witnesses, 110
 neo-Anabaptist peace networks, 92–93, 103–6
 peace witness of, 91–92, 106–7
 in post-colonial era, 97
 and reconciliation / trauma healing, 109–10
 See also Mennonite missions
Gopin, Marc, 130, 145–46, 235, 241–42
Gospel Versus Gospel (Schlabach), 90–91, 92
Graybill, Beth, 184
Grebel, Conrad, 26, 32, 255
Guatemala, 109

H

Hagenawer, Hans, 27
Hallie, Philip
  Lest Innocent Blood Be Shed, 218
Hart, Barry, 331
Hartono, Paulus, 111, 290–91
Heidebrecht, Hermann, 55
Heidebrecht, Paul, 162
Heisey, M.J., 179, 182
Henkin, Louis, 171n21
heretics, openness to, 32–33
Hergot, Hans, 22–23, 34–35
Herr, Barbara Ziegler, 61
Hiebert, P.C., 74, 75
Historic Peace Churches, 78, 92, 93, 94
historical harms, 143
historical violence, 143
Hizbullah militia, Indonesia, 111, 290
Hoffman, Melchior, 15–16, 26, 33
Holocaust, 212, 215–17, 218
hospitality, 237–39. *See also* interreligious hospitality
Hostetter, Doug, 81
Hottinger, Margret, 29
Hubmaier, Balthasar, 30–31, 32–33
Hubmaier, Elsbeth, 29
human needs theory, 120n19
human rights campaigns, 226
human rights law
  introduction to, 162–63
  creation of, 176
  goal of, 172
  impact of civil society on, 176–77
  international criminal prosecution, 168–69
  International Humanitarian Law (IHL), 163–65, 165n7, 170–71, 172
  Mennonite responses as expressions of, 173–75, 176
  Mennonite unease with, 169–70
  peace in, 172
  problems with, 170–71
  religion and, 171n21
  Universal Declaration of Human Rights, 165–67, 172
Humanism, 18–20, 31, 35–36
humility theology, 194–95
Hurst, Mark and Mary, 105
Hut, Hans, 15, 16–17, 26
Hutter, Jacob, 27, 33, 34
Hutter, Katherina, 29
Hutterites, 14, 15, 28, 35

I

IHL (International Humanitarian Law), 163–65, 165n7, 170–71, 172
imagined communities, 161
Imitatio Christi (Thomas à Kempis), 17
IMPC (International Mennonite Peace Commission), 101–3, 101n32
India, 109
Indonesia
  introduction to, 274–75
  anti-Communist pogroms, 295
  government response to violence, 281
  interfaith relations in, 109, 110–11, 289–91
  Islam in, 278–79, 280
  Mennonite influence in, 286–87, 291
  missionaries to, 39, 47
  Muria Muslim-Christian example, 287–89
  peacemaking attempts in, 281–85, 286
  "religious violence" in, 275–76
  Solo example, 110–11, 289–91
  Sunni-Shiite relations, 285–86
  violence in, 276–78, 276n2, 279–81
institutions, creating, 226
interfaith initiatives, 108–9, 111, 289–91. *See also* ecumenical dialogue; interreligious hospitality
International Conciliation Service, 84, 127
International Criminal Court (ICC), 168, 168n16
international criminal prosecution, 168–69

international experience, 132, 135, 136
International Fellowship of Reconciliation, 94
International Humanitarian Law (IHL), 163–65, 165n7, 170–71, 172
International Mennonite Peace Commission (IMPC), 101–3, 101n32. *See also* MWC Peace Commission
International Tribunal for the Former Yugoslavia (ICTY), 168, 169
Interreligious Council of Bosnia-Herzegovina, 359
interreligious hospitality
 approach to, 236–37
 Arab hospitality and, 237–39
 collaboration needed for, 244
 complexity and, 240–41
 overview of, 235–36, 249–50
 pessimism and, 235, 236, 249
 relationship-building for, 245–47
 for sustainable peace, 241–42
 theoretical basis of, 234–35
 trust-building in, 247–49
Islam
 and Christianity, 296
 hospitality in, 238–39, 246
 and Mennonites, 109, 130–31
 Qurtuby on, 296
Israel, *see* Palestine-Israel

J

Jans, Anneken, 29, 33–34
Janzen, Bill, 87
Janzen, Vladimir, 48n23
Japan, 107
Jepara, Indonesia, 285–86
Jews, *see* Holocaust; Palestine-Israel; Zionism
Jones, Jonathan, 225
Jost, Leonhard, 27
Jost, Ursula, 16, 29
Juhnke, James, 64, 75, 86
Juhnke, Roland, 66
just peace, 2, 115, 116, 117, 121, 121n23, 122

Justapaz (Center for Justice, Peace and Nonviolent Action)
 CEDECOL's Human Rights and Peace Commission and, 257, 262
 conscientious objection and, 108, 254
 Documentation Project, 268–69
 nonviolence education and, 256
 overview of, 107

K

Karaganda evangelicals (Kazakhstan), 44, 48n32, 50, 51
Karlstadt, Andreas von, 24
Kaufman, Daniel, 63
Kautz, Jakob, 28
Kazakhstan, *see* Karaganda evangelicals (Kazakhstan)
Keeney, William, 129
Kelly, Russ, 157
Kern, Kathleen, 300
Kerols, Ayman, 232
Klager, Andrew, 5–6, 7. *See also* Egypt; interreligious hospitality
Klassen, C.F., 41
Klassen, J.M., 72
Klassen, Walter
 Anabaptism, 68
Koontz, Ted, 136n83
Korea Anabaptist Center, 106
Korean Anabaptist Fellowship, 108
Korean War, 80
Kosovo, *see* Bosnia-Herzegovina and Kosovo peacebuilding project
Krabill, James and Janette, 98n23
Kratz, Clayton, 75
Kraybill, Donald
 Mennonite Peacemaking, 67, 95
Kraybill, Ron
 Bosnia-Herzegovina project and, 331
 on ego containment, 197–200
 in Mennonite Conciliation Service, 84, 128, 196n4
 mentorship for, 196n4, 202
 relinquishment in work of, 195–97
Krehbiel, Stephanie, 219
Kreider, Robert, 66

Krieder, Alan and Eleanor, 98, 104
Krisetya, Mesach, 292
Kumar, Chetan, 318

L

LaCapra, Dominick, 147
Lapp, John A., 195–96
Latin America, and Anabaptist theology, 98–99, 99n26
Latin American immigrants, 217–18, 225
Laue, James, 197
law profession, 224
Le Chambon, France, 218, 219
Lederach, John Paul
  approach to, 116, 117–18, 138–39
  Bosnia-Herzegovina project and, 331
  on collective memory, 141–42
  on conflict, 118n7
  on conflict resolution, 119n12, 123, 138
  on conflict transformation, 118–22, 118n8, 122n25
  critique of Subject assimilates the Other, 134
  Driver and, 100
  elicitive approach of, 123–24, 124n35, 130–31, 136n86
  empathetic solidarity and, 116
  framework for understanding, 135–38
  Freire and, 116n3, 123
  identity exercise of, 346–47
  impact of "experience" on, 116–17, 122–23, 124–25, 138–39
  in International Conciliation Service, 84
  on just peace, 121n23
  on Mennonite ethos and posture, 131–32
  Mennonite impact on, 117, 126–27
  on pessimism, 232–33, 240, 243, 247
  popularity of teachings by, 201
  reflexive stance of, 132
  shifts made by, 127–28
  on social change, 265
  on timeframes in peacebuilding, 328–29
  varied experiences of, 127
legacies, 143
Lest Innocent Blood Be Shed (Hallie), 218
liberation theology, 98
Liechty, Joe and Linda, 98
Lim, David, 148
Lindbeck, George, 136n85
linguistic expression, 124n37
listening/learning approach, *see* elicitive approach
literary criticism, 142
Loewen, Jacob, 99n26
Loewen, Royden, 88
LOGOS mission, 52
London Mennonite Centre, 104
Luther, Martin, 22, 23, 24, 26
Lutheran Church, 27, 96
Luyken, Jan, see *Martyrs' Mirror* (Luyken)

M

Madikela, Fifi Pombo, 191
Makhno, Nestor, 153, 153n39
Malkki, Liisa, 143
Maluku, Indonesia, 286
Manuputty, Jacky, 284
Manz, Felix, 26
Maoz, Ifat, 305
marginality, 1
Markovic, Ivo, 338, 345–46, 352, 362
Marpeck, Pilgrim, 27, 28, 29
Marpeck communities, 28
Marr, Lucille, 181, 185
Marshall, Christopher, 245
martyr stories, 209
martyrdom, medieval theology of, 16–17, 31
Martyrs' Mirror (Luyken), 9, 28, 145, 145n13
MBMSI (Mennonite Brethren Mission Service International), 327
MCC (Mennonite Central Committee)
  advocacy to governments by, 68, 76–77, 82–83, 87

Index 403

on apology, repentance, and forgiveness, 85
conscientious objectors and, 78
cross-cultural exchange and, 81
in Democratic Republic of Congo, 323
early work in USSR, 71, 73–74, 75–76, 76n11, 88–89, 154
faith foundation of, 89
founding of, 65, 71, 73, 154
historical overview of work, 155
impact on educational centers, 100–101
impartiality of service, 75–76, 87
as inter-Mennonite undertaking, 75, 78, 86–87
Mennonite Disaster Service, 80–81
Palestinian refugees and, 298, 300
PAX program (Korean War), 80
peace ministry of, 72, 72n4, 73, 86, 100
Peace Section, 78, 83, 100, 129, 196n4
peacebuilding and, 84, 85
personnel, 79–80
in post-Soviet Russia, 72
post-WWII, 80–81, 94n11
refugees and newcomers, 77, 88
relief work and nonresistance, 74–75, 78–79, 80, 86
value shifts within, 128–29, 138
Vietnam War and, 81–82
Voluntary Service program, 80
women's issues and, 84–85, 189
work of in North America, 83
between world wars, 77
WWII relief work, 77–78, 185–86
MCC Canada, 81, 82, 83, 88, 100
McKenny, Gerald, 133
McMaster, Richard, 60
MCS (Mennonite Conciliation Service), 69, 84, 127, 128, 196n4
MDS (Mennonite Disaster Service), 80–81
MEDA (Mennonite Economic Development Associates), 55, 323, 324
mediation, 174, 198–99, 198n5, 201
Memorial Society (Russia), 51

men, *see* conscientious objection
Mencoldes (Colombian Mennonite Development Foundation), 254, 268–69
Mennonite Board of Missions, 97–98, 97n20
Mennonite Brethren Mission Service International (MBMSI), 327
Mennonite Central Committee, *see* MCC; MCC Canada
Mennonite Conciliation Service (MCS), 69, 84, 127, 128, 196n4
Mennonite Disaster Service (MDS), 80–81
Mennonite Economic Development Associates (MEDA), 55, 323, 324
Mennonite men, *see* conscientious objection
Mennonite Mission Network, 97n20
Mennonite missions
  gospel preached by, 90–91
  to Indonesia, 39, 47
  in post-colonial era, 97–100, 98n23
  See also global Anabaptist-Mennonite church
Mennonite Partners in China, 105
Mennonite peace theology
  Biblical basis of, 179
  in Latin America, 98–99
Mennonite peacebuilding
  approach to, 1–2, 2–3, 4, 8–9
  basis for authentic, 161
  challenges facing, 111–12
  formation of workers for, 201–3, 202n6
  goals of book, 4–5
  historical background for, 2, 3–4, 14
  positive contributions of, 7–8
  power paradox and, 154–56
  in public sphere, 147–49
  reputation for, 200–201
  and secular peace movements, 6–7
  self-critical approach to, 7
  as snakebirds, 226–27
  traits valued in, 193–94
  See also Mennonite peacebuilding, roots of; peace; peacebuilding

Mennonite peacebuilding, roots of approach to, 14, 35–36
  centrality of Jesus and New Testament, 30–35
  experience of alternative healing community, 28–30
  experience of disillusionment and persecution, 26–28
  experience of oppression, 21–23
  Protestant Reformation, 23–25
  Renaissance Humanism, 18–20
  in Roman Catholic spirituality, 14–18
Mennonite peacemaking, 109–10, 128
Mennonite Peacemaking (Driedger and Kraybill), 67, 95
Mennonite Relief Commission for War Sufferers, 74
Mennonite women, and peacemaking
  approach to, 178–79, 192
  cookbooks and, 187
  exclusion from conscientious objector discourse, 179–80
  gendered interpretation of, 187–88
  in MCC, 80
  quilt-making and, 187
  relief work during wartime, 79, 180–83, 185–86
  and violence against women, 84–85, 188–91
  See also women
Mennonite World Conference (MWC), 43, 54–55, 69, 94n12, 96, 101–3
Mennonites
  as engaged Christianity, 146
  as exilic people, 299
  inter-Mennonite cooperation, 75, 78, 86–87
  Qurtuby on, 274–75
  See also Anabaptists; global Anabaptist-Mennonite church; *specific groups and churches*
mentorship, 196n4, 201–3, 202n6
Meserete Kristos Church, *see* Ethiopian Mennonites
Messiah complex, 134
Mexico, 64–65, 108

Meyger, Fridolin, 27, 28, 29
Michel, Thomas, 245
middle out approach, 201
Midgley, Mary, 140
military exemption, 59–63. *See also* conscientious objection
Miller, Alvin J., 76
Miller, Joseph, 128
Miller, Keith Graber, 68
Misa, Thomas, 214
modesty, 193, 194
Moluccan islands, 284
monastic asceticism, 15, 31
More with Less cookbook, 187
mourning, 348
Muria region, Indonesia, 287–89
Murray, Stuart, 104
Muslims, *see* Islam
MWC (Mennonite World Conference), 43, 54–55, 69, 94n12, 96, 101–3
MWC Peace Commission, 103, 111–12. *See also* International Mennonite Peace Commission
mysticism and spiritualism, 15–16, 26, 31
mythico-histories, 143–44
mythmaking
  introduction to, 140–41
  analytic frameworks for, 141–43
  approach to Mennonite, 141, 143–44, 160–61
  Dirk Willems myth, 144–47
  Elmira restorative justice myth, 156–59
  functions of, 143
  Russian Mennonite persecution myth, 149–50, 151–54
  silence in, 150–51

N

Nafi, Muhammad Dian, 290–91
narrative approach, 124n37, 125–26, 136
Native Americans, 213–14
neo-Anabaptist peace networks, 92–93, 103–6
Network News (journal), 104n37

New Historicism, 142
New Testament church, 34–35
New Zealand, 158
    Anabaptist Association of Australia and New Zealand, 105
Newfoundland, Canada, 80
Niebuhr, Reinhold, 67
Nigeria, 109
Nolt, Steven, 61, 66n31, 88
nonresistance, 31–32, 67. *See also* Mennonite peacebuilding; Mennonite peacebuilding, roots of; peace; peacebuilding
Non-Resistant Relief Organization (NRRO), 74, 182
Nonresistant Relief Sewing Organization, 185
nonviolence, *see* Mennonite peacebuilding; Mennonite peacebuilding, roots of; peace; peacebuilding
North American Mennonites
    American Revivalism and, 194–95, 194n2, 195n3
    Civil War and, 62
    Civilian Public Service (CPS), 66, 78, 93, 182
    enlistees to war, 66, 66n31, 78
    first immigrant wave, 59–60
    military exemption and, 59–63, 63–64, 65
    Native American expulsion and, 213–14
    new reflections on peace after WWII, 67–68, 69, 79–80, 95
    peace and, 58, 61–62, 69–70
    Russlander Mennonites immigration, 65, 74, 77
    second immigrant wave, 61
    shift from suffering to humility in, 194–95, 194n1
    third immigrant wave, 62–63
    Virgil Wiebe's family history, 209–11, 209n17, 215–17
    War of Independence and, 60–61
    World War I and, 63–64, 74
    World War II and, 65–66
nuclear weapons, 164n4

O

Omsk Mennonite Brotherhood, 46
On the Road (journal), 105
Other and Subject, frameworks for, 133–36, 137–38
Overground Railroad (ORR), 217–18, 217n47, 225–26

P

pacifism, *see* conscientious objection; Mennonite peacebuilding
Padilla, René, 99
Palestine-Israel
    approach to, 299, 308
    contact theory initiatives, 305–6
    exile for, 299, 302–5
    Mennonites peacemaking in, 298, 300
    Zochrot's initiative, 306–7
Palestinian refugees, 82
Pankratz, Hans, 66
Paraguay, 64–65, 77, 109, 110
participatory action-reflection, 116n3
PAX program, 80, 94n11
peace
    activist engagement and, 107
    evolution of concept, 59
    in Mennonite identity, 58–59
    new reflections on post-WWII, 67–68
    WWII, and rediscovery of, 93–96
    See also Mennonite peacebuilding; neo-Anabaptist peace networks; peacebuilding
Peace is the Will of God (booklet), 94
Peace Provocateurs, 284
peacebuilding
    congregational support for, 222–23
    Cousens on, 317
    ego containment needed for, 197, 200
    as integrity issue, 55
    MCC and, 84–85
    Rasmussen on, 310
    Reychler on, 309–10
    timeframes for, 328–29

peacebuilding *(continued)*
    See also Mennonite peace theology; Mennonite peacebuilding; Mennonite peacebuilding, roots of; Mennonite peacemaking; peace
peacekeeping, 175
peacemaking, *see* Mennonite peacemaking
peasant revolts, 21
Peasants' War, 22–23, 25, 26, 36
Penner, Carol, 188, 189
Penner, Peter F., 53
Pennsylvania, 59–60
persecution, of Anabaptists, 16–17, 28, 30, 33–34
persecution complex, 146–47
persecution stories, 209
pessimism
    explanation of, 232–33, 240, 247
    interreligious hospitality as antidote to, 235, 236, 249
    proxemics and, 243–44, 245
    restorative justice and, 245
    See also interreligious hospitality
Pfistermeyer, Hans, 27
Philips, Dirk, 31, 32
Piecework: a women's peace theology, 189
Pinker, Steven
    The Better Angels of Our Nature, 1
political isolation, 234–35
politics of decency, 56
Pontamina interfaith choir, 345–46, 362
power
    in mediation, 198–99, 201
    paradox of, 154–56
pre-linguistic experience, 124n37
Protestant Reformation, 23–26, 26–27, 28, 36, 46–47
proxemics, 243–44, 245
Proyecto Libertad, 225
Puidoux Conferences, 94

Q

quilt-making, 187
Quiring, Traugott, 50
Qurtuby, Sumanto Al
    doctoral work of, 293–94
    encounters with Mennonites, 274–75, 291–93, 296–97
    family history, 294–95
    on Islam, 296
    on reconciliation, 295–96

R

Rasmussen, Lewis, 310
RAV (Reconciliation and Accompaniment of Victims Project), 263–65, 267–68, 269–70
Raz-Krakotzkin, Amnon, 302–3
Rebstock, Barbara, 16, 29
Reconciliation and Accompaniment of Victims Project (RAV), 263–65, 267–68, 269–70
reconciliation / trauma healing, 109–10
Redekop, Magdalene, 179
referees, 175
Reformation, Protestant, 23–26, 26–27, 28, 36, 46–47
Reformed church, 27
Regehr, T.D., 68
Reimer, Johannes, 53
relationship building steps
    introduction to, 347
    mourning, 348
    confronting fears, 349
    re-humanizing Other, 350–51
    acknowledgment of wrongdoing, 351–52
    choosing to forgive, 353–54
    restorative justice, 354–56
religious violence, 275–76
relinquishment, 195–97
remembrance, productive, 209
Rempel, Alexander, 217
Rempel, Gerhard, 216
Rempel, Jakob, 43, 54
Rempel, John, 151–52
Rempel, Mrs. P.P., 183
Renaissance Humanism, 18–20, 31, 35–36
restorative justice, 157–59, 160, 176, 244–45, 354–56
Reublin, Wilhelm, 26, 28

Reychler, Luc, 309–10
Reynolds, Thomas, 235, 238, 239, 248
Riedemann, Peter, 27, 31, 32
Rivas, José Rutilio, 251
Roman Catholic Church
    medieval abuses of, 21–22
    medieval apocalypticism, 16
    medieval theology of martyrdom, 16–17
    monastic asceticism, 15
    mysticism and spiritualism, 15–16
    reform movements from Avignon schism, 14–15
    spirituality of, and Anabaptists, 15, 17–18, 35
Roth, John, 69, 209, 223
Rupesinghe, Kumar, 119, 119n10
Russian evangelicals, 40, 41–42, 48, 49–51
Russian Mennonites
    approach to, 37, 47–48
    denominational differences within, 48
    emigration from to North America, 38, 39, 40, 42, 62–63
    Holocaust and, 212, 215–17
    Mennonite World Conference and, 42–43, 54–55
    nonviolence and, 39–40, 50–51, 55–56, 57
    persecution myth of, 149–50, 151–54
    post-Soviet, 51–55
    standard story about, 37–38
    in Tsarist Russia, 38–39, 40, 41, 55–56, 62–63
    in USSR, 41–45, 45–46, 49–50, 56
    violence used by, 39–40, 152–53, 192
    Virgil Wiebe's family history, 209–11, 209n17, 215–17
    during WWII, 45, 215–17
Russian Orthodox Church, 49
Rutschmann, Laverne, 99n26
Rwandan Genocide, 313, 325

S

Sacramentists, 17

Said, Edward, 304–5
Saje, Vjekoslav, 358–59
Samenkorn Press, 52, 53
Sanctuary for Peace Church vision, 257–62
Sattler, Margareta, 29
Sattler, Michael, 20, 27
Scharnschlager, Leopold, 19
Schiemer, Leonard, 15, 16, 29
Schirch, Lisa, 147n22
Schlabach, Theron F., 90–91, 92, 194–95, 194nn1–2
Schlaffer, Hans, 15, 16
Schleitheim Confession, 15, 27, 31–32, 47
Schulman, Mariam, 238
Seiling, Jonathan, 180
self-care, 224–26
self-denial, 188
Sembrandopaz, 262, 266, 268–69, 270
SEMILLA, 109
Sensenig, Peter, 130
separation from the world, 31–32, 188
Serbian Orthodox Church, 333, 335, 335n7
serpent doves, *see* snakebird
Sewell, Doug, 105
Shank, David and Wilma, 98n23
Shelly, Patricia, 69
Shenk, David, 109
Shenk, Gerald, 331
Shenk, Wilbert, 98, 98n24
shepherd metaphor, 218–19
Shonholtz, Ray, 198
Sidel, John, 275
Sider, Ronald, 69, 102n33
Siemens, Ruth Derksen, 187
Simons, Menno, 17, 27–28, 32, 33, 34
Sitler, Arlene, 186
Slagel, Arthur, 76
snakebird
    introduction to, 204–5
    Brazilian, 207, 208
    call to be, 226–27
    calls of, 224
    feeding of young by, 220, 220n56
    nesting habits of, 226
    personality of, 222–23

snakebird *(continued)*
  translations of in Bible, 205, *206*, 207
Snider, Clara, 185
Snowden, Tom, 232
Snyder, Nancy Nahrgang, 182–83
Social Constructivism, 142
social justice movement, 160
social movements, 159–60
solidarity, 135, 136n83. *See also* empathetic solidarity
Solo, Indonesia, 110–11, 289–91
Somalia, 129–31
Soto, Elizabeth, 69
South Africa
  Anabaptist Network in South Africa, 106
South America, and Anabaptist theology, 98–99, 99n26
South German Anabaptists, 14, 53
South Korea, 106, 108
Soviet Union, *see* Russian evangelicals; Russian Mennonites
spiritualism and mysticism, 15–16, 26, 31
St. Petersburg Christian University, 53
state, and church, 148–49
storytelling, 140–41, 237, 348, 353
Stucky, Peter, 255, 259
Stumpf, Simon, 26
Subject and Other, frameworks for, 133–36, 137–38
submission, 188, 189
subversive engagement, 148
Suderman, Anna, 216
Suderman, Jack, 100
suffering theology, 194, 194n1
Swana, Sidonie, 191
Swiss Anabaptists, 14, 15, 26–27
Swiss Brethren, 28, 30, 31, 35. *See also* Schleitheim Confession
Swiss Reformation, 24–25

T

Ta'ayush, 306
Tauler, John, 15
teachers, 174
Ten Thousand Villages, 186

Thielman, George, 72
Thomas, à Kempis
  Imitatio Christi, 17
Toews, Elizabeth B., 183
Toews, Paul, 65
transformative justice movement, 160
trans-generational thinking, 327
trauma / reconciliation healing, 109–10
Trouillot, Michel-Rolph, 150–51
trust-building, 337
tsunami, Indian Ocean (2004), 110–11
two-kingdom theology, 59, 136n83, 148

U

Umlauft, Hans, 19
United States of America
  Civilian Public Service, 66, 78, 93, 182
  military exemption and, 60–61, 62, 63–66, 74
  See also North American Mennonites
Universal Declaration of Human Rights, 165–67, 172
universality, 235
Urry, James, 38n1
Ury, William, 172–73
usury, 27

V

Valkenberg, Pim, 237, 242, 246
van Bruinessen, Martin, 278
van den Houte, Soetken, 29
Vanier, Jean, 173
Victim-Offender Reconciliation Program, 109
Vietnam War, 81–82
Vins, Georgi, 49, 50
Vins, Lydia, 49
violence
  decline of, 1
  in Mennonite communities, 188–91
voice, 243
Volf, Miroslav, 1

Volkan, Vamik, 147
Volkskirche (church of the community), 26–27
voluntary service, 80, 202
vulnerability, 155

W

war
   laws of, 163–65
   and women, 178
War of Independence (US), 60–61
Warkentine, David, 66
warrior metaphor, 219–20
WCC (World Council of Churches), 94, 96, 102
Weaver, Edwin and Irene, 98n23
Weibel, Hans, 27
Wichert, Timothy, 162
Widmer, Pierre, 94–95
Wiebe, Virgil
   childhood spirituality of, 220–21
   family history of, 204–5, 209–11, 209n17, 213, 215–17
   as lawyer, 224
   political views of, 211–12
   secondary education of, 222
   Voluntary Service of, 217–18, 221, 225
Wiens, Peter, 49
Wijaya, Paulus Sugeng, 291
Willems, Dirk, 9, 144–45, 207–8
Wismer, Mary, 181, 184
witnessing, 175
women
   in early Anabaptist communities, 29–30
   war and, 178
   in workforce during WWII, 183–84
   See also Mennonite women, and peacemaking
world, separation from, 31–32, 188
World Council of Churches (WCC), 94, 96, 102
World War I, 63–65, 74
World War II, 65–66, 77–78, 93–96, 183–84, 214, 215–17

Y

Yoder, John Howard
   on exilic missiology, 300–301, 302
   harmful behavior of, 224n64
   on Mennonite peace witness, 67
   peace and reconciliation work of, 98n24
   Politics of Jesus, 96
   in Puidoux Conferences, 94
   in South America, 99
   What Would You Do?, 69
Yugoslavia, *see* Bosnia-Herzegovina and Kosovo peacebuilding project

Z

Zehr, Howard, 100, 158, 354
Zionism, 299, 302–3
Zochrot, 306–7
Zuabi, Amir Nizar, 307–8
Zwingli, Ulrich, 24–25, 26

www.ingramcontent.com/pod-product-compliance
Lightning Source LLC
Chambersburg PA
CBHW071227290426
44108CB00013B/1321